With warmest regards
to
Conrad & Priscilla Reining

Walter H. Sangree

Age, Prayer and Politics in Tiriki, Kenya

PLATE I. Hezron Mushenye, Chief of Tiriki

AGE, PRAYER AND POLITICS IN TIRIKI, KENYA

WALTER H. SANGREE

Published on behalf of the
East African Institute of Social Research

OXFORD UNIVERSITY PRESS

LONDON   NEW YORK   NAIROBI

1966

Oxford University Press, Ely House, London W.1

GLASGOW NEW YORK TORONTO MELBOURNE WELLINGTON
BOMBAY CALCUTTA MADRAS KARACHI LAHORE DACCA
CAPE TOWN SALISBURY NAIROBI IBADAN
KUALA LUMPUR HONG KONG TOKYO

*Printed in Great Britain
at The Pitman Press, Bath*

Xu

Basaxulu Badiliji

Foreword

THIS is the fourth in a series of studies[1] of contemporary patterns of leadership in East African Society—studies carried out by members and associates of the East African Institute of Social Research, at Makerere College in the University of East Africa.

The inspiration for these studies came originally from Dr. A. I. Richards who, as Director of the Institute from 1950 to 1956, saw the need to investigate the various ways in which Africans were responding to the political opportunities offered by the increasing devolution of authority from colonial administrations to institutions of local self-government and to the entrepreneurial opportunities offered by the increasing involvement of the region in a world economy. When the studies were first projected in 1952–3, complete political independence for the East African territories seemed a distant prospect. The trend, however, was clear and it is largely due to Dr. Richards' foresight that we now have a record, for at least some East African areas, of those political and economic developments at the 'grass-roots' level which must form the essential basis for effective independence—an independence which has come much more quickly than anyone could have predicted.

Dr. Richards and her associates had already, during 1950–52, carried out a series of studies of 'tribal' government and politics in a number of Uganda, Kenya and Tanganyika societies. A generous grant from the Carnegie Corporation of New York made it possible to extend the work by carrying out a more detailed interdisciplinary study of African leadership in two contrasting local areas. The areas chosen for further study were the Kingdom of Buganda, which forms the central province of Uganda, and the Nyanza Province of Kenya—areas markedly different both in traditional society and culture and in colonial

[1] The others are: D. Anthony Low and R. Cranford Pratt, *Buganda and British Overrule*, 1900–1955 (London: Oxford University Press, 1960).
Hugh Fearn, *An African Economy: a Study of the Economic Development of the Nyanza Province of Kenya*, 1903–1953 (London: Oxford University Press, 1961).
Lloyd A. Fallers (ed.), *The King's Men: Leadership and Status in Buganda on the Eve of Independence* (London: Oxford University Press, 1964).

experience. Buganda is a great traditional kingdom with more than a million subjects, while Nyanza is an area of extreme ethnic and political fragmentation. During the colonial period, the British Protectorate government of Uganda had been concerned primarily to foster African development through the encouragement of peasant agricultural production and the modernization of traditional political institutions. The government of Kenya Colony, on the other hand, had encouraged European settlement; consequently African participation in development has been channelled, to a much greater extent than in Uganda, through European enterprises. Political development has received less governmental attention. Careful studies of African political leadership and economic enterprise in these two contrasting areas would, it was hoped, provide some notion of the major ranges of variation throughout the region as a whole.

Previous volumes in this series have reported the results of studies carried out in both Buganda and Nyanza—some by members of the Institute staff and others by scholars who, like Dr. Sangree, had financial support from other sources but who chose to join in the common enterprise, participating in the discussions held at the semi-annual conferences of the Institute and publishing their results in the present series. Their contributions, as readers of the series will readily appreciate and as the writer, as Director of the Leadership Project can testify, has been an essential one.

In addition to its excellent account of Tiriki society and culture, Dr. Sangree's volume is particularly notable for the light it throws on two important institutional complexes: the independent Christian sects and the system of age grades. His sensitive account, based upon careful observation, of the life of the independent sects adds greatly to our understanding of the role of these groups in the development of a distinctively African Christian piety, capable of speaking to Africans in a familiar idiom and addressing itself to their peculiar religious problems in a manner which the mission churches have found it difficult to do. Together with the work of Welbourn and Taylor[1], it

[1] F. B. Welbourn, *East African Rebels; a Study of some Independent Churches* (London: S.C.M. Press, 1961).

John U. Taylor, *The Growth of the Church in Buganda: an Attempt at Understanding* (London: S.C.M. Press, 1958).

Preface

THE material for this book was gathered by my wife and myself during a period of sixteen months spent in Tiriki, Nyanza Province, Kenya, between December, 1954 and June, 1956. From December, 1954 to March, 1955, we stayed at the government rest house at Hamisi, Tiriki Location Centre, and for the remainder of the time we lived at the homestead of Mr. Elisha Shibelenge at Jebdulu, Tiriki, in the house that had just been built for his eldest son, Moses Simani. Mr. Simani, then a secondary school teacher at Kaimosi Mission, found it more convenient to live in one of the houses supplied by the Mission for its teachers; thus we had the good fortune to be able to reside in an African homestead, where English was not understood, for most of our stay in Tiriki.

The Tiriki dialect (*ludiliji*, *lu- -diliji*) was the language through which we carried out most of our investigations. Not only was the learning and use of the vernacular desirable on methodological grounds, but also it was a necessity because Tiriki with command of English were too busy as school teachers or in other occupations to be able to give us much of their time.

I do not wish to convey the impression that either of us became fluent speakers of the Tiriki dialect; our grammar remained shabby, and our grasp of Tiriki rhetoric and much of the more esoteric vocabulary remained painfully weak even to the last months.

During the second half of the field work I employed Mr. Johnston T. B. Aligula as a full time assistant, and he proved invaluable in helping us record and understand data. With only four years of formal schooling, Mr. Aligula's knowledge of English was negligible, but he could read and write both the Tiriki vernacular and Kiswahili; most helpful were his excellent memory and his extraordinary intelligence. In the last months of field work he accompanied us during much of our visiting, observing, and interviewing. In addition he spent countless hours, not only interviewing and writing texts on his own, but also helping to reconstruct, explain and amplify

xi

various incidents and details of Tiriki life that either we had observed or experienced with him or that we later recounted to him.

In accordance with the tradition of anthropological research workers in East Africa, informants were never paid for giving information; the method of informal visiting and participation in community and tribal activities, both everyday and festive, was used in obtaining most of the data presented in this book. We administered questionnaires to a sample of Tiriki governmental and church leaders and took a fairly elaborate census of two Tiriki sub-communities, one in southwest and one in north-central Tiriki. Paid Tiriki assistants were used in obtaining about half of the census data.

Readers may question the appropriateness of remaining in one community for so long and never taking up residence in a second African homestead in a different community. However, the tribe's small size and the network of roads which allows easy access to any homestead in Tiriki from Jebdulu in two hours' time or less by car and by foot, made residence in one community possible while maintaining easy access to people from every corner of the tribal territory. Even during the wet months—March to June, and August and September—the roads are rarely so muddy as to be impassable for more than a few hours a day. Indeed, a good deal of visiting was done in homesteads in all parts of Tiriki. In addition, the census data obtained in two communities in different parts of the tribe (one census was taken in the Jebdulu area) served as a basis for judging how typical the detailed information obtained during our thirteen months' residence in one Tiriki community was.

It is impossible to express adequately our heart-felt gratitude to the many people in Tiriki who freely extended their hospitality to us and excused our countless errors of speech and manners. Many of these people devoted much time to instructing us in their language and their past history and to showing us patiently how to live in their present.

Chief Hezron Mushenye welcomed us warmly and treated us with great consideration from the time we first visited the tribe. He saw in our project the possibility of furthering his plans to record Tiriki history for posterity; nevertheless, he maintained a policy of non-interference towards our research efforts. At the same time, he was most generous in his counsel and aid whenever we approached him. Without exception other members of Chief Hezron's administrative staff followed his example of minimal interference combined with friendly and generous support whenever we sought help.

Much of the credit for what is of merit in this book must go to the Tiriki elders, not only those officially selected by Chief Hezron to be members of the Tiriki Historical Committee, but many others as well. Although I refrain from mentioning them by name here, I nevertheless record my deep gratitude towards each of the several dozen elders who devoted considerable time and effort to furthering my knowledge and understanding of their tribal customs and traditions. Tiriki elders do not spend much time with young adults without a purpose, and I hope this book and papers yet to come in some measure satisfy the desire and expectation of these elder men that the tribe's history and traditions may be recorded for posterity.

Among the younger Tiriki, outside of the contemporary tribal bureaucracy, I am particularly indebted to Mr. Elisha Shibelenge, Mr. Elisha Amaganga, Mr. Moses Simani, Mr. Johnston Aligula, Mr. Sosanes Imbadu, Mr. James Abdulla, and Mr. Daudi Rono for their extensive aid, counsel and warm friendship.

Dr. Laura Bohannan, whose stay among the Wanga overlapped with ours in Tiriki, was an invaluable friend and morale-booster during the trying early days, and a fount of both sage and subtle advice.

Members of the British Administration in Nyanza Province and North Nyanza District were consistently helpful, patient, hospitable, and most generous with their time and equipment, even though generally overburdened by their regular administrative responsibilities. They were also, without exception, extremely careful not to interfere with our research efforts or to suggest in any way that we were there as government agents. Special appreciation for their aid and hospitality is due to: Mr. C. H. Williams, Provincial Commissioner, Nyanza; Mr. E. J. A. Leslie and Mr. Thomas Watts, District Commissioners, North Nyanza; Mr. John Rowlins and Mr. Roger Hosking, District Officers, North Nyanza.

Members of all the missions in Tiriki and neighbouring tribes were generous both in giving us information and in extending their hospitality to us. Special thanks are due to Mr. Fred Reeve, Mr. Kenneth Goom and Father Rostron. My wife and I remember most warmly the friendship of Dr. and Mrs. Horst Rothe, and Mr. and Mrs. Onni Rauha.

The entire field trip, including three months spent in other parts of East Africa and nearly a month in England, was financed by a grant from the United States Educational Commission in the United Kingdom (the 'Fulbright Program'). The adroit guidance and friendly interest of the Institute's Directors, Dr. Audrey I. Richards, and Dr. Lloyd A. Fallers accompanied my wife and me throughout the entire field project; a large share of the credit for its formulation and success is theirs.

My wife shares my gratitude and indebtedness to the entire staff of the East African Institute of Social Research for making their facilities available to us. The periods of rest, the conferences, the write-up time, and the relaxed conviviality that we enjoyed during several sojourns there were a most welcome antidote to the rather rigorous and intense periods of field work in Tiriki.

Both the quantity and accuracy of the field data recorded on the Tiriki were greatly augmented by my wife's efforts. She was of considerable assistance to me in devising research schemes and techniques while in the field. In addition, I am most grateful to her for the countless insights and penetrating criticisms, many borne of her first hand knowledge of the Tiriki data, which she has given me while writing up this material.

I am very grateful to Professor Fred Eggan for his counsel and support while I was writing the Ph.D. dissertation from which this monograph was largely derived, and to Dr. Lloyd A. Fallers and Dr. D. J. Stenning, for their careful editing of both the preliminary and final drafts.

I had the good fortune to be able to revisit Tiriki for two weeks in June, 1961, using travel funds made available to me by the Non-Western Program of the University of Rochester, which was supported by the Carnegie Corporation. Chief Hezron of Tiriki organized a special committee to read over and correct a draft of the monograph that I took with me at that time. The committee's suggestions have been incorporated into this final version. The draft which the committee read contained essentially all the material in this final version with the exception of the four biographical sketches of Tiriki leaders presented in Chapter IX (pp. 254–78). Members of the Committee have expressed their desire to be acknowledged in the Preface. They are: Elisha Amaganga, Benjeman Amaje, Joshua Anusu, Japetha Inyanya, R. Meshack Isiaho, Guiele Jegenou, Ezekiel Shibira and Ruben Shiguri. This work is an indication of the enormous interest of the Tiriki, both as individuals and as a tribal group, in preserving a knowledge of their history and customs for posterity. Remembrance of individuals, families, clans, and age groups, is a theme, indeed a sacred value, in Tiriki culture.

This book is an anthropological monograph, not an attempt to conform to or fulfil the Tiriki notions of what aspects of their history and customs they would prefer to have permanently recorded; and the aforementioned committee members both realize and accept this. Their desire and efforts, however, to help me 'get things straight' (*xumanya bulunji*) and those of many other Tiriki we met and worked with in 1954–56, have helped immeasurably in the preparation of this study.

To Gladys Murch I am grateful for help with proof reading, and to Felice Harris I am grateful for aid with both proof reading and indexing.

WALTER H. SANGREE

Note on the Use and Spelling of Vernacular Terms

I have included a number of Tiriki words and quotations in the text as an aid both to comparative studies and to documentation. No standardized orthography exists for the Tiriki vernacular. It is common for Tiriki to use the orthography worked out by The Friends Mission for the Maragoli when writing the Tiriki language, but with every Tiriki using his own modifications. These modifications are in large part engendered by the fact that the predominant Tiriki dialect differs considerably from the Maragoli dialect, in both phonology and morphology. Indeed, the Tiriki dialect is very similar to the dialect of Idaxo and Isuxa, which also lacks a standardized orthography of its own. There is some interest among the Tiriki in establishing a Tiriki orthography, and the Tiriki tribal historical committee asked my wife and me to devise a standardized Tiriki spelling for them.

A preliminary phonemic analysis of the predominant Tiriki dialect reveals that the currently used Tiriki variations of the Maragoli orthography fail to distinguish between two frequently occurring Tiriki phonemes, /l/ and /r/ (/l/ as in *luhya*—'meeting place', and /r/ as in *ruhya*—'little meeting place'). Other inadequacies also exist, such as frequent confusion of the /h/ and /x/ phonemes (/h/ as in *hasi*—'low', and /x/ as in *xase*—'often, frequently'). Therefore I devised my own orthography, which assigns discrete symbols to all the Tiriki phonemes revealed by my analysis, with the following exceptions:

Phonemic distinction of pitch, as exemplified by *shídélù*—'basket', and *shìdèlú*—'chin', is not indicated. Pitch contrast, although regularly indicating grammatical differences, as in verb tense, is crucial in establishing lexical differences in very few instances. I know of only one such pair of forms in addition to the example given above.

Since Tiriki phonemes, /s/ and /h/ never occur immediately adjacent to each other, graphic *sh* has been used to indicate the phoneme /ʃ/ in this paper.

xvii

For reasons of orthographic convenience, length, as exemplified by *mabele*—'millet', and *mabeele*—'milk', has been indicated in all cases by a doubling of the vowel.

The orthography, then, makes use of the following symbols:

1. *Vowel*

   i, e, a, o, u, ii, ee, aa, oo, uu; m, n; y, w.

2. *Consonant* (arranged alphabetically)

   b, g, h, j, r, s, (sh), x, z; (k, t, in some Swahili, Nandi and English loan words).

The convention has been followed in this paper of italicizing all vernacular words, with the exception of proper names. My own orthography is used in writing the Tiriki vernacular, except in those cases where the Tiriki themselves, in writing loan words and foreign names, generally employ the conventional spelling of the donor language. Tiriki is predominantly a prefixing language, with the class and number of the nouns, most modifications of the verb, &c., being indicated by changes in prefix. I have followed the practice when introducing a vernacular word for the first time, of inserting the appropriate form of the vernacular word after the given English equivalent. In the case of nouns, the singular and plural prefixes are given, followed by the noun stem; in the case of verbs, simply the infinitive prefix and verb stem are given. For example:

The people (*bandu mu- ba- -ndu*); they know (*xu- manya*).

The usual singular-plural pair of prefixes does not exist or is never used with some nouns. When this is true, the noun is followed simply by the prefix and then the stem. For example:

Eleusine gruel (*busela, bu- -sela*); milk (*mabeele, ma- -beele*).

When Terik (the language of a neighbouring non-Bantu people) words of ritual or social significance to the Tiriki are quoted, only the singular form is given unless otherwise noted, because the Terik plural forms are not commonly used by the Tiriki.

After its first appearance, a noun is simply written with the appropriate prefix and a verb is written in the infinitive form without a dash between the infinitive prefix and the stem. For example:

The people (*bandu*); they know (*xumanya*).

When vernacular phrases or quotations of two or more words are given, no special indication of the stems or prefixes is made. For example:

The people know (*bandu bamanyanga*); the people, they know! (*bandu, bamanya!*).

Most Tiriki do not voice the initial vowel characteristic of so many prefixes in Abaluyia dialects. For example, most Tiriki speakers say, '*bandu*'—'people', rather than the '*abandu*' characteristic of dialects further to the north; similarly the Tiriki generally contract 'Abaluyia' to 'Baluyia' in common parlance.

Contents

Plates

30. Elder divining with a rubbing or friction stick
    (*Lusejele*)
31. Tea House and bus stop, Jebdulu market. Jebdulu
    elders, in the background, chatting prior to hearing
    local disputes
32. Tiriki Location Advisory Council and Roger Hoskings,
    District Officer

FIGURES

MAPS

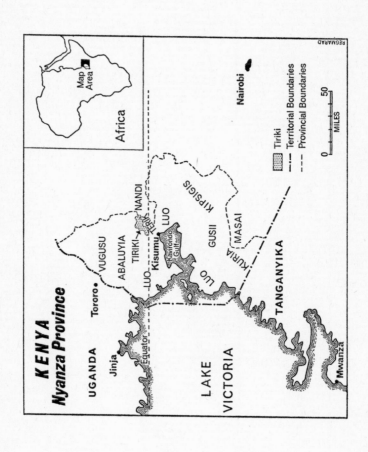

KENYA
Nyanza Province

Africa

Map Area

UGANDA

Jinja

Tororo

Equator

VUGUSU

ABALUYIA

TIRIKI

NANDI

LUO

Kisumu

Kavirondo Gulf

LUO

KIPSIGIS

GUSII

KURIA

MASAI

LUO

LAKE
VICTORIA

TANGANYIKA

Mwanza

Nairobi

Tiriki
Territorial Boundaries
Provincial Boundaries

0   50
MILES

REGMARAD

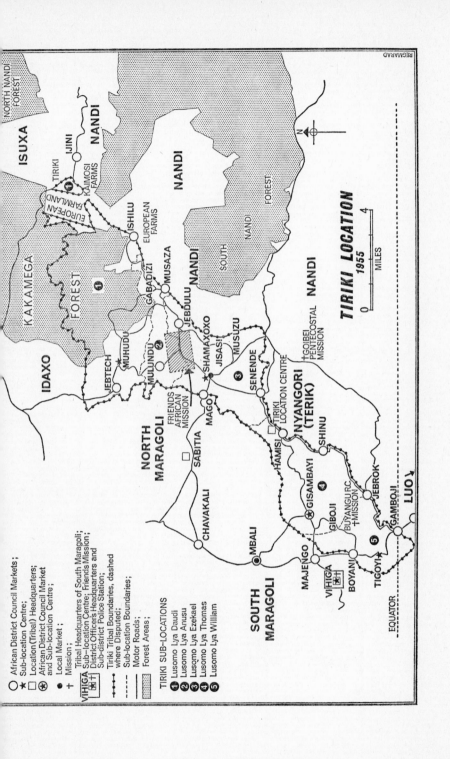

Introduction

THIS is an account of Tiriki social structure and of the main currents of change and social innovation that have arisen in Tiriki over the last fifty years, primarily as a result of European contact. The study focuses on the manner in which the indigenous Tiriki social organization, particularly in its age groups, has set the stage for the tribe's acceptance and utilization of the European-introduced church groups and tribal bureaucracy. Little attempt is made in this study to generalize about the nature and significance of age groups and Christian church organizations among other African peoples; instead the book remains essentially a case study of how five structural elements, three indigenous and two of European origin, have together served to maintain social order among the Tiriki during a period of rapid social change.

The General Problem, and the Selection of a Tribe for Study

It was my original intention to make an analysis of the significance of both the mission and 'breakaway' Christian church groups among the Tiriki. A number of considerations, both theoretical and practical, led to the decision to study church groups and to choose the Tiriki for intensive investigation. It will be seen, however, that once the study was under way its original focus was somewhat modified in order to be more in keeping with the problems that actual field research revealed to be of central significance in the contemporary Tiriki social scene.

The reading of two monographs first aroused my interest in analysing the significance of church congregations, both mission-affiliated and independent, among Bantu tribes. One of these was Bengt Sundkler's *Bantu Prophets in South Africa*.[1] In this book Sundkler describes the growth, development and proliferation of southern Bantu Christian church movements which have severed ties with their Protestant mother missions. As well as giving an overall picture of this phenomenon in South Africa,

[1] Bengt C. M. Sundkler, *Bantu Prophets in South Africa* (London: Lutterworth Press, 1948).

Sundkler examines in some detail the history and growth of several sects in Zululand, and points out how some of the traditional magico-religious and political power roles are now reappearing in not greatly altered form as power positions in these new church groups. Sundkler hypothesizes that the principal social significance of the African church groups is to be found in the outlet they afford for African leadership. His view is that the restrictions on leadership roles in mission churches, in tribal and national politics—indeed in almost every sphere—underlie the rise of all these Christian splinter groups. The second study was Lloyd A. Fallers' *Bantu Bureaucracy*.[1] In this book Fallers documents the nature of the role conflicts experienced by local chiefs working for the British Colonial Administration in Busoga, Uganda. Stated briefly, his analysis traces how conflict arises through the often mutually incompatible demands put upon Soga chiefs by particularistic and functionally diffuse kinship and clan obligations on the one hand, and universalistic and functionally specific bureaucratic tasks on the other.

When one takes the analytic orientation adopted by Fallers for his Soga chiefs and uses it to evaluate the descriptive data from Sundkler's book on separatist African churches, a clearcut pattern emerges. These churches exhibit hierarchical organizational structures that tend in the early stages to be particularistic and functionally diffuse, but their organization increasingly approaches the bureaucratic model as the churches become more established. This suggests that the growth of such sects is very likely to occur at least partly independent of efforts by Europeans to suppress African church leadership.

Most Bantu-speaking peoples of East and South Africa place a high value on power hierarchies. They structure a great many of their social activities around the explicit establishment of ranked social relationships. The establishment and maintenance of such hierarchies is generally brought about through various kinds of age grading, and also in many tribes through ranking of different clan or lineage groups. In contrast to groups such as the American eastern woodlands or plains Indians, or some of the Nilo-hamitic herdspeople of East Africa, the majority of Bantu-speaking peoples do not traditionally place a high value

[1] Lloyd A. Fallers, *Bantu Bureaucracy* (Cambridge: W. Heffer & Sons, Ltd., no date).

on the individual's independence of choice and action. Seldom does one find formally structured situations in which the individual is expected to look to himself rather than to others (either peers or superiors or subordinates) for guidance in making an important decision or for moral strength. Where such an individualistic orientation exists, it generally runs counter to the establishment of new administrative hierarchies. Most Bantu tribes, since they are relatively unaffected by such values, have little difficulty in adjusting to new power hierarchies. Generally speaking they have one major hurdle to jump in accepting and integrating a bureaucratic political framework into their indigenous social systems: the hurdle described by Fallers, that is to say, the conflict between their kin and clan-centered particularistic, functionally diffuse power relationships, and the universalistic, functionally specific demands of bureaucratic government. Protestant church groups, especially those unencumbered by strict missionary supervision, provide a ready-made framework within which a leader can fulfil some of the particularistic relationships traditionally expected of men in authority, while at the same time, with the aid of Christian ritual and symbols, increasingly eliciting more universalistic and functionally specific relationships in those areas where social, economic and political patterns have been most modified and broadened by European contact.

Any one of several Bantu Abaluyia tribes in the southern half of North Nyanza District of Kenya offered the following set of conditions, making them quite suitable for testing the hypothesis that Protestant sects, both mission-affiliated and independent, may fill a transitional political need among Bantu tribes.

First, the tribes of the region have been heavily missionized by a variety of Protestant sects. Not only have these missions been very busy evangelizing, but also, ever since their arrival in 1902, they have provided the majority of the educational and medical services available in the area.

Second, as a result of this mission activity, Christian churches, both mission-affiliated and independent, are found in abundance in this region.

Third, the tribes in the area are undergoing rapid economic, political and social change. A fast-growing population and limited land resources are making the people more and more dependent on income from wage labour in East African urban centers, on European farms, and in European homes.

Fourth, the British administration, particularly since the Second World War, has been initiating and fostering an increasingly comprehensive system of African bureaucratic administration within the tribes of North Nyanza, to supplement and supersede the weakening indigenous political forms.

The first three conditions are roughly comparable to those found in Zululand and among the other South African tribes on which Sundkler based his study, though to be sure, the contact and ensuing disruption of traditional tribal ways has gone on for much longer in South Africa. As regards the fourth point, however, there has clearly been more suppression of African leadership and political activity in South Africa. This difference supports the hypothesis that something other than the mere absence of permitted leadership roles and suppression of political activity underlies the growth of separatist churches. These separatist churches supply a transitional organizational framework more universalistic than those usually found in traditional tribal systems.

Thus tribes are to be found in North Nyanza that present a general set of conditions germane to the problem to be investigated. It seemed to me that a careful description and analysis of how any one of these southern Abaluyia tribes was responding to these conditions promised to be both comparable and supplementary to data gathered by Sundkler in his analysis of independent South African Bantu churches.

In spite of the Mau Mau rebellion among the Kikuyu 150 miles or more to the east, the modicum of social stability and European-African congeniality necessary for successful field work existed all over North Nyanza in 1954. Among the southern tribes, however, the Tiriki proved by far the most cordial towards my offer to come and study their history. Thus, other pertinent factors apparently being equal, I chose Tiriki for intensive study.

My work among the Tiriki made it clear that the Christian churches, both mission affiliated and independent, were facilitating the tribe's acceptance of the relatively impersonal bureaucratic tribal leadership being fostered by the British administration. It became apparent, however, that the indigenous age group organization was also playing a vital contemporary role in facilitating the operation of the tribal bureaucracy. Indeed, this age group organization, which the Tiriki (and only the Tiriki among the North Nyanza Abaluyia tribes) borrowed almost without modification from a neighbouring Nilo-hamitic Nandi-speaking tribe, supplied Tiriki with an indigenous social structure in which relatively universalistic and functionally specific administrative-type social roles were firmly established before the advent of the Europeans. Thus, it turned out that the Tiriki are something less than an ideal tribe to study in order to test notions about the manner in which church organizations expedite the transition to more bureaucratic-type power relationships. They are of great interest, however, because of the ongoing significance of their age-graded group organization. Indeed here is a tribe where the manifest flexibility and viability of the indigenous social organization in the face of rapid social change and extensive British administrative innovations can be in large measure traced to its age-graded age group organization.[1]

Probably the Tiriki age group organization would not in itself have proved a viable base upon which to build the contemporary bureaucratic tribal organization. The age groups, however, augmented on the one hand by a lineage-based predilection for power hierarchies, and buttressed on the other hand by auxiliary organizational hierarchies supplied by the missionary-introduced Christian church groups, have indeed remained the ongoing organizational theme of the tribe. Today the age groups continue to underlie much of the success of the new tribal bureaucracy.

Historical Sources on the Tiriki

Günter Wagner, in several field trips to North Nyanza between 1934 and 1938 (the area was then known as North Kavirondo) amassed a great deal of data on the twenty-two

---

[1] See S. N. Eisenstadt, *From Generation to Generation* (Glencoe, Illinois: The Free Press, 1956), for probably the most comprehensive survey and analysis of age groups and age grouping to date.

tribes then forming the district.[1] Much of his material has since been published in a series of articles and monographs, the most important and comprehensive being his two-volume, *The Bantu of North Kavirondo*.[2] Although Wagner makes a number of specific references to the Tiriki in his writings, most of his published material deals with the Maragoli people who live just west of the Tiriki, and with the Vugusu, who are situated in the north of the district. Enough general cultural similarity exists between all the tribes of North Nyanza for the material gathered by Wagner to provide a fair picture of traditional Tiriki material culture, and many aspects of Tiriki social custom. Also Wagner's descriptions of economic conditions and missionary and British administrative activities give a fair base for evaluating how general conditions have changed in the district during the last twenty years. A further work which has proved of great value to me because of the Tiriki's particularly strong Nilo-hamitic connexions is J. G. Peristiany's, *The Social Institutions of the Kipsigis*.[3]

My wife and I were given access to district and provincial government files in Kakamega and Kisumu, and we also had an opportunity to go over records of the Friends African Mission, Kaimosi. These files and records proved of considerable value, especially in reconstructing the early days of European contact.

The first three chapters of this study, which describe the indigenous social organization, are of necessity a reconstruction of the past based to a great extent on the recollections of contemporary tribal elders, and on their evaluations of how contemporary customs and activities were manifest and carried out when they were young. The first Tiriki contact with Europeans did not occur until the latter portion of the 1890's; thus, it falls within the life span of members of the most senior living Tiriki age group (Jiminigayi) in 1956 when the field investigations for this study were completed. Indeed contemporary elders'

---

[1] See Günter Wagner's, *The Bantu of North Kavirondo*, Vol. I (London: Oxford University Press, 1949), p. 21, for a list of the North Kavirondo tribes in 1938.

[2] *Ibid.*; Günter Wagner, *The Bantu of North Kavirondo*, Vol. II (London: Oxford University Press, 1956). See the bibliography (p. 456) for a more complete listing of Wagner's writings on the Abaluyia tribes.

[3] J. G. Peristiany, *The Social Institutions of the Kipsigis* (London: George Routledge & Sons, Ltd., 1939).

eyewitness accounts, reinforced by their memories of what they had been told by their elders when they were young, extend back into the era preceding European contact.

Tiriki: the Place and the People

The Tiriki are one of more than 17 Bantu-speaking tribes living in the North Nyanza and Elgon Nyanza Districts of Nyanza Province, Kenya Colony. In recent years, as a part of a growing sense of cultural and political identity, they have started calling themselves collectively, the 'Abaluyia'. The Abaluyia peoples in effect form a Bantu linguistic and cultural sub-area where closely related dialects are spoken and a large core of common customs and values are shared. Today they have emerged as a distinctive political bloc in Kenya politics. The Abaluyia tribes, probably numbering altogether more than half a million people (1956), live in an area of approximately 2,700 square miles that extends roughly from the equator north to the southern slopes of Mount Elgon, west to the Uganda border, and east to the Nandi escarpment. The area is predominantly very fertile and well watered, and the average altitude of about five thousand feet results in a moderate climate.[1]

Although the ruling clan of the Wanga tribe was beginning to establish military and political dominance over a number of Abaluyia tribes just before the arrival of the British, the Abaluyia tribes remain today, as traditionally, essentially a group of politically discrete tribes that recognize many common bonds of kinship, language and custom. Their sense of similarity and community is enhanced by their being surrounded on almost all sides by Nilotic and Nilo-hamitic peoples.

The Tiriki people (*badiliji, mu- ba- -diliji*) live in the south-eastern portion of North Nyanza District. Tiriki Location, the contemporary homeland of the Tiriki as legally constituted by the Kenya government, is about twenty miles long. Running southwest to northeast, the location is shaped roughly like a dumbbell; about three miles wide in the southwest, it narrows to less than a mile in width near the centre, and then grows to

---

[1] Wagner, Vol. I., *op. cit.*, pp. 3–15. Wagner, in the first volume of *The Bantu of North Kavirondo*, gives an excellent general geographic description of North Nyanza District.

over five miles in width in the relatively sparsely-populated and partially forested northeastern section. Of Tiriki Location's total area of just over seventy square miles, almost seventeen square miles in the northeast are uninhabited government-protected forest reserve, while Kaimosi Mission, in the north-central region, holds over one and one-half square miles of land. In the remaining fifty-three square miles, about 40,000 Tiriki make their homes. This brings the average population density in the inhabited part of the location close to 750 people per square mile. Overpopulation is the most pressing reason for the Abaluyia peoples' ever-growing practice of seeking employment in regions outside of North Nyanza. As the population increases so does the absolute dependency on wages from jobs in East African urban centres and on European farms. Today probably over half of the Tiriki adult males are 'off-tribe' (*mulugulu*) at any given time, for the most part performing wage labour. Mostly it is the men between the ages of about eighteen and forty who seek wage labour off-tribe; consequently, the tribal population appears to the visitor to consist almost entirely of women, children, and old men.

When I first saw the Tiriki countryside it struck me as being ideal material for a Peter Breughel landscape. Here was a bucolic beehive; the women were the workers, and the men were the drones. Women do the agriculture in Tiriki. On a morning women are to be seen everywhere; women balancing water-filled kerosene tins on their heads as they climb homewards from valley streams, little groups of women hoeing the fields, women spreading maize kernels or beans to dry on huge flat-topped granite boulders that protrude at frequent intervals from the cultivated land, women carrying loads of firewood back from the forest on their heads. Children are also much in evidence. Little boys brandishing sticks, some naked and some wearing dirty torn shirts, chase cattle out of maize fields back to the path and road edges where they are permitted to graze. Smaller children, both male and female, race around in little groups in the occasional grassy spots, often playing soccer with a green mango or some other improvised ball—even while carrying their infant charges on their left hips.

Generally the men do not become a conspicuous part of the scene until around noon. At that time the tribal elders leave the community meeting grounds, where they have passed the morning chatting and hearing cases brought before them for settlement. For the next hour or so they can frequently be seen sauntering along the pathways on their way to the nearest beer drink. Typical clothing for the Tiriki elder is an ancient army greatcoat worn over equally ancient shorts, and generally two hats—one pushed down on top of the other. One can always spot an elder on the lookout for beer, for in his right hand he will be clutching an immense wooden sheath, seven or eight feet long which encases a beer drinking tube, and under his left arm he will be carrying a battered four-legged stool. The beer pots are the centre of the elders' social life. It is while seated around a communal pot in a banana patch and sipping beer through long tubes that the elders exchange gossip, recollect the exploits of dead comrades, and discuss and, in effect, often settle, disputes of one sort or another even before they are presented to them for arbitration in the community courts. Around midafternoon, when the elders' beer drinks are already well under way, the younger men who are not off-tribe working collect around beer pots of their own, or settle in the back rooms of local African stores (*liduka, li- ma- -duka*) to drink European beer or illegally-brewed distilled liquor (*iwalagi, i- zi- -walagi*). Most of this younger set consists of men home 'on leave' from jobs off-tribe and men who hold salaried positions in the administration. During the weeks following the semi-annual harvest, when there is plenty of grain with which to make beer, drinks are virtually an everyday occurrence; from evening until after dark it is common to hear, if not to see, old men chatting as they saunter home after a lively drink. In the words of the Tiriki elders, 'It's a tough world' (*shibala shidinyu*) on those days when a beer drink cannot be found within walking distance.

Throughout most of the day one or another askari (tribal policeman or messenger) or headman can be seen pedalling his bicycle along the main road that runs the length of the Location on his way to or from the location centre at Hamisi. Occasionally an overcrowded bus travelling between Kisumu and Eldoret grinds by, covering all it passes with dust. From any high spot several primary schools are usually visible; they are often located on hilltops, and they are also easily recognizable from a distance because the long rectangular shape of the

thatched school buildings contrasts with the thatched conical
roofs of the ordinary round huts generally found in homesteads.
Children in rows doing calisthenics frequently grace the
schoolgrounds.

On Sundays many of the schools, which are run by the missions, are used as churches. Women make up three-quarters or
more of most church congregations. After the Sunday morning
services processions form at the school-church grounds and then
stream over the country paths under the midday sun on their
way to banana grove 'memorial services', singing and drumming syncopated songs of salvation.

The daily scene varies little from one part of the tribe to the
next, but as one goes towards the northeast the country grows
less crowded, the huts are progressively farther apart, and the
rusticity is more pronounced. The hills and valleys are less
precipitous, and there are fewer granite outcroppings; imported
Australian Eucalyptus trees more often break the eye's sweep,
and large tracts of dense hardwood rain forest, protected by the
Friends African Mission and the African District Council, preserve a picture of what most of northeastern Tiriki must have
looked like at the turn of the century when the last elephant
was seen roaming the area.

Tiriki Social Structure

The Tiriki indigenous social structure may be likened to a
rope of three strands; clans (*zimbamba, lu- zim- -bamba*), age
groups (*maxula, li- ma- -xula*), and territorial units (*zisomo, lu-
zi- -somo*). These three strands, although no longer in themselves sufficient to maintain the social order, combine with the
recently developed Christian religious groups and tribal
bureaucracy to form the five principal elements of contemporary Tiriki social structure.

Clanship, of secondary political significance both traditionally and today, is nevertheless the traditional organizational
arena in which a large number of significant social relationships
were carried out, and the bulk of the tribe's cultural heritage
preserved. Clan organization supplied the underlying framework for the tribe's principal religious and economic values, and
family organization can best be thought of as an integral aspect
of Tiriki clan structure. Even today, with the formal religious

and much of the economic significance of the clans gone, family allegiances and responsibilities are frequently expressed in terms of clanship; clan exogamy remains, and a man's sense of personal identity continues to be strongly linked with clan membership.

The Tiriki age group organization affects, directly or indirectly, most of the major kinds of social activity in Tiriki. The social groupings, rankings, statuses and roles it institutes are manifest in everything from the largest tribal and sub-tribal activities to everyday intra-familial relationships. Yet the Tiriki avow (and all the evidence I could muster supports their opinion) that the age group organization is not an indigenous part of their Bantu heritage; rather it is something they received from the culturally and linguistically alien Terik. The Nilo-hamitic Terik are herdspeople, a Nandi offshoot, and they were the prior inhabitants of the area now inhabited largely by the Bantu Tiriki. A few Terik have chosen to this day to remain in the region rather than take refuge in nearby Nandiland, but they are now outnumbered by the Tiriki, probably by more than ten to one. The Terik were the people who first permitted straggling remnants of Abaluyia lineages to settle in the region, and they insisted that these newcomers be initiated into Terik age groups. These age groups soon supplied the principal political and ritual basis for Tiriki corporate action. Attitudes and sentiments fostered by the age group organization continue to be very significant. For example, they underlie much of the Tiriki elder's ongoing hostility towards Protestant missionary evangelical efforts, and they also facilitate the smooth functioning of the contemporary British-instituted tribal bureaucracy.

Most traditional judicial, military and ritual activity was organized in large measure on the basis of community and sub-tribal territorial groupings that were clearly related to the age group organization. These indigenous community and sub-tribal groupings have considerably facilitated the acceptance and smooth operation of the contemporary tribal bureaucracy's hierarchy of territorially delimited administrative units. The centralized Tiriki tribal bureaucracy, and to a less extent Christianity, were both imposed upon the Tiriki by Europeans, but the manner in which these two social additions were accepted and the way they have worked to fulfil emergent social needs has been conditioned in large measure by the indigenous social structure—particularly the age group organization.

Part I of this monograph (Chapters I–V) gives a description of the traditional Tiriki social structure, and a brief analytic history of the development of the British fostered tribal administration and the spread of Christianity. Part II (Chapters VI–X) examines various aspects of contemporary Tiriki social organization and analyses the manner in which aspects of the traditional social structure have in part conditioned its development.

Part One

TRADITIONAL TIRIKI SOCIAL STRUCTURE AND THE NATURE OF COLONIAL ADMINISTRATIVE AND MISSION CONTACT

Tiriki Clans: Their Structure and Function

Clan Histories and Clan Formation

THERE are about a hundred agnatic exogamous lineage groups (*zimbamba*) in Tiriki, each with its own genealogy and history or origin myth. Nearly all of these origin stories tell of an agnatic ancestor who came from one or another Abaluyia clan (*luyia*, or *oluyia*), accepted Terik age group initiation, and thenceforth was known as a Tiriki (*mudiliji*). The Tiriki today commonly use the same term, (*zimbamba*), to refer not only to the exogamous maximal lineages within Tiriki, but also to refer to the usually larger non-Tiriki clans from which the Tiriki lineages claim they segmented. Indeed each Tiriki segment of a larger Abaluyia clan forbids marriage with all lineages of the clan, including those not living in Tiriki. No regular patterns of totemic observances or avoidances are followed by Tiriki lineages; thus traditional agnatic genealogies are the sole charters of clan identity.

Most Tiriki traditional lineage histories can be divided into the following four parts. First there is the story of the origin of the clan's putative founding ancestor. One finds three favourite origin stories repeated over and over again by the Tiriki lineage elders of different Tiriki clans, and often the elders of a lineage will disagree among themselves as to which of these origin stories they favour for their own clan. The three stories place the origin of the founding ancestor variously in Egypt, the source of the Nile at Jinja, or Mount Elgon. The second part of a lineage history recounts how the founding ancestor or his immediate descendants arrived in the region of the Kavirondo Gulf that remains the habitat of the Abaluyia. The third part tells how a member of the clan, often accompanied by his sons, left the land of his clansmen in western North Nyanza and migrated east-ward. Commonly 'a dispute over cattle' is offered as the reason why this man left his clan group. The histories often recount that somewhere a few miles west of the present day western border of Tiriki the migrant met Terik or Tiriki people who initiated him and his sons into Terik-Tiriki age groups, and thereafter accepted them as Tiriki. The fourth part of a Tiriki lineage history recounts in detail the agnatic line from the time the wandering ancestor first arrived in the region of Tiriki and was initiated into the tribe. This line may extend back for six or seven generations, which suggests that this is when migrating Abaluyia groups were first incorporated by the Nilo-hamitic Terik into their age groups. In many cases the lineage depth since incorporation as Tiriki is four or five generations.

The prestige and importance granted a lineage by the Tiriki is primarily a function of its size and of how long ago it first came to Tiriki, these two factors generally being directly related. The process of immigration of Abaluyia clan segments to Tiriki and of their incorporation into the Tiriki tribe through acceptance of Terik age group initiation has continued to the present generation. The first-generation immigrant, no matter what his clan of origin, is not considered by the tribe to be in a position to say anything of importance about his clan history. The sons, however, and even more the grandsons of an immigrant, if they come from a clan a segment of which migrated to Tiriki at an earlier time, are grouped with the older Tiriki segment of their clan, and enjoy its status in the tribe. Each Abaluyia clan, once it has been represented in Tiriki by initiated males for more than one generation, comes to function as a corporate entity within the tribe, and all subsequent immigrants from that clan, regardless of their particular lineage or lineage segment affiliation, are considered members of the same clan group. The Tiriki, when speaking of one or another of their clans (*zimbamba*) in almost every instance are referring only to that portion or those portions of the Abaluyia clan in question that became incorporated into the Tiriki tribe.

In the remainder of this paper, therefore, the word clan (*lubamba*) will be used to indicate the Tiriki portion of the clan named.

Tiriki clanship traditionally manifests itself in four clearcut ways. First, through their origin myths the clans supply their members with a sense of social identity and continuity. Second, clan solidarity is increased through clan exogamy. Third, a sense of clan solidarity, reinforced by the origin myths and the clan exogamy, is further strengthened by patterns of hospitality which are regularly extended not only to closely-related kinsfolk and neighbours, but also to all clansmen, no matter how distant genealogically. A further corollary of this is that kinship terms are regularly extended to all clansmen. Fourth, in the religious realm, a man traditionally feels his welfare is most intimately tied up with his agnatic ancestors; in the supplications to the ancestors at the homestead ancestral shrines, it is the agnatic ancestors who are most often remembered and invoked.

There are two additional areas of social interaction and control in which clan solidarity manifests itself, though less strongly in Tiriki than in Abaluyia clans outside of Tiriki. One is in cases of interclan fights which result in murder (*bulumindi bu- -lumindi*). The Tiriki elders feel that in pre-European times it was not uncommon outside of Tiriki for such an incident to result in the injured clan's avenging their clansmen's death by killing any man of the clan of the murderer. Tiriki say that such sequences of vengeance occasionally occurred, but that it was more usual for such cases of inter-clan murder to be quickly settled, and they were almost always prevented from developing into vendettas through the intervention of Tiriki elders belonging to other Tiriki clans. Such intervention generally resulted in the payment of acceptable compensation to the family of the deceased by the murderer and/or his immediate agnatic kinsmen rather than by his whole clan.

The second area in which the Tiriki clans differ rather markedly from the Abaluyia norm is in the matter of clan lands. In most Abaluyia tribes each major clan is accorded a certain political and ritual preference in the particular geographic area which has come through time to be known as the land of that particular clan. The degree to which elders of a clan actually control things within the area of their clan lands varies considerably from one region to another. Probably among all the Abaluyia the longstanding practice of inviting members of other clans (particularly sisters' sons) to live on unused portions of clan lands has minimized the political and ritual authority of an established clan over its sovereign domain. In Tiriki, however, the ideal of clan ownership of land and clan control of community affairs has consistently been submerged by the principle that all Tiriki, regardless of clan, have equal rights to all unused Tiriki land, and have equal status in community councils, by virtue of their common membership in Terik-

Tiriki age groups. It is probably this subordination of clan loyalties to the bonds of age group brotherhood that has led the Tiriki so regularly to arbitrate inter-clan murder cases on a multi-clan community basis rather than simply on an inter-clan basis.

The above generalizations hold true for all the Abaluyia clans of Tiriki, but not for the Terik clans. The Nilo-hamitic Terik (usually known as the 'Nyangori' in British administrative records) are a small but distinctive minority in Tiriki. Comprising less than 10 per cent of the population of present day Tiriki, the Terik claim that they are an offshoot of the Nandi people. They are linguistically and culturally very similar to the Nandi. Both Abaluyia and Terik clans in Tiriki agree that the Terik were the first to occupy the region now known as Tiriki, and that it was a Terik elder named Diligin who first invited members of Abaluyia clans to be initiated into Terik age groups. Terik clans are totemic groupings in which only the smaller segments form exogamous units. Although Terik clans are of significance in such matters as blood compensation, neither they nor their sub-clans seem to have been important factors in territorial control or in other aspects of social organization. Certainly the present social and political significance of Terik clan groupings in Tiriki is negligible, and I shall not deal any further with them in this study.

There are great differences in size among the various Tiriki clans. The total population of Tiriki in 1955 was approaching 40,000.[1] The two largest clans in Tiriki probably have almost 4,000 members each; the third largest nearly 1,800. These are followed in size by seven clans of nearly 800 members each, and they in turn by another three clans of about 350 members each. Finally, dozens of smaller clans complete the total of perhaps 100 clans, some being represented by only two or three families.[2]

---

[1] The Tiriki Location Advisory Council estimate of the Tiriki population in 1955 was 32,000. The 1955 Tiriki Location tax records, however, list just under 13,000 names (in theory all Tiriki males over the age of about 18 years). Assuming that this figure represents a little under $\frac{1}{3}$ of the population of present day Tiriki, I have made the tentative estimate of 40,000 for the 1955 Tiriki Location population.

[2] The estimates of clan size have been made by counting the number of men listed under each clan name in the Tiriki Location tax record for 1955, and multiplying the result by 3.

The total number of clans would be impossible to ascertain without a complete census of every homestead in Tiriki, for in western Tiriki many immigrants in recent years have settled down without being initiated into the age group system, and these people are often recorded on the tax records simply as 'members of alien clans' (*bajanganyigo, mu- ba- -janganyigo*). Indeed, this 'stranger clan' category, which in no sense refers to a corporate group, today makes up the largest single clan category in four out of five of the contemporary Tiriki sub-locations.

Tiriki Clan Formation

Tiriki clans are all products of segmentation from larger Abaluyia agnatic lineages. For the most part these segments have been incorporated into the Tiriki tribe recently enough (four to five generations) so that no further segmentation has taken place since their acceptance by the tribe. Not so with the largest clans, however. One need only look at Tiriki's two largest clans, the Baluxoba and the Bumbo, to find this process of segmentation at work within the Tiriki tribe.

Both these clans claim to share common origin with the ruling clan (Abashiseza) of the Wanga Tribe in western North Nyanza; each claims its members would not marry into the clan of the rulers of the Wanga, even though the elders of neither clan remember the name of the ruling clan (Abashiseza). Both clans

---

The major clans are as follows:

about 4,000 members
Baluxoba
Bumbo

about 1,800 members
Basuba

about 800 members
Bamabi
Bashisungu
Bamiluha
Bajisinde
Baluxombe
Badura
Bamuli

about 400 members
Barimbuli
Baguga
Basiyaniga

claim to have been the first to accept the Terik age group initiation and thus to be the founding members of Abaluyia Tiriki,
and each clan accuses the other of falsifying genealogies so as to
appear to be the first Abaluyia Tiriki clan. Long public debates
have been held between the elders of the two clans over these
matters. Occasionally an agent of reconciliation stands up who
gives a genealogy which shows that the Baluxoba and the Bumbo
are each descended from brothers who were sons of the ruling
lineage of Wanga; but always such a genealogy is shouted down
by the other elders with remarks such as, 'No, no! We marry
each other! We're not of the same clan; the man is a liar.' The
disputed names in the genealogies of the two clans generally
occur six or seven generations back. The majority of the Tiriki
elders of other clans favour the Baluxoba's story, agreeing that
the Baluxoba are those related to the Wanga ruling clan, and
that the Bumbo are a different group who followed the
Baluxoba to Tiriki by a few years. It should be noted that
the Baluxoba is a slightly larger clan than the Bumbo.

Perhaps more instructive in understanding the process of
segmentation is the case of the Bumbo and the Baluxombe clans.
The latter, with about 800 members, is one of the larger
clans, but only a quarter the size of the Bumbo. Both the Bumbo
and the Baluxombe elders have on various occasions acknowledged that the Baluxombe were descended from a Bumbo
ancestor. All of the larger clans, when tracing their genealogies,
divide their clans into clan segments or sub-clans which they
refer to as 'houses' (*zinzu, in- zin- -zu*). It is general in clan
histories for the various 'houses' to be attributed to brothers of
about four or five generations back who are all sons of the same
clan elder. Sometimes it is said that the sons are of different
wives of the elders, but generally the names of the wives are
forgotten, the houses are named after the brothers, and little
concern is felt as to whether they were full or half brothers.

The Baluxombe claim descent from a Bumbo ancestor of the
fifth ascending generation who left the area of his fathers because
of a dispute with his brothers over cattle. The name Luxombe
was not the name of this ancestor, but rather was the nickname
given him and his family by the families of other clans who lived
adjacent to the region into which he moved. Thus the Baluxombe came to live apart from their other Bumbo clansmen and

in time came to be regarded as a distinct clan group by their neighbours. Around twenty-five years ago, a Baluxombe man married a girl of a Bumbo lineage. They had children who are now in turn marrying, and recently other Bumbo and Baluxombe have started to intermarry. To marry members of one's own clan is regarded as incest (*bwixo, bw- ixo*); it is considered a very serious crime and a danger to the community and particularly to the clan as well as the couple involved. Even though the Baluxombe condoned this marriage twenty-five years ago, members of the present day Bumbo clan are very fearful about the future well-being of their clan because their sons have started taking Baluxombe for wives. The Bumbo elders so aroused the concern of other Tiriki clan leaders that several years ago it was decreed in the Tiriki Chief's weekly public meeting there should be no more marriages between Baluxombe and Bumbo. Apologists for marriage between the Baluxombe and the Bumbo point out that they live and act ceremonially as completely different units, neither extending kinship hospitality or terminology to each other. They further argue that the founder of the Baluxombe group was not a clan brother of the Bumbo at all, but rather that he was a sister's son (*mwihwa, mw- bi- -ihwa*). In Tiriki a father's sister's son is known either as 'brother' (*amwabo, a- ba--mwabo*) or as 'cross cousin' (*musiyala, mu- ba- -siyala*), either term being used almost interchangeably in this context. And there the argument is left by the elders—at the point where genealogical uncertainty can be further confounded by terminological ambiguity.

Tiriki Exogamy Rules

The relaxation of the exogamy rules between two major lineages of one Abaluyia clan is simply the final step in the dropping of a whole series of obligations and rituals which become more specific as one proceeds to the successively smaller units within the clan; i.e., as one proceeds down from the clan to the sub-clan or 'house' to the extended family or homestead (*mujizi, mu- mi- -jizi*). The Tiriki say, as do so many Bantu, that they marry the children of their enemies; in practice it is only when two lineages who can trace a common agnatic origin have ceased to function together as a clan in any way that the relaxation of exogamy rules might be condoned, and appropriate fictional adjustments made to lineage genealogies.

The Tiriki rules for clan exogamy closely follow the outline made by Wagner for all the Abaluyia tribes.[1] The general term used by the Tiriki to cover all incestuous relationships is *bwixo*. When the question of an incestuous relationship is brought up the elders will often exclaim, 'Alas! Incest will destroy the people!' (*Bayayi! Bwixo galamala bandu!*). The Tiriki believe a generalized state of ritual danger (*luswa, lu- -swa*) results from incest which imperils family and neighbour as well as the individuals committing incest. The amount of danger depends on the nature of the genealogical relationship between the offenders. Sexual union with a member of one's own or one's mother's clan is absolutely forbidden. Such a relationship would immediately be terminated by community action, and the ritual danger rectified through the cleansing of the offending couple in a ceremony (*mwiluxa, mw- mi- -iluxa*) performed by the elders of their community or communities. If sexual union were discovered to have occurred between biological siblings, or parent and offspring, the offenders would immediately be driven from the tribe.

When two people are contemplating marriage, or if they have eloped, the grandparents of both people quiz the elders of their clans and communities to see if the young couple share one or more greatgrandparents of the same clan. If any old man or woman is alive who calls both the boy and the girl 'greatgrandchild' (*mwizuxulu, mw- bi- -izuxulu*) the marriage is repudiated by the common elder kinsmen. Such an elder kinsman may not succeed in stopping the marriage, but he or she generally refuses to attend ceremonies held for the couple's marriage and those ceremonies held to celebrate the birth of their children. The third ascending generation (greatgrandparental generation) is as far back as the Tiriki kinship terms differentiate generations. All greatgrandparents and greatgrandchildren refer to each other by the reciprocal term, *mwizuxulu*, for so long as the greatgrandparents are alive. In addition, a living greatgrandfather is sometimes referred to as 'forefather' (*muguga, mu- ba- -guga*) if he is of the agnatic or the mother's agnatic line.

[1] Günter Wagner, *The Bantu of North Kavirondo*, Vol. I (London: Oxford University Press, 1949), 383.

Once a greatgrandfather dies, however, he is regularly called and known as *muguga* if he is an agnate or a mother's agnate. If he is not of these two lines, the deceased greatgrandparent becomes known simply as 'marriageable kin' (*shisoni, shi- bi--soni*), and henceforth all his or her descendants not related through a new affinal bond are also known as 'marriageable kin,' for so long as a genealogical connexion is remembered. Thus the *shisoni-mwizuxulu* distinction is not strictly derived from generational or genealogical distance; rather it indicates the nature of the relationship between a particular generational group and its third ascending generation and the resultant presence or absence of a feeling of consanguinity with non-paternal and non-maternal agnatic kin related by a link no closer than the third ascending generation.

Tiriki exogamy rules prohibit marriage with anyone belonging to one's own or one's mother's clan. Tiriki exogamy rules also prohibit marriage between two people who have any other maternal grandmothers of the same clan. In practice, however, this last rule may be overlooked and the marriage grudgingly condoned by the elders if the couple have eloped and the marriage is already in being, provided the grandmothers in question are of different sub-clans of the same clan and no other incest prohibitions have been violated. Any consequent ritual danger may then be annulled by a special ceremony.[1]

The Tiriki elders claim that present-day young people do not heed the elders' admonitions to observe the exogamy rules and that today one finds unions that would never have been tolerated in their young days. The little evidence available, however, does not support this contention. Wagner, reporting in the middle thirties,[2] describes the same general Abaluyia exogamy rules with the same sorts of border-line cases. He also describes the ceremony at the culmination of which a broken cooking pot is hung from the protruding centre pole of the hut to avert the ill effects of a mildly incestuous (*bwixo budididi*) marriage.[3] These pots are no longer seen in Tiriki, probably because of Christian Mission influence; Protestant missions in the region

[1] ibid., pp. 251–252. Here Wagner presents a description of the lustral ceremony traditionally held by the Abaluyia to remove the ritual danger believed to be caused by socially tolerable cases of minor incest.
[2] ibid., pp. 383–386.
[3] ibid., Wagner, op. cit., p. 385.

have worked hard to abolish this and any other ceremony which they realize involves sacrifices to the ancestral spirits.

Examination of contemporary cases of incest in Tiriki suggests that the general avoidance and horror of incest remains essentially unweakened. Indeed, the abolition of the broken pot ceremony may have been accompanied by an even more stringent avoidance than formerly of mildly incestuous unions, for the general belief in the danger of such unions is still very strong. Two recent cases of incest, one clearcut and the other a border-line case, may serve to indicate the contemporary reaction to incestuous unions.

One case involved a man who slept with his biological daughter and made her pregnant. When the old women of the community discovered that the girl was pregnant, she confessed that her father was responsible. The news immediately spread around the neighbourhood, and the next morning the man was found dead, hanged in his own hut. Every inquiry into the whereabouts of the girl and her baby failed to reveal what had become of them.

The second case rests right on the border-line of tolerated incest, and is a famous contemporary case. It involves a woman who is married to a man of the same clan and sub-clan as her paternal grandmother. The man, an eminent Christian and political leader in Tiriki, has on a number of occasions stood up in public or private discussions and defended his marriage. His defence is received respectfully, even though people generally end the discussion by disagreeing with him. If he were someone of less self-assurance or less stature in the community it is unlikely he could have withstood the public pressure and probably he would have left his wife. The husband defends his marriage by asserting that although a grandmother of his wife does belong to the same clan and sub-clan as he, his own agnatic great-grandfather and her grandmother's father did not have the same biological father. He admits that these greatgrandfathers did come from the same sub-clan or 'house' (*inzu indala*), but that they were from different 'doors' (*muliyango mulala dawe*) of that 'house'. Neighbours and relatives, even if willing to accept this defence based on a *post hoc* lineage sub-division, find the marriage a constant source of embarrassment because they say the husband calls his wife's grandmother by the classificatory term for father's sister (*senje, senje, basenje*); thus, following the regular Tiriki kinship usage, he should address and refer to his wife by the kinship term for 'my daughter' (*mwana muxana wanje*). People assert that incest (*bwixo*) has been committed, genealogical excuses notwithstanding, since they are able to refer to his wife both as a daughter and an in-law (*muxwasi, mu- ba- xwasi*). Thus, even though the basic rule of exogamy has not been violated by a marriage with someone of the agnatic or the mother's agnatic line, a cognatic relationship is commonly recognized to exist between the two people, and kinsmen find themselves in conflict over whether to follow cognatic or affinal kinship terminology and behaviour towards this couple. It is a 'difficult situation' (*shindu shidinyu*), the elders, kinsmen and neighbours aver; even though their considered opinion is that it probably isn't dangerous to the wellbeing of the clans or neighbourhood, they feel it is embarrassing.

Wagner neatly sums up the structural implications of such extended exogamy regulations as the Abaluyia possess.[1]

An important consequence of this far-reaching set of exogamous marriage prohibitions is that by ruling out virtually every form of cousin-marriage, extending to the most distant trace of relationship, the establishment of continued or preferential marriage relations between any two clans is prevented. If a man of clan A marries a woman of clan B this means that none of his ancestors in direct paternal or maternal line for two generations upwards have married into clan B and that none of these children or grandchildren will be able to do so again. The same holds true of the ancestors and offspring of the woman of clan B with regard to clan A. Thus, as the generations change, the clans that intermarry must likewise constantly change, and the members of any given clan are simultaneously linked by marriage with a great number of different clans. The laws of exogamy thus ensure that the network of relations which becomes established through intermarriage is as widely flung as possible. This fact has two important implications as regards social structure. On the one hand, it constitutes a strong force making for tribal integration, and on the other hand, by keeping the affinal relatives of the members of one clan in as diverse groups as possible, it clearly stresses the social preponderance of the paternal kin (and clan) over the maternal kin. It thus prevents the growth of too strong rival loyalties

---

[1] ibid., p. 387.

in the individual which, in the course of time, would weaken the principle of unilateral descent.

The Functions of Bridewealth (buxwi)

The payment of bridewealth (*buxwi bu- xwi*) is the crucial element in the legitimization of a marriage in Tiriki, as it is in so many African tribes. In Tiriki it is this payment which grants the husband's clan the right to claim the children of the union. A man customarily looks to his father for aid in paying his bridewealth. The size of the bridewealth has varied over the decades, and nowadays is affected by such things as how much schooling the girl has received. Today an average bridewealth in Tiriki totals about six cattle, two or three goats or sheep, and several hundred shillings in cash.[1] It is seldom that all of this is paid before the marriage ceremony. Indeed the most common arrangement is for the final payment to be made only after several children have been born. It is not uncommon for the wife's father to have died by that time, and thus it may be the wife's brother who actually receives the last of the payment.

Within the homestead the custom of bridewealth fosters a somewhat strained formalistic relationship between a father and his dependent sons while at the same time serving to intensify the brother-sister bond. With cattle received from a sister's marriage a man will generally do one or another of three things, depending upon the circumstances: (1) he may use the cattle to pay the bridewealth of an older son; (2) if his father has died, and he is now the head of the homestead, and acting *in loco parentis*, he may use the cattle to pay the bridewealth of a younger brother; (3) if no younger brothers can lay claim to the cattle, and his sons are still young, he may use the cattle to acquire an additional wife for himself. In practice the bridewealth is frequently paid in instalments, and no rigorous effort is made to treat the cattle resulting from the marriage of each daughter as separate units. Thus, instalments received may be immediately dispensed to pay debts contracted in one or even all of the three areas mentioned above. The ideal persists in Tiriki that the homestead head will arrange things so that an

---

[1] East African shillings. It is the practice to keep the East African shilling on a par with the British shilling (20 shillings, East Africa, equals one pound, Sterling).

elder son of his may look primarily to the father's younger sisters (to the cattle that their marriage brings into the family homestead) for his bridewealth, and that a younger son may look primarily to his own sisters.

Even though this ideal is almost always modified to a greater or lesser degree in practice, the indirect economic function that a sister may play in the marriage of a brother and/or a brother's son, is clearly recognized. Indeed this is considered reason enough for a brother's concern that a sister be well married.

The bond between brother and sister, reinforced by the custom of bridewealth, is reflected after marriage in the relationship patterns between a woman and her brother's children on the one hand, and those between a man and his sister's children on the other. A woman (and her husband) and her brother's children call and refer to each other by a special reciprocal term, *senje*. *Senje* treats her brothers' children with great warmth and cordiality; indeed they may choose to live in her homestead for protracted periods of time during childhood, and every visiting brother's child, whether the visit is for an hour or for weeks, can expect, when departing for home, to receive a live chicken from his or her paternal aunt. The one thing that the paternal aunt demands in return for this friendliness, care and solicitude is the unconditional friendliness and respect of her brothers' children. Seldom does she fail to receive this, even if she is not as hospitable as most fathers' sisters, for a paternal aunt's curse is feared above all curses as a source of sterility. Thus it is this category of kinsmen, one of whom is generally a vital economic link in the marriage of one's parents, to whom people attribute the greatest cosmic veto power over the conception of their own offspring.

A more openly ambivalent but less tense relationship commonly prevails between a man and his sisters' children. A man generally addresses and refers to a sister's child by the term *mwihwa*. *Biihwa* in turn use the term *xoza* (*xoza, baxoza*) when addressing or referring to a maternal uncle. To find a structural correlate for the ambivalence of the *xoza-mwihwa* relationship again one has only to turn to the matter of bridewealth. The homestead of the father of a young *mwihwa* inevitably has been, and often still is, in the position of owing bridewealth to the

homestead of the *xoza*.[1] The *xoza* (mother's brother) is in turn
obliged by custom to convey the hind quarter of a cow to the
mwihwa's parents after several *biihwa* have been born by his
sister and the bridewealth payment is completed. This gift of
the hind quarter signifies the termination of social avoidances
between various members of the two homesteads. The two
social proscriptions thus terminated are: (a) the forbidding of
visits between the parents of the married couple; (b) the forbidding of visiting between a man and his wife's parents.

A woman, especially during the first years of marriage,
returns to her paternal homestead for frequent and sometimes
extended visits, and almost always she brings her small children
along with her. This means that a man frequently sees a good
deal of his sister's children even while the elders of his homestead are still carefully avoiding any social relations with his
sister's husband and parents; indeed, the two groups may be in
the midst of a legal dispute over bridewealth. Thus the cards
would seem to be stacked against the cordial acceptance of the
sister's children who by birthright are members of the in-law's
homestead and clan. In point of fact, however, a *xoza* feels a real
proprietary interest in his *biihwa*, an interest which is traced and
attributed by the Tiriki themselves again to the working of their
custom of bridewealth. A marriage in Tiriki is only considered
truly consummated by the birth of at least three children.
Regardless of whether or not all the bridewealth is paid in
advance, a man can be expected to send his wife back to her
parents if she proves barren and to demand that his bridewealth
be returned.[2] If she has borne one child, or even two children,
and then bears no more, her husband may send her home to her
paternal homestead. Her father and brothers may then become
involved in the lengthy and expensive process of trying to
divine what sort of curse or sorcery is preventing further
fecundity. If the bridewealth has not been paid in advance, the
girl's family can expect to receive no more than two cattle for
each child born (the total being six cattle). Thus the birth of

---

[1] The term *xoza*, also denotes all the males of the mother's clan and generation;
indeed the plural form, *baxoza*, is used to denote as a group all the mother's clans-
people regardless of generation or sex.

[2] Neither the wife's biological sister nor anyone from her sub-clan (*inzu*) may be
substituted for a barren wife. Indeed no form of sororal polygyny is permitted in
Tiriki.

each sister's child brings a tangible material increase to the homestead of the *xoza*.

The Tiriki fully recognize, and often speak of, the importance of the mother's clan, especially the importance of the mother's brother. The formalized aspects of the *xoza-mwihwa* relationship are manifest in obligations that the *xoza* has towards his sister's daughter at the time of her marriage, and in certain rites that a sister's son must be ready to perform following the death of his *xoza*. Also tradition smiles upon an agreement between a *xoza* and his sister's son which leads to the sister's son's learning a special craft or skill from his *xoza* such as basket making or divining. Finally, a man will often ask a sister's son to come settle near him if there is land available, and even become a member of his homestead.[1]

[1] The maternal (or paternal) matriline, in contrast, has virtually no structural or functional significance in the Tiriki social system. Any talk of matrilineages seems ludicrous to the Tiriki. They are quick to tell you that a woman owns nothing—indeed is nobody—in her own right. She has her clan by virtue of her father, and she achieves her status as a mother and a grandmother thanks to her offspring and the payment of the bridewealth (*buxwi*) by her husband and his family. A woman owns some pots and cooking utensils which are given her, for the most part, by her parents. Also she may acquire some livestock and fowl. Upon her death, however, these animals generally go to her husband or his clansmen.

A daughter may learn certain skills in medicine and sorcery from her mother; add to these skills the prerequisite disposition of temperament, or 'blood' (*masayi*) as the Tiriki put it, which leads to interest in and mastery of these skills in medicine and sorcery, personal clothing and a few bits of jewelery, and you have the sum total of personal attributes, skills, and property acquired from the matriline; and these things are of course only handed from mother to daughter, never from mother to son.

The mother's brother (*xoza*) traditionally plays an active role in the wedding arrangements and bridewealth settlement of his sister's daughters (generally—everything else being equal—the particular mother's brother most involved is the one who received most aid towards his own marriage settlement from the cattle received from his sister's marriage). Since he prospered from his sister's marriage he is now expected to see that the family into which his sister married prospers through his sister's daughters' marriages. Also the mother's brother in some cases has a specific ongoing economic stake in the marriage of a sister's daughter, for the last instalment of the bridewealth for his sister may still be owed him or his family, and he can demand this final payment from the cattle received by the marriage of his sister's eldest daughter.

When an elder dies it is traditionally a sister's son who climbs onto the roof of the elder's hut and removes the stick protruding from the centre of the roof (*shisejese, shi- bi- sejese*), thereby announcing to all that the hut's owner has died. It is fitting (and interesting to note) that the *shisejese* is removed by a member of the very category of relatives whose birth had assured the deceased of the bridewealth necessary for the establishment of his own family.

The distinctive nature of the *xoza-mwihwa* relationship is also manifest informally in many little ways that make it seem more typical of relationships between Tiriki siblings than of inter-action between Tiriki of adjacent generations.

A *mwihwa*, when visiting his *xoza*, cannot be refused his little demands; the *xoza* is an 'easy touch' for pocket money, articles of clothing, and the like. Conversely when a *xoza* meets his *mwihwa* at the market place, or sees him while visiting his sister, the relationship is reversed and the *mwihwa* can be asked for a small gift, must run errands, and do the *xoza's* bidding. This should not be perceived as evidence of the *mwihwa's* possessing proprietary rights over the *xoza's* personal belongings or skills or vice-versa. Rather, this limited area of demanding and giving is in keeping with the relationships between siblings. Siblings both of the same and opposite sex always feel free to make little demands of each other which they expect will be gratified. The demands between a *xoza* and a *mwihwa* are first made through the *mwihwa's* mother as intermediary; then later on as the *mwihwa* grows up this relationship between the *mwihwa* and *xoza* continues without the intermediary.

A man first looks to his father for instruction in a special craft or skill such as basket weaving or divining. If, however, the son does not feel inclined to follow the vocation of his father, an alternative is to go to his *xoza*. For example, a man who wants to learn the art of divining with a rubbing stick (*lusejerele, lu- zi- sejerele*), may have a father and father's brothers skilled in ironworking and other hand-crafts, but untutored in divining. If he has a *xoza* who is such a diviner he may go to him with a goat and make his desire known. If the *xoza* accepts the goat the *mwihwa* becomes his apprentice and in the months that follow he is instructed in divining. He cannot practice until the diviner's death, but from then on he can practice his divining skills and also has the right to pass his knowledge on to his own sons and, if he choses, to his *biihwa*. The possibility of passing skills down through the lineage of one's *biihwa* as well as through one's own lineage has resulted in such a wide dispersal of arts and crafts that today it is hard to find a traditionally important skill such as iron working or divining that is not known by members of at least one sub-clan in every major Tiriki clan. Remembrance still persists, however, as to which clan or clans first brought a particular skill to Tiriki.

A *mwihwa* may turn to his *xoza* for land as well as skills. In both cases, however, the *mwihwa* may not demand, but only request, such things of a *xoza*, and the *xoza* can always refuse. When granting land to a *mwihwa* not only must the *xoza* be willing, but he (the *xoza*) must also get the consent of his brothers, neighbours (*barende, mu- ba- -rende*), and the community elders (*basaxulu bu luhya*). Such a grant is not considered binding unless the *mwihwa* pays the *xoza* a goat, sheep, or perhaps only a chicken. The boundaries of the land are walked and the payment made in front of community witnesses. Just as with skills acquired from the *xoza*, the payment affirms the *mwihwa's* right to pass on the land received to his own children, or to grant it, with community permission, to his own *biihwa*.

The *xoza-mwihwa* relationship finds a supernatural correlate in the sanctions which, as almost always in Tiriki, flow from the elder to the younger generation. It is said that a *xoza's* displeasure but not his curse, may bring the offending *mwihwa* a case of skin-itch, or a cloud of flying ants swarming around his head—appropriate distress to accompany a sometimes awkward ambiguous relationship. In addition, a *xoza* may curse his *mwihwa* with sterility or barrenness.

The Socio-Religious Ideal of Remembrance

A basic element in the Tiriki feeling towards clan, sub-clan, and family, is the Tiriki concept of remembrance. The Tiriki feel that everyone wants very much to be remembered, both those who have died and those who are still living. The clan and sub-clan form the principal framework within which remembrance is made manifest.

The Tiriki have only a weak concept of a man's being remembered for his works; mighty warriors and famous doctors are remembered for their deeds by their age group and even the whole tribe, but for the most part even they are remembered and boasted of only by descendants; it is through his own offspring, through descendants of his clan brothers, and to a less extent, through his sister's children (*biihwa*) that a person primarily feels his desire to be remembered will be gratified.

A man wants sons, 'so that there will be people to remember me.' A man invites his sister's children to come and live with him primarily because he has extra land and wants their help and support; but for the second reason he will usually say, 'because they are my sister's children, and I want those people to remember me.'

It is felt that the dead want to be remembered by the living just as strongly as the living want to be remembered by their heirs. Furthermore, the welfare of the living is believed to be intimately tied up with the beneficent disposition of the dead. An ancestor who feels forgotten may let sickness or some other disaster strike one of his descendants.

The naming of a newborn child reflects both of these beliefs. During the first few weeks of his life a child is presented one after another with names of deceased relatives of the father's and mother's clans. It is carefully observed which names the infant received with a smile, and which ones are followed by whimper-ing and tears. Generally the elders first try the name of a clans-man of the father or the mother who died shortly before the baby's birth. A name is eventually selected which the grand-parents and other elders feel pleases the child. In the weeks that follow if the baby gets sick elders will be brought in to think of deceased ancestors (*baguga*) who may feel forgotten and who are thus causing the child to suffer; the most likely name will then be chosen and given the child as a second name. If the baby's health then improves, the name will be used occasionally thence-forth along with the first name. A sickly baby may in this manner build up a repertoire of several ancestors' names.

It is common for a young Tiriki man as he starts his own family to nurture the dream of having many sons and, through them, a large progeny to remember him, all of whom will trace their origin directly back to him. The young man does not say he wants to start a new clan, but when sketching the picture of how his descendants will proliferate and branch out, he follows the identical model he has heard the elders use when discussing clan genealogies. At such a discussion an old man held in esteem for his genealogical knowledge will stand up and speak more or less as follows:

'B was the first man of our clan to come to Tiriki; he was the son of A (usually the clan name with the person prefix). B had seven sons; one of these got lost, went off to Nandi to live, but the remaining sons were . . . ' Here he names the six sons of generation C, throwing a stick down onto the ground after naming each son, so that upon finishing he has six sticks lying in front of him representing the six sons and their respective descendants. 'Now each of these six sons formed one of the "houses" (*zinzu*) of our clan; each founded the "house" which bears his name.' Next the elder gives a detailed account of the agnatic lines of his own 'house' (sub-clan) which is usually from three to five generations in depth; then any elders present belonging to other sub-clans step forward in turn to recount in detail their patrilineages.

A common variation on such a discussion is for the ancestor of B generation to have just one son; then it is C who has many sons who form the sub-clans.

To return to a young man's dreams of his progeny-to-be, no

matter how many brothers he may have, the young man tends to see himself as the potential head of a clan, i.e., as the father of many sons, rather than as the potential head of a sub-clan or 'house', i.e., as himself one of many sons. The young father likes to view himself as the head of a growing homestead (*mujizi*) which after the years have passed will be viewed by his descendants as the origin of several lineage segments (*zinzu*), each segment having been founded by one of his sons. Before many years have passed a wealthy man may procure a second wife with the hopes of having more sons; if his first wife has borne many daughters but few or no sons, he will very likely use cattle received at the marriage of one of his elder daughters to pay bridewealth for a second wife. The ideal of the eldest son of each of a man's wives forming a separate house or lineage segment is sometimes brought up by the elders in genealogical discussions, but in practice this ideal is seldom bothered about or made manifest. A seniority is generally remembered in genealogies, but it is the seniority of succession of birth, neither the mother's names and their order of marriage, nor even their clans generally being remembered back beyond the second or third ascending generation.

A Father's Obligations Towards His Sons

Once a young man has been initiated into the tribe and is ready for marriage, he becomes a very mixed blessing to his father, for he has become a rival. The father is prone to try to further his dream of heading a large homestead to which many sons and their families are attached, while each son in turn nurtures a similar dream for himself. Custom decrees that every father should help his sons acquire bridewealth so that they can marry. The unmarried mature sons are expected, for their part, to help their father amass wealth in livestock; nowadays this means that an unmarried son working away from the tribe is expected to send home the greater part of his earnings so that the father may buy cattle, a good portion of which will later be used for that son's bridewealth. The actual planning for the acquisition of the bridewealth is primarily the father's responsibility. Today, with the son often away, the father may take this responsibility rather lightly. It is not at all uncommon for a son to return after several years away working to find that his father has used the money he has sent home to acquire another wife for himself instead of having amassed a herd for his absent son's bridewealth. In such a case the son may appeal to his grandfather and other clan elders for support in obtaining bridewealth from his father. Strong pressure would then be put on the father by his clan elders to apply whatever extra wealth he had to acquiring bridewealth cattle for the son and to reserve all future excess for that purpose. The son, however, might be only partially successful in his appeal if he had not previously sent home money or engaged in some other activity of direct social or economic aid to his father. Sons are careful to inform brothers, grandparents and other relatives and friends about what they have done for their father so that if such a mishap occurs they will have people to speak for them in their appeal to their clan and community elders.

A son is not always blameless in his relation with his father over bridewealth. A son often tries to force his father's hand by running off and eloping with his favourite sweetheart. Marriage by elopement is in fact today the most common form of marriage, and probably was in traditional times as well. But it is not, nor ever was, the type of marriage preferred by the families of the couple. When a couple elope they generally go by night to a prearranged rendezvous, the house of a mutual friend sufficiently distant from their respective parents' homesteads so that it will not be very easy to find them and interrupt their tryst on the very first night. If they are not discovered and chased home by their kinsfolk before the first night is over, they generally continue to live at the friend's house for several days until the father of the girl has had a chance to lay his demands for immediate payment of the bridewealth before the father of the boy and the elders of the boy's community. Then the couple may return and live in an empty hut in the vicinity of the boy's home, eating food cooked by his mother. Perhaps the boy's father will be able to forestall any payment of bridewealth until after the birth of the first child, but after that he will be liable to pay at least one animal on demand, no matter what hardship it may cause him. An elopement by a son who is known by his clansmen not to have given (and is thenceforth still not willing to give) his father aid in acquiring cattle, puts the son in the bad graces of all the clan elders. When, in future, the son needs the elders' economic aid, judicial intercession, or anti-witchcraft medicine, he will find them loath to help him. Actually, what happens in most cases of marriage is that a father tries to postpone his son's marriage for as long as possible, while the son, after he feels he has worked and waited long enough, will force his father to procure the marriage cattle by eloping or threatening to elope.

When a son marries it is up to his father to assign fields for his new daughter-in-law to work, and to designate the place for his son to build his house. Sometimes the fields are assigned and the house built before marriage, but generally not until afterwards. The father usually gives his eldest son a house site and fields directly adjoining his own, for it is the eldest son who usually becomes the economic and ritual leader of the homestead upon the senility or death of the father. The succeeding sons may be provided with a home on any of the father's properties, or if they so choose they might emigrate to a mother's brother's (*milimi, ja baxoza*) or new lands (*milimi jimbiya*). Usually, however, a son prefers to accept his right to a house site and land on one of his father's fields during the early days of his marriage.

Inheritance of Land and Other Property

Several months after an older man's death, a well-attended meeting of the sub-clan and neighbours is held to make final distribution of his property. It is at this time that all people, related or not, come forth to state whatever claims they may feel they have against the estate of the deceased. At such a meeting (*lubego, lu- zim- -bego*) of the sub-clan it is generally the eldest member of sound mind and in good community standing who acts as leader of the meeting, and who is the person depended on to reflect the general feeling of the sub-clan and reserve its final veto. A younger man of that sub-clan who fulfils the general Tiriki requirements for a good leader, but who is not an actual son of the deceased, acts as the executive leader of the meeting, deferring to and voicing the opinions of the elder spokesman. The general opinion of the sub-clan is arrived at through discussion led by the younger man.[1]

[1] The data given above and which follows on the *lubego* is drawn from hearsay, systematic questioning, and from what my wife and I observed when we attended a *lubego* in the autumn of 1955.

Clan sentiment about remembrance and property contrasts with and counterbalances the individual's personal desire to be remembered. The same man who is interested in furthering his own acquisition of land and cattle, and through them wives and offspring, regardless of the better interests of his father, brothers and sons, becomes very protective of the greater interests of the clan, sub-clan and all members of the deceased's homestead in those cases where his own immediate personal gain is not involved. In such situations he identifies with the clan, and becomes concerned that the welfare and growth of the larger group be put ahead of any of the more individualistic wishes and personal ambitions of particular clan members. Younger men say they feel it right that the very old men of the sub-clan be the ones who have the final word in deciding how property should be distributed, because they feel that very old people, provided they are shown respect, and are given shelter, food, and beer are too aged to have any material wants for themselves. Furthermore such very old men are regarded as the 'fathers of their clan', and as such they are expressly forbidden by Tiriki custom from themselves moving into huts or utilizing other property that is already being used by their 'sons'.[1]

At the large post-funeral meetings (*zimbego*) the grants of land made to the mature sons by the father before his death are reviewed and accepted, or contested and revised. The eldest son is generally recognized as the spokesman for those sons not yet mature, and he is usually given the responsibility of distributing the remaining land to the younger sons as they reach

[1] Elders of the sub-clan (*inzu*) are in most cases those who have the final say about property distribution at a *lubego*. This does not mean, however, that a sense of pride in and loyalty towards one's sub-clan exists that is comparable to that commonly felt towards one's clan. Rather the Tiriki simply view the sub-clan as the logical group to tend to matters such as inheritance, because they are the largest group within the clan who generally have intimate knowledge of each other's genealogy and affairs. In the absence of any formalized group of clan leaders in Tiriki it is felt only right that the sub-clan elders should be the final arbiters in any decision involving the disposition of a man's property.

The term sub-clan (*inzu*), although it is purported to refer to a particular group of agnates the founding ancestor of which is definite and fixed, in practice is used to refer to any group of agnates which at a given time is acting corporately in an economic or ritual capacity. The sub-clan to which a man will say he belongs when asked, 'What is your sub-clan?' is generally a larger, more geographically dispersed lineage group than the lineage segment that he turns to in times of family or personal crisis, and with which he regularly interacts in such matters as inheritance settlements.

maturity, providing the mother or mothers of these immature sons (i.e., widow or widows of the deceased) are past child-bearing age. In the case of young widows of child-bearing age, the meeting inquires what members of the sub-clan might be interested in inheriting them as their own wives. Sometimes a clan brother of the deceased has already made inquiries that have been received favourably by the young widow, in which case this fact will be made public, and the proposed liaison may be approved by the meeting. In other cases, preliminary inquiries are made at this time and final arrangements are postponed until a later date, when a small meeting of the sub-clans is called just for that purpose. Generally the man inheriting the widow is a full or half-brother of the deceased, or at least a member of the same sub-clan.[1]

The Tiriki do not look at widow inheritance as increasing the family and estate of a deceased clan brother; rather it is viewed as a way of caring for the widow and children of the deceased and of helping the clan to grow through the fullest utilization of the widow's child-bearing capacity. The clan brother who takes on this responsibility has his own reward through becoming the *pater* as well as the *genitor* of any children borne him by his inherited wife. The widow's new husband is given charge of whatever portion of the deceased's unassigned lands the sub-clan elders decide will take care of the widow's own needs. He is also assigned some additional land to help meet the future needs not only of the widow's immature sons, but also of the immature sons of her new husband by his other wife or wives. The amount of land accompanying the inherited wife varies from case to case. It is said that the new husband's name as well as the name of the deceased clan brother will thenceforth be on the land accompanying the inherited wife whether or not more children result from the union. When the sons of the inherited wife by her deceased husband come of age they have the right to one half of the land assigned to the care of their foster father. The latter, however, may divide the other half between all his own sons regardless of which of his wives have borne them. It is common for the youngest son of each wife eventually to receive for his

---

[1] In the neighbouring Abaluyia tribe of Maragoli a son of a senior wife may inherit a junior wife of his deceased father, but this is not allowed among the Tiriki.

own use the fields and house assigned for use by his mother. Provision is made, however, for the aged mother to continue to live in the house if she chooses, or in another house to her liking, and a garden is reserved for her own use.

Inheritance of Livestock

When a homestead head dies his cattle are divided fairly equally among his sons. The eldest son often takes over the deceased father's role as homestead head, and assumes responsibility for the cattle of his immature brothers. In such cases it is to the eldest brother that each unmarried son later turns for aid in acquiring bridewealth. If the eldest son has not yet come of age the clan brother who inherits the deceased man's widow generally takes over the homestead leadership and bridewealth responsibility. Although no formal scheme exists by which a man is expected to plan for the inheritance of each of his sons, a thoughtful father gives a great deal of consideration to this matter and also makes it clear to his brothers and others clansmen whence he intends to acquire bridewealth cattle for each son. Indeed, a man who has a number of cattle and/or daughters who will in time bring in cattle, is obliged to account to his brothers and affines for the future disposition of each animal. In this way he is able to excuse himself, without hard feelings, from innumerable requests to lend cattle to brothers, brother's sons, and other kinsmen. It is common for a man to farm out (*xw- ejexa*) cattle to various categories of relatives who then receive the offspring of the cattle as compensation for their care. Another common practice is for two neighbours (generally non-kin) to buy a cow or bull in partnership; an heir of either receives part ownership in livestock and the accompanying mutual responsibilities that attend such a relationship.[1] Thus the eldest brother or the clan brother who is appointed guardian falls heir to a complicated network of rights and obligations over livestock which generally express themselves sooner or later as litigation about bridewealth payments. For example, a father-in-law sues before the community elders (nowadays it may go directly to a gazetted African Court) for payment of his

[1] Joint ownership of cattle in Tiriki seems to follow the same conventions described by Wagner for the Maragoli. See Günter Wagner, *The Bantu of North Kavirondo*, Vol. II (London: Oxford University Press, 1956), pp. 103–4.

daughter's bridewealth. His decision to sue may have been precipitated by a younger brother's persistent demands for cattle for his own bridewealth. The sub-clan and maternally linked relatives of the person sued, and sometimes even non-kin, may all be involved since they may be obliged to make immediate repayment of loans if the case is lost. It is not the purpose of this chapter to analyse the nature of livestock ownership and litigation, but it is relevant here to point out the sort of network of mutual obligations towards clan kin and neighbours into which a person is usually drawn through inherited or acquired rights in livestock.[1]

Attitudes Towards Land and Land Rights

Until recent times land elicited a markedly different set of feelings from those manifest towards livestock. In the first place, land has never been used as a medium of ritual exchange, while animals have; and secondly, until the present generation land has always been readily available. Although frequently talking about the identification of clan and land, the Tiriki have not felt it mandatory for the ritual and political control of a particular region to remain through the generations under the control of the first Abaluyia lineage to settle the region. The ideal of clan lands is in practice subordinated both politically and ritually to the pan-tribal Terik-Tiriki age group organization, which cross-cuts clan and territorial groupings. The result is that clans are probably of less political significance in Tiriki than in any other Abaluyia tribe. Further, the Tiriki are an Abaluyia frontier community. Unlike some of the other southern Abaluyia tribes, the Tiriki never felt the pinch of limited land resources until the last decade or two. Directly east of Tiriki there are great stretches of field and forest uninhabited except for occasional wandering Nandi. It is a Tiriki tradition for the adventurous, the crowded, or the refugee from a family feud to open a new homestead in Nandi land. Until about 1906, when the British administration was able to establish fixed tribal

---

[1] Wagner gives an excellent account of rights in land and livestock, particularly among the Maragoli, in Vol. II of *The Bantu of North Kavirondo* (op. cit.), Chap. IV, pp. 75–138. Much of the material that Wagner presents here on Maragoli cattle rights is in keeping with Tiriki custom.

boundaries in the region, there was a continuous movement of
Tiriki eastward. This migration was accompanied by Tiriki-
Nandi raids interspersed with peace oaths made possible by
related age group structures and common peace rituals. But the
infiltration into Nandi land was so slow that the Nandi with
their pastoral interests never felt any need to make a concerted
effort to curtail the Tiriki settlers. Once he had cleared bush for
his hut and a garden for his wife, a Tiriki pioneer would call for
clan brothers, sister's sons, and even his wife's brothers to come
and settle around him, to make his life less lonely and more
secure from Nandi cattle raids. These Tiriki settlements then
expanded naturally.

The facility with which new land could be obtained meant
that sons were often indifferent to the precise division of their
father's land. It was only considered important that one son,
generally the eldest, should settle down in a homestead that
was an extension of, or adjacent to, his father's. This was the
son to whom the father would confide his proprietary affairs,
and who would generally be recognized as the guardian of the
father's estate after the latter's senility or death. Other sons
might stay and use some of the land assigned them by their
father, or they might go to live with a maternal uncle (*xoza*) or
other relative, or decide to open up new land.

It is not uncommon, as the reader will recall, for a man to
dispense some of his land to people who are not his sons. He
frequently gives some land to his sister's son (*mwihwa*), and less
commonly, to his brother-in-law (*muxwasi*), son-in-law (*naxobizala*, — *naxobizala*, or, *guga*, *guga*, *baguga*), or simply an
unrelated friend (*mulina*, *mu- ba- -lina*). Before making such an
allotment a man must get the consent of his own immediate
elder kin, the sub-clan elders living in the vicinity, and his
neighbours (*barende*, *mu- ba- -rende*). Then, with the community
elders (*basaxulu wu luhya*) present as witnesses, the land to be
transferred is walked, the boundaries clearly defined, and a payment of chickens or hoes, or perhaps a goat, is made by the
recipients. The giving and receiving of the animals or tools is
viewed not as an exchange equal in value to the property
received, but rather as a way of legitimizing the transaction and
of transferring the rights of use and inheritance of the land to the
new owner. According to the Tiriki, the gift puts the name of the

new owner (*mwene mw- -be- -ene*) on the land.[1] If the new owner thenceforth makes use of the fields by making his principal homestead there, or by establishing a second or third wife there, his sons will have the right to inherit and divide these fields for their own use.

A man can make private arrangements to let a relative or neighbour use some of his fields for a year, and then if both parties so choose they may renew that agreement in a subsequent year. This is clearly felt to be different from making a grant of fields where clan and community elders are called in to witness the exchange. A private arrangement which continues for years, however, becomes tantamount to a legal transfer of ownership. A son whose father has transferred rights of use over one of his fields year after year, even if no money or goods have changed hands, will, at best, get the elders to concede him only a small share in the land. The main rights are distributed among the sons of the regular occupier and user.

This permissive structure of land rights is, needless to say, changing now that land is becoming very scarce. It is not uncommon today for a man to try to claim a share in land that his father or grandfather had granted to a relative of another clan, or to a non-kinsman. If such a plaintiff belongs to one of the first clans to occupy the region he sometimes tries to win support by appealing to the concept of clan land as it has developed in Maragoli[2] and other Abaluyia tribes. He points out that his clan was the first to occupy that land and that consequently he has a permanent claim to a share of the land of his agnatic ancestors. Such a case usually stands or falls, not on clan priority, but on the ability of the user to produce testimony that he or his father was granted rights to the land in the presence of the community elders (*basaxulu wu luhya*). If witnesses are found (not necessarily those same elders who witnessed the actual

[1] See Wagner (ibid.), pp. 76–100, for a rather full account of Maragoli land tenure. The distinction in rights which the Maragoli make between an 'owner' (*omwene*) and a man who has purchased rights to occupy land (*omumenya*) (pp. 76–80) doesn't really exist in Tiriki where no land is held to be solely under the charge of a particular clan. In Tiriki there was traditionally no office of clan elder (*eligutu—liguru* in Lutiriki) (see ibid., pp. 75 *et passim.*, and pp. 87–90, for a description of the Maragoli office of *eligutu*); land disposal in Tiriki was handled instead by the elders of the sub-clan and community involved.

[2] ibid., Chap. IV. Note especially pp. 87–88.

transaction) and their testimony judged sound, the plaintiff receives no land. Otherwise the plaintiff is generally granted a portion of the fields.

Grandparent–Grandchild Relationships: Attitudes Towards the Aged

The ancestor cult in Tiriki is traditionally maintained and administered by the elders, particularly the most senior elders. It can best be understood, initially, in terms of Tiriki attitudes towards the aged. Three themes manifest themselves again and again in relationships with the aged. First, there is the warm, informal, solicitous nature of the grandparent–grandchild relationship. Second is the belief and feeling that the aged are closest to the ancestors (*baguga*) and thus are best able to obtain the good will of the ancestral spirits (*misambwa, mu- mi- -sambwa*). Third, there is the belief that most supernatural and magical power is obtained and retained by the aged. The belief in the old people's near-monopoly of magical power is further reinforced by the view that the most powerful forms of sorcery carry with them the property of making the practitioner sterile; thus with few exceptions only those past child bearing age will ever use such power. It can be seen that attitudes towards the aged run the gamut from the most friendly and informal to the most fearful and sinister.

The reader will remember that a man usually views the marriage of his sons with strongly mixed feelings, if only because the need to provide for their bridewealth often curtails his own desire for more wives and sons. In contrast, grandchildren are usually viewed by their grandparents as an unmixed blessing. Grandparents generally have few responsibilities towards their grandchildren; but they are living evidence that their names will probably be remembered after they die.

During the first few weeks of a child's life its grandparents, especially on the paternal side, take the initiative in choosing its name, and in asking the ancestral spirits to bless it. Also they are asked to give counsel and aid on those occasions when the baby is sick or ailing. Before a baby is able to get about by himself he will have made innumerable trips to his grandparents on the hip of the child appointed to look after him. After he is able to walk he continues to think of his grandparents' hut as a favourite place to visit, and in his turn often goes there with his infant

charges.[1] When a child reaches the age of six or seven, about
the time when he has his front lower incisors knocked out,[2] he
is expected by his parents and brothers and sisters to stop sleeping in his mother's hut and to start sleeping at the hut of a
widowed grandparent until he reaches puberty. He will then
join the peers of his own sex in a sleeping hut (*lisabo li- ma-*
-sabo). The boys and the girls have separate sleeping huts. The
girls' hut is usually under the supervision of an old woman.

Grandparents and grandchildren banter a great deal. Their
joking is often sexually toned, and expressions of endearment
such as 'sweetheart' (*ijolwa*), 'my little wife' (*muxali wanje*
mudididi), or 'my husband' (*musaza wanje*) are frequently used
when addressing or referring to a grandchild of the opposite sex.
These two categories of kinsmen would never be permitted to
marry, however. In the evening a grandmother will often tell
her young grandchildren stories and teach them songs. Grandfathers generally remain more distant from the very young than
grandmothers. In the days before schools were established it
was common for men of the grandparental generation to gather
before a fire in the evening and tell stories about the famous
warriors of the past, and other manly stories, to the older boys
who were approaching the age for circumcision. Later in life, if
a man is in trouble, for example over a matter like his expectation
of bridewealth, it is to a grandfather that he naturally turns for
support. When a person has been cursed by an elder, or is the
victim of sorcery (most notably *bubila*), he usually looks first to
his father for aid (a girl generally turns first to her mother) who
may send him to his grandfather for his intercession and aid.

In return for this solicitude and warmth of feeling, grandparents expect their grandchildren to do chores and run errands
for them, and to show respect and quick obedience. As a child
grows up and comes to realize the ritual magical and religious
power held by his ageing grandparents, disrespect towards
them becomes untenable; it is quite literally viewed as a sure

[1] Generally girls are selected by parents to serve as nursemaids for the infants,
but it is not uncommon for a young boy to be given the task of looking after a
younger sibling.

[2] The practice of knocking out the front lower incisors, although universal in
pre-European times, is now practised only by a few pagan Tiriki and very few, if
any, Tiriki Christians. See Wagner, Vol. I (op. cit.), pp. 27–28, and pp. 40–41, for
brief discussions of this traditional practice.

road to madness (*bulalu, bu- -lalu*). Everyone in Tiriki agrees that the old people have the power to drive the young insane; at every large market there is usually to be seen at least one mentally disturbed person whose madness is attributed to an elder's curse.

A man's assumption of grandparenthood coincides with that time in his life when he is expected to take an active part in the judicial affairs of the clan and the community and also to assume an increasingly important part in the ritual aspects of clan and community life. After experiencing the easy warmth and special concern showered on them by their grandparents, children begin to see these same grandparents officiate at ceremonies after each sibling's birth, and preside at ceremonies held for themselves or others at times of illness and other misfortune. Thus the image of the grandparent as someone wonderful and friendly, but also awful and powerful, is firmly established.

As they grow older and their descendants increase in number, most grandparents find a growing satisfaction of their own familial aspirations through caring for their own grandchildren and other infants and youths of the clan. Grandchildren are the agents through which grandparents achieve the remembrance that their cultural experience from early childhood has taught them to cherish. Grandparents are aware that some of their grandchildren's children and grandchildren will bear their names and give them special remembrance. Thus, the Tiriki man's dream of being the 'father of a nation', of becoming a clan father, so rudely jolted by his sons' marriages and their demands for help with bridewealth, are soon afforded new encouragement by the birth of his sons' sons. A Tiriki grandfather finds a new and increasing gratification of his own paternalistic ambitions through identification with his clan as a whole, and particularly through care of his own children and other infants and youth of the clan.

These characteristic attitudes between grandparents and grandchildren may be extended to embrace any kin of the second ascending or second descending generation; and even, in attenuated form, to members of the second ascending and descending generations with whom one has no kinship bonds. This extension of behaviour patterns is in harmony with the kinship terminology. A Tiriki most commonly refers to, and addresses, all male relatives of the second ascending and second descending generations as *guga*, and females as *guxu* (*guxu*, *baguxu*). These terms are often also extended to non-kin of senior or junior generations towards whom one feels especially friendly or respectful. *Guga* and *guxu* are regularly used, for example, when addressing one's parents-in-law after avoidances of behaviour and speech have been relaxed. It is fruitless to make too much of the relationship between kinship terms and behaviour patterns, but it is interesting to note that the reciprocity of concern which grandparents and grandchildren feel towards each other should be paralleled by terminological reciprocity.[1]

In summary, grandparents view their grandchildren as those who will remember them after they die and as those who assure the continuation of the clan. In other words, grandparents generally understand, often in ways that they can express in words, that their grandchildren are the agents through which their most precious personal ambitions will be realized. Grandchildren in their turn come to view grandparents not only as very kind and pleasant people, but also as the story tellers and tutors of worldly wisdom, and, most important, as the people they can depend on to help most in times of real trouble or distress. Grandparents and grandchildren view each other as the trustees of their respective destinies.

Religion and the Ancestor Cult: Traditional Tiriki Views on Cosmology, the Moral Order, and the Supernatural

Traditional Tiriki religious beliefs are quite in harmony with the prevailing Abaluyia and general Bantu idea that the spirits of the deceased have a continuing influence over the fortunes of the living. A crucial aspect of the relationship the Tiriki feel exists between the living and the dead is the distinction they make between the fairly recently deceased paternal and

[1] Alternative vocative kinship terms are often employed between grandparents and grandchildren that extend terminological reciprocity to grandchildren and grandparents of the opposite sex. It is not uncommon, for example, for an old woman to address her grandson by the term *guxu*, even though *guxu* in a referential sense denotes a female, i.e., grandmother, or granddaughter. The grandson when addressed as *guxu* by his grandmother then uses the same term (*guxu*) when replying to her.

maternal agnatic ancestors (*baguga*), and the generalized ancestral spirits (*misambwa*).[1]

The term *misambwa* (hardly ever used in the singular) generally denotes 'spirits of the deceased', but without any strong lineage connotation. *Baguga* (*mu- ba- -guga*, seldom used in the singular), on the other hand, when used to refer to the spirits of the deceased, generally also denotes lineage, and in addition carries a strong connotation of a personal relationship arising from a prior intimacy with the persons whose spirits are being denoted. The *misambwa* are the ancestral spirits of both kin and allies who live together in a world more or less apart from the world of the living. The Tiriki pagan elders are not sure exactly where the *misambwa* generally reside or what sort of existence they lead, but they agree that the *misambwa* continue to have access to the world of the living and that they can strongly influence their welfare. It is felt to be of paramount importance, therefore, to get and keep the support of the *misambwa*. This support is gained through the rites of supplication which are most commonly held at the homestead ancestral shrine (*lusambwa, lu- zi- -sambwa*). In times of supplication it is common for the presiding ritual elder (*musaalisi, mu- ba- saalisi*) first to beseech one or two of his deceased *baguga* whom he names; on other occasions he may simply call on *baguga* generally, without mentioning any names. Then he supplicates the *misambwa* for

[1] This distinction is more implicit than explicit and also is blurred by two terminological ambiguities. Nevertheless the distinction is clearly manifest in the ancestor cult through the manner in which the living relate themselves to the spirits of their deceased ancestors. One of the terminological ambiguities is that *misambwa* is a rather general term which may be used to denote not only the genealogically more distant ancestral spirits, but also is sometimes used to refer to the spirits of forebearers who were alive recently enough to be remembered by living elders; and it is this last category of ancestral spirits which are more commonly known as *baguga*. The second ambiguity is between the term *baguga* (*mu- ba- -guga*), referring to the spirits of deceased kinsmen (principally agnatic and mother's agnatic) who were known and are remembered by living elders, and the kinship term *baguga* (*guga, baguga*), the plural form of the term denoting grandfather, grandchild, etc. The Tiriki are very explicit about their feeling that *guga, baguga*, and *muguga, baguga* are two different concepts, but in practice they often use the term *guga* when evoking the spirit of a particular greatgrandparent, or even more distant agnate; also they frequently employ *muguga* when speaking of an agnatic elder who is still alive. The linguistic picture is further muddled by the occasional use of *muguga, baguga* to denote agnatic ancestral spirits of the long dead; in such cases, however, the speaker is usually referring exclusively to his own agnatic ancestors or to the agnatic ancestors in some other specific lineage rather than to the ancestral spirits in general.

help and assistance. The ritual elder acts on the assumption that the way to get the *misambwa*'s attention, and to get them to give strength to him and his progeny and charges, is by first remembering and praising his own deceased *baguga*. The *baguga*, pleased to be remembered and praised, may then feel moved to solicit the aid of the *misambwa* in general on behalf of their living descendants.

Wagner gives a succinct description of the traditional Maragoli beliefs and attitudes towards the spirits of the deceased.[1] In spite of fifty years of increasing Christian mission activity, one finds many of these beliefs and attitudes still held by both Christian and pagan Tiriki; but most of the ritual that accompanied these attitudes in earlier times has been forgotten, modified, or displaced. The form and ritual of the ancestor cult *per se* is now nearly defunct. Only a generation ago Tiriki elders report it was normal for a sub-community area of about two or three hundred people to contain one or two dozen family ancestral shrines. Today often only one or two homesteads in such a community might retain ancestral shrines. Thus, perforce, the following account of the traditional ancestor cult is based as much on hearsay as on observation.

The homestead (*mujizi*) ancestral shrine (*lusambwa*) is the place where the rites of the ancestor cult are most often performed. Ideally, the keeper of a homestead ancestral shrine is also the homestead head, and the eldest son of the deceased homestead head. In practice, however, the position is often held by a father's brother, even though the jural and economic responsibilities of the homestead may be primarily in the hands of the father's eldest son. An adult son who is considered fit to run the everyday affairs of the homestead he has inherited from his father is often, nevertheless, unqualified to officiate at the ancestral shrine because he is still too young. Such duties are considered the rightful province of the ritual elders (*basaxulu basaalisi*), who are drawn from the senior age grade in Tiriki.[2] In such cases the primary ritual responsibility for the homestead is in the hands of an elder clansman who is expected to come in and officiate at the shrine at times of supplication.

---

[1] Wagner, Vol. I, op. cit., pp. 159–67.

[2] See Chap. II, pp. 68–70, for a description of the Tiriki age grades and the traditional duties of each.

The homestead ancestral shrine is usually placed under the eaves of the granary (*shyaji, shy- by- -aji*) in which the crops of the homestead head's senior wife (*muxayo wu mwene*) are stored. Millet from this granary is used to make the beer used in supplications at the ancestral shrine. The granary is usually fifteen to twenty feet in front of the entrance of the senior wife's hut. The ancestral shrine, situated on the side of the granary facing the hut, consists of two parts. One part is a slender branch of the *lusiyola* tree (markhamia platycalyx), which is renowned for its great size, toughness, and resistance to rotting. Known as the 'branch of the ancestral shrine' (*musaala gu lusambwa*), it is placed so that it extends from the ground up to the eaves of the granary. The second part of the shrine consists of several, usually three, small stones called 'the stones of the ancestral spirits' (*majina ji misambwa*) placed around the base of the *lusiyola* branch. One stone is for the deceased father of the homestead, one for the present homestead head (*mwene*), and the third is added by the homestead elder, usually for his eldest son, after that son has a wife and children of his own.

In times of trouble or stress, or in times of transition and celebration there are supplications to the ancestral spirits at the *lusambwa*. Illness, for example, may induce a homestead head to hold a supplication. Perhaps with a diviner's aid, the homestead head has decided that the illness may have come because the ancestral spirits are feeling forgotten and consequently are no longer giving their strength to the people of the homestead. Thus, it may be decided to hold a special supplication and gathering of remembrance (*lizuxiza, li- ma- -zuxiza*) at the ancestral shrine. Supplications and offerings are inevitably made at the ancestral shrine of the homestead principally involved on the occasion of wedding or funeral celebrations, at the conclusion of a youth's initiation, &c.

When a major supplication is to be held at the ancestral shrine, the homestead head has some beer brewed, usually by his first wife, and an especially selected chicken (*ingoxo ingasizwe*) slaughtered. Then, in the company of the ritual elders (*basaalisi*) of the community and as many other elders (*basaxulu mu- ba- -saxulu*) of the community (both clansmen and neighbours) as wish to attend, the homestead's ritual elder puts a few drops of blood from the slaughtered bird on each of the ancestral stones. Next he places a bit of eleusine porridge or mush (*busela bu bule* or *bushuma bu bule*) on the stones, and finally tops the offerings with drops of beer (*malwa, ma- -lwa*). As the homestead ritual elder sprinkles the beer he supplicates the ancestral spirits and asks their blessing. The supplication is generally simple and direct, and repeated at each stone. The following is an example:

Guga belu mungwi malwa bulahi!
Xumenyi ni milembe!
Bandu bosi bizanga; misambwa yanzi mungwi malwa bulahi.
Xandi xujendi bulahi; xumenyi bulahi.

Our forefathers, drink up the beer!
May we dwell in peace!
Everyone is gathering; please drink up the beer, ancestral spirits.
And may we be well; may we remain well.

The traditional way of showing friendship, hospitality, indeed of doing anyone a special favour in Tiriki, is to serve food followed by beer. Thus, it is appropriate that this should be done for the ancestral spirits when trying to restore their favour and aid. The *basaalisi*, and other elders of the community who come to help beseech the ancestors, eat the sacrificial chicken (on very special occasions a goat or some other large animal may be used instead) and drink beer through tubes (*zinsexa, lu- zin- -sexa*) from a pot which has been placed between the ancestral stones. After the beer drinking is over, a small pot of beer is left for the ancestral spirits who may be dwelling far away.

There are many different occasions, all more or less marked by stress, on which the ancestral spirits are beseeched and remembered at the homestead ancestral shrines. Not only are supplications at the *lusambwa* held as part of the regular *rites de passage*, and at times of illness, but they are also performed as part of special lustral ceremonies (*miiluxa*) performed to purify warriors after they have killed in battle, to restore peace between kinsmen or neighbours who have been fighting, and to neutralize the particular contamination (*buxwana, bu- -xwana*) believed to accompany the birth of twins.[1] Also the occurrence of any of a whole category of acts and events which the Tiriki and other

[1] See Wagner, 'The Abaluyia of Kavirondo,' *African Worlds*, ed. by Daryll Forde (London: Oxford University Press, 1954), pp. 49–50, for a description of the nature of such ceremonies.

Abaluyia believe are unnatural and dangerous (*luswa*)[1]
demand that lustrations be held by the ritual elders to prevent
disaster from befalling the individual, persons, or groups involved. Although many of these lustral ceremonies are not held
at the ancestral shrines, when they take place it is common to
leave offerings of food and beer and to supplicate the ancestral
spirits at the ancestral shrines of the homesteads involved. The
underlying concern seems to be that the ancestral spirits should
feel that they are remembered and welcome participants at all
important occasions. Thus will their continued support be
assured.

Supplication of the ancestral spirits is by no means confined
to the homestead ancestral shrines. On first emerging from his
hut in the morning, the homestead head traditionally spits
towards the rising sun and asks the ancestral spirits to bless the
coming day. The ancestral spirits are also beseeched by the
ritual elders at family, community, and sub-tribal ritual fire
ceremonies (*bwali, bw- -ali*) held to bless a newly-built hut, to
bless the planting and the harvest, and to bring luck to proposed
cattle raids and to certain other occasions. A married woman
who has borne several children and who has been granted a
cooking hearth (*mahiga, ma- -higa*) of her own by her husband's
family, may have her own separate ancestral shrine (*lusambwa
lya baxali*). It consists essentially of a sacred branch stuck in the
floor of the matron's hut near her cooking hearth. The three
stones that serve as a trivet in the cooking hearth are the nearest
equivalent she is permitted to the ancestral stones surrounding
the sacred branch at the homestead altar. Female elders from a
woman's own clan generally come to set up such a shrine. Offerings and supplications are made at these shrines in connexion
with pregnancy, childbirth, and the health of the mother and
small children. These supplications are in addition to, and in no
way a substitute for, the supplications made by the men at the
homestead shrine.[2]

Contemporary Tiriki elders, both pagan and Christian, agree
that the Tiriki traditionally have no conceptualizations of a

---

[1] ibid., p. 45.

[2] The inroads made by Christianity are even greater among the women than
among the men. In 1955 the writer failed to find any women in Tiriki who still
maintained women's ancestral shrines.

'high God, Creator of all things', comparable to the Mission-taught Biblical God, or comparable to the Northern Abaluyia creator Wele.[1] Today (1956) Tiriki apparently remember only scattered myths about the origin of the sun, moon and other natural phenomena which, when viewed together and compared to one another, manifest no readily apparent integrating theme or dominant cosmological focus. Tiriki elders trace all pre-European Tiriki custom (*miima, mw- mi- -ima*) to their clan ancestors, with one exception, and that is the body of custom defining and regulating circumcision and initiation and the related structure of age groups and grades. This body of custom is called (*idumi, i- -dumi*). Idumi, the elders aver, was borrowed from the Terik, and originally came, fully developed unalterable, from '*ging*' (*idumi yarula ging*). The Tiriki say that *ging* is a Terik word which may be interpreted as meaning simply, 'long long ago' (*xale munonono*). Tiriki folk tales give instances of specific phenomena and types of behaviour which are good or bad and then offer particularistic explanations as to why they exist; they also support the popular contention that the ancestral spirits are the only generalized source of power. If the *misambwa* are indifferent about or angry towards you, you will not receive their strength and consequently will probably soon fall on bad times. The ancestral spirits are never, either in myth or in common pagan judgment, conceived of as themselves a source of evil or misfortune.

Dangers arising both from human and other natural and supernatural causes are often illustrated in Tiriki myths, but these dangers are not related in any conscious or formalized way by an overall cosmological tradition. Man-eating giants (*manani, gu- ma- -nani*) are probably the most frequent superhuman agents of evil alluded to in Tiriki myths.[2] Wild animals, enemy tribes, those phenomena traditionally considered to bring a state of ritual danger (*luswa*), and the actions of sorcerers, are other often cited sources of danger. Today, as in pre-European times, one class of sorcerers, the witches (*baloji*,

---

[1] Wagner, 'The Abaluyia of Kavirondo,' op. cit., pp. 27–28.

[2] Alta Howard Hoyt, who for many years was a Friends missionary at Kaimosi Missions in Tiriki, has collected and translated a number of Abaluyia folk tales. See Alta Howard Hoyt, *Bantu Folklore Tales of Long Ago* (Wichita, Kansas: Alta H. Hoyt, printed at Day's Print Shop, Wichita, 1951).

mu- ba- loji), are regarded as inherently bad (*damanu*). Witches
are believed simply to enjoy using their powers to make people
barren or to make them sicken or die. They get their evil nature,
it is said, either from a disposition of blood present in their
family (some sub-clan segments are recognized as carrying a
predisposition towards witchcraft), or from having been cor-
rupted and trained by a practising witch.

Every Tiriki community is concerned about the problem of
curbing the activities of witches. It is believed dangerous to
declare someone a witch, for that makes the accuser a prime
target for the suspected malevolent power of the accused. Most
overt anti-witchcraft activity is sustained by the community
elders acting as a group, thereby lessening the danger of individuals being singled out for the witches' wrath. On a number of
occasions during the year, such as the annual first-fruits ceremonies, it is common for the community elders collectively to
curse the witches, no specific names being mentioned, and to
ask the ancestral spirits to drive them away. Occasionally a person is openly accused by the community elders of being a witch.
If the accused fails to clear his (or her) name of the charges
through one of the several kinds of ordeal, or some other
method, it is not uncommon for the accused to be cursed by the
elders and driven from the community, or severely beaten and
warned never to indulge in witchcraft again. Sometimes a witch
would be clubbed to death by the whole community. The advent
of British justice has curtailed the beatings, ordeals and club-
bings for witches. It has even made community accusations of
suspects extremely rare because the accusations can no longer
lead to any definite social sanction. Indeed an accusation may
boomerang and lead to a slander suit against the accusers.

The ancestral spirits' intolerance of witches is unquestioned.
It is through invocation of the ancestral spirits that witches are
publicly cursed by the elders, and when deemed necessary it is
in the name of the ancestral spirits that an individual alleged to
be a witch is driven from the community or killed. The spirits
of deceased witches are not welcomed by the ancestral spirits
(*misambwa*); indeed it is said that they chase such evil spirits
(*binanyenzo, shi- bi- -nanyenzo*) into a limbo lying at the bottom
of Lake Victoria.

There are many sorcerers (*balyuli, babila*, &c.) in Tiriki who are not witches (*baloji*). They use their supernatural powers primarily to protect their families and clients from the medicine and spells of witches and enemy sorcerers. Sorcerers are believed occasionally to turn their art against other people, principally for two reasons. One reason is jealousy (*imbodoxa, i- zi- -mbodoxa*), over a neighbour's children, or over ownership of land. Jealousy, however, is believed to characterize witches, and any known sorcerer who seems by disposition to be especially prone to jealousy may come to be suspected as a witch. Thus, both sorcerers and those untutored in the arts of magic make every effort to appear free from jealousy. The second reason is vengeful anger (*burima, bu- -rima*). A sorcerer may feel this against someone, particularly a younger person who has treated him disrespectfully, and consequently may make him ill; or he may endeavour to harm by sorcery someone whom he suspects of having harmed a member of his family.

No one in Tiriki, either young or old, is felt to die simply because his or her time has come. At every death a human agent is suspected unless there is clearcut evidence before the person's death that he had fallen into a state of ritual impurity (*xugwa luswa*) and had not been properly purified, that he had violated an oath where the sanction was death, or that he was being troubled by a ghost (*shisyuxu, shi- bi- -syuxu*) seeking vengeance or company. It is the role of the elders, particularly the sub-clan elders, to comfort the immediate family of the deceased and to allay and smooth over any public accusations of sorcery that might be uttered at the graveside.[1] Also it is to his sub-clan elders that a person first turns for medicine to protect him from the sorcerer who, he believes, killed his close kin. It must be remembered that nearly all magical power—preventative, curative, and destructive—is controlled by the old people in Tiriki. Young people are not allowed to practise, nor are they even instructed in, most of the more important magical arts until they have reached middle age. Thus at times of death the elders are viewed as those who have, above all others, the power to preserve the well-being of the living, but also as those who can kill. The death of an elder does not serve to weaken the potency ascribed to the aged; rather, in the eyes of the Tiriki

---

[1] See Wagner, *The Bantu of North Kavirondo*, Vol. I, op cit., pp. 485-7, for a description of the traditional role of the 'comforter' (*omuseni*) among the Abaluyia.

it reaffirms it by suggesting there are other elders around as powerful as, or more powerful than, the one who just died.

There are, as we have seen, four significant alternatives to the predominant practice of attributing the underlying cause of death to a living human agent. One is belief in the killing power of the state of ritual impurity called *luswa*; the second is the killing power attributed to certain oaths if violated; the third is the notion that occasionally someone who knew you very well while alive may be lonely for you, and call you to join him; the fourth is the belief that the restive or evil ghost of someone recently deceased may kill you out of vengeance or jealous spite. The first two causes clearly can be avoided by not doing things that involve falling into ritual impurity or violating a mortal oath. If, either inadvertently or knowingly, one does fall into ritual impurity or violate a major oath there are specific lustral rites (*miiluxa*) which may be performed to save the violator's life. Dealing with troublesome ghosts, however, can be delicate in the extreme.

All living people are viewed as having a body (*mubili, mu- mi- -bili*), and a spirit or 'shadow' (*shinini, shi- bi- -nini*). After death the spirit becomes a ghost (*shisyuxu*). The Tiriki believe that nobody likes to die and that after death a person's ghost takes some time to get reconciled to the fact that it is no longer a 'shadow' (*shinini*) but indeed a ghost (*shisyuxu*). Thus the ghost generally lingers in the vicinity of the corpse (*mulambo, mu- mi- -lambo*) for a few days. If the funeral ceremonies are well-attended and suitable to the status of the deceased, and if the elders are successful in averting or allaying specific charges of sorcery or other foul play, the ghost usually becomes reconciled to death, gradually leaves the vicinity of the corpse, and eventually joins the *misambwa*.

Sleep is believed to be a vulnerable time for the living, for a person's spirit (*shinini*) may leave him then. A sleeping man's spirit may be called to a *rendezvous* with a ghost of a friend or relative several years dead. The meeting may be simply a friendly visit initiated by the ghost because it is lonely for its former companion, or the ghost may be angry and scold the spirit because in his waking life the living friend seems indifferent and has not even sought to avenge his dead friend's demise. After awakening, a person knows of an encounter between his spirit and a ghost because he remembers it as a dream. Such a *tête-à-tête* with a ghost is undesirable, whether or not the ghost is friendly. When the ghost is angry the situation is considered extremely troublesome, for a ghost which has never departed to join the *misambwa*, but instead has remained near the vicinity of the corpse to haunt (*xu-syuxa*) people, may first appear to them in dreams. Such a vengeful ghost will often severely harass its victims, occasionally killing them. When the ghost is friendly the situation is considered to be potentially no less dangerous because one such meeting may be followed by others until the spirit actually feasts with the ghost. If a person's spirit eats with a ghost, the Tiriki believe that if he awakes the dreamer knows he can expect soon to die. All he can do is quickly arrange for the elders to perform lustral ceremonies (*miiluxa*) to avoid the consequences of having eaten with a ghost. If he is lucky, the person will then escape death and even all harm; or he may have only a serious illness.

A ghost which remains lingering near its corpse and haunts living people in their waking as well as their sleeping hours is known as a *shinanyenzo*. A ghost may become a *shinanyenzo* for two major reasons. First, out of vengeful anger (*burima*), and second, out of *jealousy* and pure *malice* (*imbodoxa*, *budamanu*). These two motives, it will be remembered, are also felt to underlie the activities of witches (*baloji*). A murdered man's ghost commonly feels vengeful anger against his murderer and those who passively witnessed or condoned his murder, and a man's ghost also feels vindictive anger towards all those relatives and friends who seem indifferent about his death. Failure to provide an appropriate funeral, failure to attend the funeral if attendance is possible, and failure of one's family to seek redress for death are considered as evidence of indifference. Only the ghost of an evil person such as a witch, however, will haunt the living out of jealousy and malice.

Various medicines and charms may be acquired by the haunted to chase away a *shinanyenzo*. The most effective countermeasure is to burn the corpse of the haunting ghost. This is considered particularly dangerous to those who do the burning; only very old men with protective medicine will undertake such a task, and then not unless heavily reimbursed by their client. *Binanyenzo*, as well as causing aches and pains, especially in the sides and backs of those they haunt, are believed on occasion to strangle and smother their victims to death. Once a *shinanyenzo* has fulfilled its vengeance or has been chased away by medicine or the burning of its corpse, it retires to the company of the *misambwa*. If the *shinanyenzo* has been haunting purely out of evil and jealousy—in other words, if it is the ghost of a witch (*muloji*)—the *misambwa* will not accept it when the living have successfully chased it off; they also cast it out and relegate it to the bottom of Lake Victoria. There are no evil spirits among the *misambwa*!

The Organization and Function of Tiriki Clans and Lineage Groups: A Brief Analysis and Summary

Tiriki patrilineages are primarily of significance in the religious, affiliative and economic spheres. Tiriki clans (*zimbamba*) and sub-clans (*zinzu*) supply their members with answers to the questions: 'Where did I come from? Who cares whether I live or die? Upon whom can I depend for food, land and shelter? Who will remember me after I die?' In short, Tiriki clans and sub-clans offer their members a sense of social affiliation and continuity, and they give their members both economic and supernatural support.

Tiriki clan exogamy fosters a sense of social and economic unity within the clan group. The numerous additional exogamy rules prohibiting marriage to all but the most distant non-agnatic kin serve indirectly to further clan solidarity by preventing the clustering of clans into several affinally linked tribal subsections. In spite of the resulting sense of clan brotherhood and the frequent lip-service the Tiriki give to the importance of clans, they are really of secondary significance in the judicial and political spheres. The Terik-Tiriki age group brotherhood (*idumi*), into which all Tiriki males are initiated during adolescence without regard to clan, supplies a series of age-graded affiliative bonds that put a strong check upon clan loyalties as a basis for judicial or political action. At the same time the age groups serve as a major basis of community (*luhya*), subtribal (*lusomo*), and tribal (*badiliji*) integration.

The clan is of significance in economic and religious affairs, but in effect its significance in these respects is limited to agnatic sub-groups or sub-clans (*zinzu*) of three to five generations in depth. Inheritance of property is recognized as primarily a concern of the sub-clan of the deceased, but in inheritance disputes the intervention of the multi-clan community elders (*basaxulu wu luhya*) is often sought in determining questions of inheritance because of the frequency of cases in which grants of property have been made by the deceased to sisters' sons (*biixwa*), in-laws (*baxwasi*), and even unrelated friends (*balina*).

Sub-clan affiliation serves as the basis for a set of crucial authority relationships in the religious and economic realms. Mandatory so far as immediate agnatic kin are concerned, these relationships may also be extended to less immediate agnatic kin and sometimes even to non-agnatic kin. Thus, in their broadest manifestations they can be viewed simply as a set of crucial power relationships between kinfolk of different generations. These relationships are bracketed by what might be succinctly labelled the '*baguga* triad'. This triad, when viewed in its entirety, consists of three alternating terminologically equated generations.

The grandparental *baguga* are the balance point of the triad; they serve as the ritual mediators between their grandchildren (*baguga*) whom they perceive as those who will be sure to remember them when they die, and their own grandparents (*baguga*), now dead, but still remembered and regularly beseeched in supplications at the ancestral shrine. A ritual elder does not expect distant deceased agnates or the whole body of ancestral spirits to hear his supplications directly, but he does believe that their aid can be rallied through his own deceased grandfathers and other kin of his grandparental generation. By remembering, flattering and beseeching his grandparental ancestors the ritual elder prevails upon them to beseech preceding generations until a large ancestral group of all generations has been recruited to give aid to him and his dependants.

The complement of this ritual triad of three alternating generations is a second triad composed of three adjacent generations, the grandparental, parental, and filial. Here the relationships are essentially economic and authoritarian in nature. A child is expected to respect and obey his father; and a father, in his turn, is expected to discipline his children, provide for their economic needs, and arrange for the bridewealth of his sons. Competition between siblings over cattle and other property is checked and arbitrated by the parental generation, while competition between father and son over cattle is controlled primarily by members of the grandparental generation. To be sure, members of the grandparental generation are by this time generally entering their dotage and are growing more and more dependent economically upon their middle-aged sons. The sons, however, are dependent upon their ageing fathers for leadership in the ritual sphere. Thus the senior elders retain a potent weapon with which to guard both their own and their grandchildren's rights. The tense, ambiguous grandfather-father-son triad is the relationship overtly represented and reinforced by the three ancestral stones generally found at the ancestral shrines; but perhaps the three stones derive effectiveness as religious symbols at least partly from covertly symbolizing the harmonious *baguga* triad.

Another element of Tiriki social organization which serves to control and rechannel intergenerational conflict is the system of semi-generational graded age groups (each covering an age span of approximately 15 years) which in effect divide the whole tribe into two moieties. It will be shown in Chapter II that this moiety division generally occurs so as to place father, son, and grandson in the same moiety.

Tiriki clans are the basis of a wide network of persisting affiliations. Clans traditionally serve to answer the questions, 'Where do we come from?' and 'Where are we going?', for Tiriki primarily remember their deceased agnatic ancestors, and in turn expect to be remembered primarily by their agnatic descendants. Each Tiriki man wants to have a large homestead of his own with as many heirs and followers beholden to him as possible. Desire to attain these ends sometimes fosters intense conflict between father and son, particularly over cattle. Maternal, and to a lesser extent, affinal, connexions supply alternate intergenerational power relationships through which the individual can endeavour to receive aid or extend his influence. Through circumcision and initiation customs (*idumi*) adult men's loyalties are integrated into a pan-tribal age group organization which overrides clan and kin loyalties at the community, subtribal, and tribal levels. This suppression of clanship as a major basis of political organization has fostered the development of multi-clan territorially-based organizational units of several sorts. Chapter II will describe the initiation customs and the resulting graded age groups. Chapter III will outline the nature of Tiriki territorial organization.

Tiriki Age Groups and Age Grades

TIRIKI age groups and age grades were traditionally perpetuated by two sets of rituals, the male initiation ceremonies (*idumi*) which included circumcision, and the ceremonies by which the formal status and duties of warriorhood were handed from the incumbent age group to the succeeding age group. This chapter will start by outlining the nature of the Terik-Tiriki initiation. Next, the nature and function of the age graded age groups will be presented. Finally, the movement of the age groups through successive age grades will be discussed.

Tiriki Initiation Ceremonies

The Tiriki word *idumi* designates the whole series of ceremonies performed when adolescent boys are initiated into an age group (*lixula*) and achieve adult status. *Idumi* is derived from the Terik-Nandi word, *tum*, which in its broadest context can be roughly translated as 'ceremony'; but the Tiriki also often use *tum* to refer specifically to the age group initiation ceremonies.

Idumi is usually held at four or five year intervals. Until the *idumi* of 1920–21 the Terik and Tiriki ceremonies are reported to have been one and the same, and to have remained substantially unaffected by European contact. Since then it is clear that a number of innovations have taken place which have affected the initiation practices even among the segment of the Tiriki population that has remained avowedly pagan. Also since then Terik-Tiriki interaction has steadily decreased in the sphere of initiation as well as in other respects. Nevertheless, Terik and Tiriki are still initiated together in some parts of Tiriki and Nyangori Locations where the two peoples continued to live as neighbours.

The following outline of *idumi* is primarily based on detailed accounts given by two Bantu Tiriki who were initiated in the traditional manner prior to the innovations which started in 1921; they have lived all their lives in predominantly Bantu areas of Tirikiland and know only a few words of the Terik

48

language. No initiation was held while I was doing field work
in Tiriki (1954–56). Because of the secrecy surrounding these
customs in Tiriki today it was not possible to make more extensive inquiries about the nature of *idumi*, and no account was
obtained of *tum* from a Terik elder. Members of the Tiriki
committee which read and edited a draft of this volume in the
summer of 1961 (see p. xv of the Preface) do not sanction the
following description of the initiation rites (pp. 49–67). They
say it contains many mistakes and inaccuracies. Being themselves good initiated Tiriki they gave me no corrections and
offered no further comments.

The Tiriki and the Terik both assert that their initiation is the
same as (*halala na*) those of the Nandi and Kipsigis tribes. When
descriptions by Hollis[1] of the Nandi initiation (*tum*) and by
Peristiany[2] of the Kipsigis initiation (*tumda*) are compared with
each other and with the version obtained from the Tiriki many
differences of detail are found. Nevertheless, the three ceremonies are generally similar in outline and share a great many
identical traits. It is quite common to hear of Terik who have
been initiated in Nandiland, of Nandi youth initiated in Kip-
sigisland, and *vice-versa*. Tiriki elders assert that it is possible for
their youth to be initiated in any of these tribes rather than at
home; in practice, however, seldom if ever is a Tiriki initiated
anywhere other than with his fellow Bantu Tiriki or with Terik.

Initiation is organized on a territorial basis. The area traditionally inhabited by the Terik and Tiriki is divided into about
ten or twelve territorially discrete major socio-ritual units or
sub-tribes (*zisomo*).[3] Each *lusomo* has a sacred grove (*gabogorosiyo*)[4] situated on a hilltop, and a circumcision grove (*shibanda, shi- bi- -banda*, or *gabunyonyi*[5]) located in a valley. Each
sacred grove is under the care of a ritual elder (*musaalisi wa*

---

[1] A. C. Hollis, *The Nandi: Their Language and Folklore* (Oxford: At the Clarendon Press, 1909), pp. 52–57.
[2] J. G. Peristiany, *The Social Institutions of the Kipsigis* (London: George Routledge & Sons, Ltd., 1939), pp. 6–24.
[3] The Terik word for *lusomo* is *jemilot*. The total number of *zisomo* and the exact boundaries of each in many cases changed from year to year with the fortunes of war.
[4] The Tiriki employ the Terik word (singular form), but synthesize their own Bantu plural form, *zigabogorosiyo*.
[5] The Terik name for the initiation grove, *gabunyonyi*, is often employed by the Tiriki.

gabogorosiyo) who is assisted by other renowned ritual elders (*basaalisi bagali*) living in the sub-tribe.[1] These elders in effect form a sub-tribal ritual council. When the head priest grows too feeble to carry out his ritual duties the council chooses one of its members to succeed him. Everything else being equal, a near clansman of the retiring head is customarily chosen.

Every circumcision grove is under the care of a ritual leader. This leader, as well as being a member of the ritual council that officiates at the sacred grove, is chief circumciser and leader of the entire initiation ceremonial sequence (*idumi*) of his sub-tribe (*lusomo*). Thus he may be called not only *musaxulu wa gabunyonyi* (elder of the circumcision grove), but also *mushebi wuxuranga* (first circumciser), or *mwimili wi idumi* (initiation chief). This man is probably the most ritually powerful and most revered personage in the whole sub-tribe; certainly his pre-eminence is unchallenged at initiation time. During the actual rituals of initiation, the initiation chief is looked to as the final authority in all matters, although most of the actual rites are directed by lesser elders.

The initiation chief is assisted in his duties as circumciser (*mushebi, mu- ba- -shebi*) by a number of men who have learned the technique and ritual of circumcising from their fathers. Many of these assistant circumcisers are too young to have achieved priestly status, but it is from their elder members that a new initiation chief is chosen by the retiring initiation chief and the other sub-tribal ritual elders. He is chosen on the basis of his former prowess as a warrior, his character, wisdom, lineage and family. As with the elder of the sacred grove, it is felt most fitting to choose whenever possible someone of the same clan and sub-clan as the retiring initiation chief.

It is customary for initiation to be held every four or five years. Tradition decrees that the first move to open a new initiation period should be made by the ritual leaders of the most south-

[1] The term *musaalisi* (literally, 'one who supplicates') is used to refer to any man who is fulfilling a priestly role, whether for the homestead (*mujizi*), for the community (*luhya*), or for the sub-tribe (*lusomo*). If one wants specifically to refer to the caretaker of the *gabogorosiyo* one is obliged to say *musaalisi wa gabogorosiyo* (priest of the sacred grove), or *musaxulu wa gabogorosiyo* (elder of the sacred grove). On other occasions, however, the same priestly position may be referred to by other descriptive titles such as, *musaalisi wuxuranga wu lusomo* (first priest of the sub-tribe), etc.

westerly sub-tribes where nearly all of the population is Terik.[1] If the Terik elders think it a good time to hold initiation their opinion is passed on to the ritual leaders of sub-tribes lying successively further to the northeast, until all the sub-tribal ritual councils have debated the question. These discussions are held towards the end of the main harvest (usually in July). In the discussions such things as the availability of grain for food and beer, absence of epidemics, relative peace with tribal neighbours and the number of 'boys' (*bayayi mu- ba-yayi*) ready for initiation, are reviewed. When enough time has elapsed for the discussions to have been held in all the sub-tribes and for the comments to have filtered back to the southwestern sub-tribes, the Terik ritual leaders of the southwest make a final decision as to whether or not to hold initiation that year.[2]

An affirmative decision is announced by their singing a special initiation song (*lwimbo lyu buxulu*). Although the Tiriki do not know the meaning of the words of the song, the tune and its significance is recognized by all.[3] In a matter of hours the song has been taken up by the ritual elders of all the sub-tribes. Immediately every sub-tribe settles down to the business of organizing and carrying out its own initiation. The sub-tribal initiation chief and his council of elders (henceforth this group including its leader will be referred to simply as 'the initiation elders' (*basaxulu bi idumi*)) retire to the circumcision grove to start the initiation rites. Their first action is to slaughter a white goat and inspect its entrails to divine whether or not it is auspicious to hold circumcision in that grove. If the signs are unfavourable the slaughter and divination is repeated the next day. When the results of the divination are negative for three days in

[1] Although most of the Terik still live in the southwestern portion of what is now Tiriki Location and in Nyangori Location immediately to the south, there is probably no sub-tribal division remaining in Tiriki or Nyangori where the Bantu population hasn't grown to outnumber the Terik population during the last decade or two.

[2] My informants felt that the final decision as to when to hold initiation was probably made by several south-western *zisomo* leaders in conference. They did not know how the final decision was reached—whether through consultation of oracles or diviners, or by other conventions not involving recourse to the supernatural. For the Tiriki the decision was simple; they merely followed the lead of the Terik sub-tribes.

[3] It seems likely that these as well as the other ritual songs of initiation have words that are in an archaic form of the Terik language.

a row the circumcision grove is abandoned and the people of the sub-tribe either establish a new circumcision grove or join the initiation rites of a neighbouring sub-tribe.[1]

Every sub-tribe is divided into about five or ten communities (*zimbihya*).[2] It is the responsibility of the elders of each of these communities to select the initiates (*baxulu, mu- ba- -xulu*).[3] The community elders divide the initiates into groups of 15 or 20, and then with the help of the initiation elders they select a young man for each of these groups to act as its counsellor (*mudili, mu- ba- -dili*). The counsellors are recruited from the age group just senior to that of the initiates. Such factors as behaviour while in initiation, bravery and skill in warfare, and recognition as a leader among their own age group, are prime considerations when selecting counsellors. Many communities have only enough initiates to warrant one initiation group and counsellor, but others need two or more. In those cases where a community has less than a dozen or so initiates it may arrange for its youth to join a group of a neighbouring community.

A counsellor's first duty is to arrange for the construction of a seclusion hut (*shirumbi, shi- bi- -rumbi*) in an unfrequented forest area. It is here that he and the initiates in his charge will live in seclusion during the six month initiation period following circumcision. During the next two or three days while the huts are being built the parents of each initiate arrange for a kinsman or friend with an ample supply of grain to sponsor (*xu-shebela*)

[1] An extensive exposition of the many rites and rituals performed during the six months long initiation period would probably offer little additional insight into the nature and function of the age groups. Thus only an outline of the major ceremonies and events is given in this account. For the most part only those ceremonies which seem explicitly or implicitly to emphasize the establishment of status, status ranks, and positions of leadership are described here in any detail.

[2] The contemporary division of Tiriki into sub-tribes (sub-locations), each under the charge of a headman, only roughly approximates traditional sub-tribal divisions (see Chap. IV, pp. 110–11). The estimate of five to ten communities per sub-tribe is based on reports of contemporary elders. It should be noted, however, that the contemporary elders disagree among themselves both as to the numbers and the boundaries of the pre-European tribal divisions and sub-divisions.

[3] The Tiriki elders assert that traditionally a youth wasn't circumcised and initiated until he was well past puberty and mature enough to take an active role in warfare and other adult activities. By 1929 the usual age for initiation had dropped to around fourteen to sixteen years of age. In the present decade, with school and jobs away from the tribe cutting more and more into the free time of older boys, the age of initiation has dropped as low as eleven years of age with twelve to fourteen years being the most common age.

their son during the initiation period. It is the duty of the sponsor's womenfolk to supply and cook food for the initiate during the entire six months. Eventually the sponsor is paid a goat by the initiate's family in recognition of this service. Another preparatory task is arranging the order in which all the initiates of the sub-tribe will be circumcised.

The first (*jibuledi*), second (*waxabidi*), and last positions are especially desirable. These positions are assigned by the initiation elders primarily on the basis of the esteem and status granted the initiates' fathers. The honoured holders of first, second, and last positions are not usually members of the same community.

On the day before circumcision the counsellors of each initiation group confiscate the clothing from their initiates and in return supply them with headdresses made from a special creeper called *isenende* (*i- zi- -senende*, Terik, *senendet*). Nude except for these headdresses the initiates of the whole sub-tribe gather at a central meeting ground and dance before their watching relatives and neighbours. Soon the whole community joins in the dancing which is performed to special drumming and songs. At dusk the merriment stops and the initiates are taken to the homestead of one of the more venerable initiation elders. There, after dark, the initiates are led one at a time into the unlighted interior of the hut where several of the initiation elders are waiting. Each boy, as he stands alone in the hut with the elders, is asked to confess all the traditionally forbidden acts (*mijilo*, *mu- mi- -jilo*) he has committed. The elders ask him specifically whether he has stolen property, or taken the life of certain animals that it is tabu to kill. Then he is questioned in detail about any sexual activity he may have had either with other people or animals. Sodomy and sexual connexions with children and animals are stringently forbidden everyone, while only males who have been circumcised are permitted to have sexual intercourse with mature females. The sound of bull roarers (*masobi*, *li- ma- -sobi*) which the uninitiated are told is the roaring of giants (*manani*), the administration of an oath believed to bring disease to a perjurer, and various other techniques are used to persuade and terrify the initiate into telling his forbidden activities. One threat used is that the initiate will bleed to death when circumcised if he doesn't confess all. If an initiate is particularly obdurate several robust elders who are waiting under a large skin in the back of the hut rush forward under their furry cloak and grab him. The attendant elders tell him he has been seized by a giant, and they then describe how the giant will kill him by committing sodomy with him unless he confesses all without further delay.

At the end of his confession the initiate agrees to pay the elders a fine at a later date to compensate for his absolution. The fine may be a chicken or even a goat, depending on the number and nature of the violations. The elders thereupon absolve him of his errors and admonish him henceforth to leave behind childish ways and assume behaviour appropriate to a man. They end by telling him to be brave and not to cry out or try to run away when he is being circumcised. Then he is led from the hut and seated with the other confessees away from those who still have to confess.

At daybreak the initiates return to their family homesteads where they are feasted and ceremonially blessed by the homestead head. Around mid-morning the counsellors of each community lead the initiates in their charge to the sub-tribal circumcision grove. The women and children follow to the grove's edge, but only the initiates and initiated are allowed to enter.

Then the initiates are seated behind and a bit to one side of the grove's cleared ceremonial centre so that they cannot see the circumcision of those who precede them. After opening supplications and benedictions by the circumcision leaders, the initiate chosen to be first (*jibuledi*) is led forth and circumcised. The initiate may either stand or kneel while being circumcised. If he flinches or tries to move away counsellors come forward and hold him; if he cries out all the elders start singing to drown his cries so those women and children waiting outside the circumcision grove won't hear him. The operation is very painful[1] and the initiates are admonished to prove their manliness by bearing it without flinching or uttering a sound. It is reported that in spite of this initiates fairly often flinch, yell out, and even try to run away. The first initiate is operated on by the initiation chief; the succeeding initiates, however, are merely touched by the initiation chief and then circumcised by one of the younger

---

[1] For a description of the actual operation which coincides with the description given the writer by the Tiriki, see Peristiany, op. cit., p. 13.

circumcisers. After the operation the initiate is led to a spot in front of the circumcision place where he can sit and watch the other initiates being circumcised. At midday when all have been circumcised an eleusine gruel is served the initiates to help them recover their strength. The initiates then surrender their vine headdresses to the counsellors who carry them out of the initiation grove and present them to the initiates' waiting mothers. If the counsellor throws grass on the mother of an initiate as he hands over her son's headdress the mother knows he was brave; if, however, the counsellor cuts off a bit of the headdress vine before handing it over his relatives will mourn, for this is a sign that the initiate was cowardly. Sisters of the initiates then put on the headdresses and run to the central subtribal meeting place where they dance together; thus all can see from the headdresses who was brave and who was not. At dusk the sisters carry the headdresses home and hang them from the hut roof over the cooking hearth. It is said that this will help the sisters bear children easily after they marry.

Once they have finished their gruel the initiates are each issued a short leather apron. Then the different initiation groups are led out of the circumcision grove and conducted by their counsellors to the seclusion huts. As they move from the circumcision grove to their seclusion huts each group is surrounded by a cordon of older initiated men who beat off and chase away all uninitiated onlookers.

Life during the six months' seclusion period is characterized by strict regimentation and a focus on group activities to the exclusion of all privacy or individual undertakings. All the initiates of a hut eat, sleep, sing, dance, bathe, do handcraft, &c., all at the same time and only when commanded to do so by their counsellor. Even the smallest details of living are regimented. For example, if an initiate wants to leave the hut at night to urinate he must first awaken the initiate whom the elders have chosen as the hut leader (*jibuledi*). The hut leader then awakens all the other initiates, and the whole group accompanies the boy while he goes out to urinate.

The circumcision operation is believed to bring on a state of contamination which gradually decreases as the circumcision wound heals. For the entire seclusion period the initiates are forbidden to touch or eat food with their fingers in the customary

Tiriki manner. Instead each boy is given his own gourd,
wooden spoon and pointed stick with which to receive and eat
his food. The only regular item of Tiriki fare the initiates are
forbidden to eat is roasting bananas.

The six months' initiation and seclusion period following
circumcision is divided into four stages, each of which is begun
by a beer drink sponsored by the families of the initiates. The
circumcision elders decide when these drinks should be held
and make sure the parents brew the beer at the appropriate
times.

The first beer drink, called, 'the beer of clothing' (*malwa gi
zingubu*), is held about five or six weeks after circumcision.
During the interval between circumcision and this beer drink
the initiates are kept fairly quiet so that their wounds will heal
and their strength will return as quickly as possible. Their
principal activities are nightly descents to bathe in a swiftly
flowing stream, and daily song practice led by their counsellors.
Also they begin to weave puttees and masks that they will wear
during later stages in the initiation. The first beer marks the
end of the initiates' convalescence and their readiness to
undertake more active training. The initiates themselves do not
partake of 'the beer of clothing', but the day following the drink
families send them, via their counsellors, new leather clothing
to replace the short aprons worn while their wounds were still
open. The latter are destroyed. The new clothing is in effect a
leather cloak which forms the basic traditional garment
(*isumadi, -si zi- -sumadi*) for Tiriki male elders. The elder wears
such a robe draped from one shoulder by day and sleeps on it
at night. The initiates thus are provided with a style of clothing
for the rest of their seclusion period which they will subsequently
have to discard until they themselves are elders.

The second stage of initiation which follows 'the beer of
clothing', is devoted in large measure to learning and practising
special dances. The initiation masks (*zingolole, i- zi- -ngolole* or,
i- zi- -ngolose) which were started in the first stage of seclusion
are completed during this period. Also during this period instruction in how to make and shoot bows and arrows and in how
to use the spear and shield are begun. The counsellors, assisted
by other members of the warrior age group, are the principal
tutors for these skills.

About three months after circumcision the elders instruct the parents of the initiates to brew 'the beer of the fires' (*malwa ga masambu*). On the morning of this beer drink the initiates make their first public appearance since circumcision. Completely covered and disguised by the wearing of their newly completed initiation masks, their leather cloaks, rope girdles and leggings, all the initiates leave their seclusion huts and gather at the sub-tribal meeting place where their parents, neighbours, and indeed most of the sub-tribe, are already waiting for them. Then they dance the steps they have just learned. While the dancing goes on, each initiate's mother seeks out the counsellor in charge of her son and gets him to point out which dancer he is. If the son appears to be wearied by his efforts the mother cries out, 'Oh! Who is taking his food!' (*Ish, bayayi! Wina abugu-langa byuxuliya bye!*). In the afternoon the initiates, wearied by their strenuous dancing, return to their seclusion huts. Their parents hurry home, build fires, and take the headdresses which have been hanging over the cooking hearths and burn them. Late that afternoon and evening at the beer drink the groups gathered around the beer pots speak of how good it is to have burned the headdresses because circumcision is past now, and it would not be good for the initiates to return home and find the headdresses still hanging there. In the days that follow the initiates return daily to the meeting ground to dance, always wearing the mask and clothing described above. When not dancing they stay in the forest near their seclusion huts, practise using their spear and bow and arrow, hunt small game, and work on various kinds of handicraft. They also have nocturnal song fests and continue to bathe nightly in the river.

Around four or five months after circumcision the elders instruct the initiates' parents to prepare 'the beer of the back' (*malwa gi shigongo*). The morning of the drink the initiates gather at the meeting ground wearing special big headdresses (*bugoxwi, bu- -goxwi*) made of branches in addition to their regular masks and clothing. As they dance each initiate tries to break his headdress by violently bobbing and shaking his head. Each time an initiate succeeds in breaking his headdress he is loudly cheered. The initiate who managed to break several headdresses in the course of the morning is remembered for his strength and endurance. That evening the parents of the initiates deliver pots of beer to the circumcision grove where the initiates, counsellors and the initiation elders have gathered for a special all night session.

Before evening darkness descends the initiation elders examine each initiate to see whether or not his wound has completely healed. A special salve is applied to those initiates whose circumcision wounds are infected or have not completely healed. Also, in the presence of his counsellor, each boy is asked if he has been abiding by all the rules of the seclusion period and whether or not his counsellor has been doing a good job of looking after him.

Following this the initiation elders all seat themselves in one side of the clearing in the grove and instruct the initiates to sit on the opposite side. Then one by one all the initiates are called forward in the order in which they were circumcised and are made to kneel down before the initiation chief. 'Never tell the initiation rites!' (*uxabola idumi dawe!*), the initiation leader begins. The elder's admonitions to the kneeling initiate continue roughly as follows:

Everything you learn during the *idumi* you must obey and remember forever! You must never tell a person not initiated in the Terik-Tiriki way what you learn and see. If someone threatens to kill you in order to find out let him kill you, but don't tell! If someone offers you a cow to tell, remain silent! If you ever tell the *idumi* to the uninitiated you shall develop a terrible itching of the skin, and then you shall die!

After each of the above phrases all those present add their agreement by saying in chorus, *Mmmmmmmmmmmmmmmm!* Finally the kneeling initiate, having agreed aloud that he will never tell, is dismissed and the next initiate steps forward.

When all the regular initiates have in this manner been sworn to silence, a new category of initiates is asked to step forward. These new initiates are those previously circumcised adults who have recently immigrated to Tiriki from other Abaluyia tribes where, of course, the Terik-Tiriki initiation and age groups do not prevail. The Tiriki and Nandi speaking peoples regard such circumcised aliens as a higher order of life than an uncircumcised person, but still not fit company for members of their age groups. Such a person (called a *jebusabageni*) is expected to undergo the last portion of initiation if he wants to settle among the Tiriki. He must first, however, pay the circumcision elders one bull. This is known as, 'buying initiation' (*xu-gula idumi*). He follows the regular initiates in swearing never to divulge the circumcision customs, and for the rest of the initiation period he joins one or another of the initiation groups. He wears the initiates' leather cloak, rope girdle and puttees; he sleeps, eats with, and follows the routine of the other initiates; but he doesn't wear a mask, and because of his greater age he is treated as an unofficial leader by the regular initiates.[1]

After all the initiates have been sworn to secrecy a few of the most mature initiates are invited to join the initiation elders and the other tribal elders at the beer pots which have been set up at several spots in the circumcision grove. All initiates are henceforth considered eligible to partake of beer at the beer drink, but the elders, who on all occasions have the right to control who has access to the beer pots, limit participation on this occasion to the seniormost initiates so that there will be more than enough beer to satiate those who do join the drink. While the elders and lucky eldest initiates grow mellow and then tipsy, the counsellors go to the homes of each of their initiates and say in effect, 'Your son is dying! Give me a chicken to take to the initiation elders so that they may make your son come back to life.'

The more gullible (or more obliging) mothers quickly hand over chickens for delivery to the circumcision grove. By now the beer drinkers are quite high, and gleefully start to make a series of sounds simulating the cries of the hyena. Thoroughly frightened or aroused by these dreaded cries, even the more sceptical mothers quickly surrender chickens at the second visit of the counsellors. The noise from the circumcision grove grows steadily louder and wilder, and it is simple enough for the counsellors to extract more and more food from the initiates' mothers on subsequent visits by telling them that their sons have done something very wrong, are terribly ill, will die, and that the only hope is to bribe the initiation elders with more and more food so that they will bring them back to life and good health. Soon the festivites in the circumcision grove take on the dimensions

---

[1] The adult immigrant to Tiriki who has not been circumcised is obliged to undergo the circumcision and initiation ceremonies in their entirety.

of a drunken brawl; the counsellors rush thither and yon
raiding fields of the initiates' parents for ripe maize or whatever
other edibles then can find. Any protests from the parents are
brushed aside by vivid descriptions of how their sons are ailing,
dying, rotting in the grove, and by assertion that consequently
the appetites of the elders must be appeased at all cost. Everyone in the grove is thoroughly satiated with food or beer or both
by daybreak.

As morning dawns the initiates are instructed to leave the
circumcision grove and to stagger back to their seclusion huts
as if very weak and hardly able to walk. The procession of
masked initiates that stumbles from the circumcision grove, in
many cases their staggering being more genuine than spurious,
is said to present a very convincing picture of the extreme weak-
ness that might reflect a brush with death.

For the next three days and nights the initiates don't stir from
the vicinity of the seclusion huts and refrain from singing,
speaking loudly or making any sounds that might be heard by
those outside the seclusion area. The counsellors instruct the
initiates' sponsors to cook and send up nothing but the thin eleusine gruel (*busela, bu--sela*) traditionally served the very ill. On the
fourth day the counsellors visit the parents of the initiates and
ask them for meat, chicken and vegetables, because miracu-
lously their sons are now beginning to show signs of recovery
and need lots of the best food to speed the return of their
strength. That night the initiates sing, although ever so feebly,
for the first time since the all-night session in the circumcision
grove. The counsellors repeat the request for extra food for
several days, and each successive night the initiates sing a bit
louder to show their parents that they are recovering. Finally,
on the seventh night they sing loud and clear for several hours
and thus announce to the world that they are fully recovered.
During the next month or so (during the latter part of the fifth
and the early part of the sixth months of initiation) the initiates
go out, still garbed in their initiation clothing and ceremonial
masks, and herd cattle by day. Groups of girls frequently come
up and ask the herding initiates to dance for them. The girls
may in turn dance for the initiates, but no initiate is allowed to
engage any post-pubescent girl in conversation. The initiate
may arrange during this period for his counsellor to deliver a

carved baton which he prepared earlier during his seclusion to a girl of his choice who is approaching marriageable age. The girl may refuse to accept the baton if she doesn't like the boy, or she may take it at first and then change her mind and send it back before the seclusion period has ended. If a girl keeps the baton she thereby gives a tacit invitation to the donor to come and sleep with her in the girls' sleeping hut (*lisabo*) after his initiation is over. The initiates while herding cattle may stop any man they meet who is not initiated in the Terik-Tiriki manner and demand a payment of a chicken or some other edible on pain of beating him up if he does not comply.

The beginning of the fourth and final stage of initiation is celebrated by 'the beer of leaving' (*malwa gi shyaluxu*) which is held about six months after initiation. The ceremonies immediately preceding this beer drink bring to an end the seclusion of the initiates. These ceremonies require each Tiriki initiate to have an elder Terik woman act as his ceremonial aid or sponsor. The arrangements for having such an aid are made by the initiate's family prior to this phase of the initiation. It is common for the same Terik woman to sponsor all the sons of a Tiriki homestead when they get initiated, and then for the Terik woman's daughter or one or more of her close relatives to sponsor the grandsons of that Tiriki lineage when they in turn are initiated.

On the morning of the 'beer of leaving' the initiates go to the sub-tribal meeting ground where their Terik sponsors are waiting for them. First the initiates dance. Towards midday the dancing is called to a halt and each initiate goes up to his Terik sponsor, who is usually accompanied by a grown daughter. Each sponsor has prepared a gourd of butter (*magura, ma- -gura*) and a string of beads made from threaded seeds. While her daughter assists by holding the gourd of butter the sponsor reaches up under the mask of the initiate, smears his head with butter, and says, '*bamwayi*'. The initiate answers, '*bamwayi*'. By the utterance of this reciprocal term a lasting bond of friendship and mutual concern is related between the Terik sponsor and the initiate. Then the initiate removes his mask in public for the first time since he entered seclusion, and his Terik sponsor slips the string of beads around his neck. Thus the initiate's period of seclusion and his need to go masked in public are ended. Thenceforth he is no longer referred to as 'initiate' (*muxulu*); instead for the rest of the initiation ceremonies he is called, 'bride' (*mwiha, mw- bi- -iha*). Each Terik woman sponsor is then feasted and presented with a gift of iron bracelets by the family of her *bamwayi*. The Tiriki say they are obliged to get a Terik woman to remove the mask from their initiates because Terik women are 'circumcised' (*shebwa*), that is, clitoridectomized, and therefore people of social and ritual significance (*jebusabageni*), while Tiriki women are not and are therefore no more eligible to partake in the initiation ceremonies than a child would be. The beads given the erstwhile initiate by his Terik *bamwayi* are cherished by him for the rest of his life.

While the Terik women sponsors are being feted in the homesteads of the initiated youth, the 'brides' and the circumcision elders retire to the circumcision grove. There the circumcision chief tells the 'brides' his work is finished. He reminds them of their promise never to reveal the nature of the initiation rites, adding that whoever does shall be cursed, itch, ail, won't father children, will be like a barren woman, a barren cow, an impotent bull, will die badly! Then he admonishes them to remember that they are no longer children and henceforth to behave in a way suitable to grown men. Soon beer is brought to the circumcision grove. This time all partake, though not to the point of satiation. The evening and early part of the night are passed in the circumcision grove with singing and dancing. On this occasion the elders and 'brides' mock those unfortunate 'brides' who were cowardly (*jibgwalogwalo*, or *jibede*) when circumcised. The mocking is done through jeering songs in which the cowards' names are mentioned. Those sung against must feign indifference; perhaps they can draw some comfort from the knowledge that the mocking will never be carried on in the presence of the uninitiated, that only their peers and elders will know of the exact nature of their cowardice, and that it would not be permitted for any uninitiated person ever to mock them for their cowardice.

A little after midnight the initiates leave the circumcision grove and proceed, still singing circumcision songs, to a spot several miles from the circumcision grove where a huge bonfire has been made. After they have all gathered at the bonfire, each 'bride' finds himself a stick, and at a signal given by the circumcision elders all the 'brides' rush out into the darkness away from the fire and hurl their sticks before them as if they were spears. They must not look back and if they stumble they may lose their potency. Thence the 'brides' go directly to their seclusion huts. Each group builds a fire in which they burn the wattle fence built around the hut and all the branches and leaves used as bedding while in seclusion. The huts are left to rot. Then the youths simply lie down outside the hut near the fire and sleep away what is left of the night.

At sunrise the 'brides' put on new clothes which their families provide for them (traditionally short skin aprons which cover the genitals and posterior but leave the right leg exposed) and turn over to the elders the skin capes they have been wearing during the preceding several months. Then the 'brides' leave the seclusion spot for good each carrying a carved baton (*lusibwa, lu- zi- -sibwa*) similar to the one that they may have had delivered to sweethearts. All that morning they go about singing a special song called, 'the song of departure' (*lwimbo lu saluxu*), and begging girls and whomever else they meet to give them bracelets and other trophies or 'blessings' (*migasa, mu- mi- -gasa*) to hang on the ends of their batons.

In the afternoon each 'bride', accompanied by the other youths who made up his seclusion group, visits his family homestead. All the family greet him in front of an archway (*shilibwa, shi- bi- -libwa*) especially constructed at the entrance to the homestead yard to honour his return. It is similar in form to the archway built to honour a girl when she is being brought to the home of her bridegroom for the first time. There is one difference, however; the girl's archway is made of banana plants and banana leaves, while the one for the youth returning from initiation is made from *lusiyola* branches (the same tree that is used for the sacred branch at the homestead ancestral shrine, and on other occasions where men are presiding or being honoured). The 'bride' of the homestead goes through the archway first, followed by his seclusion-mates and finally by his family. Inside the homestead ritual elders bless all the 'brides'. Thence the 'brides' go to the homestead of another seclusion-mate and so on, until the round of all their homes has been made.

The seclusion is completely over, but it is not yet considered good for those who have been initiated to return to their family

homes. Consequently the initiates of each seclusion group sleep
and eat together for the next three weeks at the hut of an elder
widower, their families bringing them their food. During this
period they have no set responsibilities and they may talk and
visit with whomever they want; a good deal of every day is spent
in walking around and begging girls and other passers-by to
hang small gifts on their batons. About two weeks after the 'beer
of leaving' the sub-tribal ritual elders call all the 'brides' of the
sub-tribe to a meeting of the sub-tribal meeting spot. A bull is
strangled and butchered, and subsequently a lustral ceremony
(*mwiluxa*) is performed. The ceremony is concluded by the
elders conferring their blessing on each of the 'brides.' Then the
bull is roasted and elders and 'brides' sit down together and
eat the meat.

Four or five days after the lustral ceremony and feast the
sub-tribal ritual elders lead the 'brides' for the first time into the
hilltop sacred grove (*gabogorosiyo*). There they are introduced to
the mystery of the roaring noise which they undoubtedly had
already heard coming from the hilltop grove on ceremonial
occasions. The roar is made with a friction drum. The drum is a
large earthenware pot (*inyungu, i- zi- -nyungu*), like those used
for brewing beer, over the top of which has been stretched and
tied a scraped sheepskin. With the pot sitting mouth up, one
end of a vertically held stick is placed against the skin. Then the
skin is made to vibrate and thus the pot to roar by sliding first
one hand and then the other down the stick in a milking-like
motion. Each 'bride' is given a chance to make the pot roar,
'to milk the cow' (*xushela ingombe*), in order that he may acquire
many cattle and grow wealthy.

The last formal rites of the initiation period are held about
four or five days after the visit to the sacred grove. At the
beginning of the closing rites the 'brides' gather by a river,
remove their clothes and have all their head and body hair
shaved off by the initiation counsellors and sub-tribal elders.
The following day the 'brides' again gather in a valley by a
river, bathe, and then, while still naked, are smeared with
butter by the counsellors. Thence they retire to the sub-tribal
meeting place and dance, naked, for the rest of the day. It is a
great holiday and all the sub-tribe comes to watch the initiation
group perform their final dances. That night, for the first time

since circumcision, the initiated youths may return to their homesteads to eat; indeed, their families welcome them home with a feast. For the succeeding two weeks or so the youths (no longer known as 'brides') visit various paternal and maternal relatives, eating and sleeping one night first at one relative's house, and the next at another's. In addition to a fine feed and a place to sleep, each relative so visited also gives the initiated youth a live chicken to carry home.

The Tiriki initiation customs (*idumi*) are far and away the most elaborate and extensive ceremonial complex of the tribe. Youths emerging from initiation find themselves with a completely different social status and role from those they had when they entered initiation. There is no counterpart to such a ceremony or abrupt status change in the lives of Tiriki women. Marriage, followed by the successful bearing of three children, usually firmly establishes a place for a woman in her husband's homestead, but this change from girlhood to womanhood, with its accompanying changes in residence, social contacts, duties and responsibilities, occurs quite gradually, and without benefit of nearly as much ceremonial reinforcement as the male transition from childhood to adulthood.

Scores of differences between the social behaviour of a person before and after initiation give expression and content to the formal status differentiation established through initiation.

One of the most striking of these differences is, of course, that an initiated male may legitimately indulge in sexual intercourse, while uninitiated males are forbidden to do so. Of course Tiriki females do not have any comparable restriction regulating their introduction to active heterosexuality; the prevalent Tiriki view *vis-à-vis* females on this score is comparable to that held in some of the rural and isolated regions of the United States, which American wags have summed up as, 'If they're big enough they're old enough.' Intercourse with a girl who has not yet started to menstruate or who has not yet developed her secondary sexual characteristics is considered a serious and dangerous deviation from the natural (*luswa*), and the man involved is regarded as the one primarily at fault. Other than this no regularly maintained sanctions exist regulating the time of a female's introduction to active heterosexuality.

Other differences between the behaviour of the initiated and the uninitiated clearly separate the activities of men from those of women and children. The uninitiated youth (*muyayi*) eats with other children and the womenfolk; he also has free run of the cooking section (*isisi, i- zi- -sisi*) of a hut which is considered the women's part of the home. After initiation a man (*musaza, mu- ba- -saza*) is expected to eat in the company of other men, and he must never go into the cooking section (*isisi*) of huts of people not of his own generation for as long as the women of the huts are of childbearing age.[1] Further, it is considered dangerous to the health of a man to pick up any infant who hasn't learned to walk yet and is still spitting and spewing. If obliged to do so the man feels it is necessary to cleanse himself by a thorough scrubbing with water and sand of all those parts of his body touched by the baby (in recent years *Lifebuoy* and *Boy* soap have come to be regarded as an adequate substitute for sand, and consequently the scrubbing is no longer such an arduous affair). During initiation the initiates are explicitly instructed and drilled in the above mentioned and literally dozens of other differences of behaviour that they will be expected to observe upon the completion of their initiation.

Initiation does much more than establish a youth's status and role as an adult, sexually active male. It also formally incorporates him into his age group (*lixula*) and schools him in the status and role expectations ascribed to his age group within the total age-graded age group system. During the many evenings in the seclusion hut and at the special ceremonial meetings in the circumcision grove he is taught by his counsellor and by the initiation elders the host of duties, responsibilities and privileges that accompany age group membership. The initiate learns he must respect and defer to members of age groups senior to his own. Also he comes to feel a special bond of brotherhood with all members of his own age group, and after initiation often uses a special term (*mugugwa*) when addressing or referring to them. He learns he must never marry the daughter of a member of his own age group, for it is felt that would be like marrying the daughter of a brother; in point of fact it would set up serious obstacles to age group solidarity by establishing within the age

---

[1] This restriction, as well as daughter-in-law avoidance, is allowed to lapse when a man is very old and past the age of sexual potency.

group tension-ridden father-in-law–son-in-law (*naxobizala*) oppositions with their customary social avoidances.

The initiation elders instruct the initiates during seclusion in how to kill someone who is many miles away through the use of sorcery. The initiate is also taught, however, that such sorcery deprives the user of his ability to father children. Thus the initiate comes to realize that the very old men of the tribe would feel no loss in using a power to kill that he himself would probably never choose to use until very old. The initiate also learns that some very old men of the ritual elder age group have additional knowledge of sorcery, in which they instruct only chosen members of the immediately junior judicial elder age group. The initiate is told in detail of the curse which the elders may utter collectively against a witch (*muloji*), a betrayer of the initiation secrets, or against any other Tiriki man who has erred sufficiently to evoke the elders' collective wrath. This curse is in effect an expulsion from one's position in the age group system; it is not believed necessarily to bring immediate sickness and death, but it deprives one of any age group recognition and support and promises failing health and 'a bad end' (*alaxuza damanu*). In pre-European days instruction which began during initiation in the skills of armed combat was continued with increasing diligence in the months following initiation. This preparation for warfare was under the direction of the initiation counsellors and other members of the age group immediately senior to the initiates, namely, the warrior age group.

The Structure and Function of Tiriki Age Groups

There are seven named, sequentially-arranged age groups, each embracing an age span of about 15 years. The system is cyclical as well as hierarchical; about 105 years elapse from the time a named group starts through the cycle until it appears again at the beginning of the cycle. Before the abolition of tribal warfare by the British around 1900 and the forbidding of the formal handing over of warrior status from one age group to the next, the age group immediately senior to the age group of the initiates was expected to occupy itself in raiding and warfare. Traditionally about every fifteen years ceremonies were held which retired the warrior group from active warrior status and replaced it by the initiates' age group. Thenceforth the group immediately following the newly-installed warrior group was declared 'open', and it was into this newly-opened initiation age group that youths were initiated every four or five years, until they in turn were installed as warriors, and the succeeding age group opened for initiation. Each time a new warrior group was installed the retiring warriors assumed the next higher status position of elder warriors and executive-type leaders at public meetings. The elder warriors in turn moved on to the status of judicial elders, while the judicial elders became the ritual elders. Members of the retiring ritual elder group who still had strength to fulfil their priestly roles were regarded with special veneration but were not considered a separate age grade. The final age group, once it had been deprived of all its members through death, eventually reappeared at the beginning of the cycle as the set embracing those boys to be initiated when the current initiation group succeeded to warrior status.

The Tiriki have no specific titles or words by which they designate the five age grades; furthermore, in practice the duties and functions of each grade overlap and intergrade. Very likely the overlapping and intergrading have increased since the abolition of the formal instatement of a warrior group and age grade change over, but the Tiriki persist in viewing their regular complement of five adult age groups as ranked and as possessing differential statuses and duties which are nowadays gradually passed from one age group to the next. Tiriki elders, when discussing the contemporary age groups, generally agree that the age group immediately senior to the age group open to initiation would traditionally be the principal warrior age group (*lixula lya balulu* or *lixula lya bandu bi lihe ligali*). Of the group immediately senior to this they speak with less certainty, but generally state that such people would not only have been the spokesmen, as they are today, of such affairs as post-funeral inheritance settlements, but that those who had gained reputations as warriors in earlier years might continue to direct raids, and would be active in community defence. The Tiriki usually sum up their traditional role by saying that people of this age group would have been the elder war leaders (*lixula lya biimili basaxulu bi lihe*) and also minor community leaders (*biimili badididi bu luhya*). All elders agree that today, as in traditional times, the principal duty of the next more senior age group is to

FIGURE 1
TIRIKI AGE GROUPS

1939 Age-Graded Duties (Traditional)	1939 Age Groups	1939 Membership Age Span (approx.)	Modern Age-Graded Social Roles	1954 Membership Age Span (approx.)	1954 Age Groups	1954 Age-Graded Duties (Traditional)
Elders (Deceased or Senile) [ELDERS]	(gibgoymed) KABALACH	86–100	Senile or Deceased	—	—	—
Ritual Elders [ELDERS]	(andalo) GOLONGOLO	71–85	Ritual Elders	86–100	(andalo) GOLONGOLO	Elders (Deceased or Senile) [ELDERS]
Judicial Elders [ELDERS]	JIMINIGAYI	56–70	Judicial Elders	71–85	JIMINIGAYI	Ritual Elders [ELDERS]
Elder Warriors	NYONJE	41–55	Administrators or away at work	56–70	NYONJE	Judicial Elders [ELDERS]
Warriors	MAYINA	26–40	Away at work	41–55	MAYINA	Elder Warriors
Initiated / Uninitiated	JUMA	25 / 11	In school and away at work	26–40	JUMA	Warriors
Small Boys	SAWE	0–10	Babies, baby tenders	25 / 11	SAWE	Initiated / Uninitiated
—	—	—	Cattle herds and School-boys	0–10	(gibgoymed) KABALACH	Small Boys

serve as the community and sub-tribal judicial elders (*lixula lya basaxulu bi biina*). And all concur that the seniormost age group (or age groups) traditionally fulfils the ritual and suppli- catory duties of the homestead, community and sub-tribe (*lixula lya basaxulu basaalisi*).

Figure 1 lists the seven Tiriki age groups, and the traditional duties ascribed to each in 1939 and then in 1954. It also gives the approximate population age range covered by each group and lists the principal contemporary age-graded social roles fulfilled by each age group in 1939 and 1954.

It should be noted that neither 1939 nor 1954 were initiation years; rather both dates fell several years prior to the opening of new age groups for initiation.[1]

Traditionally the warrior group enjoyed certain liberties and prestige granted no other age grade. Through deeds of cunning and valour while on raids, men in this age grade came to enjoy the praise and respect of other age groups and of the unmarried girls of the tribe. It was in large measure from his ability as a warrior that a man earned his reputation as one fit to lead and worthy of being followed, both among his age peers and among his age group juniors and seniors. Many of the stories and songs told and sung around the beer pots and recounted to the youth around the community fire described the bravery and skill of warriors still active and those long retired or dead. The pleas- ures of the bachelor huts were for the most part confined to the warrior age grade. Many Tiriki warriors married before the

[1] The names of the seven age groups listed on the diagram are those most widely used by Tiriki elders today. There is complete agreement about the name and order of the five age groups containing initiated members still alive today (1956)—namely (listed in order of decreasing age of members) Jiminigayi, Nyonje, Mayina, Juma, and Sawe. Only partial agreement is found with regards to Kabalach and Golongolo, several other names sometimes being used in their stead, but there is unanimity about there being seven age groups in the cycle.

The confusion as to whether Kabalach or Golongolo are the two additional age groups, or whether Gibgoymed and Golongolo are their present names apparently stems from the practice of occasionally substituting a new name for the name of an age group that was unsuccessful in warfare or was virtually wiped out in battle. In such cases the initiation elders sometimes decided to give the group a new name when it came time to open it for initiation at the beginning of a new 105 year cycle. The Tiriki elders recall the names of three age groups that are not used any more, Bandanin, Gamanyeli, and Damamudi; and one more, Andalo, was used by some sub-tribes in the previous cycle instead of the more widely used Golongolo.

succeeding age group formally took over their warrior status, but marriage did not prevent the warrior from continuing to accompany his unmarried age peers on nocturnal *rendezvous* with unmarried girls. Once, however, an age group had passed through the warrior age grade, the members began to give up the practice of meeting together in sleeping huts with unmarried sweethearts, and it was considered ludicrous for someone to try to join in the amorous activities of men in the age group junior to his own. Thus regular access to the unmarried girls was primarily a privilege of the warrior age grade.[1]

A man's position following the retirement of his age group from warriorhood was neither as glamorous nor as well defined as before retirement. In the early years after retirement the better known warriors of the elder warrior age grade sometimes continued to accompany and even lead segments of the warrior age grade on raids. Also members of this elder grade were generally depended on to sound the alarm and organize defensive action when the Nandi and other hostile tribes staged surprise raids. Then, as time went on, members of the elder warrior grade who showed the proper sort of leadership characteristics found themselves called on to chair post-funeral property settlements and eventually to join the age group immediately senior to them in helping to arbitrate various disputes within the community. There is no evidence to be found today that the graded functions of any of the age groups did not always overlap markedly with those of the age groups immediately junior and senior to them. This does not mean, however, that every Tiriki did not have a clear picture of the sorts of activities commonly regarded as *most suitable* for each age group during its occupancy of any given age grade. Certainly today the concept of fixed progression by the age groups through successive

---

[1] Today men, both married and unmarried, generally court the favours of unmarried girls in informal neighbourhood groups consisting of members of their own age group. Initiated members of the initiate age grade and members of the traditional warrior age grade remain the two groups most occupied with such amatory activities.

The Tiriki elders recount that traditionally the warriors might allow initiated members of the immediately junior age group not only to join them in raids but also to entertain girls in the warriors' sleeping huts. The warrior group, however, had the right to exclude the members of the junior group from the warriors' raids and amatory activities if they so chose, and naturally the warriors kept the pick of the girls for themselves.

social statuses is an openly expressed part of the way the Tiriki
conceptualize their own society both past and present.

It is difficult today, over fifty years after the termination of
large scale raiding and tribal warfare, to evaluate with much
certainty the role of the age groups in the war organization.
The oldest Tiriki men still alive (1956) are members of the
Jiminigayi age group. At the time of the last raids they were the
initiates, and they were never formally installed as warriors;
thus they were never responsible for the organization and carrying out of raids. A few elders still survive who took part in both
defensive and offensive fighting under the direction of more
senior age groups, and even those who did no raiding seem to
have a general idea of how raids were organized from what they
observed as youths and from what their elders told them. It
seems worth while, therefore, to sketch briefly the manner in
which the elders believe the raids were organized.

All the age grades had their specialized roles in planning,
carrying out, and forestalling the possible adverse effects of a
major raid. It was usual for scouts (*baluri, mu- ba- -luri*) of the
warrior and sometimes of the elder warrior age grade to keep
track of the major concentrations of enemy cattle and enemy
warriors. When the reports of the scouts seemed particularly
favourable, war leaders from the warrior grade under the
guidance of some of the more outstanding elder warrior leaders
might draw up a plan of offensive action, and then start
recruiting men from their own sub-tribe to join the proposed
raid. In some cases warriors from neighbouring sub-tribes were
also solicited. The warrior age grade made up most of the
recruits, but some of the initiates and elder warriors also
frequently joined in.

If a large raid was proposed and many recruits were obtained
the ritual elders were then asked to pass on its auspiciousness
and to decide the best time for the raid. In order to do this the
ritual elders retired to the sacred grove, where they observed
certain omens such as how the wind carried the smoke from a
ritual fire, the colour and shape of the entrails of a ritually
slaughtered animal, the flight of certain birds, &c. In some cases,
especially in raids conducted by primarily Terik sub-tribes, an
elder from a clan of Terik diviners (said to be related to the
Masai 'laibon' diviners living in Nandi) was asked to hold a

seance to ascertain the propitiousness of and the best date for the raid. Once the date had been set for a major raid the warriors from each sub-tribe gathered at the sub-tribal sacred groves to receive the blessings of the ritual elders. The Tiriki elders recount that it was not uncommon in major raids for elder warriors renowned for their leadership and fighting skill to lead members of the warrior age group into actual skirmishes with the enemy. Initiates directed by some of the more active and adventuresome judicial elders sometimes followed the raiders to help drive home whatever cattle were captured by the warriors. Elders disagree on precisely how the cattle and other spoils obtained through these raids were divided up. They mostly concur, however, that only those men who took an active part in capturing and/or conducting home such booty had any claim to it. After a raid those warriors who had killed enemies were not allowed to return to their homes and regular activities until they had been purified from the danger to themselves and others which was believed to adhere to anyone who takes a person's life. This purification entailed seclusion of the warriors who had killed from all people not so tainted for a number of days, during which they bathed, shaved off all their body hair, and had a lustral ceremony held on their behalf by the ritual elders.

Age group solidarity and age grading were traditionally manifest not only at initiation, in raiding, and in the carrying out of the more formalized community and sub-tribal activities in the judicial and ritual spheres, but also at more or less informal occasions such as beer drinks. Tiriki elders view the social organization of contemporary beer drinks as being little changed from traditional times.[1] The predominant practice is for beer drinkers to gather in age-group clusters. At a contemporary

[1] Reference is being made here only to beer drinks at which locally brewed beer is served in the traditional manner in pots and drunk through long beer tubes— each pot thus simultaneously serving several, even as many as two dozen, people. It is becoming increasingly common in Tiriki, especially in the southwestern part of the tribe that has been heavily settled by Maragoli, for an individual to purchase a tinful (*muhoda, mu- mi- -hoda*—approximately a quart) of locally brewed beer for -/50, East African currency (about seven U.S. cents), or larger amounts for correspondingly higher prices, which he then carries home and drinks from a cup either alone or in the company of a few friends. The Tiriki claim that the practice of selling and drinking small orders of African beer started in the urban centres of East Africa and has been taken back to the tribal areas by younger men who fancy the practice as 'modern'. Also a preference is growing among the younger groups for the much more expensive (three to four shillings—about fifty U.S.

beer drink the ritual elder and judicial elder age grades often sit around a common pot of beer, while the younger age groups— those that traditionally would have occupied the 'elder warrior' and the 'warrior' age grades—usually have another pot some distance from the elders. Today such a high percentage of the younger men are away from the tribe working in urban centres and on European farms that the elder groups may outnumber the younger groups. At very large drinks the drinkers may further subdivide, and one may find the seniormost age group around a small pot, the judicial elders with their own pot (or pots) and then one or two additional pots for the elder warrior and warrior grades. The divisions at beer drinks are affected by the total number of participants and by other incidental factors, but the drinks usually subdivide by age groups when there are enough men over the entire adult age span to permit this. In every case the seniormost members of the senior age group drinking at each pot have the greatest authority in saying who should be invited to join the circle of drinkers and in controlling their conduct.

Age group solidarity also asserts itself at funerals. Each age group cherishes and preserves the memory of its own leaders and distinguished warriors. When a man dies members of his own age group sing and organize dances to honour him at his funeral. If the deceased was an important elder, members of his age group arrange for the running of a herd of cattle to his grave. Then, in a night ceremony, his age group friends gather and sing the special set of songs (*buxulu, bu- -xulu*) otherwise only sung at initiation time. Finally, through speech and song, the mourners of his age group recall his prowess in battle and his other noteworthy accomplishments.

An age group, even after all its members are dead, continues to be viewed as a corporate entity by the members of junior age groups. The ritual elders, when they are asking the ancestral spirits to bless the people and the crops at community or sub-tribal supplications, generally call on one or more age groups of deceased elders for special consideration and aid. The

cents—a quart) for the lager beer brewed and bottled commercially at several East African urban centres. In northern Tiriki participation in the communal type traditional beer drinks are still the rule rather than the exception among all age groups.

present-day elders, for example, might call on Golongolo or Sawe (meaning the most recently deceased groups of those names). It should be noted that in spite of the practice of viewing each age group as a distinct social entity, the members of an age group, today at least, apparently do not identify themselves with the group that carried their age group name in previous centuries. Identification seems instead to be with all the age groups, past and present, that make up the ongoing seven-part cycle, rather than with the particular name group to which one belongs.

Age Group Succession: A Discussion and Comparison of the Tiriki, Kipsigis and Nandi Procedures

It has already been mentioned that the Tiriki no longer perform any ceremony through which warriors are retired and members of the following age group are granted warrior status. Indeed, the contemporary Tiriki elders profess to have no recollection as to the nature of the traditional method or methods by which successive groups became warriors and how age groups were opened to initiation. They merely assert that the Tiriki used to follow the lead of the Terik in such matters, and that the actual rituals (*miima*) followed by predominantly Tiriki sub-tribes on such occasion were just the same as the Terik, Nandi and the Kipsigis customs. In recent years, both the opening of a new initiation period and the opening of a new age group to initiation have been decided in Tiriki by the initiation elders, subject to the final sanction and approval of the British-established tribal Chief. The opening of a new age group now-adays occurs coterminously with the opening of every third or fourth initiation period and does not entail any special ceremony or the establishment of a warrior group. The occurrence of initiation and the opening of new age groups in Tiriki apparently continue to be coterminous and in phase with the Terik initiations and age groups.[1]

[1] My information on the years in which initiation was held in Tiriki since 1900 is not completely consistent, while the information on when initiation was held in Terik areas now in Nyangori Location is even less certain. The Terik-Tiriki agree, however, on the names and order of the contemporary extant age groups. Furthermore, with the exception of the most recent initiation period (1958 in Tiriki and 1957 in Nyangori), I have no evidence that the Terik and the Tiriki ever held initiation on differing years.

The Tiriki elders feel it is most probable that in traditional times the decision to open a new age group to initiation was guided by two traditions. These two traditions are maintained to the present day, not only among the Tiriki and Terik but also among the Kipsigis and the Nandi. The first of these traditions is that a son is not allowed to be initiated into the age group immediately following his father's (his own biological father's) age group. The second tradition is that there are only seven age groups in the total age group cycle, and it is prohibited for an age group to be opened for initiation when the corresponding age group of the preceding cycle still contains living members. It would not be permitted, for example, for Jiminigayi age group to be opened for initiation in future years until all members of the elder Jiminigayi group had died . . . even if a member of this group were to live to be 120! The Tiriki elders point out that no cases are remembered of difficulty having arisen because elders lived too long, but that the elders are concerned not to have the age span during which age groups receive new initiated drop below about fifteen years for fear that the cumulative result would be to have seven age groups initiated before all men in the seniormost group had died.

The above two traditions serve to maintain the graded age groups as a system of semi-generational stratifications. Of course a younger son may be initiated into an age group three below his father's, but the vast majority of Tiriki men belong to the age group two below their father's. Today, for example, most men of the Mayina age group are sons of men of the Jiminigayi age group, while their sons are now being initiated into the Sawe age group. The Tiriki assert that when a number of youth in a community reach the age when they might be initiated, but the age group open for initiation remains that directly succeeding their fathers', the sons prevail upon their fathers and other members of their fathers' age group to see what can be done about opening a new age group. The fathers in turn consult with their own fathers, who are for the most part members of the age group two above their own. It is among these old men of the grandparental generation, most of whom are members of the judicial elder age grade, but a few of whom are probably members of the immediately senior ritual age grade, that one finds the initiation elders who have the traditional authority to open a new group for initiation. Thus when a dozen or more years have passed since the current initiation group was opened, the conversation around the elders' beer pots tends more and more to turn to the question of opening a new initiation group. In recent decades the decision to open a new age group to initiation has been subject to the final approval of the British-appointed tribal Chief, but the initiation elders still feel that it is primarily their responsibility to see that the changeover is made.

Today a mild but widespread element of rivalry is evident in relationships between members of adjacent age groups. For example, at small beer parties where participants are disinclined to establish separate beer pots for each age group, members of the senior group at a pot are very careful to maintain their position of control over members of the immediately younger group, and are quick to discourage any efforts of the junior group to foster an atmosphere of easy equality. It will also be recalled that the counsellors (*badili*) during initiation are members of the age group just senior to the initiates. These young men are the principal disciplinarians and task masters for the initiates. Of course they are selected by the initiation elders and their duties are under the ultimate direction of the elders, but it is reported that the counsellors receive considerable encouragement from other members of their own age group to be zealous in their efforts to discipline the initiates in their charge.

In pre-European times it is probable that a fairly intense rivalry existed between the initiate group and the immediately senior group that they would soon replace as warriors. Further, it is rather likely that this rivalry, coupled with the relatively depressed statuses of the initiate and elder warrior groups when compared with the warrior and judicial elder groups, tended to produce an informal coalition of alternating age groups. Unfortunately, the Tiriki have no remembrance of the mechanism through which the initiate group was declared warriors and the warrior group retired to a more advisory role. It seems reasonable to postulate, however, that the Tiriki initiates (or the Terik initiates if the Tiriki segments of the tribe were merely passive imitators of the Terik) may have solicited the aid of their fathers who in turn brought the matter to their fathers—just as today when youth want a new age group opened for initiation.

It must be remembered that most of the initiate group's fathers would have been members of the age group serving as elder warriors. Thus through aiding their son's ascendancy to warriorhood they would not only remove from warrior status the very group that displaced them from this coveted position, but they would also be working for the establishment of their own age group as judicial elders. The grandparental age group, enfeebled and depleated by old age and death, would not lose status but simply gain needed recruits for its ritual responsibilities through a change over; thus members of that group would probably be easily prevailed upon to set the ritual machinery in motion whereby their grandsons would ascend to warriorhood.

Jacobs, in an essay, 'Age-Class Systems and Political Organization in East Africa', has pointed out how a moiety division within an age grouped society, resulting from the coalition of alternating age groups, may serve, in the absence of a chieftainship, to control hostility between adjacent age groups, and also may implement the changeover of age group statuses.[1] The Tiriki do not recall that a formal or even informally recognized moiety division consisting of alternating age groups ever existed in Tiriki. Almost certainly competition between adjacent age groups has decreased in Tiriki as a consequence of the virtual demise of the warriors as a distinctive status group, resulting from the British Administration's prohibition of warrior installation ceremonies and the suppression of tribal warfare. Also the establishment of tribal chieftainships, both in Nyangori Location (where many Terik live) and in Tiriki, now supplies centralized machinery for the regulation of age group succession. In the absence, however, of clear-cut evidence as to how the Terik-Tiriki managed their changeover in aboriginal times, the moiety hypothesis seems worth tendering. Further, to the extent that a moiety division was functionally manifest in such matters as succession to warriorhood, it would have helped maintain clan solidarity at one of its weakest points, namely in the area of father–son interaction. It will be recalled that father–son solidarity is a clan ideal and is ritualized in the ancestor cult. Nevertheless father–son competition, especially over cattle for

[1] Alan H. Jacobs, 'Age-Class Systems and Political Organization in East Africa,' *Anthropology Tomorrow* (Chicago: Publication of the Department of Anthropology, University of Chicago, June, 1956), Vol. IV, No. 3, pp. 29–37.

bridewealth, sometimes gets very intense, and the whole father–son relationship tends to be rather formal and somewhat precarious. The graded age groups almost certainly helped to neutralize latent father–son hostility by providing semi-generational alignments that placed adjacent generations in complementary rather than competing statuses.

To date no information has been gathered from the Terik either by myself or by any other researcher known to me on the the details of Terik age group organization. Fairly detailed published reports do exist, however, describing the nature and function of both Nandi and Kipsigis age groups and age grading.[1] In view of the Tiriki assertion that the Terik-Tiriki age group organization is like, indeed the same as (*xolandi, na halala na*), the Nandi and Kipsigis age groups and age grading, it seems worth while briefly reviewing what is reported of these two systems.

Peristiany gives a succinct account of the traditional Kipsigis procedure by which a new age group was opened to initiation, the old warrior group retired, and the newly initiated members of the succeeding age group installed as the new warriors.[2] Two major aspects of this procedure are worth noting here, one for its contrast with and one for its similarity to what is remembered and remains of the Tiriki system. First, the initiates were also the warriors in Kipsigis, except for a period of a year or less (out of about fifteen years) when those first to be initiated into a newly opened age group had not yet emerged from initiation. The rites which marked the closing of the current and the opening of the succeeding age group to initiation were part of one continuous ceremonial sequence that culminated in the *saket ap eito* ceremony whereby the warrior group was retired and the new initiation group installed as warriors. This identity of the initiate and warrior group is not in keeping with what the Tiriki elders remember of their own traditional system, and thus must be regarded as an area in which the Tiriki and Kipsigis systems probably differed. Second, it was through a ritually formalized pairing of the age group waiting to be initiated and installed as warriors with the second and fourth ascending age

---

[1] Hollis, op. cit.; G. W. B. Huntingford, *The Nandi of Kenya* (London: Routlege & Kegan Paul, Ltd., 1953); Peristiany, op. cit.

[2] Peristiany, op. cit., pp. 32–37.

groups senior to this group that the retirement of the old and the formulation of a new initiation-warrior group was implemented. A similar, though strictly informal, coupling of the interests and efforts of alternate age groups is manifest in contemporary Tiriki when it approaches time to open a new age group to initiation. Finally, it should be noted that Peristiany does not report the existence of any formally recognized moiety division for the Kipsigis in his monograph; nor does he describe the alignment of alternating age groups in any other social context.

There are a number of inconsistencies between the reports given on Nandi age groups by Hollis[1] and Huntingford.[2] Very likely these reflect variations of age group customs between different Nandi-speaking tribes and sub-groups and also variations of these customs through time. Nevertheless the accounts given by Hollis and Huntingford clearly portray an overall age group structure and age grading similar in most respects to the Tiriki and Kipsigis systems. All three tribes have seven age groups which cover an age span of about fifteen years each, and which re-appear cyclically approximately every 105 years. For the most part the age-graded statuses through which the groups pass are similar but not identical, and at any given time the ages of men of all three tribes within each age group are roughly comparable.

Huntingford's account indicates that the Nandi method of implementing age group status changeover differs markedly from the Kipsigis procedure. Huntingford claims that every second blooming of a shrub, called *setiot* by the Nandi, which flowers only every six or seven years, is the signal for the opening of a new age group to initiation. Following the second blooming of the flower, permission may be obtained separately by members of each Nandi maximal territorial unit (*pororiet*) from the *Orkoiyot* who is the high priest or supreme prophet of all Nandi, to open a new age group for initiation.[3] There was not the rigid demarcation between warriorhood and the other age-graded statuses that was characteristic of the Kipsigis system. Rather there were apparently two groups that acted as warriors during

[1] Hollis, op. cit., pp. 12–13.
[2] Huntingford, op. cit., pp. 53–75.
[3] ibid., pp. 62–4.

the greater part of any fifteen year period, one junior and one senior group. Furthermore, each age group was subdivided into junior and senior sections. It seems as though the formal installation of a new age group to warrior status and the retirement of the previous warrior group did not occur until about eight years after the opening of a new age group to initiation. During this eight year period the former initiate age group, especially its senior section, was informally taking over the duties of the warrior group; the senior section of the warrior group was in turn informally assuming the role of tribal elders. Thus when the changeover ceremonies (*saket ap eito*) were finally held, both the incoming and the retiring groups were in effect simply assuming the formal statuses appropriate to the social roles they were already fulfilling.[1]

Huntingford finds no evidence of rivalry between incoming and retiring warrior groups in Nandi such as Peristiany reports for the Kipsigis.[2] If Huntingford's material is correct, apparently the gradual process through which the shifts in roles were effected, coupled with the non-human agent (the flowering of the shrub) for determining the time and the centralized priesthood for regulating the manner of changeover, all worked together to preclude the development (or utility) of inter-age group rivalry.

It is impossible to say on the basis of what the Tiriki elders remember whether the Terik-Tiriki system resembled more closely the Kipsigis or the Nandi, or whether they had evolved a third quite dissimilar system. Very likely, as both groups profess, the Tiriki did follow the lead of the Terik in these matters. Thus careful and systematic inquiry of the Terik elders would probably be the best remaining way of getting a more complete picture of the traditional Tiriki age group system.

Summary

The Terik and the Tiriki share the same male circumcision and initiation rites (*idumi*). Occurring after puberty, these rites

---

[1] ibid., pp. 54–59. Robert Wiltsey, *Age Class or Sets, and Age Grades* (Unpublished manuscript, University of Rochester, Rochester, N.Y., 1959), points out the utility of differentiating between status and role when trying to systematize and summarize Huntingford's account of Nandi age grading.

[2] Huntingford, op. cit., p. 68.

not only mark the transition from childhood to adulthood, but they are also the ceremonials through which adult males attain membership in an age group, and thereby tribal membership. The extended initiation rites instruct the initiates in their obligations towards their own age group, other age groups, and all initiated Tiriki. The initiation rites help the initiates become fully aware of the age-graded statuses through which all the age groups progress. The two major statuses, adulthood and elderhood (*buhindila*, *bu- -hindila* and *busaxulu*, *bu- -saxulu*) are further divided into a total of four grades, each with its own prerogatives and social responsibilities. Thus each of the four adult age groups normally found at any given time has its own social status, which it occupies for about a fifteen year period and then surrenders to the immediately junior group in favour of the next higher status. Age group loyalties cross-cut clan ties and serve as the principal traditional basis for community, sub-tribal, and tribal cooperation.

III

The Traditional Tiriki Territorial Organization

THE traditional Tiriki territorial organization strongly reflects both the tribe's Abaluyia origins and its recent Terik affiliations. The settlement patterns superficially resemble those of other southern Abaluyia tribes, but upon analysis the organizational patterns reveal themselves as being perhaps closer to those characteristic of the Terik and those which Evans-Pritchard outlines for the Kipsigis.[1]

Joseph Thompson in 1883 made a journey through what are now parts of North Nyanza and Elgon Districts of Kenya.[2] He is the first European known to have traversed the region. His route took him 30 or 40 miles north of Tiriki, through a region that remains even today much less densely populated than Tiriki and other southern Abaluyia tribal regions. Thompson reported that most of the inhabitants lived in homesteads scattered rather widely across the countryside. In some regions of the area Thompson found people living in walled and moated villages from which they emerged by day to graze their cattle and till their fields. These fortified villages were constructed, the Abaluyia say, primarily as protection against bands of Masai marauders. After the establishment of peace under the British they were abandoned in favour of the pattern of dispersed homesteads, each with surrounding fields, so characteristic of the region as a whole.

In Wanga and other tribes in the north of the Abaluyia area, where the population density per square mile to this day remains relatively low, a number of homesteads, each containing several huts, are found scattered over the flanks and crests of the low hills which typify the topography of that part of Nyanza Province. Each low hill or ridge (*olugongo*) is generally separated from adjoining hills by valleys that contain bogs or little

[1] J. G. Peristiany, *The Social Institutions of Kipsigis* (London: George Routledge & Sons, Ltd., 1939), pp. xx–xxiv.

[2] Joseph Thompson, *Through Masai Land* (new and revised edition), (London: Sampson Low, Marston & Co. (no date), pp. 278–285.

streams. This has no doubt encouraged the development on each ridge of a community life to a great degree independent of that found on other ridges. Generally each ridge has its meeting place where the elders from the homesteads on the ridge regularly convene to exchange news and settle local inter-homestead disputes. It was customary to build a fire at such meetings to dispel the chill of the morning air; thus, the Abaluyia aver, the local meeting place came to be called the 'bonfire' (*luhya*, or *oluhya*).

In the southernmost part of North Nyanza, including the area of present day Tiriki, the hills are generally steeper and more irregular in contour than in the north. The enormous and increasing population density, now surpassing 1,000 people per square mile in some regions, has caused the people to extend regular settlement down into the valleys. The contemporary view from a Tiriki hilltop presents a virtually unbroken panorama of small cultivated fields, dwelling huts and granaries, with no apparent preference being shown for either hill or valley habitation. No break occurs between the settlement of one hillside and that of the next, and homesteads are so close together as to often make the division between huts of adjacent homesteads imperceptible to the hilltop observer. The continuous blanket of cultivation and habitation is punctured in spots by the occasional boggy valley and by jagged outcroppings of rock, by a sprinkling of hilltop sacred groves and valley bottom circumcision groves, and by the occasional grassy clearing which serves as the community meeting place (*luhya*).

The community centres or meeting places, which may occur on any terrain so long as it is not too steep, are regularly used for grazing cattle. In pre-European times some of the community meeting places served as markets where goods were bartered with people of neighbouring areas, other tribes, and itinerant Swahili merchants. Nowadays some of those meeting places that fall along the motor roads have become officially established as African District Council market places. The African District Council (A.D.C.) is a British-established executive body that embraces all the tribes of the District. The A.D.C. grants a limited number of plots to local petitioners who then may erect permanent brick-walled tin-roofed stores from which to sell their wares. Often today a portion of a community meeting place which has no official market serves as the site of a mission church or primary school.

Tiriki settlement does not cluster around the community meeting place, nor does it tend to thin out in regions coterminous with boundaries between adjacent communities. Indeed the meeting places themselves offer the only conspicuous visual evidence of tribal socio-political sub-divisions. In point of fact, however, the communities are only one of three distinctive sets of territorial divisions within the tribe. These three sets of divisions are: the homestead (*mujizi*), the community (*luhya*), and the sub-tribe (*lusomo*) officially known today as the sublocation. The boundaries of every territorial division, be it homestead, community, or sub-tribe, are well known to the majority of the elders living in the division and in the immediately adjacent areas. It is quite clear that concern over the precise delineation of land division boundaries has grown enormously in the last few decades since the British have curtailed most of the eastward migration into Nandiland. Also the population has greatly increased during the last fifty years, further stimulating a possessive attitude towards the increasingly hard-pressed land resources. This growing concern over boundaries is especially evident in the case of homestead lands where the traditional view that all sons have equal claim to the land of their father is leading to even smaller homestead holdings. In many parts of Tiriki the terrain is so choppy that a community of three or four hundred acres may embrace several hills, valleys, and rivulets. It is not even uncommon to find the land of one homestead straddling a little valley. Thus in all three types of territorial divisions streams and valley bottoms are often ignored as boundary markers. Instead boundaries are often located and remembered simply by such commonly agreed upon landmarks as designated rocks, trees, and shrubs.

The Homestead

The homestead (*mujizi*) and its (usually) surrounding farmlands is the smallest territorial unit of judicial and economic significance in Tiriki.[1] The eldest active male member of the

---

[1] Extended family units embracing three generations and usually a dozen or more people are today the exception rather than the rule in Tiriki, but they remain the preferred form of family arrangement. Tiriki elders claim that such extended families were the rule rather than the exception two generations ago.

homestead usually acts as its head and spokesman. He generally is the arbiter of disputes within the homestead, and also speaks for all its members in disputes with other homesteads over property damage, boundaries, and the like. The homestead head also directs the family's use of its land. It is his responsibility to assign fields each season for the use of his wives and the other women of the homestead. It will be recalled from Chapter I that the homestead traditionally serves not only as the minimal jural and primary economic unit, but also as the minimal ritual group. Most homesteads had their own ancestral shrine which was tended by the homestead head, often with the assistance of the eldest active male member of the same clan who lived in the same or a nearby community.

A further traditional function of the homestead, completely eliminated since the establishment of the British Administration, is defence. Each homestead was completely surrounded by a thorn fence (*lugaga, lu- zi- -gaga*) that had only one gate (*shilibwa*). The fence served as protection against the nocturnal marauding of large predatory animals and enemy cattle raiders. These fences are no longer constructed, for the increase in population density has driven away the large animals, and *pax britannica* has virtually eliminated cattle raiding in the area. The Tiriki never had any village or community fortifications such as the walled and moated villages of Kabras and Wanga to the north; thus the thorn fence around the homestead was the only fixed fortification. In case of a cattle raid or a major enemy attack the homestead or homesteads affected immediately raised a cry that warned members of neighbouring homesteads to grab their spears and guard their homesteads' gates. In each community several men living in different homesteads held the inherited position of keeper of the horn (*imbumi, i- zi- -mbumi*).[1] Any sustained uproar occasioned their blowing the horns; thus were all men aroused to the common defence of the community. Tiriki elders claim that community defence was the principal responsibility of the elder warriors. Large scale

[1] A person's right to inherit his father's position as horn keeper was contingent upon both his father's and the community elders' approval; if they felt the heir-apparent did not fill the requisite qualifications of bravery, wisdom, and prowess in battle, the elders could if necessary confer the position upon someone in no way related to the former keeper. Such contingency is characteristic of most inherited positions in Tiriki.

raids from hostile tribes were evidently infrequent enough so that the system of arousing the community to a general defensive effort through blowing of the horns was generally sufficient to avert complete disaster.

The Community

Inquiry as to the nature of the traditional community reveals two aspects of community life that are now defunct. One of these is the community's significance as a defensive unit which was briefly mentioned in the previous paragraph. The other is the community as a ritual unit.

The ritual unity of the community was most regularly manifest in the annual first fruits ceremony, held shortly after the slackening off of the long rains (usually early June) when the principal grain crops were about ready to harvest. This is usually a time of food shortage and disease, when the supplies from the previous harvest are nearly used up and when malaria and other diseases are on the increase from the hunger, dampness, and relative coolness of the season. The ritual elders, through examination of the growing crops, decided the day for the ceremony. Early that morning they kindled a small fire at a central spot in the community where two or more pathways cross. Making a small fire for ritual purposes is known as making *bwali* (*xulomba bwali*). Green leaves were thrown on the fire and from the manner in which the smoke rose the elders augured the fortune that would befall the community in the following months. Then elders and onlookers, under the direction of the most venerable ritual elder, each picked up a stick and waited in readiness while the elder beseeched the ancestral spirits and the most recently deceased age group to bless the health, crops, and cattle of the people of the community. The supplication ended with an entreaty to the ancestral spirits to drive the witches (*baloji*) into the bottom of Lake Victoria. At this moment, the dramatic climax of the ceremony, the leader cast his stick in the direction of the distant lake (about twenty miles to the southwest, and only visible from a few south Tiriki hilltops), and the onlookers followed suit. The formal ceremony ended here, but for the rest of the day the fire was kept burning, no one worked in the fields, and every passerby threw a handful of grass, a leaf, or some foodstuff on the fire, 'to bless the land'

(*xugasiza shibala*). After the ceremony the people of the community were free to harvest their crops.[1]

Community *bwali* ceremonies were not restricted to this one
annual occasion. At any time of stress, be it defeat or fear of
defeat in battle, epidemics, famine, or earthquakes, community
elders might decide to perform *bwali* in order to call the ancestral spirits to the community's aid. By 1955, however, organized
pagan religious activity, such as the first fruits ceremony and
rituals held in times of stress and disaster, were no longer performed at the community level. A few elders still pray at their
homestead ancestral shrines at such times, but all members of
the community, Christian and pagan alike, now look to the
European-organized or inspired health and hospital services,
governmental agencies, and church leaders, to help the community both materially and spiritually in times of crisis. The
pagan elders openly proclaim that they have abdicated all
community-wide religious activity, asserting that the Christians
with their European[2] backing forced them to stop such ceremonies as the first fruits *bwali*. They also, of course, disavow any
responsibility for all present day community misfortune and
disaster, saying it is the Christians who have ruined the manners
and morals of the people and who now let the witches roam
freely to spoil the land (*baguristayo na baloji badamana shibala*).

The community today, as in former times, is an important
judicial unit. The elders say that the contemporary community
judicial procedures are for the most part essentially the same as
in traditional times. It should be noted, however, that certain
striking limitations have been placed on the jurisdiction of the
courts. The judgment of certain serious crimes such as murder

---

[1] The preceding description is based on conversations with Tiriki elders, and a
reenactment of the ceremony that the elders of Jebdulu, Tiriki, held for me in
June, 1955. The elders reported on that occasion that such a community first
fruits *bwali* had not been regularly held in Tiriki communities for a decade or more.

[2] The Tiriki use the term *Musungu* (*mu- ba- -sungu*) to refer to all people of
European extraction, be they American missionaries, Italian mechanics, British
administrators, Boar settlers, or German anthropologists. The American Negro
is a special case; in the abstract, he is classified as an African (*Mumwamu, mu-
ba- -mwamu*)—literally, 'a black person'; in the two brief encounters, however,
that the Tiriki had with American Negroes during the writer's stay in Tiriki, the
American Negroes were both quickly pronounced to be '*basungu bamwamu*'
(black Europeans), and considered very strange indeed. Those Tiriki who have a
knowledge of English almost invariably translate *Musungu* as 'European'.

and manslaughter have been completely removed by the British, not only from both community and tribal jurisdiction, but also from the jurisdiction of the multi-tribal African Tribunal. Also today it is possible for a plaintiff to appeal, or take his case directly, to the sub-tribal or tribal courts, or, if he chooses, to the multi-tribal African Tribunal, which is the lowest court granted statutory recognition by the colonial government, whereas in traditional times the community courts usually offered a man his only legal recourse.[1]

The judicial elders who habitually gather at the community centre in the mornings may always be prevailed upon by any man in the community to arbitrate a dispute. Boys, girls, and women customarily have their grievances presented by an adult brother or father; a husband, in those cases where he is not the defendant, may represent his wife. The plaintiff pleads his own case or the case of the aggrieved woman or child in his charge, and he may bring as many witnesses as he wants to substantiate his story and give supporting evidence. The defendant, or his or her guardian, then presents his own case and names witnesses whom the judicial elders may then summon to give testimony on his behalf. During the entire proceedings all adult men and elderly women present may ask the judicial elders for permission to express their opinions on the case, or add further evidence, and the elders may themselves call on anyone, including women and children, to present testimony.

The matter upon which the judicial elders finally pass judgment is not necessarily that which the plaintiff first presented. Indeed, the original accusation may be judged irrelevant to some other question that arises during the trial which is deemed of greater importance by the elders. The original defendant may even be acquitted and final judgement made

---

[1] Three factors work to preserve much of the utility and authority of the community courts. First, the higher courts tend in most cases to uphold the decision of the community courts; and in those cases where the plaintiff has bypassed the community court in favour of a higher court, his chance for a favourable verdict is jeopardized by the prevalent practice of calling and deferring to the judgement of elders from his own community. Second, frequent use of the multi-tribal tribunal is discouraged by the relatively high court fee which must be paid in advance. Third, the factor of simple convenience favours the continued utilization of the community courts. They convene near the homestead of the plaintiff, and the local elders will hear a case usually the same day it is presented to them.

against someone else—even the plaintiff. In short, once a case is presented, the whole life and character of the accuser and the accused are potentially on trial, and to a lesser extent this is also true of the witnesses. There is really no such thing as a simple dismissal of a case, for in any event the plaintiff's good judgement is on trial. If his accusations are disproved or rejected, but otherwise he is judged guiltless, the plaintiff will characteristically be laughed at by the elders for his stupidity (*busilo bwe*), and of course he will be obliged to pay the elders a chicken or some other fee for having heard his case. If the plaintiff is successful in the presentation of his case the defeated party must compensate the elders for having heard the case and then perform whatever else the elders direct as indemnity to the plaintiff and the community.

Ritual elders frequently do not attend judicial hearings, but when present they are granted extreme deference. Their testimony and judgement is regularly sought in cases involving incest and witchcraft, where their greater memory depth and their ritual power and protection are deemed necessary.

In traditional times community courts could administer certain kinds of ordeals to reveal guilt and also could employ several oath-taking rituals, some Nandi in origin (*xuliya muuma*), and some common among the Abaluyia peoples (e.g., *xuroza murembe*). All ordeals and pagan oaths have been outlawed by the British Administration with the exception of the *murembe* (*mu- mi- -rembe*) oath (*xuroza murembe*) which is still occasionally administered under British sanction, but only at the multi-tribal District-administered African courts. One takes this oath by publicly making one's declaration and then thrusting a spear into the trunk of the *murembe* tree (*Erythrina Abyssinica*). If the declaration is false, it is believed that the power of the tree will bring much sickness and death to one's family and probably one's own death during the next several years.

The jurisdiction of the community court is for the most part confined to cases where both the plaintiff and defendant live within the community. Cases heard cover such diverse things as domestic squabbles, especially between husband and wife, thievery, inheritance disputes, delinquency in bridewealth payment, and assault. Murder and manslaughter, now always under the jurisdiction of British magistrates, in traditional times usually involved groups outside the particular community or communities involved; for these were clan affairs, whether the killing occurred within one clan or between members of two clans, and elders of most, if not all the larger Tiriki clans, are found residing in a number of different Tiriki communities. Consequently, final settlement, although usually made at the community of the deceased, generally involved judgement by elders of several different communities, and sometimes even other sub-tribes. Witchcraft and sorcery accusations still occur occasionally in the community courts, but they seldom bring the plaintiff much satisfaction any more; for the British instituted reforms have not only forbidden the administration of ordeals, but also have ruled such accusations null and void unless material evidence of witchcraft activity can be produced, which is rarely possible.

One further traditional duty of the community which is still retained is to help select youth for circumcision and to arrange for the building of seclusion huts (*birumbi*) for their youth undergoing initiation. Thus the seclusion groups during initiation are for the most part community groups. It will be recalled, however, that the circumcision and principal initiation rites held in the circumcision groves and hilltop sacred groves were and still are performed by larger multi-community organizational units (*zisomo*) that can be called sub-tribes.

The size of the community, judging by contemporary evidence, often approximated a square mile in area, and embraced a population of perhaps three or four hundred people in the period just prior to European contact, although certainly in the regions bordering Nandi to the east, the communities were often smaller in population and probably possessed only tentative boundaries on their eastern frontiers.[1] The problem of overcrowding was evidently obviated by the practice of emigration to empty land to the east and the subsequent formation of new communities.

[1] These population estimates are based on a careful consideration of the population, boundaries, and social organization of specific communities as the elders report they existed when they were young (roughly the decade prior to the First World War). Such information from the elders might not be too meaningful if it had not been elicited in large part by questioning based on the detailed demographic and organizational data which I gathered on two contemporary Tiriki sub-communities.

Tiriki Sub-tribes

The next larger set of Tiriki territorial divisions are the sub-tribes (*zisomo*).[1] Because the information on the traditional sub-tribes gathered to date contains a number of contradictions and is none too ample, the sketch presented below must be regarded as tentative.

The Tiriki use the word *lusomo* in several contexts. They use it to refer to the contemporary Tiriki sub-tribes (more correctly, sub-locations), the boundaries of which were fixed by the British. The Tiriki also occasionally use *lusomo* in a more generic sense, however, to refer to any major land division. For example, it is not uncommon to hear elders speak of *lusomo lya Jebdulu* (the territory of Jebdulu [community]), and in the next breath speak of *lusomo lya Shibila* (the [sub-tribal] territory presided over by [the Headman named] Shibila), which is a larger contemporary sub-tribal land unit embracing not only Jebdulu community but several other communities as well. When referring to the maximal traditional Tiriki sub-divisions, each of which embraced several communities and had its own sacred and circumcision groves, the elders use either the word *lusomo* or the word *ibololi* (*i- zi- -bololi*).[2] They generally favour *ibololi* when referring to one of the warrior sections or armies associated with each of the traditional maximal sub-divisions, but some-times *lusomo* is also used for this. When pressed, the elders recognize a distinction between these two terms, namely that in traditional usage *lusomo* referred to geographic or land unit, while *ibololi* referred to a collectivitity of people.

The consensus among Tiriki elders is that traditionally an *ibololi* was an army, *i.e.*, a major autonomous military unit. Its members were all those initiated men who had been or still were active in the military affairs of the unit. By extension, all people actively or formerly associated with an *ibololi*, and all their dependants, male and female, are spoken of as people of that *ibololi*. Contemporary Tiriki elders, when reconstructing the traditional offensive military organization, list ten *zibololi* that existed at one time or another partially or completely within the area of what is now Tiriki. Not all of these *zibololi* existed at the

---

[1] Terik elders living in Tiriki report that the Terik word for *lusomo* is *jemilot*.

[2] The Terik elders say that *ibololi* is the Tiriki equivalent of the Terik *proriyet*, (pl.) *proriyosiyak*.

same time, nor did each *ibololi* always occupy precisely the same territory. It will be recalled that the Tiriki have for a number of generations been moving steadily eastward, leaving some of their former lands in the west to the Maragoli tribe. Thus the territory under the control of a particular *ibololi* was frequently diminished or extended through the vicissitudes of warfare and migration. Also, whenever a fairly substantial group of Tiriki moved into the eastern frontier from an area further west, the immigrants formed a new *ibololi*.

Tiriki elders cannot agree on the precise traditional boundaries of the ten *zibololi* they list; nevertheless they claim that at any given time each offensive military unit had its own discrete territory, which did not overlap with the territory of any other offensive unit. Elders of the Terik minority disagree with this; they say that the Abaluyia Tiriki are wrong in thinking that each traditional army was recruited from those living within a fixed territorial domain. Several heated discussions took place in 1955–56 between these two groups of elders over this matter. The fact that the Terik elders were never able to convince the Tiriki elders that a real distinction existed between the traditional armies and the traditional major territorial units may reflect a major difference between the traditional organizations of the predominantly Terik and the predominantly Tiriki areas. Certainly the present day difference of opinion is in keeping with current values of the two groups, for the traditionally pastoral Terik living in Tiriki and Nyangori, although they have in recent decades become agriculturalists, still exhibit a less possessive attitude towards land than do the traditionally agricultural Tiriki.[1] For the rest of this chapter I shall follow the lead of the contemporary Abaluyia Tiriki elders and use

---

[1] Probably in traditional times each Terik military offensive organization (*proriyet*) was independent of or only loosely connected with a major tribal territorial unit (*jemilot*). Peristiany's discussion of the Kipsigis *puriet* is suggestive in this area (Peristiany, op. cit., pp. 161–3). He reports that there were four Kipsigis armies (*puriesiak*) all of which had their Nandi counterparts, and that army membership rather than being territorial was inherited from the father regardless of where the father or son chose to live. The father could, however, under certain conditions, change the army affiliation of some of his sons.

Perhaps careful field work conducted in the Terik language would even at this late date yield sufficient information to allow an adequate reconstruction of the traditional relationship between the armies and the sub-tribal units in Terik; such field work still remains to be done.

lusomo and *ibololi* interchangeably when referring to the maximal
indigenous territorial sub-divisions, rendering them both into
English as 'sub-tribe'.

The major offensive fighting units were organized on a sub-
tribal basis. Each sub-tribe chose its own war leaders (*biimili bi
lihe*) and scouts (*baluri*). Every sub-tribe planned its own strategy,
carried out its own raids against Tiriki enemies, and divided
the plunder within its own group. At times two or more sub-
tribes joined forces for a major offensive, but this was the exception rather than the rule, and on each occasion involved the
active assent of the sub-tribes involved.

Each sub-tribe generally had within its bounds at least one
hilltop sacred grove (*gabogorisiyo*) and valley circumcision grove
(*gabunyonyi*). Annual *bwali* ceremonies were held in the sacred
groves during the long dry season in late December or early
January before the fields were prepared for the principal
planting. This yearly sub-tribal *bwali* was held not only to bless
the land and drive away malevolent people, but also involved
specific entreaties for success in war during the coming season.
At other times during the year the ritual elders, at the behest
of the war leaders, occasionally held *bwali* at the sacred grove
to augur the fortune of a proposed raid, and, if the omens were
favourable, to ask the spirits of deceased warriors for help in
accomplishing victory. In times of disaster such as general
defeat in war, famine, or disease, spirits of the deceased were
often entreated through *bwali* ceremonies held at the sacred
groves, just as they could also be supplicated at the community
level.

Community affairs, when contrasted with sub-tribal activities,
were rather sporadic and intermittent. It will be recalled from
Chapter II that the circumcision and initiation rites were
performed on a sub-tribal basis, but these only occurred during
about six months out of every four years. When an important
man died his age group peers from the entire sub-tribe would
inevitably gather at the graveside to sing the initiation songs
and praise his memory. People from other sub-tribes might
also come, but their attendance at funerals was spotty compared
to the virtually universal participation of age peers from the
deceased's own sub-tribe.

The Tiriki elders say that whenever conditions warranted

judicial sessions were held at the sub-tribal level. In each sub-tribe there was one (or sometimes two) centrally located community meeting ground commonly used for holding sub-tribal court sessions. The elders differ in their opinions as to what sorts of problems were heard at the sub-tribal courts, and agree simply that whenever a case involved people from two or more communities and could not be satisfactorily settled by the elders of the plaintiff's community, it might be discussed and arbitrated by the most respected elders drawn from the whole sub-tribe.

The Traditional Basis for Tribal Unity

Prior to the coming of the British (around 1896 or shortly thereafter) the Tiriki had no centralized tribal authority. Each *lusomo-ibololi* unit was virtually autonomous; the only permanent bond tying the different sub-tribes together was the almost mystical sense of brotherhood that was felt between all those who had been circumcised and initiated according to the Terik-Tiriki customs (*idumi*). Initiation established a special comradely relationship (*bagugwa*) between all members of the same age group. Even though an age group comrade was secluded in the hut or huts of a different community, and was initiated in a different sub-tribe, a man felt a binding obligation to show him hospitality, eat with him, and give him a place to sleep in his hut. A general sense of brotherhood or sense of relatedness was extended to all people, regardless of age group, initiated in the Terik-Tiriki manner.

Everything else being equal, this sense of relatedness extended not only to the Tiriki but also to the Nandi, Kipsigis, and all other peoples sharing the Nandi-type initiation and age groups. In practice, only with the Terik was the ritual affiliation flowing from initiation not honoured more in the breach than in the observance; but sometimes Tiriki individuals and Tiriki communities would use common initiation customs as the basis for establishing peaceful relationships with one or another Nandi community or family.

In contrast, adult males who did not partake in the Nandi-type initiation and age groups were considered not to be true men at all; they were viewed as little better than women and children, and as such, not worthy of a properly initiated man's

respect or trust.[1] To be sure, many Tiriki families had clan
ties with Abaluyia living in other tribes where they did not
practice the Terik initiation customs. In times of peace such
clan obligations were often honoured, but if ever a choice had
to be made, loyalty to one's own *ibololi* and to other Terik-Tiriki
always overrode loyalty to clansmen and kinsmen of other
tribes.

Summary

The Tiriki differed from other southern Abaluyia groups in
assigning no formal importance to clanship as a basis for
community organization and control. The homestead with its
associated lands was the only case where a geographically discrete division was associated with kin and clan-based social
organization. In the case of community organization the Tiriki
followed the lead of the Terik in bestowing full power for the
management of all community affairs upon the community
elders. The elders from each homestead purportedly had equal
opportunity to achieve recognition as leaders of particular merit
regardless of relative numerical superiority or inferiority of their
clan in the community. The basis for community solidarity was
the feeling of fraternity established through the initiation rites.
The community had important defensive military, judicial and
ritual functions.

The sub-tribal units, consisting in most instances of probably
from four to six communities, each had their autonomous
military units. The functional solidarity of the sub-tribe was
ritually reinforced through the major initiation rites, and also
through the periodic and occasional ceremonies and sacrifices
performed by the ritual elders at the sub-tribal sacred grove
(*gabogorosiyo*).

---

[1] The Terik and Tiriki make a distinction between the man (or woman)
circumcised (or clitoridectomized) and initiated according to some custom other
than that which initiates a person into Terik-Tiriki age groups (such a man or
woman is called a *jebusabageni*), and the person who hasn't been circumcised and
initiated at all. The former, while in no wise a full-fledged Terik-Tiriki, is nevertheless ritually a social entity and worthy of some respect. Clitoridectomized
Terik and Nandi women fall into this category. Even the Tiriki who will not
tolerate clitoridectomy for their own women, recognize the status that Terik and
Nandi women achieve through clitoridectomy and initiation rites. The uncircumcised man or woman (including Tiriki women) is considered no better than a
child, perhaps worthy of consideration, but rarely of respect.

Loyalties incurred through initiation helped check the tendency on the community level for the numerically predominant clan or clans of the community to usurp all the power positions. Initiation loyalties, springing as they did in great measure from rites performed by the whole sub-tribe, served as a unifying base for military, ritual, and judicial endeavours of the sub-tribe. Finally, at the tribal level, in the absence of any centralized political machinery, initiation-spawned loyalties provided continuing basis for cooperation between sub-tribes.

IV

The Development of the Contemporary Tiriki Tribal Administration

Historical Factors

During most of the British Administration the Abaluyia have been administered as one District.[1] Within this District the autonomy of the different Abaluyia tribes has been recognized and preserved to a fair degree. Nevertheless, it is clear that the major decisions regarding the formal administration of the Tiriki under British rule have been formulated for the most part on the basis of what the British administrators have considered to be the nature and needs of the District as a whole rather than on the basis of the particular characteristics and needs of the Tiriki.

The British Administration of North Nyanza (known as North Kavirondo until 1946) had its beginnings in 1894 at

---

[1] The boundaries of the almost one hundred per cent Abaluyia District of North Nyanza (called Kavirondo before 1946) are given in Günter Wagner's, *The Bantu of North Kavirondo*, Vol. I (London: Oxford University Press, 1949), in the map on page 2, and they are listed on page 4 of the same volume. On page 21, (ibid.), Wagner lists all the Abaluyia chieftaincies and the populations of each as of 1932.

In 1939 an area then called South Tiriki (now Nyangori Location) of roughly thirty square miles was transferred from Central Kavirondo to North Kavirondo (Nyanza Province Annual Report, 1939). In 1955 North Nyanza District was divided into two districts. The new boundary line was drawn at the River Nzoia. The following tribes south of the River Nzoia continued to form the district of North Nyanza, with its headquarters at Kakamega:

Isuxa, Idaxo, North Maragoli, South Maragoli, Tiriki, Nyangori, Bunyore, Marama, Buholo, South Wanga, North Wanga, East Wanga, Bunyala, Kabras, Butsotso.

The following tribes north of the River Nzoia became members of the newly formed Elgon Nyanza District, with its headquarters at Kimilili:

Kimilili, Elgon, Malakisi, South Bukusu, Iteso, Buxayo, Marach (minutes of the African District Council, Kakamega, 4th July, 1955).

It should be noted that there are some differences between the listing of tribes in 1937 by Wagner, and the 1955 listing given above. These differences are due to several changes in tribal boundaries, administrative units, and tribal names that have occurred during the intervening eighteen years. The writer has no record, however, of any changes in the outside boundaries of the district from 1937 until 1955 when the district was divided, except for the addition of South Tiriki in 1939.

Mumias, a pre-European trading community, and centre of the Wanga chieftaincy. The Abashiseza clan of Wanga Chiefs was the only clan among the Abaluyia which had in any definitive manner extended its authority beyond its own tribal domain in pre-European times. Consequently the British Administration, when first establishing its dominion over the District, appointed Mumia, who was the ruler of Wanga, the Paramount Chief of all the tribes of North Kavirondo District.[1] In the immediately succeeding years, Mumia, with the support and backing of the British, strengthened his hold over several nearby Abaluyia tribes, in each case either by appointing a member of the Abashiseza clan to be tribal Chief, or by choosing an amenable leader of the outstanding clan of the tribe to rule in his (Mumia's) name. Tiriki, lying about 50 miles from Wanga on the southeastern boundary of the District, was not reached by Mumia's agents as soon as most of the other tribes, and never strongly felt Mumia's authority. It probably was not until 1899, when taxation was introduced in the District,[2] that Mumia first sent some of his troops to Tiriki. Mumia's military agents appointed a Tiriki war leader named Mwanga to be Chief of all Tiriki and demanded a tribute of cattle for Mumia, which Mwanga was obliged to obtain. Other duties or honours conferred upon Mwanga by Mumia's emissaries evidently have been forgotten. Mwanga was an important war leader in northern Tiriki and also a member of the Baluxoba clan, the largest clan in all Tiriki. Most members of the Baluxoba clan live in northern Tiriki, which was the part of the tribe first visited by Mumia's agents. It is not surprising, therefore, that Mumia's agents, accustomed to selecting subordinate Chiefs from the predominant clan of a region, should have chosen Mwanga in preference to other war leaders of equal status in the eyes of the Tiriki who belonged to smaller clans.

C. W. Hobley was probably the first British administrator with whom the Tiriki had direct administrative dealings. The contemporary Tiriki elders say that in 1901 Hobley appointed Mujela, another outstanding Baluxoba war leader, to be tribal Chief. There is much uncertainty and some conflict among the elders as to whom Hobley appointed as Mujela's assistants

[1] Wagner, op. cit., p. 14.
[2] ibid., p. 31.

at that time and what jurisdiction each was given. Probably the most widely accepted story is that Mujela, as well as being Chief of the whole tribe, held the job of headman in the northern-most sub-tribe of Tiriki, where the Baluxoba were the dominant clan group.

Most elders feel that Isiyaho, a member of the Mumbo clan (second largest clan in Tiriki) was appointed headman over the sub-tribe just south of Mujela's, where the heaviest concentration of Bumbo clan members live. Isalano of the Badura clan is credited with being Hobley's appointee to the position of head-man for the sub-tribe just southwest of Isiyaho's area, and Mushenye of the Bamuli clan was put in charge of the south-westernmost Tiriki sub-tribe. All of these leaders were impor-tant war chiefs in their respective regional armies (*zibololi*), and all had many clansfolk in their respective sub-tribes. It should be noted, however, that the Badura were probably not the largest clan group in the sub-tribe where Isalano was headman. Details as to the exact boundaries of the four sub-tribal areas originally recognized by the British, and how they were drawn up, are not available; nor are the duties and privileges of this early Chief and his headman clearly remembered.

The founding of the Friends African Mission at Kaimosi probably at first encouraged the Tiriki's traditional movement eastward into Nandi territory. Certainly the establishment of this mission on what was then the easternmost limit of Tiriki habitation played a role in eventual stabilization of Tiriki tribal boundaries. The mission also proved (and remains until this day) a most powerful force for change in many areas of Tiriki life.

The American Quakers, Willis Hotchkiss, Arthur Chilson, and Edgar T. Hole, founded Kaimosi Mission. They arrived in Kisumu on Lake Victoria in 1902, having made the trip from Mombasa on the newly-completed Kenya and Uganda rail-way.[1] The newly established Kenya Provincial Administration at Kisumu arranged for the three men to take a guided tour of North Kavirondo so that they might find a suitable spot to establish a mission. After about six weeks of looking about they chose an area that contained both a small river suitable for

[1] Douglas and Dorothy Steere, *Friends Work in Africa* (London: Home Service Committee, 1955), p. 31.

damming and a hillock from which one could gain a view of the surrounding forest. Known as Kaimosi, the region was uninhabited, lying east of Tiriki and west of Nandi. The Friends bought 850 acres of Crown Land at Kaimosi, and later leased an additional 150 acres. Headman Isiyaho, whose territory was nearest to Kaimosi, was commanded by Hobley to take special care of the new missionaries and to help them in every way possible to get established.

One consideration which may have loomed large in the British Administration's decision to grant the Friends such a large tract at Kaimosi was the hope that their presence would help stop the fighting and cattle raiding between the Tiriki and the Nandi. Certainly the Tiriki during these early days viewed the missionaries mostly as helpful allies who could be counted on to help defend them against Nandi raids. With this point of view, many Tiriki started homesteading in the uninhabited regions directly east and north of the Mission. Meanwhile, the predominantly Terik sub-tribes to the southwest of the mission continued their habitual cattle raiding against the Nandi to the east. Also, the advent of new Tiriki settlers east of Kaimosi clearly did nothing to discourage Nandi raids against the Tiriki and the Terik. Finally, in 1905, the Nandi were further piqued when African guards hired by the mission (it is unclear what tribes these guards were from) stole some Nandi cattle. In retaliation a group of Nandi warriors raided Kaimosi and killed a missionary named Wendt. Other Nandi raids in 1905 included assaults on the railway line to Kisumu, and an attack on Dutch settlers near Sergoit to the northeast of Nandiland.

The British Administration, anxious to stop all this, dispatched a field force against the Nandi with subsidiary movements against the Terik to the south of Kaimosi.[1] This put an end to all major hostilities between the Nandi and the Terik and Tiriki. In 1907 the boundaries of Nandi were fixed, and further eastward extension of the Tiriki boundaries was curtailed. The Tiriki retained all the land they had moved into north and east of Kaimosi Mission and received some of the uninhabited

[1] ibid., p. 32.
G. W. B. Huntingford, *The Nandi of Kenya* (London: Routledge & Kegan Paul Ltd., 1953), p. 41.

region just beyond. The Nandi, however, were granted most of the remaining uninhabited area.[1]

Mujela served as Chief of Tiriki until his death in 1909, when he was succeeded by his son, Shagome. In 1911 Lubuze, son of Mwanga, replaced Shagome as Chief. Lubuze remained Chief until 1924 when Amiani of the Badura clan succeeded him. We lack specific information about the development of the British-instituted tribal government in Tiriki prior to Amiani's becoming Chief, but certain information concerning developments in the District as a whole can be gleaned from District and Provincial reports[2]:

In 1902 Kavirondo (which included what is now North Nyanza) was separated from Uganda and added to Kenya Colony and Protectorate.

A Hut tax was collected in the district in 1904 by Administration employed Swahili soldiers.

Rinderpest broke out in 1910 killing 50 per cent of the cattle within the district within six months. A large amount of migration outside the district to obtain employment was noted that year, perhaps stimulated by this enormous loss of wealth.

In 1913 the supervision of native tribunals was instituted, with a fixing of court fees.[3] These courts were generally administered at the tribal level.

In 1919 the District Headquarters was moved from Mumias to Kakamega, which is only about twenty miles from the northern border of Tiriki. The move was made because several District Commissioners had died of Blackwater Fever at Mumias, and it was felt that Kakamega afforded a more healthy climate for Europeans.[4]

The advent of Amiani to the Chieftainship of Tiriki in 1924 marked the beginning of a new era in Tiriki tribal government.

---

[1] In 1920 several large European farms were established in the uninhabited part of the Nandi area bordering Tiriki. Known as Kaimosi Farms, the area is now the site of several European coffee and tea estates. The whole region is slowly being purchased from its European owners by the Kenya Government and returned to the Nandi. The Tiriki claim that one small portion of Kaimosi Farms of about three square miles was alienated from that part of the uninhabited inter-tribal land originally assigned to the Tiriki tribe in 1907. A number of Tiriki squatters now live in this area, and the tribe hopes that it will eventually be returned to the Tiriki by the Kenya government.

[2] See Wagner, op. cit., pp. 32–35, for a summary listing of some of the events discussed in these reports.

[3] ibid., p. 34.

[4] Nyanza Province Annual Reports, 1919 (kindness of the Provincial Commissioner, Kisumu, 1955).

Many people are still alive who served as governmental assistants under the formidable Amiani, and they assert that he was a giant both in physical stature and in personality. Today, over a decade after his retirement from the Chieftancy, the popular mythology which has grown up around his career remains unmatched by the stories told about any other Tiriki, past or present. It is safe to say that the concept of a centralized tribal authority and tribal chieftaincy never really took hold among the Tiriki until Amiani, aided by his successful solicitation and employment of British support, won the awe and fear-mingled respect of the whole tribe.[1] The colour and forcefulness of Amiani's personality were such that he has left an impression of power and regality on the minds of both European Administrators and Africans of North Nyanza second only to that left by Paramount Chief Mumia of Wanga.

Amiani was ceded large estates by the British authorities in accordance with the policy current at that time. These lands provided him with food for feasting followers and supplied him with enough cash income through grain and cattle sales to buy newly-introduced European products on a much larger scale than any other person in the tribe. Also the British Administration allowed Amiani to retain some particularly fierce Terik warriors to act as tribal police. During the early years of his chieftaincy Amiani's awe-inspiring personality effectively fused these two adjuncts to power into a rustic version of, 'the velvet glove covering the iron fist'.

In 1926 and 1927 two district-wide innovations were introduced that had direct bearing on tribal administration. First, a Native Court of Appeals was established at the District Headquarters in Kakamega. Until this time, except for the possibility of appeal to the Paramount Chief at Mumias or appeal directly to the District Commissioner's office, the highest native court of appeals for the North Nyanza African had been the British-supervised court of his own tribe, which was presided over by the tribal Chief or Assistant Chief. A Tiriki of the Bumbo clan named Lujaja was appointed to be one of the judges of the new Native Court of Appeals at Kakamega. His appointment,

---

[1] Amiani became Chief after a thirteen year term as headman in southern Tiriki where he had succeeded Isalano. The major steps in Amiani's career are presented in Chapter V.

plus the relative proximity of Kakamega to Tiriki, made appeal
beyond the tribal court much more feasible after this time.
The second innovation was the introduction of a system of
salaried headmen (called *mlango, m- mi- -lango*)[1] by the British
Administration. This marked the beginning in North Nyanza
of the development of a system of tribal rule by African civil
servants. Prior to this time tribal chiefs and headmen had
received their rewards of office through portions of the taxes
collected from their subjects and through other payments of
tribute,[2] and/or through lands granted them by the British for
their personal use. The salaried headmen (*milango*) were no
longer granted such privileges.

The *milango*, supposedly chosen from the predominant clan
of the region under their charge, were assigned the task of representing the tribal Chief at the local level, and of representing
their local constituents in tribal administrative affairs. The
mlango's clan-derived basis for local authority and representation was antithetical to the traditional Tiriki ideal of community
and sub-tribe leadership based on merit demonstrated within
appropriate age group activities. Nevertheless the *mlango*
system proved to be less satisfactory in many of the Abaluyia
tribes with clan based traditional political institutions than it
did among the Tiriki. In Tiriki, traditional expectations and
attitudes made it imperative that a local headman chosen from a
numerically dominant clan treat members of other clans almost
on an equal footing with members of his own clan. In tribes
such as Maragoli, however, where each community was traditionally dominated politically, ritually, and socially by one
clan, favouritism shown by the headman towards members of
his own clan grew in frequency and flagrancy.

The establishment of the *mlango* system ushered in another
administrative innovation in Tiriki. Around 1926 the four old
tribal subdivisions were abolished as administrative units and

---

[1] *Milango* is the plural form of the Swahili word *mu- mi- -lango*, meaning 'door'.
The Tiriki form of word is *mu- mi- -liyango*. Both the Swahili and Tiriki forms are
commonly employed by Tiriki when referring to this salaried office and office
holder.

[2] The writer never clearly ascertained what portion of tribute taxes held back
by headmen and the Chief was officially condoned and what portion was taken
on the sly.

PLATE 2. Young girl and her infant charge

PLATE 3. Magozwe, Tiriki elder, making rope

PLATE 4. Elders offering beer and making supplications
at homestead ancestral shrine

PLATE 5. Children playing with an improvised wheelbarrow

PLATE 6. Children playing a pebble game, *Majina*, similar to Jacks

PLATE 7. Tiriki initiates, Kaimosi, Tiriki
(*photograph by Onni Rauha*)

PLATE 8. Tiriki–Idaxo soccer match

PLATE 9. Homestead at harvest time

PLATE 10. Eastern Tiriki homestead

Plate 11. Sunday morning loungers

Plate 12. Cattle market frequented by Tiriki

PLATE 13. Tiriki blacksmith

PLATE 14. Working blacksmith's bellows

PLATE 15. Elders and litigants locating a disputed boundary

PLATE 16. Isugudi drummers

PLATE 17. Tiriki women preparing field for planting

PLATE 18. Young children removing maize kernels from the cobs

PLATE 19. Girls cooking maize porridge (*bushuma*)

PLATE 20. Serim market

PLATE 21. Serim market

PLATE 22. Basket maker

PLATE 23. Buying sugar at a local shop

PLATE 24. A Tiriki Israel congregation on the march

PLATE 25. Hymn singing members of a Tiriki Israel
church congregation

PLATE 26. Men and women leaders of the Tiriki Israel church

PLATE 27. At beer, elder group

PLATE 28. Beer drink, younger men

PLATE 29. A meeting of the Tiriki Historical Committee
and onlookers

PLATE 30. Elder divining with a rubbing or friction stick (*Lusejele*)

PLATE 31. Tea house and bus stop, Jebdulu market. Jebdulu elders, in the background, chatting prior to hearing local disputes

PLATE 32. Tiriki Location Advisory Council and Roger Hoskings, District Officer

replaced by two sub-tribes known as North and East Tiriki.[1] North Tiriki extended northeastward from the tribe's southwestern borders to include the community of Shamaxoxo; East Tiriki included the areas immediately adjacent to Kaimosi Mission and all areas north and east to the Isuxa and Nandi borders.[2] Amiani was Chief of the whole tribe, while Assistant Chief Shimoli (Bumbo clan), appointed in 1926, held court and handled most of the executive matters in East Tiriki.

The headmen appointed in Tiriki under the *mlango* system did indeed come for the most part from large clans, but sometimes they came from the numerically superior clans of the traditional sub-tribe in which they lived rather than from the most heavily represented sub-clan in their own immediate jurisdiction. For example, all five *milango* appointed in 1926 to serve under Shimoli were members of either the Bumbo or the Baluxoba clans, the two largest clans in East Tiriki (also the two largest clans in the whole tribe). There is evidence, however, that these two clans were not numerically superior in all five of these *mlango* areas; furthermore not all of the East Tiriki *mlango* replacements appointed during the following decade were members of these two clans. It is quite clear that the Chief and the elders of each region tended to pick the man they most wanted for *mlango* and then employ whatever sophistry necessary to justify his clanship to the British Administration.

The *mlango* system proved unsatisfactory over the district as a whole, and in 1936 the British Administration took steps to abolish clanship as the major basis for local authority. In its stead they established a system of community government that was supposed to encourage a territorially based leadership divorced from clanship. It seems probable that the Swahili word *mlango* meaning 'door' had been chosen as the title for the clan-based local administrative leaders because the metaphor 'door' or 'doorway' is so often used by East African tribes to designate a clan or lineage head. It is customary among the Abaluyia, for example, for the head of the homestead to have a special place reserved for his stool by the doorway of his hut;

---

[1] The date of this change (1926) is based only on verbal reports—no documentary evidence.

[2] Again no documentary evidence; only the verbal reports of the contemporary tribal elders.

thus the Abaluyia feel that *mlango* was an appropriate title to confer on a man of authority who served as an intermediary between his own lineage or clan and other and larger social groupings. Under the new system the leader was not necessarily to be chosen from the dominant clan of the local group, so the title *mlango* was dropped and replaced by the title *olugongo*, which in *luhanga* (the dialect of the Wanga tribe) means, 'the hilltop'. It will be recalled from Chapter III[1] that it is characteristic in Wanga for each community (*oluhiya*) to occupy its own separate hillock; thus the Wanga derived the notion of calling the community leader the *olugongo*. How much the official change from clan to strictly territorially-based representation was more than merely a change in name I am not prepared to evaluate; certainly in many, probably most, parts of North Nyanza the leaders of the newly drawn up local administrative units continued to be members of the dominant clans of each region.

A number of changes took place in Tiriki governmental organization between 1936 and 1946, some of which were clearly in no way connected with the official district shift from *mlango* to *olugongo* local administrators. In 1936 the twenty-four tribal courts of the district were amalgamated into six divisional courts.[2] The Tiriki were assigned to the division that had its headquarters at Mbale, Maragoli. This did not mean the abolition of the Chief and the Chief's elders as arbitrators of tribal litigation, but it did take away from their weekly tribal meetings formal sanctioning and supervision by the British as courts of law, and thereby relieved the Chiefs of their formal jural responsibilities to the British Administration. Consequently, when Assistant Chief Shimoli of East Tiriki retired in 1938, it was feasible for Chief Amiani to take over Shimoli's duties himself instead of appointing a new Assistant Chief. Thenceforth Chief Amiani held two weekly meetings, one early in the week at Gisambayi in North Tiriki, and a second one later in the week about sixteen miles northeast of Gisambayi at Ishilu.

The following year (1939) Amiani's duties and responsibilities were further increased by the incorporation of Nyangori into Tiriki Location. Soon after the British established their rule in

[1] See pp. 83–4.
[2] Wagner, op. cit., p. 35.

Nyanza Province, several predominantly Terik areas (*zisomo*) had been set up as Nyangori Location, under an administration separate from that of the heavily Bantu Tiriki areas further north, and incorporated into the same administrative district as the Nilotic Luo people living below them in the Nyando plain.[1] Unfortunately I have no information as to precisely when or why this administrative division between the Terik and the Tiriki was made, but apparently it happened quite early, very likely as far back as the punitive expeditions of 1905–6 (see p. 101).[2]

The Terik had always been unhappy about being a part of the Nilotic Luo-dominated Central Nyanza District. Then two additional factors arose between 1926 and 1938 that finally stirred the Administration to transfer Nyangori Location to North Nyanza District and incorporate it as part of Tiriki Location. First, from about 1926 onwards an increasing number of Bantu Maragoli had been emigrating from their over-crowded tribal areas to relatively empty Nyangori, which for a short distance borders South Maragoli Location. Some of the early Maragoli immigrants were initiated into the Terik age groups, but the majority were Christian converts, and on religious grounds they refused to have anything to do with Terik initiation ceremonies. The second factor was the increasing hostility that developed between the pagan elders and the Christian converts in Tiriki during the late 1920's and early 1930's. This hostility, which grew much stronger after Chief Amiani's conversion to Christianity in 1927, flared forth most strongly at initiation times when the mission converts refused to let their sons be circumcised and initiated in the traditional Tiriki manner. A number of instances of houseburnings and

[1] The Nyando plain is in Central Nyanza District (called Central Kavirondo District before 1946) which has its headquarters at Kisumu.

The term 'location' is currently used by the British Administration to designate a formally established and recognized tribal administrative unit. In North Nyanza the locations in every case form maximal units of tribal administration, and each is presided over by a different tribal Chief. The tribes of North Nyanza are grouped together as an administrative district under the authority of a British District Commissioner.

[2] It seems a bit strange in retrospect that the Terik should have been administratively grouped with their traditional enemies, the culturally, linguistically alien, uncircumcised Luo, instead of having been administratively grouped with their close relatives, the Nandi.

kidnapping of Christian youths for initiation occurred both in Tiriki and Nyangori. The houseburnings were a terror tactic of the Terik and Tiriki pagan elders intended to deter Maragoli and Tiriki Christians from boycotting and revealing the initiation customs. Forceful intervention by the District Commissioners of North and Central Nyanza reduced the kidnapping and arson to a minimum, but not before they had made the Christian Maragoli in Nyangori very willing to support any move to have Nyangori administratively joined with the Bantu tribes of North Nyanza.

Amiani and the Tiriki Christians who were still a small minority in Tiriki probably felt that the annexing of Nyangori, where the Maragoli Christians very likely already outnumbered the Terik, would help their cause by increasing the proportion of Christians in the location. Terik and Tiriki pagans, for their part, saw new hope for preserving the initiation customs if they and the Terik were formally joined together as one location. Thus nearly all groups in both tribes were united in desiring the transfer of Nyangori to North Nyanza. Some Terik undoubtedly would have preferred to have been administered as part of Nandi District, while the Maragoli in Nyangori mostly wished to see Nyangori united with South Maragoli. The obvious compromise was to make Nyangori part of Tiriki Location, thereby reinstating the traditional Terik-Tiriki alliance and at the same time bringing the Maragoli immigrants to Nyangori under overwhelmingly Bantu tribal authority and North Nyanza District jurisdiction.[1]

After the merger Nyangori became known as South Tiriki. Amiani encouraged further immigration of Maragoli people into South Tiriki and further increased his Christian backing by arranging for the sale of land in North Tiriki to predominantly Christian Maragoli immigrants. Contemporary Tiriki elders, both pagan and Christian, assert that Chief Amiani received a 'commission' from each of the Maragoli immigrants for having granted them permission to settle in Tiriki and for assuring their safety once they had moved into their new

[1] The preceding analysis of factors leading up to the 1939 Nyangori-Tiriki administrative merger is entirely an *ex post facto* reconstruction derived solely from discussion with contemporary Tiriki and a few Terik elders, and without benefit of official records of the administrative debates leading up to the merger (if such records exist). Thus, it must be regarded as tentative in nature.

homesteads. Thus Amiani's continued encouragement of immigration from Maragoli to Tiriki was regarded with disfavour by Christian and pagan Tiriki alike, and it is safe to say that for every Maragoli that Amiani admitted to Tiriki after the merger he lost the support of two or more Terik and Tiriki. A major threat offered by the continued influx of Maragoli was their rapid occupation of the few remaining bits of unused land still available in the Location, but the explicit issue around which Tiriki and Terik began to rally feeling against the immigrants was, again, their refusal to accept Terik-Tiriki circumcision and initiation.

The Contemporary Tiriki Administrative Divisions

By 1945 the anti-Maragoli feeling among the Tiriki and the Terik had reached a new high, and the aging Amiani had become strongly identified in the popular mind as the man who had favoured the Maragoli at the expense of his own people: Amiani, with the British Administration's encouragement, decided to resign, and on December 17, 1946, Hezron Mushenye was elected to the Tiriki Chieftaincy, a position which he holds to the present day (1956).

Three major administrative changes followed Hezron's election to office. First, in July, 1947, South Tiriki was re-established as a separate tribal Location and its name was changed back to Nyangori Location. It continued, however, to be administered as a part of North Nyanza District. The administrative dissociation of Nyangori from Tiriki rid Chief Hezron of a large portion of two rather difficult minority groups —the extremely conservative, culturally and linguistically alien Terik, and the Maragoli immigrants. The second change was a reorganization of the administrative sub-units in Tiriki. Hezron, who fell heir to Amiani's system of two tribal meetings a week, one in the northwest at Gisambayi, and one in the east at Ishilu, quickly instituted a plan for the establishment of a new tribal centre at Hamisi which lies near the geographical mid-point of the tribe. His plan received the wholehearted support of the British Administration, and Hamisi became the official meeting place for the whole tribe. The third change was the establishment of a new semi-official office at the sub-community level, entitled the *Liguru*. The establishment of one tribal centre resulted in the dissolution of North and East Tiriki as separate administrative entities; thenceforth the Tiriki tribe (Tiriki Location) was simply divided into five major administrative divisions (sub-locations), each under the charge of a salaried headman (*olugongo*). This system prevails to the present day (1956). Each sub-location is further divided into several smaller jurisdictional sub-divisions each presided over by a salaried sub-headman (*isubuhedeman, i- zi- -subuhedeman*; sometimes currently referred to as *mlango* or *muliyango*—the title conferred upon headmen prior to 1936). Roughly comparable in area and often in boundaries to traditional community divisions (*zimbihya*), these judicial sub-divisions within the sub-locations range from six in number in the large centrally located sub-location of Olugongo Ezekael, which has it scentre as Shamoxoxo, down to two each in the two easternmost Tiriki sub-locations of Bumbo and Buluxoba.[1]

Contemporary sub-location boundaries conform neither with traditional sub-tribal areas of the first decades of the century nor with the *mlango* areas of the 1920's and 1930's. Clearly, however, they more closely approximate the traditional military and ritual sub-tribal divisions (*zibololi* or *zisomo*) than did the division of the tribe into three major administrative units— South, North and East Tiriki. The contemporary sub-divisions within the sub-locations often have boundaries identical with or close to the boundaries of traditional communities, and they are usually referred to in the Tiriki dialect either as *zisomo* or as *zimbihya*. Population density, however, has in most areas in Tiriki increased markedly since the turn of the century so that the number of people living in each of these contemporary communities may be three or four times as great as in traditional times. This has resulted in a dilution of the intensely personal 'face-to-face' quality of community organization, a fact which very likely might have seriously weakened the authority of the local judicial elders were it not for the recent introduction of a set of semi-official neighbourhood sub-divisions within each community.

The decision to sub-divide all local communities into semi-official units was the result of an innovation advanced by the

---

[1] All 'contemporary' descriptions, unless otherwise indicated, refer to things as they were in 1955–6. In 1956 there were a total of nineteen headmen in Tiriki.

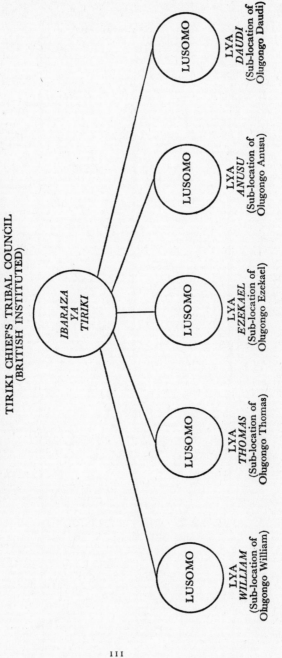

FIGURE 2

TIRIKI ADMINISTRATIVE UNITS (1955)
BRITISH INSTITUTED CENTRALIZATION OF TRIBAL AUTHORITY

TIRIKI CHIEF'S TRIBAL COUNCIL
(BRITISH INSTITUTED)

IBARAZA YA TIRIKI

LUSOMO

LYA WILLIAM
(Sub-location of
Olugongo William)

LUSOMO

LYA THOMAS
(Sub-location of
Olugongo Thomas)

LUSOMO

LYA EZEKAEL
(Sub-location of
Olugongo Ezekael)

LUSOMO

LYA ANUSU
(Sub-location of
Olugongo Anusu)

LUSOMO

LYA DAUDI
(Sub-location of
Olugongo Daudi)

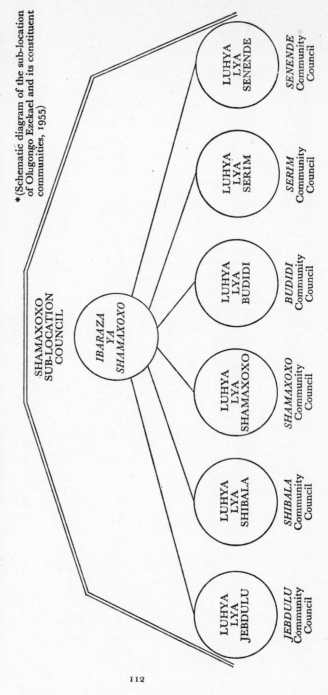

FIGURE 3

TIRIKI ADMINISTRATIVE UNITS

RELATIONSHIP BETWEEN A TIRIKI SUB-LOCATION AND ITS CONSTITUENT COMMUNITIES (ZIMBIHYA)*

*(Schematic diagram of the sub-location of Olugongo Ezekael and its constituent communities, 1955)

SHAMAXOXO
SUB-LOCATION
COUNCIL

IBARAZA
YA
SHAMAXOXO

LUHYA
LYA
JEBDULU

JEBDULU
Community
Council

LUHYA
LYA
SHIBALA

SHIBALA
Community
Council

LUHYA
LYA
SHAMAXOXO

SHAMAXOXO
Community
Council

LUHYA
LYA
BUDIDI

BUDIDI
Community
Council

LUHYA
LYA
SERIM

SERIM
Community
Council

LUHYA
LYA
SENENDE

SENENDE
Community
Council

CLAN COMPOSITION OF A TIRIKI COMMUNITY
(SCHEMATIC CHART)

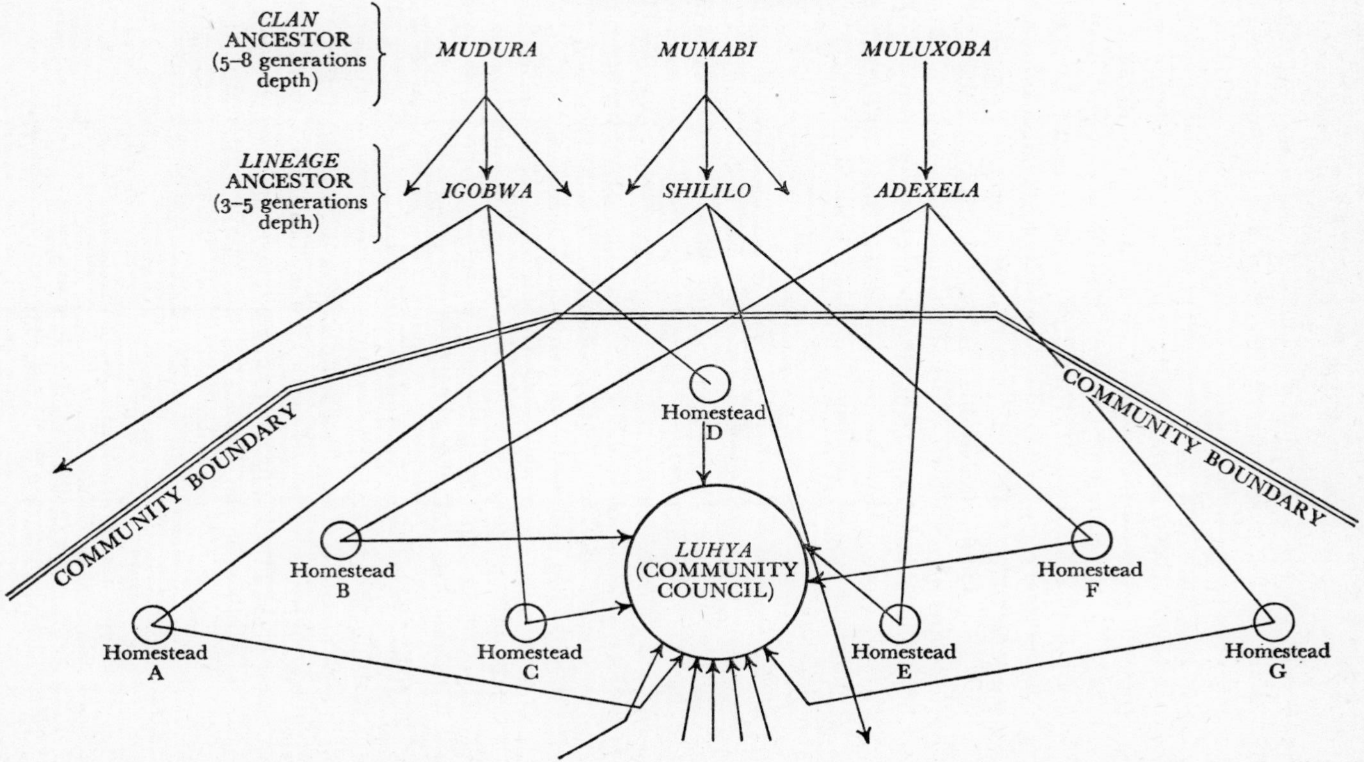

CLAN ANCESTOR (5–8 generations depth)

LINEAGE ANCESTOR (3–5 generations depth)

MUDURA   MUMABI   MULUXOBA

IGOBWA   SHILILO   ADEXELA

LUHYA (COMMUNITY COUNCIL)

COMMUNITY BOUNDARY

Homestead A
Homestead B
Homestead C
Homestead D
Homestead E
Homestead F
Homestead G

British for the whole district. The innovation was prompted by the Administration's desire to try to do something to check soil erosion in North Nyanza. Overcrowding and soil erosion are just beginning to be serious problems in Tiriki, but in neighbouring North and South Maragoli and nearby Bunyoro they have been grievous problems for nearly two decades. In 1947 Norman Humphrey, Senior Agricultural Officer in Kenya, published a small book giving the results of his research into African land usage and land tenure in North Nyanza, and making some suggestions for the future control of land usage in the district.[1] These suggestions, at least in part, guided the Administration's efforts to establish this new order of semi-official neighbourhood leadership throughout the tribes of the district. The following is a *précis* of Humphrey's statements about traditional village (or neighbourhood) leadership among the Abaluyia:

In aboriginal times Abaluyia village or neighbourhood authority was in the hands of the people who belonged to the dominant descent group or sub-clan. The leadership of such villages was granted to the eldest surviving man of the senior segment of the village's dominant sub-clan provided he was regarded as generally competent; in other words leadership was confined to one senior lineage and was bestowed through the principle of primogeniture whenever feasible. This leader, known in several Abaluyia tribes as the *liguru*, exercised his powers by the will of the people. He was trustee of any unallocated lands, director of the agricultural methods of the village, protector of the village public resources such as pathways, springs, and salt-licks, and was chief arbiter of inheritance disputes.[2]

The North Nyanza District Administration decided in the early 1950's to try to reinstitute (or to institute) village or neighbourhood *liguru* leadership as Humphrey had outlined it. They hoped thereby to tackle at the local 'grass roots' level some of the pressing problems of land tenure and soil erosion.

The office of the *liguru* (*li- ma- -guru*)[3] was instituted in

[1] Norman Humphrey, *The Liguru and the Land* (Nairobi: The Government Printer, 1947).

[2] ibid., p. 14–18.

[3] The title, Liguru, traditionally used in Wanga and Marach, is another case of a metaphorically derived honorific. Liguru (*li- ma- -guru*) is the name of the long upright posts that support the part of a hut's roof that overhangs beyond the walls to form a small porch. Such a post-supported overhang, common in Wanga,

Tiriki in 1952–53, and official buttons were issued to all the *maguru* in 1955. The office was established in Tiriki without too much difficulty. Each community, under the supervision of its sub-headman, was divided by its elders into several sub-communities or neighbourhoods (*zisomo* or *madala, li- ma- -dala*).[1] Then the elders of each of these sub-communities nominated a man to act as the area's *liguru*, i.e., as its official jural spokesman. Usually the elders' first nominee was accepted by the Chief and the British District Officer, and officially installed as the *liguru*. Some Tiriki communities are divided into as many as nine *liguru* areas while others are divided into only four; five or six *liguru* divisions per community are common.

The *liguru* is not salaried by the British Administration; he cannot, therefore, be indicted for receiving bribes or for indulging in other corrupt governmental practices. His only remunerations are his official governmental recognition and button, and the *kudos* he receives from his fellow tribesmen. The *maguru* have for the most part served very successfully as jural spokesmen in their respective neighbourhoods; in matters of soil conservation and maintenance of pathways they have been of less aid. Most *maguru*, however, have coveted their formal status enough to comply, minimally at least, with their sub-headmen's commands to mobilize their neighbourhoods into digging occasional drainage ditches, and to bring to the community court men who have flagrantly disobeyed the district conservation ordinances on their farms.

Few Tiriki, either young or old, are under any illusion about the *liguru* having been a traditional Tiriki office. Many contemporary Tiriki elders, although illiterate and unable to understand English, are aware both of the Wanga origin of the term *liguru* and that Humphrey's investigations were

---

is not customary in Tiriki. The local elder who was considered the leading authority on lineage and land affairs would often stand in the shade of the porch leaning against one of the posts while arbitrating disputes brought before him. Thus he came to be known as the Liguru.

[1] *Lu- zi- -somo* is, of course, the generic term for a geographic division. *Lidala* is an Abaluyia word meaning 'homestead'. The Tiriki say that it was seldom used by the Tiriki, and that they employed the word *mujizi* instead when referring to a homestead. The early missionaries used *lidala* to refer to the church-centered Christian communities that they attempted to establish for their early converts; in recent years *lidala* has come to be widely used in Tiriki to refer to any small cluster or grouping of huts or homesteads.

instrumental in starting the contemporary district-wide *liguru* organization. It is noteworthy, therefore, that the office of *liguru* had been well received. I think that the reasons for its success in Tiriki are threefold.

First, no attempt has been made in Tiriki to make the office fit Humphrey's assertion that the *liguru* was usually the senior member of the dominant sub-clan of each local area. Such an attempt would have inevitably led to difficulty because no such sub-clan political priority exists in Tiriki. Even at the sub-community level homesteads of several different clans and sub-clans will be found adjoining each other without the numerically dominant or seniormost sub-clan having any traditional or formal claim to area leadership. This does not mean that the largest sub-clan or clan of a region (be it sub-tribe, community, or sub-community) does not tend to dominate the region's power positions. Everything else being equal, Tiriki usually do favour their own clan and lineage members; but numerous instances, both past and contemporary, are found where members of relatively sparsely represented clans and sub-clans are chosen for power positions.

Second, most Tiriki communities, although they often have not grown in area during the last sixty years, have increased several-fold in population. Furthermore, all evidence indicates that the amount of litigation to be settled at the community level has increased at an even greater rate than the population. Thus the new sub-division has not only helped provide a sufficient number of local courts to handle the increasing litigation, but also has re-established a new minimal judicial unit more in keeping with the size and informality of the traditional community courts.[1]

The third and probably most important factor fostering the acceptance of the office of the *liguru* is the high regard felt by the community elders themselves towards any plan which promises to bolster their declining power and prestige in community and tribal affairs. During the last two decades a larger and larger proportion of the formal administrative posts have

[1] A preliminary analysis of census data I gathered in two *liguru* areas in 1955–56, one in east Tiriki and one in northcentral Tiriki, reveals populations of about 350 for each of these two areas. One area covered 204 acres and the other covered 169 acres.

been assigned to younger literate men, mostly of the elder warrior age grade. It is quite in keeping with the traditional age
grading that these younger men should fill executive type offices,
but ultimate power sanctions of course traditionally rested with
the judicial and ritual elders. Contemporary conditions of rapid
social change, demanding quick decisions about matters for
which there is no traditional answer, have made the British
administrators and the tribal elders themselves depend increasingly on younger mission-schooled tribal officials to fulfil
judicial as well as executive functions. It is true that the Chief's
court, as well as the courts of the headmen and sub-headmen,
have continued to call on the more distinguished community
elders to act as judges in all cases concerning 'native custom';
nevertheless, the establishment of the office of the *liguru* was
interpreted by the community elders as a long overdue formal
accreditation and reinforcement of their positions of power both
within the community and in the tribe at large.

In concluding this discussion of tribal administration, a few
words should be said about the relationship of the *liguru*'s sub-
community court to the community court. Squabbles between
neighbours over such matters as a disputed boundary between
adjoining fields, trampling of crops by a neighbour's cow, petty
thievery, and domestic disputes between husband and wife
that have not been successfully settled within the homestead,
may all be presented to the local elders for arbitration. If it is
a dispute between people living within the same sub-community,
the affair will generally be settled before those local elders who
live within the sub-community, with the *liguru* acting as spokesman. Usually such a sub-community court is held in a clearing
along a pathway rather than at the community meeting ground.
If the dispute is between people living in different sub-communities, it is usually heard before elders from the whole
community at a meeting held at the community meeting place
(*luhya*), and presided over by the sub-headman.

Summary

The contemporary Tiriki political structure consists of a neat
hierarchy of appointed, salaried, tribal administrators, each
with specific administrative duties within his assigned territorial
domain. At the lowest level there are nineteen sub-headmen,

each in charge of a community. Over them are the five headmen, each in charge of a sub-location, and each aided by his sub-headman. At the apex is the Chief, who is responsible to the British District Administration for all tribal (Location) affairs. The Chief is aided by his five headmen. Finally, outside of the salaried administration are the community elders—several hundred of them *in toto*—and their 100 or so officially accredited sub-community spokesmen, the *maguru*.

The elders act as the tribal judges. Most of the elders frequently attend the semi-official *liguru* court sessions of their own sub-communities. Many regularly serve as judges in the community court sessions held weekly by the sub-headmen, and a substantial minority of the more respected and more vigorous elders are urged to attend the weekly courts of their respective headmen. Finally, twenty or thirty of the most venerable elders of the tribe who still have the vigour to walk or bicycle to the Chief's weekly court at Hamisi are urged to do so by the Chief and his headmen.

The *maguru*'s courts are held whenever a local case arises and a convenient time can be found; the courts of the sub-headmen, headmen, and Chief, however, are regularly held on different days of the week so as not to conflict with each other. Thus a distinguished Tiriki elder may spend most of the week attending court sessions at one or another court level. The elders, although they receive no salary, nor any regular customary pay for their services, except in the courts of the *maguru*, gain local respect and sometimes tribe-wide prestige for their efforts, and they are never forgotten when feasts or beer drinks are held.

The Tiriki administration retains to a high degree the informality and flexibility one associates with governmental procedures in a small intimate face-to-face group, in spite of the size of the tribe and the administration's formal, bureaucratic, hierarchical nature. Crucial in the maintenance of this intimate quality is the presence of the sub-headmen and usually several elders from each community at the Chief's as well as at the headman's weekly court and administrative sessions. Thus the formal chain of authority from the Chief via the headmen, sub-headmen and *maguru*-represented elders to the people in the sub-communities is supplemented by the personal awareness of both the sub-headmen and community elders of what has taken place at all levels. This intimacy at the local level of intermediate and top-level administrative affairs serves in Tiriki to foster the smooth acceptance of the administrative activities of the tribal bureaucracy. The same intimacy, however, could just as well serve to harass and obstruct tribal administration, as indeed it did during the latter part of Amiani's rule.

V

The Spread and Acceptance of Christianity in Tiriki: A Brief History of Tiriki Factionalism

CHAPTER III sketched the indigenous territorially-delimited social units of the Tiriki. Chapter IV traced the development of the contemporary British fostered tribal government. It also outlined the major formal changes that have occurred in the tribal territorial divisions and administrative bureaucracy after Chief Hezron assumed office in 1946, and concluded by mentioning the improved manner in which the tribal government has functioned during the last few years. These recent administrative innovations are clearly not in themselves sufficient explanations for Chief Hezron's current success; Hezron's skill and luck in helping the Tiriki Christian and pagan factions regain a common sense of tribal identity and purpose has also done much to foster the recent political unity and well being of the tribe.

This chapter falls into two parts. The first part describes the early efforts of the Friends Missionaries to establish themselves and win Abaluyia converts. It also portrays the acceptance and spread of Christianity in Tiriki under Chief Amiani and the growth of a Christian-pagan factional division. The second part traces the factors leading to the Tiriki Christians' reaffirmation of their Tiriki ties, and describes the manner in which Chief Hezron was able to end the political division of the tribe into pagan and Christian groups, and establish the unity of Tiriki against outsiders.

I

The Early Years of Missionization, 1902–1924

Members of the Tiriki tribe have been in continuous contact with Christian missionaries longer than any other Abaluyia tribe. Kaimosi Mission, which is today surrounded by Tiriki land, was the first Christian mission to be established in the District. It has remained since its founding in 1902 the principal centre of Friends work in North Nyanza. It is a bit ironical, therefore, that Friends missionaries feel the Tiriki were and still remain (even though by 1954 the majority of Tiriki had become professing Christians) the Abaluyia tribe most resistant to Christianization. Contemporary Friends missionaries generally feel they do not understand as fully as they would like the factors underlying the relatively slow response of the Tiriki to evangelization. They recall two 'explanations' that have grown up for Tiriki indifference to the Mission over the years. One is that the Tiriki were not a tribe at all in pre-European times, but simply the riff-raff and outcasts from other Abaluyia tribes to the north and west. In other words the notion is that the Tiriki even before European contact were a relatively truculent and disorganized group. The other 'explanation' is that the Tiriki hold on to their special brand of depraved circumcision rites with a stubbornness characteristic of those slow to learn. Most of the present group of Friends missionaries are not content with either of these explanations, recognize the long-standing nature of Tiriki–Friends Mission hostility, and seek to ameliorate the situation, whatever its origin might have been. Unfortunately, the District and even colony-wide professional and executive responsibilities of the contemporary Friends missionaries, coupled with the perennial shortage of mission workers, do not leave much time for them to explore and try to rectify the long standing coolness of the Tiriki towards Friends' evangelical and educational activities.

The first decade of Friends Mission work was primarily a pioneer homesteading operation. At first, African-type mud-and-wattle huts were built to serve as homes, chapel, infirmary and classrooms. Soon a wagon road was surveyed and laid from the mission to Kisumu, twenty-eight miles away, and the damming of a river allowed the installation of a sawmill and flour mill. African porters were of necessity recruited during this period through local African headmen under orders from the British Administration. Probably the greatest share of this porterage fell upon those Tiriki who lived directly west and north of the mission. By 1911 things were beginning to get established on a permanent basis; that year, for example, the mission doctor, who had first arrived in 1903, supervised the completion of the mission's first permanent hospital building.[1]

In 1906 a Friends Mission station was established at Vihiga, South Maragoli, about fourteen miles from Kaimosi. Then stations were started at Lirhanda (Isuxa Location), twelve miles to the north, in 1907, and, much farther away in the northern part of the district, in Kitosh Location in 1912.[2] Emory Rees, who was in charge of the station at Vihiga, immediately set himself the task of rendering the Luragoli dialect into writing. Before the advent of the First World War he had succeeded not only in teaching a number of Maragoli to write their own dialect, but had also, with their aid, translated the entire Bible into a utilitarian, though hardly elegant, version of Luragoli. Knowledge of the Scriptures is, of course, held to be of paramount importance by the Friends as well as by other evangelical Protestant sects, so the missionaries found this translation a tremendous spur to their proselytizing efforts. Nevertheless, the number of Africans who actually achieved church membership was very small during the first years, coming to a total of only forty-three members by 1914.[3]

These initial converts were, in the vernacular of the missionary, for the most part 'dedicated individuals', and during the next decade their proselytic zeal, backed as it was by the careful preliminary work and planning of the missionaries, was amply rewarded by a growth to over 2,000 Abaluyia Friends Church members, with an estimated weekly attendance of over 6,000.

Many factors undoubtedly lay behind this enormous wave of converts after the initial slow start. For one thing, by the second decade major misunderstandings and resultant disillusionments over the nature of the Christian message had had time to resolve themselves. One such misunderstanding was the Africans' misinterpretation of the Christian promise of immortality. The Friends evangelists preached that 'whosoever believed in Jesus Christ would not perish, but have everlasting life.' This was literally interpreted as meaning that the believer in Jesus Christ would never die—a possibility that Tiriki elders

[1] Douglas and Dorothy Steere, *Friends Work in Africa* (London: Home Service Committee, 1955), p. 34.

[2] Friends African Mission notes, Kaimosi Mission (kindness of Fred Reeve, Mission Secretary).

[3] Steere, op. cit., p. 35.

as well as Abaluyia from other tribes found most exciting, but also most unlikely. The Tiriki report that the first time an Abaluyia convert to Christianity died (he was a member of a neighbouring tribe to the north) many Tiriki elders joined the multitude that gathered from miles around to attend the funeral and see for themselves whether or not the Christian really continued to live. Interest in the missionaries was somewhat damped when the deceased convert failed to come to life again.

It appears that it was not so much the growth of clearer understanding of Christian beliefs and theology as the role the missionaries began to play as the dispenser of European goods, services and schooling that lay behind the sudden enormous growth of Christian membership during the second decade of mission contact. A number of factors worked together to encourage greatly the growth of Abaluyia interest in European goods and European education during this second decade. From 1910, the year of the rinderpest epidemic,[1] increasingly large numbers of Abaluyia sought jobs outside the district in the growing commercial centres such as Nairobi, Mombasa, and Nakuru, and on the farms that were being developed in the highland country opened up by the railway. During the First World War the recruitment of Abaluyia into African regiments and intensified utilization of African manpower throughout the colony greatly increased Abaluyia contact with the European world, and fanned a growing curiosity about and desire for European life and know-how. Finally, during the famine of 1918, the Friends, as well as the missions of several other denominations that had by them become established in the District, worked tirelessly to help the British Administration distribute imported maize meal to help alleviate starvation. This evidently did much to diminish Tiriki suspicion of the mission. Older Tiriki remember the famine relief efforts with real gratitude, and they say that from that year on maize started to gain wide acceptance and soon surpassed eleusine as the most feasible and widely-used, if not the most highly cherished, crop.

From the very earliest days the Friends missionaries found that their greatest Abaluyia response and support came not from the Tiriki but from the neighbouring Maragoli. This may

---

[1] Günter Wagner, *The Bantu of North Kavirondo*, Vol. I (London: Oxford University Press, 1949), p. 33.

have been due in part to accidental factors such as those that placed Mr. Rees among the Maragoli and thus determined that Luragoli rather than Lutiriki be chosen as the Abaluyia dialect for Biblical translation, but most of the evidence suggests that the Maragoli from the very first seemed more eager both to aid and to learn from the missionaries than did people from any other Abaluyia tribe.[1] The Lirhanda Mission in Isuxa Location also got much more support from the Isuxa people than the Kaimosi missionaries were able to muster from the Tiriki. The Isuxa and Tiriki dialects are almost identical, which means that the Friends missionaries' Luragoli grammar and Scripture translations were as alien to the Isuxa as they were to the Tiriki. Thus clearly the selection of Luragoli as the dialect for instruction was not in itself an important factor in the Tiriki's slowness to respond to mission teachings.

Why then the long term resistance of the Tiriki to the Friends missionary efforts? There is no evidence that the granting of 1,000 acres of land at Kaimosi to the Friends Mission initially aroused Tiriki hostility, for the Tiriki did not feel any particular claim to that land. Perhaps the inevitable demands for portering and other services that the Kaimosi missionaries made upon the nearby Tiriki during their first years annoyed the Tiriki; indeed any number of a host of possible factors now long forgotten may

---

[1] Several socio-cultural factors may have predisposed the Maragoli to a quick and eager acceptance of alien benefactors. Linguistic and other cultural evidence, including the Maragoli's own traditional clan histories, indicate that the Maragoli are relative newcomers to North Nyanza, and that the bulk of the Maragoli clans are derived from lineages that split off from Abagusii clans now living in South Nyanza. The Maragoli, although considered one of the Abaluyia group, are to this day linguistically and culturally the most divergent of all the southern Abaluyia peoples. Bordered by the completely alien and intensely hostile Luo to the south, and surrounded by the fairly divergent and often unfriendly Bunyoro, Idaxo and Tiriki tribes to the west, north and east, the Maragoli, by the turn of the century, were already hard pressed to find enough land for their growing population.

The Maragoli are a group of agnatic lineages recognizing common descent from a putative common ancestor, Mulogoli, who is accredited with having come from the land of the Abagusii in South Nyanza. Each Maragoli lineage traditionally has its own territorial domain. The whole group of lineages possess no formal traditional tribal unity other than that derived from an awareness of common origin and a relatively weak ritual supremacy granted two senior lineages.

A preliminary perusal of the evidence suggests that each Maragoli lineage group was eager to gain a supremacy over other lineages, through the patronage of the missionaries. Thus, both internal and external pressures probably worked together to encourage Maragoli interest in the missionaries. A more systematic analysis of these factors lies beyond the scope of this paper.

have got mission-Tiriki relations off to a poor start. There are, however, two factors clearly remembered by the Tiriki elders which spawned an early dislike of the missionaries' proselytizing. First was the hostility the missionaries expressed towards the secret Tiriki-Terik circumcision and initiation customs (other Abaluyia tribes do not perform their circumcision ceremonies in seclusion, nor are their ceremonies followed by such lengthy and secret initiation rites). The second factor was the feeling of disgust that the Tiriki soon came to harbour towards the mission because of the aliens, outcasts, witches and irresponsible youth (by Tiriki standards) that the missionaries willingly recruited for their first African helpers and converts.

It will be recalled that the Tiriki circumcision and initiation rites are the ceremonies that institute membership into the all-important age graded age groups. Thus these rites were not only of enormous importance to the organization and maintenance of both warfare patterns and peacetime activities, but they were also the principal symbolic basis for a sense of tribal identity and unity. It is not surprising, therefore, that the Tiriki disliked the missionaries for their attempts to block or discourage their circumcision and initiation practices.

The second Tiriki objection to the Kaimosi missionaries warrants further explanation. Verbal accounts from African Friends of several different Abaluyia tribes clearly indicate that even prior to the First World War the missionaries at Kaimosi recruited the largest proportion of their African house servants, students, evangelists, and teachers from the Maragoli tribe. The Idaxo and Isuxa tribes supplied the second largest number of recruits to Kaimosi, while the Tiriki were a poor third. Thus there was real substance to the Tiriki contention that the majority of Africans working in the mission were from alien tribes.[1] It is not possible to document with precision the proportion Tiriki attached to Kaimosi Mission who were in fact witch suspects or 'irresponsible youth'. Quite likely pagans began to

[1] Members of the Tiriki tribe were migrating westward and thus Kaimosi Mission was rapidly being surrounded by Tiriki on all sides. It should be recalled that the Tiriki shared with the Terik the feeling that all men not initiated according to their customs were aliens. According to Tiriki sentiment all those people from other tribes moving to Kaimosi Mission should by rights have agreed to go through the Tiriki-Terik initiation ceremonies and thus become, so to speak, naturalized members of the Tiriki tribe.

spread witchcraft rumours about people just because they did go to the missions, and it is also quite probable that a youth's taking a serious interest in mission affairs was *ipso facto* interpreted by some conservative pagans as a sign of irresponsibility. A fair proportion, however, of the Tiriki men who became devoted adherents and workers at Kaimosi are widely believed to have been witches (*baloji*) before they went to the mission. Formerly, as today, anyone whom the community felt to be a witch or witch suspect had little chance of becoming an important community elder, and was in continual danger of being publicly cursed by the elders. In pre-European times ordeals were occasionally administered to one openly accused of being a witch, and sometimes the accused was stoned or clubbed to death by the incensed community elders.[1] With possibilities for attaining positions of high esteem within the community and tribe blocked, plus the ever present danger of being publicly cursed, outcast, or even killed, it is quite probable that witch suspects turned to the mission for protection and support. There are no stories of female witch suspects having been among the first Tiriki converts, but in several instances Tiriki girls who later married mission converts from other Abaluyia tribes first came to the mission as runaways from unhappy marriages.

Friends missionaries followed a policy of trying to induce the British appointed tribal leaders to send sons to the mission at Kaimosi to learn to read and write and hear the Christian message. Several Abaluyia tribal Chiefs and headmen, very likely encouraged by the British authorities, soon took up the practice of sending perhaps one of their own sons and several other children of their clan to Kaimosi to live and to learn what the missionaries had to offer. Joseph Ngaira, of the Idaxo tribe, one of the first and most outstanding Abaluyia Friends clergymen, went to Kaimosi Mission as a youth under such an arrangement. Tiriki's leading and seniormost contemporary Friends elder, Joshua Dungu, was in like manner sent to the Friends missionaries by his elder brother, Headman Mushenye. No one has ever intimated to me or my wife that these two men or any of the early converts sent to the mission by headmen or

[1] See Wagner, op. cit., for several passages on witches (*baloji*) among the Abaluyia, especially among the Maragoli and the Vugusu tribes. Note particularly Wagner, ibid., pp. 111–32.

Chiefs were ever suspected of being witches. Several other early Tiriki converts who are purported to have been free of any suspicion of being witches came to Kaimosi because they were attracted by an early mission offer (only extended briefly) to let Africans homestead on mission land if they would agree to attend regularly mission meetings for worship.

To summarize, it does indeed appear that most of the early Tiriki Christian converts at Kaimosi were either sons or younger clansmen of Tiriki chosen by the British to rule parts of the tribe, or young men and women finding refuge from distinctly unfavourable conditions in their home communities. The headmen and Chiefs saw advantages in risking an offspring and several younger relatives to exposure to unsavoury mission company because of the useful knowledge and skills they might acquire, but it is not difficult to appreciate why most Tiriki did not want to expose themselves or their children to the company of so many aliens and witches.

The Spread of Christianity in Tiriki During Amiani's Rule as a Christian Chief

The rate of Tiriki conversion to Christianity, although increasing through the 1920's, continued to lag behind that of Maragoli, Idaxo and Isuxa. The conversion of Chief Amiani to Christianity in 1927, however, marks the beginning of a new period in Tiriki missionization. Amiani's actions immediately following his conversion helped fan into flame the smouldering resentment over mission attitudes towards Tiriki circumcision, and a full blown pagan-Christian factional split quickly came into being. During the remaining years of his Chieftaincy Amiani was the principal Tiriki Christian leader as well as tribal Chief. Thus an account of the development of Christianity in Tiriki from 1927 until Amiani's retirement as Chief in 1946 can perhaps be most economically presented by being interwoven with a sketch of Amiani's political and religious career as a Christian Chief.

Amiani became a headman in the Gisambayi region of northwestern Tiriki in 1911. At the time he was a young man renowned for his great physical stature and forceful manner. He was a member of the Jiminigayi age group, which was by traditional reckoning in the warrior age grade at that time. In

1921 Amiani spent six months at Kaimosi Mission learning to
read and write. He remained a pagan, however, and by 1925,
a year after he was appointed Chief of the entire Tiriki Location, Amiani is reputed to have had thirty wives, whom he kept
together in one enormous compound at his homestead at
Gisambayi. The Friends missionaries built a church near
Amiani's homestead, continued to curry his favour, and in 1927
their efforts were rewarded by Amiani's formally joining the
Friends Church. No particular event seems to have led to his
becoming a Christian, although there are several popular
anecdotes offered to explain this—as there are to explain all the
major steps in his career. One story is that the missionaries
convinced him that having so many wives (few polygynists in
Tiriki, it seems, had more than three or four wives) was more
of an economic liability than an asset, and that he would be a
richer man without them. Whether or not this was a factor in
his conversion, Amiani did in fact pension off all but one wife
during the decade following his conversion to Christianity.

Circumcision was held in 1927, and as in the past at initiation
times, friction began to mount between the Christians at Kaimosi and the Tiriki pagans. During several previous initiation
periods Tiriki pagans had severely beaten a number of Christian
Tiriki girls who worked or attended school at the mission, and
had kidnapped for circumcision and initiation the sons of
several Tiriki Christians who professedly did not want their sons
to go through the traditional initiation ceremonies. Also some
of the Christian men, both Tiriki and alien, had been beaten
and threats had been made to burn their houses. Pagan terrorist
tactics had evidently first started in earnest after September
1920, when a Tiriki was first inveigled by the missionaries into
revealing the secret initiation rites at a Friends Meeting held at
Malava in Kabras. In 1927, almost certainly with missionary
encouragement, a half dozen or more young adult male
Tiriki converts 'confessed' the initiation secrets to a Friends
Quarterly Meeting group at Kaimosi which included Tiriki
women and a number of non-Tiriki Abaluyia. It is not clear
whether Amiani was among the group that actually confessed,
but he fully supported their action, and immediately thereafter
ordered all the circumcision groves (*gabunyonyi*) in Tiriki to be
cut down. The order was carried out in North Tiriki, where

Amiani himself lived and had been headman before becoming
Chief, but the headmen in East Tiriki, responding to the virtually universal sense of outrage felt by the tribal elders, refused
to cut down the groves in their areas.

Amiani and the other Tiriki Christians did not want to
abolish circumcision, but they were in favour of its being done
in the open and without the accompanying secret initiation
rites. Furthermore they wanted the period of seclusion and
initiation after the operation to be reduced from six months to a
simple one month period of recovery. In other words, they
wanted the special and secret Terik-Tiriki *idumi* to be abolished
entirely and only adolescent circumcision, accompanied by a
minimum of seclusion and ritual, to be preserved. When, in
1927, the circumcision and initiation period actually began,
the beatings and kidnappings characteristic of the two previous
initiation periods again took place. In the weeks that followed,
however, the beatings of Christians and aliens reached a new
frequency; the violence culminated in the burning of a mission
school at Maguji in East Tiriki, and in the burning of the homes
of two of the Tiriki Christians who had publicly confessed the
initiation secrets. The District Commissioner rushed to Tiriki
from Kakamega to restore order, and declared that thenceforth
all Christians should be circumcised either at the mission hospital or in a shortened African ceremony in the open, the decision
being entirely up to the initiate and his parents, while all pagans
should be circumcised and initiated according to the traditional
secret customs with no restraint or interference from the missionaries or Christian Africans. That year, and for several successive initiation periods, the pagans of North Tiriki had to
turn to Terik circumcision groves in Nyangori for their ceremonies, but as a result of the District Commissioner's pronounce-
ment the groves cut down on Amiani's orders were allowed to
grow back again, and today they are again in use.

The District Commissioner's intervention stopped the open
violence between the Tiriki Christians and pagans, but it in no
way lessened the feeling of righteous wrath the Tiriki elders felt
towards those who had so flagrantly violated the sacred oaths of
initiation by revealing the rites to the uninitiated. It will be
recalled from Chapter III that such a betrayal is believed to
evoke automatically certain supernatural sanctions that bring

disease and loss of fortune. The Tiriki who had confessed the
secrets in 1920, however, was still alive in 1927, and the elders
deemed it propitious on this occasion to pronounce their collective curse against the violators of the secrets. During the
1927–28 initiation period a special meeting was held in one of
the circumcision groves at which those who divulged the initiation secrets were named and cursed (to curse—*xu-nyega*, or
xu-suha) by the initiation elders. This procedure was in keeping
with traditional action that could be taken against violators of
the initiation oaths. Then a group of pagan elders gathered on a
roadway at the border of Kaimosi Mission and in unison recited
the names of the Tiriki betrayers of initiation secrets, including
Chief Amiani, and wished them all a speedy demise and final
oblivion at the bottom of Lake Victoria. Similar public cursings
were repeated on several occasions during the following months.

A public cursing of this sort by Tiriki elders carries no
specific sanctions of disease, death, or complete ostracism;
rather it is a proclamation of intent to withhold from the
accursed the normal aid and services of all the elders of good
standing in the community and tribe. It is in effect an announce-
ment to the culprit (or culprits) and to the tribe that thenceforth this person is to be *persona non grata* at all beer drinks and
public gatherings. It is also an assertion that the cursed person
cannot count on any future aid from the elders, be it religious,
magical, medicinal or jural. Such a public curse goes a bit
further than this, however, because it also embodies an appeal
to the ancestral spirits, sometimes implicit, or sometimes
explicitly stated in the curse, to withdraw their supernatural aid
and assistance from the accursed and 'to finish his line' (*xumala
inzu ye*), that is, to deprive him of offspring. Finally, curses
pronounced in public, either by individual elders or by a body
of elders, may be followed up at a later date by specific acts of
sorcery designed to bring a more speedy and more certain
demise to the cursed person.[1]

---

[1] There are a number of types of sorcery practised in Tiriki today that reputedly
are not connected with those magical practices divulged in the initiation ceremonies. Although witches (*baloji*) are believed to employ various types of sorcery
in attacking their victims, respected elders, whom no one credits with the possibility of being witches, also in some cases have skill in some of these other forms
of sorcery. Such elders may use their knowledge not only to harm personal enemies
and enemies of the community, but also they are much sought after because of their

Unfortunately it is not possible now to ascertain the immediate reactions of these Tiriki Christians after they were cursed; apparently none of them quickly repented their actions. They were able to find support through the generously given moral and medical aid of the missionaries, through the Christian religious beliefs they had come to profess, and through the British backed political and judicial assistance of their fellow outcast, Chief Amiani. With the social and moral support of each other and African converts from other tribes, they were able to lead quite satisfactory lives without recourse to or dependence upon the Tiriki pagan elders. The missionaries, of course, were adamant in their assertions that pagan curses and sorcery were probably all superstition and certainly all 'workings of Satan' (*miima giisadani*), and that a Christian could find strength to combat and forget such things by standing steadfast in his faith in Jesus. Today, nearly thirty years after they were cursed, most of these Tiriki Christians are still alive, in good health, and with numerous relatively prosperous and healthy children and grandchildren. Indeed they, plus just a few additional Christian Tiriki, form the core of the contemporary Tiriki Friends Church leadership. It is strikingly evident that the career patterns of those cursed Tiriki Christians form a composite picture which contrasts markedly with the sporadic service and shifting religious allegiance of most of these Tiriki Christian men who did not reveal the initiation secrets.

Chief Amiani was for at least three reasons the prime focus of the pagan elders' wrath. First, he was the eldest of those involved in the confessions. Amiani was a member of the Jiminigayi age group which in 1927 was graded as the elder warrior group; all other Tiriki who confessed at that time of whom I have knowledge were either Nyonje, then warriors, or Mayina, which was still open for initiates. Second, he ordered the cutting down of the circumcision groves. Third, his position as the British appointed and supported tribal Chief gave him

---

knowledge of antidotes and cures for the malignant medicine which a person (usually with the help of a diviner) may come to feel is being used against him by a witch or hostile sorcerer elder. See Wagner, op. cit., pp. 132–143, for a discussion of various kinds of sorcerers among the Maragoli and Vugusu.

extraordinary powers. A tribal (location) Chief in North Nyanza had and has a very good chance of being able to trump up a fine or short jail sentence against any individual (or small group) in his tribe who proves troublesome; there was no question but that Amiani had the power to subvert traditional custom and justice in many little ways, and in general make life miserable for the pagan elders or any other group in the tribe. Pagan elders quickly came to feel that Amiani had to be brought to a more submissive attitude as soon as possible or they would stand to lose a large portion of their traditional prerogatives.

No clearcut evidence has been uncovered as to why Amiani decided to defy the elders by supporting the revelation of the initiation secrets. Everything indicates that Aminai was quite popular and highly respected by his subjects, both young and old, prior to his anti-initiation activities. He ruled as headman and then Chief with vigour and dash, initially gathering the support of his constituents primarily through his tremendous physical vigour and commanding manner. The British Administrators seem to have been very much impressed with his leadership attributes, and as mentioned earlier, aided him liberally through their formal support, through allowing him to keep a sizeable police force of Terik warriors and through granting him sufficient productive land so that he was able to entertain his followers on a lavish scale. All evidence indicates that Amiani was never a person to do things in halves. His acquisition of a white horse, and then of a touring car (the first to be owned by a chief in North Nyanza) shortly after the First World War, both of which quickly succumbed to the environment—the former to disease, and the latter to the roads—are just two of many indications of his tendency to be drawn to the dramatic, with little concern about the cost of consequences. It seems probable that Amiani's efforts to discredit and end the pagan initiation ceremonies arose more from his enthusiastic embracement of a new religion than from any calculated planning or personal vendetta against the pagan elders. He probably both underestimated the degree to which the tribal elders would be enraged by this new violation of the initiation secrets and overestimated his ability to cope with whatever objections might be made. During the years of Amiani's rule as headman and during his first years as tribal Chief his relative youth had

granted him under the traditional age grading system the right
—indeed had made it almost mandatory for him—to be a
dashing, fierce warrior type of leader. By 1927, however, people
of his age group were beginning to assume the more restrained,
advisory role of the traditional judicial elder age grade which
clearly was less compatible with Amiani's temperament and
character. Thus personal conflicts arising from the changing
implicit role behaviour that society was beginning to demand of
him may have helped provoke Amiani's rather precipitous
defiance of the elders' authority in 1927—a defiance first manifest by his conversion to Christianity, and then, much more
blatantly, by his disavowal of the initiation rites.

The political consequences of Amiani's actions regarding
initiation were highly disruptive both immediately and in the
years to come. The District Commissioner's visit ended all the
major violence, to be sure, but in the months and years that
followed Amiani was continually faced with a truculent body
of judicial elders who found little ways to obstruct and impede
his executive and judicial tasks, whereas before this time they
had generally been prone to support him actively. Perhaps a
fear of the elders' powers of sorcery, perhaps political considerations—indeed probably both of these factors—led Amiani
around 1930 to pay some of the more venerable pagan elders an
enormous sum of money [*sic!*] to perform a reconciliation ceremony to rescind the curses uttered against him and reinstate
him as a member of his age group. It is not clear whether the
pagan elders extracted any promises from Amiani on this
occasion, but in the years that followed Amiani never again did
anything to aid or abet the violation or discouragement of the
initiation customs, nor did he ever do anything to weaken or
circumvent the District Commissioner's edict that pagan and
Christian be allowed to circumcise and initiate separately, each
in their own manner.

In 1932 Chief Amiani resigned from the Friends Church and
joined the Salvation Army. The incident that immediately preceded his resignation from the Friends Church is both rather
amusing and revealing of Amiani's character. The Friends were
building a church at Munsazi, not far from Amiani's Gisambayi
homestead, and Amiani was contributing over 1,000 shillings
towards its construction—a large proportion of the total cost.

One day a quarrel arose between Amiani and Fred Hoyt, a Friends missionary who had for many years been in charge of the industrial and building programmes at Kaimosi. The dispute was over whether four or six cross beams should be used in building the roof. Amiani favoured six cross beams, and reminded the missionary that his opinion should be honoured since he was meeting most of the construction costs for the church. Hoyt insisted that he knew his job as a builder and that he would build the church with only four cross beams. Hoyt's stature and temper almost matched Amiani's and witnesses say the two men nearly came to blows. In the end Amiani took his grievance to the District Commissioner in Kakamega. The District Commissioner supported Amiani, saying that since Amiani was paying for the church he should have the number of cross beams he wanted. So the Friends Church at Munsazi was built with six cross beams. Shortly thereafter Amiani left the Friends Church for the Salvation Army, citing his dispute with Mr. Hoyt as a reason for his switch.

The Salvation Army, up until the time that Amiani joined it in 1932, had mostly confined its activities and membership enrolment to Nairobi and several other East African towns. A few converts, however, returning from the towns in the Salvation Army uniforms, had initiated interest in tribal areas of Kenya. One of Amiani's many sons had become a Salvation Army member while working in Nairobi, and it is probably through him that Amiani first became interested in the Salvation Army.

Once he joined the Salvation Army Amiani threw himself into its activities with his usual vigour. He soon convinced most of his headmen, tribal policemen (askaris) and other tribal employees that they too should join the Salvation Army. In the decade that followed Amiani did much to aid the establishment and growth of strong Salvation Army congregations in Tiriki, Nyangori, Maragoli and Bunyoro. He built a large church at Jimamoyi, just a few hundred yards from the Friends church at Munsazi, to serve as the centre of Salvation Army activities in southern North Nyanza. Amiani also travelled far and wide, both to participate in Salvation Army training programmes in Nairobi and other towns and to help organize Salvation Army groups in other tribal areas throughout Kenya.

In the early 1930's Chief Amiani handed down a number of judicial decisions in the tribal courts which proved to have a great bearing on subsequent recruitment of Tiriki women to Christianity. Traditionally it was a wifely duty to brew beer for one's husband whenever he commanded, and in the early years of mission activity a number of cases of wife beating occurred because Christian women, following the missionaries' admonitions, refused to brew beer for their pagan husbands. It was quite in keeping with Tiriki custom that a husband should administer a severe, but not crippling, beating to his wife for such a breach of her traditional duties towards him. Until Amiani's interference the beatings had successfully induced Christian wives not to extend the mission's testimony against alcoholic beverages to their preparation. Amiani, however, started handing down rulings in his courts exonerating all Christian women from beer preparation and fining for assault those husbands who beat their Christian wives because they refused to brew beer. It is not surprising that release from the labours of brewing should have been appealing to the women, because, with the exception of those past child-bearing age, women could not participate in any of the Tiriki beer drinks, and thus reaped no reward from their labours as beer makers except for the occasional gourdful of brew which they might drink on the sly, away from the scolding glances of elder women who wanted all such filched 'nips' for themselves. The women's responses to Amiani's rulings were at first cautious, but when months passed and it was seen that fined husbands indeed were having to turn elsewhere for beer, a few more Christian women risked and in some cases suffered beatings. Amiani continued to confirm his ruling with similar jural decisions, and soon the small group of Tiriki Christian women all gave up beer brewing. Once such a situation began to prevail among Christians it wasn't long before Christian wives succeeded in recruiting pagan co-wives into church membership. Soon neighbour was following neighbour, sister sister, daughter mother and *vice versa*, until by 1950 or so the recruitment of adult women to Christianity began to fall off— but only because by then the vast majority of Tiriki women had already joined one or another Protestant church. Thus Christianity ultimately swept Tiriki through its being

embraced by the principal adult uninitiated tribal segment—
the women.

Amiani's judicial support of the missionaries' testimony
against alcohol triggered the main stream of female Tiriki
conversions to Christianity; in Chapter VI we shall see that the
tentative and indirect manner in which women were included
in the traditional Tiriki social structure underlay their sustained commitment to Christian church membership and
participation.

Amiani's edict did not succeed in making Tiriki a beerless
tribe; it did, however, shift the burden of beer preparation
from the women to the men. Further, the traditional millet
(eleusine) beer was completely forsaken for beer made from
maize, in which the fermentation process is seeded by the addition of a few millet sprouts. The shift to maize beer undoubtedly
would have taken place even if the women had continued to
make beer, because of its relative cheapness, quickness and ease
of preparation; tradition, however, which assigned all grinding
to women, obliged the men immediately to turn to maize flour
as the base for their beer because maize could be ground into
flour at the mission-introduced power mills, while eleusine had
to be ground by hand.

Chief Amiani regained some of his Tiriki support and popularity through his dissociation from the Friends and through his
Salvation Army activities. The Salvation Army during the
early 1930's had no European mission stations or missionaries
in North Nyanza; even today (1956) the nearest Salvation Army
European officer lives in Kisumu over twenty-five miles from
Tiriki. Thus Amiani became a bearer of European Christian
enlightenment and education (both of which were beginning to
be held in high esteem by an increasing segment of the population) without being under the immediate control of European
supervisors. Even the Tiriki pagan elders, angry as they were
over his previous defection concerning initiation and his contemporary moves against beer making, were impressed by his
growing acclaim as a religious leader throughout the District.
The pagan elders were especially pleased by his success in
organizing and encouraging a dynamic church group that
effectively broke the religious and educational monopoly of the
Friends Mission in Tiriki.

II

Factors Underlying the Reuniting of Pagan and Christian Tiriki.
The Final Results of Amiani's Maragoli Immigration Policy.

Chief Amiani's growing popularity with the pagan elders was
short-lived because, starting in the early 1930's, Amiani showed
himself increasingly friendly towards Maragoli immigration
into North Tiriki. The situation in North Tiriki was not comparable to the early Maragoli migration to Nyangori Location,
which had already begun by this time, because Nyangori was
still relatively sparsely populated; furthermore many Terik
were quite willing to sell their land to Maragoli immigrants for
cash and then move on themselves to settle in Nandiland. The
population density in Tiriki, however, was already high and
extensive immigration of Maragoli most likely would not have
occurred if it had not been officially encouraged and the immigrants sponsored by Chief Amiani. Amiani himself owned
considerable land in North Tiriki, part of which he sold to
Maragoli immigrants, while other Tiriki, protected from the
wrath of their Tiriki neighbours by Amiani's police-backed
authority, sold part or all of their land and then moved to the
remaining unoccupied land in East Tiriki to get as far away as
possible from the proximity of both Maragoli immigrants and
Chief Amiani. It is fairly certain that Amiani got a remunera-
tion from all Maragoli land buyers for having sponsored their
immigration, but it is not clear whether Amiani's motives for
encouraging Maragoli immigration to North Tiriki were primarily pecuniary or political.

It will be recalled that the Maragoli immigrants, mostly
Friends Mission converts before their arrival in Tiriki, would in
most cases have nothing to do with Tiriki-Terik initiation. Thus
their continued presence in Tiriki was tolerated by the pagan
elders only because they were powerless to defy the protection
that Amiani granted the immigrants. Initially the immigrants
found friends among some of the Tiriki Christians. The Maragoli minority steadily grew in numbers during the 1930's, and
eventually became, along with the Tiriki Christian minority,
Amiani's most dependable source of support in tribal meetings;
together they became the group he called on most often for
executive and clerical aid in running Tiriki affairs.

12

After the merger of Nyangori and Tiriki Locations in 1939, with the subsequent increased tempo of Maragoli immigration to South and North Tiriki, anti-Maragoli sentiment began to develop among the Tiriki Christians, who suddenly found themselves outnumbered, crowded and bettered within their own tribe by the generally more educated Maragoli immigrants. By the early 1940's Amiani not only had again fully estranged the Tiriki pagan elders, but had also started losing the active support of the Tiriki Christians.

The Development of a New Tiriki Tribal Unity

The Tiriki Christians, more disgruntled with each passing year, were greatly aided in regaining a sense of identification with the Tiriki tribe by an event which occurred in 1940. An elder named Sagwa of the Baluxoba clan was the hereditary initiation chief (*mushebi muxulundu*) for the *ibololi* traditionally associated with central Tiriki (roughly from Senende to Jebdulu, including the Serim region). Sagwa intended that his son, Charles Lumbede, eventually should succeed him as initiation chief. Lumbede, however, joined the Salvation Army in the late 1930's. The Tiriki initiation elders informed Sagwa that because of this they would not allow Lumbede to inherit his position. Sagwa was so upset at the elders' refusal to sponsor his son that he himself joined the Salvation Army, and in 1940 he became initiation chief for the Tiriki Christians.

From 1928 until 1940 the Christians in Tiriki had no consistent policy regarding initiation. Some Christian families averted their gaze when community elders took their sons off to pagan circumcision and initiation, and then postured dismay in front of the missionaries and African Christians at Kaimosi. Others either encouraged, or failed to prevent, missionaries from having their sons circumcised at the mission hospital, with no accompanying ceremony at all. A third group had their sons circumcised in a shortened public ceremony such as the Maragoli had adopted, which substituted Christian prayers, hymns and sermons for pagan ritual, followed by only a five or six week seclusion period that was essentially nothing more than a quiet period for convalescence. These alternative types of circumcision were ranked by the pagan elders in the following manner: The Maragoli type circumcision rendered the initiate a

'person'—that is, no longer just a child or womanlike creature—
but still a person of no account in Tiriki; in other words such a
circumcision failed to make the initiate a Tiriki. The hospital
circumcision, on the other hand, while it rendered the circumcised an adult, not only left the person a non-Tiriki but also
branded him as a coward.

After Sagwa's defection to the Christian ranks, the Tiriki
Christians, under his leadership, developed their own circumcision and initiation ceremony which preserved some of the
distinctive features of the traditional Tiriki-Terik initiation.
First one and then several Christian circumcision groves were
established where the traditional practice has been followed of
excluding all uninitiated witnesses. The Christian Tiriki
ceremony has followed the traditional practice of performing the
circumcision operation so as to leave a small fold of foreskin
bunched on the lower side of the penis. Then, during the course
of a shortened convalescence and seclusion period of about six
or seven weeks, the Christian initiates are instructed in most of
the traditional canons (*malago, li- ma- -lago*) of adult behaviour
and are drilled in the sorts of behaviour and respect to be
observed by initiates towards Tiriki men of elder age groups.
The initiates get brief instruction in the rope-braiding, wood-
carving and weapon-making traditionally given in initiation,
and they are given condensed accounts of the power traditionally ascribed to the elders' curse and powers of sorcery. Finally,
just as in the traditional ceremonies, they must swear not to
reveal what they have learned to those not initiated in the
Tiriki manner. Most of the tabus and cautions which surround
the pagan initiates during seclusion have been dispensed with—
Christian prayers and iodine evidently being considered
sufficient to remove the psychic and disease dangers traditionally
associated with the convalescence and seclusion period. The
Christian initiates are still instructed in some of the traditional
initiation songs, but Christian hymn singing has been substituted for most of the traditional nocturnal initiation songfests.
Traditional initiation dance instruction and public perform-
ances have been dropped in the Christian ceremony.

It is probable that the Christian Tiriki initiation ceremonies
carry only a small portion of the emotional impact of the
traditional ceremonies, with their much longer seclusion, much

more rigorous and regimented routine during seclusion, and dramatic secret rituals and public dances. There is some indication, however, that parts of the traditional ceremonies are beginning to seem anachronistic and ridiculous even to the older pagans, and conversely, there is a great deal of evidence that the shortened Christian initiation is much more than a fleeting experience for those being initiated. Christian-initiated Tiriki manifest for the most part an even greater concern over not betraying any of the initiation secrets than do those initiated in the customary manner. It is clear that the Christian initiates feel strongly identified with, but also 'marginal' to, the main stream of Tiriki tradition.

Sagwa in 1940 supplied the mantle of traditional ritual and legitimacy that greatly helped the Tiriki Christians to regain a strong sense of identity with the tribe. What was still needed was a Tiriki leader who could minimize or reduce the remaining hostility between the Christian and pagan Tiriki sufficiently so that the two factions could begin to work together towards the achievement of their common political desires. Amiani simply no longer had the popular support to do this. Not only had his continued policy towards Maragoli immigration won him the profound distrust of both pagan and Christian Tiriki factions, but also the time had long since passed when he should have forsaken his aggressive executive manner and made more dispassionate judicial activity the principal motif of his actions as Chief. Without any traditional precedent for the behaviour appropriate to a tribal Chief, there is no reason to think that Amiani could not have continued to be accepted as such even if, as he grew older, he had joined his Jiminigayi age group peers in assuming the relatively sedentary and sedate behaviour[1] expected of judicial elders. Contemporary elders recount that most Tiriki found it increasingly ridiculous and distasteful to see the ageing giant pedalling from meeting to meeting on his bicycle, occasionally stopping to box the ears of a bystander who did not raise his hat to him, and then at regular gatherings yelling forth his edicts and judiciary decisions in a manner suitable to a war leader directing his band of warriors. It was

---

[1] Emphasis should be placed on, '. . . *relatively* . . . sedate behaviour . . .,' because certainly by British norms there is very little about the behaviour of even the Tiriki elders that could be called sedate.

not an easy problem, however, to find a younger man who might take his place. A new candidate had to be someone who had had sufficient previous administrative experience, and, if possible, education, to be acceptable to the British authorities, and who at the same time wouldn't be anathema either to the pagan or Christian factions in Tiriki. Hezron Mushenye, chosen Chief in 1946, probably came closer than anyone else in Tiriki to meeting these requirements, and his actions during the subsequent decade have demonstrated his great suitability for the office he holds.

During the late 1930's and early 1940's Hezron was labelled by both Europeans and Tiriki Africans as being one of the brighter and more ambitious Tiriki young men. His father, Mushenye, had been a headman in western Tiriki shortly after the British Administration was first established, and Hezron at a tender age was sent to a Friends primary school. He had completed his primary school education before he underwent traditional Tiriki initiation. After initiation he spent several years working in European areas of Kenya. Finally, after a total break of six years, he resumed his formal education—this time at the newly established Pentecostal Mission in Nyangori Location. Hezron completed his teacher's training at Nyangori Mission School, and remained there from 1930 to 1933 as an instructor of carpentry. Then, after a brief interlude spent working as a carpenter at the Kakamega gold mines, Hezron took a job teaching in a school at Tigoi, a large Friends school on the Maragoli-Tiriki border. He held this position for five years and during this time came to be regarded by the missionaries and African Christians as one of the most forthright and promising young Tiriki Christians.

It is easy to perceive, after the fact, the large number of factors that worked together to favour Hezron for the Chieftaincy. Of course his pleasant personality, intelligence, and mission schooling were much in his favour. His membership in the Friends Church and long-standing connexions with the Pentecostals were an enormous asset in his dealings with Europeans (especially missionaries) and Christian Africans, but hardly brought him favour with the Tiriki pagans, though the fact that he was initiated into the Mayina age group in the traditional Tiriki manner and never revealed or violated the initiation oaths, made him a tentative candidate for pagan backing.

Hezron had other connexions, however, that admirably equipped him for a career in tribal politics. For one thing, the Tiriki tend to favour for leaders men who are sons of comparable leaders, and Hezron's father had been a headman under the British. Also Hezron's clan, the Bamuli, is not only one of the largest clans in western Tiriki, but also is one of few Abaluyia Tiriki clans having sub-clans which intermarried with the Terik and adapted both female initiation and the Terik language, in short, which became assimilated Terik. Hezron himself belongs to one of the sub-clans that remained Abaluyia, but the fact that he has clan relatives among the Terik undoubtedly adds to his Terik support. Finally, one of Hezron's elder sisters (a biological daughter of Headman Mushenye) was the woman that Chief Amiani kept as his Christian wife after his conversion to Christianity (Amiani pensioned off his other wives). Because Headman Mushenye had died while Hezron was still a youth, Amiani offered him not only the hospitality and respect traditionally maintained between brothers-in-law, but also owed him additional consideration and respect because Hezron was the senior surviving male member of his (Amiani's) wife's immediate family.

Very likely both these affinal ties and Amiani's awareness of the large number of clansmen and friends Hezron had in southern Tiriki were factors in Amiani's decision to appoint Hezron, in 1938, to be a judge at the new Mbali African Court. Hezron was still in his early thirties, but he filled the educational requirements deemed desirable by the British Administration for such a post better than most adult Tiriki. Certainly the Tiriki elders would have preferred to have seen one of their own number chosen for the appointment, but the British had set the precedent of selecting several young literate men to serve along with the majority of middle aged respected elders chosen for these regional courts. Thus Hezron's appointment was not an innovation.

Amiani failed to gain popular support through Hezron's appointment; indeed, once he was established in the powerful and influential position of regional judge, Hezron quickly became a spokesman for those groups in Tiriki opposed to

Amiani's rule. As a judge Hezron not only held a position from which Amiani could not remove him without showing sufficient 'cause' to the British Administration, but he was also in a most advantageous position from which to point out to the British administrators some of the shortcomings and questionable procedures of Amiani's rule. By 1945 the British Administration had been well alerted to the growing wave of Tiriki hostility towards Amiani. When a series of violent outbreaks occurred that year between the Terik and Maragoli in South Tiriki over the question of circumcision, the British decided the time had come for a change. The ageing Amiani had grown obese and was rapidly losing his physical vigour; thus he was quietly retired on the grounds that he was no longer able to keep the peace because of failing health.

Three candidates were chosen to run for Tiriki Chieftaincy; each one ostensibly represented not only one of the three major regional divisions of the combined tribe but also one of the three major factional divisions. A young literate Terik named Antonio, who was assistant chief of South Tiriki under Amiani, was the South Tiriki candidate who claimed to champion the Terik minority. The candidate from East Tiriki was a pagan elder named Logosi. He was an outspoken and able spokesman for the conservative anti-mission, anti-Maragoli Tiriki faction. Logosi was also favoured by his membership in the Baluxoba clan, Tiriki's largest, with its numerical dominance in several eastern Tiriki communities. Hezron was the candidate from North Tiriki. His court experience, relatively high educational attainment, and church connexions made him the favourite among the Tiriki Christians, and the Maragoli immigrants generally favoured him over the other two candidates not only for these reasons but also because, after his own retirement had been announced, Amiani advised his Maragoli supporters to back Hezron. Finally, those Terik and Tiriki pagans displeased with their respective faction's candidates, could support Hezron without violating their initiation-bond loyalties because Hezron was a member in good standing of his age group.

Missionaries, Christian Tiriki and Maragoli living in Tiriki all rallied around Hezron, hailing him as a soldier of progress and light, while Logosi was painted by them as a herald of pagan darkness and savagery. The election was held by having taxpaying adult Tiriki males (who identified themselves by showing their tax receipts or, in the case of tax exempt elders, their tax exemptions) line up behind the candidate of their choice. Not only did the election procedure make little pretence of successfully controlling voter intimidation, but also it proved to be a most time-consuming procedure for the District Commissioner, who conducted the election by walking by and counting the men in each line.[1] By successfully rallying a small portion of the pagan elders as well as the backing of the Maragoli and Tiriki Christians, Hezron received a substantial plurality of the votes. One reckoning of the vote count was:

Hezron, 2,153; Logosi, 1,165; Antonio, 1,105.[2]

It will be recalled from Chapter IV that shortly after Hezron attained office South Tiriki was administratively reseparated from Tiriki Location, thereby removing from Hezron's jurisdiction the majority of the Maragoli immigrants who had helped put him in office. It is not absolutely clear whether Hezron was in favour of the loss of South Tiriki from the beginning, but once it was *fait accompli* he was quick to capitalize on the potential political opportunity the move afforded him, and immediately banned all further Maragoli immigration to Tiriki Location. All Tiriki, other than Maragoli immigrants, were delighted by this move, and for the first time in nearly two decades Tiriki pagans and Christians found themselves politically united behind their Chief over a major tribal issue.

Hezron's ban on all further Maragoli immigration was a grand beginning to his efforts to try and reunite his tribe, but in itself it was not enough to maintain his wide popular support for long. Hezron succeeded in maintaining and currying the favour of the pagan and Christian factions during the following decade primarily by three tactics: first he won support from educated Tiriki and Tiriki Christians (most of the educated Tiriki are either professing Christians or ex-Christians) by working hard to increase the number and quality of Tiriki schools; second he rallied the support of both Christians and pagans by attacking

---

[1] This procedure for electing Chiefs in North Nyanza was later abandoned, and today (1956) the Provincial Commissioner simply selects a new Chief from candidates who have been proposed by the tribe and passed by the District Commissioner.

[2] Kindness of Elisha Shibelenge, Jebdulu, Tiriki Location (personal communication).

the missions for favouring the Maragoli in the schools (both for employing mostly Maragoli schoolteachers for Tiriki schools and for favouring Maragoli over Tiriki students), and for not developing the school system more rapidly in Tiriki. Finally Hezron did much to win the more lasting confidence of the pagans by himself resuming the practice of drinking beer (to be sure Hezron drinks only European bottled beer) and then by taking a second and later a third wife. Of course the Friends African Church reprimanded Hezron for drinking, and withdrew his church membership after he became a polygynist. Today Hezron describes himself as, 'a man of God and a believer in Jesus Christ, but a man without a Church.' Most Tiriki, both pagan and Christian, today accept Hezron's current religious position as one with which they can sympathize, if not concur.

Hezron did much to encourage the widespread current practice in Tiriki of blaming the missions, especially the Friends Mission, for not supplying more adequate educational facilities with which to meet the enormous demand for schooling that has arisen in Tiriki since the Second World War. In recent months Hezron has made frequent statements, both publicly and informally, favouring the establishment of non-denominational District Education Board Schools in Tiriki. Several such schools have already been established in other tribes in the District, but it is the District Education Board's policy to subsidize and supervise the mission school systems rather than to embark on an extensive government school programme. Whatever discrimination the Friends missionaries may have practised against the Tiriki in years past (and there is considerable evidence that they did favour in several ways other tribal groups over the Tiriki) there is no evidence whatsoever that such a policy is being continued today. So far as schools are concerned, Tiriki now ranks near the top in the District in the number of primary schools and school teachers in proportion to the population. To be sure the recent enormous growth in school facilities in Tiriki probably has in part resulted from Hezron's needling and campaigning, but all evidence indicates that the Friends as well as the other three mission groups currently involved in Tiriki education are straining their resources to the limit, deserve praise for their efforts, and are in no way guilty of obstructing current educational development in Tiriki.[1]

Hezron's assertions that the missions were obstructing rather than fostering the expansion of the school system very likely did little to stimulate directly the missions' educational efforts, but

[1] Contemporary (1954) North Nyanza District Education Board information indicates that in North Nyanza only North and South Maragoli Locations clearly have a higher proportion of primary schools and teachers for their population than the Tiriki.

Education is administrated in Tiriki today by four different missions. The following table indicates the number of primary schools of each denomination in Tiriki (1954) and also shows the number of schools receiving financial assistance from the Kenya Government's District Education Board.

	Aided	Unaided	Total for each denom.
Friends African Mission	9	4	13
Salvation Army	2	6	8
Pentecostal Assembly of East Africa	6	3	9
Mill Hill Mission (Roman Catholic)	2	2	4
Combined Protestant Missions	1	0	1
TOTALS	20	15	35

(The above figures were obtained through the kindness of Roger Hosking, District Officer, Vihiga, South Maragoli, 1956.)

In addition to the above listed primary schools there are two coeducational intermediate day schools (roughly equivalent to American grades 5th to 8th) in Tiriki; one is run by the Friends and the other jointly by the three Protestant missions. Both of these schools are situated near the Tiriki-Maragoli border, and both have many Maragoli students.

Also, there are (1954) three boarding schools at Kaimosi Mission: an intermediate girls' school, a secondary boys' school (which was moved from Kaimosi to Kimilili, Kitosh Location, in 1956), and a Bible school. These boarding schools at Kaimosi Mission are intended to serve students of the entire North Nyanza Districts, and beyond, without any partiality or restrictions based on tribal background. Such a policy is quite feasible beyond the primary level, because today from the intermediary level on up all instruction is conducted in English.

It is the policy of the Friends Mission to assign teachers to their schools without regard to their tribal affiliations. Only in response to particular family needs and other hardship cases will the Friends normally arrange for a man to teach at a school within daily commuting distance of his family homestead. In the case of Tiriki, however, the Friends have clearly relaxed this policy. Although they would be against their Tiriki schools being staffed entirely by Tiriki, they have in the last few years yielded to popular pressure in Tiriki and have increased the number of Tiriki teachers in Tiriki until they now comprise over half of the total staff in Friends primary schools in Tiriki. At the intermediate level, however, only one of the total of six teachers in the two Tiriki schools are Tiriki. It should be noted that in 1954 it is doubtful whether as many as six Tiriki men could have been recruited for intermediate day school teaching, either because the few Tiriki sufficiently trained already had more lucrative positions, or because they were still continuing their advanced education.

they probably did have the effect of helping to break down the widespread earlier tendency in Tiriki to identify education with Christianity, missions, and, in particular, with past Friends policy. Thus pagans began more widely to favour education for their children, and the overall demand for schooling grew larger.

Many Tiriki youths during the last several decades started their education at mission schools only to discover, after a six months absence for initiation, that the schools were loth to take them back, both because the teachers claimed the initiated youth were often unruly and hard to discipline after initiation, and because the shortage of teachers and schools made it auspicious for both the African teachers and the missionaries to favour those students who did not disrupt their education by such a long absence. Chief Hezron himself was one of the few men of his age group who had undergone and remained faithful to the traditional initiation ceremonies and at the same time had managed to return and receive more education after initiation. Among the factors growing from, and further encouraging the growth of, a demand for education in Tiriki is Hezron's recent success in persuading the circumcision elders to shorten the traditional initiation procedure from six to three months. The age of initiation has steadily declined in recent decades in response to an increasing concern that youth not leave the tribe for work in other areas of East Africa before being initiated. Recently, with education rapidly becoming such an important asset in the eyes of many Tiriki, the initiation elders grew concerned about the danger of losing an increasing number of young boys to the Tiriki Christian ceremony—or even to hospital circumcision—if they did not lower initiation age to the pre-adolescent, pre-school or primary school age. Such an innovation was regarded by the elders with extreme repugnance on the grounds that pre-adolescents are much too young to appreciate or even endure the rites and rigours of traditional initiation. Hezron offered the proposal of shortening the initiation to three months as an alternative to the distasteful prospect of initiating pre-adolescents. The initiation elders accepted and put into practice a three months version of initiation for the first time in 1952–53. In return for the initiation elders' having granted this concession, Hezron has agreed to try to increase the

average age of youths going to initiation in future years by
fostering a postponement of the next initiation period beyond
the usual four year lapse.

The current three-month initiation period shortens the loss of
school time to part of one term. This loss, although probably
of not too great significance for the primary school student, still
works a major hardship on the student attending the highly
competitive intermediate schools. It is rumoured that Hezron
has hopes of eventually persuading the elders to cut the total
initiation period down to two months or less so that no loss of
school need be involved.

Hezron's personal actions and administrative policy have
greatly encouraged a convergence of pagan and Christian
interests in Tiriki, but it was Initiation Elder Sagwa's acceptance of Christianity and his consequent establishment of a
Christian Tiriki initiation ceremony that supplied the needed
symbolic and ritual basis for a reaffirmation of legitimate tribal
membership by the Tiriki Christians. The pagan elders have not
granted their active support to Sagwa's Christian initiation, but
neither have they made concerted efforts to contest its legitimacy. Thus Sagwa, probably quite unwittingly, has supplied the
ritual-symbolic innovation that has allowed Hezron to establish an on-going pagan-Christan tribal political unity.

Sagwa's success in establishing an acceptable Christian initiation warrants further consideration. Sagwa's inherited position
in the tribe, his personality and his personal integrity were all in
his favour. As a member of the enormous Baluxoba clan he was
heir to the social and economic security that a host of clansmen
affords. Then, as heir to, and legitimately appointed holder of,
one of the ten (or fewer) venerated positions of initiation chief
in Tiriki and Terik, he is the traditional recipient of the
enormous prestige that goes with that position. It will be
remembered from Chapter II that initiation chiefs are regarded
as the supreme authorities on all matters involving initiation.
Indeed it is most likely that only a man who was himself an
initiation chief could have carried out the innovations in
initiation procedure that Sagwa instituted and still have the new
initiation retain any of the traditional legitimacy of the procedure it replaced. The position of initiation chief, it will be recalled, is not automatically inherited by the eldest son, or even

necessarily any of the sons, of the former incumbent; his sons are simply given first consideration. A son is only chosen to succeed his father if he shows himself eminently suitable for the position through possession of the requisite characteristics of respectfulness and obedience to his elders, courage, sagacity, and diligence when young in aiding, assisting with and learning the duties of the initiation elders. Also any major defects in character or physique disqualify a young man from being considered for the job. That Sagwa had been chosen to be initiation chief before he became a Christian is proof enough of his having been regarded as an exemplary sort of person prior to his conversion.

Most of the pagan elders were deeply shocked and troubled when Sagwa became a Salvation Army member; in doing so he clearly flaunted the elders' advice and personal wishes. To this day, however, Sagwa is credited with never having done anything expressly forbidden by the initiation rites, and it also seems that he never fostered any change in the initiation rites that opposed the social relationships and values supported by the traditional ceremonies. The sacred core of the initiation rituals (as of 1920–30, at least) clearly centred around those rites which stressed the following: (1) the distinctive *adult* status of all those who had been circumcised compared to the non-adult or lack of status of the uninitiated—including the women; (2) the unique and superior adult status of all men initiated according to the Tiriki-Terik customs; (3) the essential brotherhood of all Tiriki-Terik initiated men regardless of clan or tribal origin; (4) the importance of conferring respect upon all members of age groups senior to one's own; (5) the power of life and death (through the curse and sorcery) which members of the elder age groups may employ against members of younger age groups who violate their initiation vows and also against the uninitiated; (6) the supreme sin of divulging the initiation ritual to the uninitiated.

Sagwa, in deference to Salvation Army testimony, has given up his rightful place at the beer drinks of his age group, but in no major way has the general respect shown him by his peers (there are few men alive today who are his seniors) been impaired, nor has his stature as a judicial elder suffered appreciably. Whether it be a wedding party, a funeral, a decision over a disputed inheritance, or an adultery case, Sagwa's presence is always welcome and his advice often sought.

There is every indication that the Tiriki who have been initiated in Sagwa's Christian ceremony adhere to the values supported by the initiation customs with fully as much zeal as their traditionally initiated peers. Those initiated by Sagwa are not rejected or scorned by their pagan peers, but they are somewhat pitied for having missed the beer and dancing, and occasionally chided for having escaped the hardship and excitement of the traditional ceremonies. Those Christian initiates who continue to abstain from beer drinking after initiation (and only a few do continue to abstain) are treated in a manner similar to those college fraternity members in America who cling tenaciously to their Sunday School abstinence oaths; they are initially teased, and later respectfully pitied. Those Tiriki initiated by Sagwa regard the mission hospital or Maragoli-initiated men, as well as those Tiriki who have divulged the initiation secrets, with as much distaste as do the pagan Tiriki; Sagwa's initiates, however, are generally more discrete in voicing their disapproval of them than are the pagans. This is easily understood if one realized that most of his Christian initiates have close kin in one or the other of these categories.

The contemporary Tiriki elders are not as willing to accept fully the Sagwa-initiated Christians as are the young pagans; consequently there is little hope of immediately combining Sagwa's Christian Tiriki initiation and the traditional initiation. A growing minority of younger Tiriki leaders, however, feel that in the none-too-distant future, after the pagan ceremony has been shortened to two months, the pagan and Sagwa-type ceremonies will be merged into one combined ceremony for the whole tribe.

Part Two

CONTEMPORARY TIRIKI SOCIAL
ORGANIZATION AND LEADERSHIP

VI

Christianity, the Supernatural, and the Secularization of Authority

THERE is a marked and consistent difference between the sort of interest and response the Tiriki have manifested towards the religious and political innovations brought to (or foisted upon) them during the last fifty years, primarily by European agents, and their reaction to economic innovations.[1] The Tiriki tend to view the world in political rather than in economic terms. Religion is important, but in large measure as an adjunct to or re-enforcer of power relationships. Since European contact most of the explicit, formally organized efforts of Tiriki communities, sub-tribes, and the tribe as a whole, have centred around maintaining old power relationships and developing new authority patterns between social groups rather than developing and organizing new modes of 'getting and spending'.

Women still perform the hoe agriculture which remains the *sine qua non* of Tiriki economic life. Political and religious institutions have been maintained, modified, and replaced, but in such a manner that the traditional subordination of the women to the men has been in large part preserved. It would almost appear that so long as the subservience of women is maintained, economic activities (so basic a portion of which are carried out by the women) will continue to receive little formal attention from the men. Even while earnestly debating most of the post-European religious and political developments, the Tiriki have until the present decade remained relatively passive recipients of the myriad economic innovations and opportunities brought in from the outside. They have evaluated and utilized such opportunities primarily for their perceived utility in obtaining cattle for bridewealth, procuring extra food for hospitality and

[1] Traders and shopkeepers of East Indian extraction have also been of major significance in drawing the Tiriki into a money economy. African shopkeeping activities in Tiriki are today (1956) essentially subordinate to, and the hand-maidens of, Tiriki political interests. For a description of markets, trade, etc., among the Abaluyia in the 1930's, see Günter Wagner, *The Bantu of North Kavirondo*, Vol. II (London: Oxford University Press, 1956), pp. 161-81.

entertainment purposes, and getting clothes and various manufactured items for their curiosity and prestige value.

Until the coming of the British nearly all of a Tiriki man's social and economic activities were pursued within his own community and immediately neighbouring communities. Only cattle raids took him farther afield. A Tiriki married, visited, and traded almost exclusively with people living within a radius of ten miles or less; indeed, it is safe to say that only an unusually adventurous Tiriki or the occasional outcast ever attempted to settle new land or even raid enemy cattle further than twenty miles away from his parental homestead. There are no accounts among the Tiriki comparable to stories about Masai, Nandi, and other Nilo-hamitic warriors who went on raids into enemy territory lasting several days or weeks. Perhaps some Tiriki warriors took part in such extended raids, but very likely only in company with and under the direction of their Terik allies.

The Tiriki never made so much of either warfare or cattle herding as did the Terik, Nandi and other Nilo-hamitic tribes. Cattle were, however, the most socially rewarding and acceptable form in which to amass surplus wealth among the Tiriki, and cattle raiding was the method by which men might quickly increase the size of their herds. Cattle were, and remain, an integral part of every Tiriki marriage settlement. Through cattle a man procures wives; wives bear children; children not only increase the clan but also are traditionally those people who support their parents when they are old, and remember and praise their names after they die. Cattle were, and still are, of great instrumental aid in the attainment of community influence. A wealthy man lends cattle to less fortunate kinsmen and friends and thereby increases the circle of people directly beholden to him; such economic dominance in itself does not bring political and social eminence, but when sagaciously employed it does much to bolster one's community standing. Traditionally, to be sure, warriors received *kudos* from their peers and sweethearts and bolstered their reputations in the sub-tribe through success and bravery in battle. But, probably even more important, every cow captured helped assure the capturer of a larger circle of indebted or dependent people to listen to his boasts and to praise his name.

Today cattle raiding is defunct; occasionally Tiriki youth attempt, sometimes successfully, to steal a few cows from a Nandi herd, and *vice versa*, but cattle raiding as a regular pattern of social activity was successfully suppressed by the British in 1906. Tiriki cattle herds, probably never of impressive size, have clearly not kept up with the increase in population since 1906. Today a pre-adolescent child, occasionally aided by an elderly relative, can generally manage the herd of a homestead which is seldom as large as a dozen head, and usually consists of only two or three cattle.

Tiriki young men of the warrior age grade were, in effect, left unemployed by the British suppression of cattle raiding and inter-tribal warfare. Well established traditions relegating virtually every aspect of the traditional hoe agriculture to the women have curtailed the men's taking up agricultural pursuits except in those few cases where a man owns enough level land to practice plough agriculture to economic advantage. In the last few years a small number of men, under the direction and encouragement of district agricultural officers, have planted and tended coffee bushes in areas of their homestead lands too hilly to be used unterraced for maize or other regular crops. Many regulations governing where and how the bushes should be planted and tended, and limiting the total planting to 100 bushes or less per homestead, have curtailed widespread efforts to grow coffee. Indeed until the early 1950's numerous restrictions and regulations controlling the growing of coffee in Kenya were manipulated by the British Administration so as to prevent all coffee cultivation by Africans in North Nyanza. To date (1956) only a small number of Tiriki have planted coffee bushes, and not sufficient time has yet passed for the bushes to mature, so this endeavour still has no economic significance whatsoever.

Several factors combined to start and then establish the current Abaluyia pattern of men seeking employment outside of their tribal areas. In 1910 a combined hut and poll tax was introduced, and the same year rinderpest struck, killing about half of the cattle in the district. The economic exigencies created by these two events were the first major economic incentive for seeking employment. Then the widespread recruitment efforts launched by the Europeans during the First World

War drew a sizeable number of Abaluyia men into labour and army battalions. Once the initial practice of seeking employment outside the tribe had been established, it grew in strength and was reinforced by the prestige that men enjoyed when they returned to their tribes with stories of the European areas, with manufactured articles they had bought in towns, and with cash they could use to purchase cattle. Today the Tiriki are firmly tied to the Colony, and indirectly to the Commonwealth, economic system. Indeed, during the last few years they have become dependent on these wider economic networks for their very subsistence. Although the traditional hoe agriculture of the women still provides most of the staple foods for the Tiriki, it is very doubtful that the tribe could still keep its growing population from starvation through subsistence agriculture alone. There is little prospect that the recent efforts in coffee planting will provide sufficient cash to pay for the growing necessity to buy grain from outside sources, let alone supply money to satisfy the increasing desire to buy manufactured goods and provide formal education for the young; thus everything suggests that the present practice of labouring in European and urban areas for cash wages will continue to grow.[1]

At present (1956) not only do the majority of young unmarried and newly married men with pre-adolescent children seek employment outside the tribe, but also a growing minority of middle-aged men with many children, some of whom are adolescent or even married, spend periods working away from the tribe. In some cases these older men seek outside employment because of dire economic necessity, but more often it is because they want the money with which to buy prestige-laden products, and because they want to be able to send their

[1] In a brief return visit to Tiriki in June, 1961, I found that not only has coffee become a rather widely planted cash crop in Tiriki since 1956 (in spite of a general decline in the world coffee market), but in addition the men are now beginning to grow tea on their homesteads to sell commercially. I also found that since the end of the Mau Mau Emergency in 1959, and the return of the Kikuyu to Nairobi and other Kenya urban centres, Tiriki and other Abaluyia have been replaced by the more educated and urbanized Kikuyu in many labouring and semi-skilled positions. Drought and growing uncertainty about the political situation in 1960 and early 1961 have adversely affected the general economic condition of the Colony with a resultant ever increasing number of Tiriki young men returning to their family homesteads after losing their off tribe jobs. Thus it is not surprising that the men of the tribe are planting cash crops with such eagerness today.

children to school. Although most of the cost of running the predominantly mission-run educational system in North Nyanza is borne by the Kenya government, all students must pay tuition fees.[1] These fees, while modest at the primary school level, mount rapidly at the intermediate school level, and are very high indeed at the secondary school level when compared to the usual wage paid an African labourer. Today among the middle-aged Tiriki (the Mayina age group), the condition and furnishings of a man's home, ownership of a bicycle and various other imported manufactured articles, and the educational attainments of his children, are factors of prime importance in the informal evaluation given him by his peers. Wealth as indicated by number of cattle and/or wives and offspring are also factors of considerable weight, but they have nothing like the social importance that was attached to them by nearly all Tiriki a generation ago, or still granted them by most of the contemporary tribal elders of the Nyonji and Jiminigayi age groups.

The Importance of the Christian Churches in Maintaining and Reintegrating Women's Economic and Social Activities

The economic activities of Tiriki women have been much less affected by the coming of the Europeans than have those of the men. Women's lives have changed markedly in the religious realm, but the core of their economic and domestic duties remains much as it was. The status of women is still clearly subordinate to that of the men, and their social tasks and responsibilities, in the eyes of both men and women, remain relatively mundane. Women still care for the young, perform almost all the agricultural tasks, prepare the food, and do almost all the household chores. Only when a woman fails in one or more of these areas do people take any formal notice of women's activities or speak of their importance.

A father instructs his son, today, as yesterday, never to trust his mother with any secrets or important information (or today with money), because not only is she considered a bit foolish

[1] A small proportion of Tiriki children receive tuition assistance each year from the funds of the Tiriki Location Advisory Counsel. Most of these educational grants-in-aid are given to children from homesteads where clearly there is little possibility of any of the adult members of the homestead being able to earn the tuition fees.

(*busilo*) like all women, but also because she is not a member of their clan. It will be recalled that a Tiriki woman has no jural status in her own right; when young, even after marriage, a woman is generally her father's responsibility; during middle age her husband is usually legally responsible for her, and in her aged widowhood, sometimes a father's brother, but more often a son, looks after her.

In the religious sphere the changes in women's formal activities are as striking as the paucity of change in the economic and judicial spheres. Women, of course, did not participate actively in the homestead ancestor worship; instead they merely had their subsidiary women's rites, which were believed to bring aid principally in the realms of childbearing and women's health. Today membership in the Christian church supplies the women with judicial sponsorship outside of their immediate kin group, provides them with a needed basis for economic cooperation, and last but not least, gives them an active role in what has become the dominant religion of the tribe. If one keeps in mind the lack of formal status and lack of direct participation in most of the principal tribal rites, and finally, the absence of any formal status-conferring or expressive organizations for women *qua* women comparable to the men's age groups and beer drinks, it becomes easy to appreciate not only the rapidity with which the women responded to Chief Amiani's judicial policy on beer making and Christianity and became Christians in order to escape the drudgery of beer making but also it appears quite reasonable that women should have become such active participants in church organized social activities.

One may argue that the absence of formalized women's social groupings doesn't necessarily mean that women were discontent or socially disorganized. Indeed, homestead and community work and social activities for women were organized, with the male homestead and community elders' ultimate sanction and approval, by the senior wives and elder women of the homesteads and neighbourhood. During the last generation, however, with the increasing absence from the tribe of a sizeable portion of the middle-aged married men as well as most of the young unmarried men, a pronounced lack of social direction and organization became prevalent among the younger women. If a woman's husband and his brothers, plus most of her male kinsmen, were away at work, the number of kinsmen whom a younger woman might conveniently turn to for jural, religious, and economic support in times of crisis or trouble became very few in number, and sometimes such kinsmen were entirely unavailable. The local Christian pastor has filled this growing hiatus in male sponsorship available for Tiriki women. A Christian woman will now often call on her pastor to arbitrate a minor dispute with a neighbour; also, when her husband is absent, it is fairly common for a woman to have her pastor represent her when she is involved in a serious dispute that has been brought before one of the regular courts for settlement.

Christian pastors have also attempted to become the upholders of the traditional code of sexual behaviour for married women. In keeping with the Christian tradition, local pastors occasionally preach that all sexual activity should be limited to the bounds of matrimony. Their major efforts, however, are directed towards upholding the traditional value placed on married women remaining sexually faithful to their husbands. Their efforts are none too successful; pagans and Christians both assert that the sexual fidelity of married women has suffered a marked decline during the last several decades. The pagans generally attribute this to the evil effects of Christian doctrine and political influence, which have made it possible for Christian women to refuse to submit to traditional supernaturally sanctioned tests of fidelity that are believed to punish the adulteress by sickness and difficulty or death at childbirth. The Christians generally feel that it is only natural for adultery among women to have increased with husbands away for such long periods of time. Christians also concede that continued utilization of the traditional supernaturally sanctioned tests of fidelity would discourage this adultery, but they generally feel that the use of such tests would be a recourse to 'the works of Satan' (*miima giisadani*) and a greater sin than adultery.

It remains a man's prerogative and duty to assign and clear the fields that women of his homestead are to use for agricultural purposes. The actual regulation, however, of how the agricultural activities are carried out remains most usually entirely in the hands of the women. Commonly either the mother-in-law or the senior wife directs a woman's agricultural or domestic activities. In those homesteads containing several wives with older children it is common for each such wife to be assigned separate fields which she then cares for with the aid of her unmarried daughters and perhaps with the help of a junior wife or daughter-in-law. A large portion of the agricultural work is done in women's work bees (*zishiliga, -i zi- -shiliga*). These were traditionally more or less informal groups of about a dozen or more women who lived in neighbouring homesteads. They worked each others' fields on successive days, with food and drink being supplied by the women whose fields were being worked that day. It became the practice for Christian women, who in the early years of Christianity were more or less ostracized by their pagan peers, to work together in parish groups when performing their agricultural tasks. Today, with nearly all women now professed members of one or another Christian denomination, the traditional neighbourhood cooperative work groups have been supplanted by groups based on church affiliation.

One seldom finds today that women of one sub-community all belong to the same Christian denomination; indeed women of the same homestead occasionally belong to differing parishes. There are currently very few homesteads anywhere in Tiriki not within a mile and a half of parish churches representing at least two different denominational groups, and in most places the concentration of churches of different denominations is much higher. Furthermore, in the few remaining areas where one or more alternative denominations are not within easy walking distance, there is nothing to prevent individuals from starting a prayer group in a private homestead to carry on the religious practices of an unrepresented sect; indeed, this is the usual first step in establishing a new parish. Consequently denominational affiliation among the women tends to reflect patterns of differential association, both within the homestead and the sub-community. It is common for the Christian co-wives of a pagan elder who live in the same homestead, but are assigned separate fields, to belong to the same parish—and consequently be members of the same parish agricultural work group. If, however, as is sometimes the case, the two wives follow a pattern of formal but minimal cooperation within the homestead, they are almost certain to belong to different denominations, which means that they also belong to different

work groups. A daughter-in-law is obliged by custom to work
on the fields of her mother-in-law until her husband has been
granted or obtained land and a hut of his own. This in no way,
however, precludes the possibility of a woman and her
daughter-in-law belonging to different denominations and par-
taking in different work groups; only rarely would a mother-
in-law be displeased to accept aid from and serve tea to the
church work group of a daughter-in-law who belongs to another
sect. Neither geographic propinquity to a church of a particular
denomination nor concepts of neighbourhood loyalty are very
important determinants of denominational affiliation among
the women. Consanguineal and affinal kinship ties seem to be
somewhat related to choice of church, as do doctrinal preferences
in some cases. Most important, however, seem to be factors
that might best be subsumed under the ruberic of 'personal
friendships' (*balina banje*), and compatibility as work partners.
Inability to cooperate with a member or members of one's
denominational work group, whatever the underlying cause or
causes of this inability may be, is clearly an important factor in
women's denominational switches.[1]

Age is not an important variable in denominational choice
among the women except for the women past menopause, who
may be permitted to join in some of the men's beer drinks.
During the last several years quite a number of old women
have joined the Catholic Church, but relatively few younger

[1] The four major Protestant denominational groups in Tiriki today (1956) are
as follows:

The Church of Israel (Dini Israel), an independent African sect, with chief
headquarters in Nyangori Location (this sect split off from the Pentecostal Assembly
of East Africa in 1942); The Friends African Meeting; The Pentecostal Assembly
of East Africa; The Salvation Army.

The Friends have no estimate of their Tiriki membership since they have not
reckoned membership on a tribal basis. The other three groups have estimates of
membership in Tiriki, but since the lines between 'adherents' and 'members' are
drawn differently in the three groups the official figures cannot be easily compared.

The Catholic Mill Hill Mission has recently won a number of 'catechists',
especially among the very old and the children. The Salvation Army and the
Friends probably have the largest following in Tiriki today, but the two other
Protestant groups and the Catholics also have substantial Tiriki followings. In
addition to these groups there are a few Church Missionary Society (Anglican)
converts in Tiriki, and converts to at least two other independent African Christian
sects which have their origins and principal followings in other tribes. Finally,
there are a few dozen Tiriki Moslems, and from the men in the Moslem group
come the contemporary livestock slaughterers in the tribe.

ones have become Catholics. Several factors have militated
against the widespread acceptance of Catholicism in Tiriki.
An important factor is the recency of its arrival in Tiriki and
the relative paucity of Catholic churches; indeed, there is only
one Catholic priest working in the tribe. Some old women
evidently feel that they can combine the best of two worlds, so
to speak, by joining the Catholic Church. Catholic affiliation
saves them from many taunts and lectures on hellfire by their
Christian neighbours, and also gives them assurance of having
whatever supernatural benefits Christianity has to offer. But
Catholic Church membership does not prohibit them from
drinking beer. Consequently they are free to ask permission to
partake in the drinks of the pagan elders, and at the same time
they are too old to be expected to participate much in beermaking activity. On the other hand, Catholic church membership fails to afford younger women (whom the elders do not
permit to drink beer anyhow) a legitimate reason for not assisting their menfolk in beermaking. Thus the Catholic view on beer
serves to discourage the membership of younger Tiriki women.

It would be fallacious to suggest that Christian churches have
a vital place in the lives of Tiriki women principally because
they supply them with a way of organizing their group agricultural activities and because Protestant church membership
relieves them from the drudgery of brewing beer. Clearly,
however, among the women both of these factors are significant
adjuncts of church membership.

We have seen that Christianity has given Tiriki women a
much greater role in religious activities than they had traditionally. Women, as a result of their conversion to Christianity,
have also become much less dependent religiously on their
immediate consanguineal and affinal kin, particularly male
kin, than formerly. In the remainder of this chapter I shall
briefly examine the principal religious and magical practices
widely held in Tiriki today, and then trace how the ultimate
focus of tribal authority has shifted from the ritual elders to the
British Administration.

Contemporary Attitudes Towards the Supernatural

The religious and magical revolution wrought by the advent
of Christianity is neither so profound nor so far-reaching as it

might appear to be at first blush. The Christian church and Christian beliefs are in effect a new method, perhaps as effective as the ancestor cult, for obtaining solace and aid in standing up to the dangers of a world replete with uncertainties still ascribed by the Tiriki to sorcery (*bubila, -bu- -bila,* etc.), witches (*baloji*) and bad luck (*ixabi indamanu*). Traditionally the ancestral spirits were solicited and praised when it was felt that strength (*zingulu- zi- -ngulu*) to fight off witches was low and one's luck was bad because of ancestral indifference. In addition, it was believed that persistent difficulties and diseases often also had more immediate magical causes, and the diviner and herbalist were sought for diagnoses and counter-medicines. Today Christians, both men and women, generally view both prayer and hymn singing as mechanisms for bringing them God's grace and good luck, and also as powerful deterrents to haunting ghosts and to many forms of sorcery. Nevertheless, the pagan diviner and herbalist with antidotes for troublesome ghosts and various kinds of sorcery are still often sought out by Christians as well as pagans. In addition, a wide variety of medicine and ritual drawn and synthesized from the magical and medicinal practices of the many tribes and peoples with which the Tiriki now mingle are used by pagans and Christians to combat sorcery, troublesome ghosts, and other ills. Several of the most educated Tiriki—some of those who have finished their secondary school education—are openly sceptical of the traditional beliefs in witches, ghosts, and the like; and a handful of the most ardent Tiriki Christian church leaders feel that prayer, hymn singing and Bible reading are the most effective ways of combatting such evils. But the observations of both my wife and myself strongly suggest that most of these sceptics and Christian zealots have a preoccupation about poisoners and being poisoned far beyond that of most other Tiriki, pagan or Christian. For them evil or hostile humans, using a pharmacopoeia of poisons, have replaced magically armed evil or hostile humans and quasi-humans as bearers of individual misfortune.

Traditional magical and religious rituals have in many cases been displaced or discarded since the coming of the Europeans. In very few instances, however, have the underlying magical and religious belief systems been discarded; instead they have generally been reorganized, and sometimes augmented, by the coming of Christianity. The Christian concept of Satan and his works has supplied a conceptualization and personification of *all evil*, whereas before beliefs about witches served as a looser, rather less inclusive focus for beliefs about evil. Also the Christian concepts of heaven and hell give a much more vivid picture of the afterlife and its rewards or punishments than did the sketchy traditional feelings about 'the world over yonder' (*shibala sha xale*) of the ancestral spirits and the direct relegation of witches and bad ghosts to the bottom of Lake Victoria. Perhaps the largest change to traditional cosmology accompanying conversion to Christianity is the establishment of God and his son Jesus as the fountainhead of good, and the relegation of the ancestral spirits (*misambwa*) to the side of Satan. The early missionaries were adamant in their assertions that belief in sorcery, witches, ghosts, and ancestral spirits, was evil, and that all these things were clearly works of Satan. The contemporary missionaries generally sum up all such beliefs and practices as being mere superstition and don't dwell much or at all on their satanical nature.

Most contemporary Tiriki Christians seldom deny (and clearly believe in) the reality of these supernatural forces, but all agree that the concept of the *misambwa* is simply a mistaken primitive notion, a misunderstanding that people had (still stubbornly held on to by a few pagans) about the nature of God (*Nyasayi*) prior to the coming of the missionaries with their Christian message. Tiriki Christians generally assert that the *misambwa* are in fact nothing more than evil ghosts (*binanyenzo*) that should be driven away at all cost.

A displacement of the ancestral spirits (*misambwa*) by the Christian God (*Nyasayi*) does not entail a complete deviation from Tiriki traditional beliefs, for the Christians in effect disavow only one of the two aspects of the traditional veneration of the ancestors. The Christians find nothing satanical about attributing helpful power to remembering their deceased *baguga*.[1] Indeed, elaborate church services are held in remembrance of deceased *baguga*, both Christian and pagan, and the traditional way of naming a newborn infant for a deceased *muguga* remains essentially unmodified among both pagans and

[1] See Chap. I, pp. 34–5, for a discussion of *baguga*, and the *baguga—misambwa* distinction.

Christians. Thus it is only the depersonalized aspect of the ancestral spirits (*misambwa*) that the Christians have relegated to the side of Satan, and in their stead they have accepted the Christian God (*Nyasayi*) as the *ultimate* source of power and goodness.

Tiriki Christians continue to hold the traditional belief that no one is happy to die, and that consequently something must be done by the living to prevent the deceased's ghost (*shisyuxu*) from becoming a vengeful ghost (*shinanyenzo*) which may linger near the corpse and trouble the living. Drastic and dangerous measures such as burning the corpse[1] are sometimes still resorted to in those cases where a troublesome ghost cannot be persuaded to leave by other means, but a big funeral with a subsequent memorial gathering are usually felt to be sufficient to reconcile the spirit of the deceased to its new condition. To-day most of the wealth of ritual traditionally employed at post-burial remembrance rites (*zimbego*) has been abandoned by the pagan elders, with an occasional dance being the only supplement to the beer drinks held to honour the memory of a recently deceased pagan comrade. The Christians, however, have taken up where the pagans left off. Several months, or sometimes several years, after a person dies Christian members of his or (less often) her immediate family may make arrangements with their local pastor for the holding of a remembrance service (*lizuxiza*) to which all friends, relatives, and members of nearby church congregations are invited, regardless of denomination. Such a meeting is usually held out of doors near the home of the deceased. Starting shortly after noon on a Sunday, it generally continues until early evening unless dispersed earlier by a thunderstorm. It is customary for one preacher from each of the attending denominations to give a sermon and offer a prayer, and for a woman song leader from each church to lead a round of hymn singing. The excitement and fervour generated by some of the preaching and prayers, and the passion expressed

---

[1] The traditional procedure of disinterring and cremating the corpse has been superseded in recent years by the practice of driving a stake into the ground so as to penetrate the head of the corpse, pulling out the stake, filling the hole with gasoline and lighting the gasoline. This procedure, felt to be much less dangerous than disinterrment for the person performing the deed, is also believed to be less certain, for there is always the possibility that the stake did not penetrate the head of the corpse in which case the evil ghost will not be driven away.

through the singing of, and often dancing to, the hymns, has to be witnessed to be believed. Little mention is actually made of the deceased in whose memory the service is being held, and remembrance services are never avowedly held by the Christians either to bring the deceased's supernatural blessing to the living or to prevent the deceased's ghost from haunting the living. If it appears, however, that a deceased person's ghost is in fact returning to trouble the living, or if the luck of the deceased's family takes a turn for the worse, failure to have held a memorial service is widely offered by Tiriki Christians as a likely cause. Whatever their other functions, the Christian memorial services supply Christian men and women with a stage for dramatic and social expression. Today the Tiriki pagans still hold their beer drinks (very often on Sunday afternoons), but the Christians have their memorial services.

Christianity in Tiriki today is much more than an alternative and supplement to the traditional religious system, for in effect it has succeeded the ancestor cult as the predominant religious organization. During the last two decades, particularly during the last ten years, Tiriki juridical and ritual elders have withdrawn from most forms of religious activity. Few of the elders have espoused Christianity, but even fewer have maintained the formal aspects of the traditional ancestor worship. Only a small proportion of the elders qualified by age and family position to keep an ancestral shrine are actually maintaining such shrines today (1956). Elders have forsaken their homestead shrines just as they have forsaken community and sub-tribal ritual fire (*bwali*) ceremonies. They also have given up, with perhaps one exception, care of the sacred groves (*gabogorosiyo*) situated within the boundaries of present day Tiriki Location. Several sacred groves are still maintained in Nyangori Location, however, and it is to these remaining groves in Nyangori that pagans in the tribe retire at certain points in the initiation ceremonies.

The Demise of the Ancestor Cult

The pagan ritual elders have given up most of their traditional religious duties, but not because they have come to believe that the traditional beliefs about the ancestral spirits and their relationship to the welfare of the living are false. They have given up their religious efforts because they believe that recent events have stacked the cards against the ancestral spirits' ability to exert their control over the activities of the living. Recent developments, they claim, have allowed bad people and bad forces to gain so much power that the *misambwa* are foiled in their efforts to help people live good healthy lives. The elders point out that witches, both accused and suspected, have for years found protection and solace by becoming Christians, and that, similarly, thieves, adulterers, and disobedient wives and children can all often find refuge at the missions. Christian converts, even as they consult pagan diviners by night, by day preach against and refuse to partake in traditional sanctioned rituals to bring health and luck, to test fidelity in marriage, to drive away witches, and so on. Furthermore, younger male Christian converts, many of whom are literate and have travelled more widely than their pagan elders, have sometimes threatened to have pagan elders prosecuted under the British administration's anti-witchcraft ordinances if they continued to practise the traditional religious rites. I know of no actual convictions of ritual elders under any anti-witchcraft ordinance, but Chief Amiani, after his conversion to Christianity in 1927, is reported to have admonished pagans on numerous occasions against trying to force Christian converts to participate in one or another traditional religious ceremony. The Tiriki elders are not a sentimental lot. Whatever their personal preferences may be, they have come to realize that the principal power sanctions reinforcing the traditional beliefs in the ancestor cult may now be ignored with seeming impunity by those who choose to do so. Instead of finding themselves regularly praised, or at least deferred to as those most important in maintaining the community's health and good fortune, the ritual elders nowadays may be ignored in their religious capacity; and in addition they have often had their ritual functions condemned and ridiculed by missionaries and Christian converts as works of Satan (*miima giisadani*), and even as causes of social and individual distress. Rather than continue to administer a cult which has lost its general social significance, and in so doing expose themselves to charges of being responsible for contemporary social woes, the Tiriki elders have abdicated their principal ritual roles. Today, on those occasions when pagan elders are still called upon to perform a cleansing or reconciliation ceremony (*mwiluxa*), it is quite common for them to beseech not only *baguga* and the *misambwa*, but also the Christian God (*Nyasayi*), thereby acknowledging His contemporary *de facto* authority.

The ritual elders are now free of most of their ritual duties, but they still receive much of the deference and respect traditionally shown them by junior members of the tribe. The demise of the ancestor cult has but little affected their standing as leaders of the initiation ceremonies; also, most people feel that they continue to possess the power of life and death over their juniors through the potency of their curse and their ability as sorcerers. The initiation rites do much to maintain the status of the elders through continuing to stress the age grading of the age groups, the deference which each age group should show towards senior age groups, the supernatural power readily available to the elders.

The elders are fully aware of the importance of the initiation rites in maintaining their status in the community and tribe, and they remember with vividness that it was only the intervention of the District Commissioner in 1927 that prevented the forceful disruption of the traditional initiation by the Christian convert Amiani's tribal administration. After 1927 Amiani received only tentative support from the Tiriki elders, but he would almost certainly not have received even that much support if the pagan elders had seen any alternative to compliance with the authority of this British-backed Chief which would not involve loss of their British-sponsored judicial role in the tribe. Under Chief Hezron things have changed remarkably. No longer are the elders obliged to support a Chief who clearly would, except for the higher authority of the British Administration which also gives him his office, destroy the traditional basis of the elders' judicial authority. Chief Hezron has not only taken an outspoken stand against the abolition of the traditional initiation rites, but he has also, through his own break with the Church, made himself even more acceptable in the eyes of the pagan elders. During the last decade, with an astute and sympathetic Chief to act as their mediator in their disputes with the Christians and uninitiated immigrants to the tribe, the Tiriki elders have come to depend ever more willingly upon the British-instituted tribal authorities to preserve and reinforce the prestige and judicial role traditionally alloted them by the initiation-instituted age grading system. The judicial and ritual elders during the last decade have in essence transferred their former concern with the ancestor cult to a dedicated support of the British-instituted tribal government. Certainly their duties as judicial elders within the contemporary tribal bureaucracy, plus their almost fanatical concern about preserving the ritual, sacredness, and secrecy of the initiation customs, comprise the major community activities of the contemporary judicial and ritual elders. Where formerly the religious sanctions of the ritual elders stood behind their judicial authority, today the authority sanctions of the British-sponsored tribal administration support their judicial decisions. The magical sanctions of the elders, today as formerly, are for the most part held in abeyance, and thus remain relatively untested and undisputed.

In summary, the widespread acceptance of Christianity in Tiriki has been accompanied by a marked secularization of the tribe's principal authority sanctions. No longer do the elders look to supernatural forces for the principal support of their privileged status and judicial authority. But in matters connected with individual and family fortune, birth, death, and disease, most of the traditional religious attitudes persist, though now largely clothed in Christian dogma and ritual.

VII

Christian Church Separatism in North Nyanza and Tiriki

ONE reason why I initially decided to study the Tiriki was because it looked as though Christian church organizations, both mission-affiliated and 'separatist', were playing an important role in the tribe's transition from the relative isolation and self-sufficiency of pre-European times to an ever-increasing involvement in colonial, emerging national and world affairs. It will be recalled from the Introduction (p. xxxi) that I had some notions I wished to test and develop about the significance of church groups, particularly separatist churches, to the contemporary acculturative process among Bantu tribes. As my field work progressed in Tiriki it became clear that church groups and Christian religious practices are indeed of enormous significance to contemporary Tiriki life and acculturation. On the other hand, I found that Christian separatist or splinter groups were not as dominant an element in the Christian scene in Tiriki as I had originally supposed. Indeed, compared with other southern Abaluyia tribes, the Tiriki have viewed Christian church separatism with considerable scepticism and caution. Nevertheless there are a substantial and growing number of separatist church members and adherents in Tiriki, and no picture of contemporary Tiriki religious life would be complete without a description of the colourful activity of these separatist sects. Also an analysis of why the Tiriki have been relatively wary of separatist churches affords a striking example of how traditional attitudes towards authority, particularly the authority of the dream prophet, continue to affect Tiriki social behaviour. This chapter gives a brief picture of contemporary Christian church separatism in North Nyanza generally and in Tiriki in particular, and presents an analysis of why the Tiriki response to separatism has remained somewhat more tentative and conservative than that of North and South Maragoli and the other southern Abaluyia tribes.

Separatist Church formation is a fairly widespread response

of eastern and southern Bantu peoples to Protestant evangelical missionization. It seems principally, however, to be confined to regions where several mission groups of different denominations have competed for members. Among the Tswana in Bechuanaland, for example, where Christian activity has generally been restricted to one denomination in any given area, separatism has not been prevalent,[1] nor has it occurred much in Uganda, where Christian missionization has been almost exclusively in the hands of the Roman Catholics and the Anglicans. In contrast, throughout Kenya and South Africa several Protestant missions of differing denominations have often worked in the same or overlapping areas; and in both areas missions of many Protestant denominations have been plagued by a rash of Christian separatism. The presence of an economically and politically dominant white settler population and the extensive alienation of African land are, of course, the two most striking features that Kenya and the Union of South Africa share when contrasted with Uganda and Bechuanaland. These two factors have almost certainly indirectly, if not directly, worked to encourage the growth of separatism in these two areas. It is noteworthy, however, that separatism has been as prevalent in North Nyanza, which has been free of land alienation and direct settler domination, as in the settler-dominated areas of Kenya. A careful examination of developments in Kenya, especially in the district of North Nyanza, reveals that European interference and innovation in the political sphere have occurred in varying manner and degree during the six decades of British administration. This interference and innovation indeed probably has been a major cause of Christian separatism. A distinction must be made, however, between political suppression and political interference and innovation. Political suppression *per se* probably is a negligible or only minor factor in the growth of Christian separatism in North Nyanza.

Kaimosi Mission, it will be recalled (see Chap. V, p. 121), was the first mission to be established in North Nyanza. Founded in 1902, and situated in the middle of present day Tiriki, it was quickly followed by the establishment of missions of other denominations throughout the district. Today (1956)

---

[1] I. Schapera, 'Christianity and the Tswana', in S. and P. Ottenberg, eds., *Cultures and Societies in Africa*, p. 496.

the Friends, the Church of God, the Pentecostal Assembly of East Africa (primarily Canadian sponsored), the Salvation Army, the Church Missionary Society (Anglican), and the Mill Hill Fathers (Roman Catholic), each have substantial organizations in North Nyanza; all have African adherents numbering in the thousands. Along with their evangelical and pastoral commitments, these missions run a number of hospitals and dispensaries and administer virtually all the educational facilities of the district.

During the early years of missionization each mission group in North Nyanza had, by mutual agreement with the British Administration, separate tribal areas in which to pursue their mission activities; but tribal intermarriage and increasing African residential mobility fairly soon gave rise to denominational mixture throughout the area. A considerable amount of friction developed not only between Protestant and Catholic missionaries but also between the different Protestant groups over what they interpreted as encroachment into their respective legitimate tribal spheres of influence. Not only did the Africans have the unedifying experience of seeing different mission groups squabbling over converts and areas for churches, but also schisms arose within Protestant missions over matters of changing doctrine, mission policy, and religious practice. In the late 1920's, for example, seizures and trance states, apparently encouraged by the Pentecostals' condoning of visions and 'speaking in tongues', reached almost epidemic proportions in several African Friends congregations in the south of the district, especially among the women. The Friends missionaries, while generally opposed to such displays of uncontrolled emotionality, were divided as to how the situation should best be dealt with. One prominent missionary favoured probationary status or other severe disciplinary measures for those converts who persisted in such behaviour, while another missionary felt that prayerful counselling and admonishment to seek quieter expressions for one's religious zeal was the proper procedure. When the latter was transferred to a distant mission station (for reasons that had little direct bearing on his views on this matter) many of the seizure-prone African converts interpreted this as a defeat for them, and under an African leader they seceded from the Friends African Mission and formed their own independent church. This church is popularly known today sometimes as *Dini Ya Roho* (Church of [the Holy] Spirit) and sometimes as *Yawoha* ('breakaway'). Its official title in colony records is, The African Church of the Holy Spirit, commonly abbreviated to A.C.O.H.S.

Dini Ya Roho now has branches in all the southern Abaluyia tribes. Long white robes with red crosses sewn across the chest, white bandanas for the women, and white turbans for the men form the Sunday uniforms of this sect; also, the men generally wear beards. Drumming, flag bearing and marching, after the manner of the Salvation Army, take up part of their Sundays, while dancing, spirit possession, public confessional and dream interpretations are an integral part of their regular services. Faith healing and a number of ritualistic avoidances, such as not shaking hands or eating with non-members, also characterize this sect. It is rumoured both in European administrative and mission circles and among Africans that some of its members feel themselves to be the spiritual heirs of the suppressed anti-European *Dini Ya Misambwa*.[1] Most of *Dini Ya Roho*'s members live in North and South Maragoli Locations just west of Tiriki, and in Isuxa Location immediately to the north. The church headquarters are in Isuxa. Tiriki membership in *Dini Ya Roho* is small and limited almost exclusively to one small parish located in Tiriki almost adjacent to the Isuxa border.

A number of factors worked to limit my first hand familiarity with the *Dini Ya Roho*, not the least of which was the time it would have taken to build up a close working rapport with its principal leaders. Separatist church leaders and parishioners mostly shied away from inviting or encouraging me to visit or participate in their worship services. If approached directly, they were usually most willing to arrange a meeting for me with their principal leaders and pastors; and at such meetings questions concerning the history and growth of the sect, membership, theology and ritual were solicited and gladly answered. They would characteristically, however, dodge my requests to

[1] A fanatical religious sect, principally drawing adherents from Kitosh, and other tribes in the Elgon region. Elijah Masinde, leader of the sect, an ex-Friend, was deported with two of his assistants after a riot resulting from the sect's activities at Malakisi in 1948. The sect was outlawed after this and several other acts of violence, culminating in the murder of two European policemen and a District Officer in Suk country in 1950.

visit regular church services by saying that the present service
was about to end or that it was a special memorial service
intended only for the relatives and friends of the deceased, or
by using some other equally unlikely excuse to indicate that I
really wouldn't be welcome. Separatist church leaders and
parishioners were aware enough of the suspicions with which
they were viewed by most Europeans to cause them to fear that
one or another aspect of their ritual or worship activity might
cause offence or be misinterpreted; consequently they had
developed a fairly standard set of procedures for dealing with
the curious or suspicious European. Of course, after my wife and
I had lived in Tiriki for about a year and had become known
and generally accepted, or at least regarded as fairly harmless
American students of their tribal history, we were able generally to drop uninvited into church services of all sects in the
tribe with little or no resultant malaise or disruption; but no
such acceptance was ever achieved by us outside of Tiriki.

My wife and I on one occasion did elbow our way un-
announced into a regular Sunday afternoon worship service at
Dini Ya Roho's central church in Lirhanda, Isuxa. The part of
the service we attended, which is recounted below, proved to be
quite similar in content and mood to a number of worship
services, both of separatist and Pentecostal denominations,
which I witnessed on a number of subsequent occasions in
Tiriki.

One day after we had become fairly well known and
accepted in Tiriki, the Tiriki elder of the small local Tiriki
parish of *Dini Ya Roho* invited my wife and me to attend a
Sunday service of his church; but the invitation happened to be
for a Sunday when we were scheduled to attend a conference in
Uganda. Using his invitation and our ability to be present that
day as an excuse for our entrée, my wife and I decided to pay a
call on the High Priest of the *Dini Ya Roho* at his Lirhanda,
Isuxa headquarters. We started out early one Sunday afternoon
accompanied by two Tiriki young men, who were good friends
and who were as curious as we to learn more first hand about
the *Dini Ya Roho*. On the road to Lirhanda we passed through
part of North Maragoli and met a local procession of *Dini Ya
Roho*. We asked if they were going to a church service and were
answered with shifty glances and mumbled words about there

being only a monthly meeting for business today. Deciding quickly that another Sunday would be just as good for Lirhanda, we asked if we might attend. The request caused some consternation and a number of attempts to feign that they did not understand our question. Then someone said that they were not going to the monthly meeting but were on their way to a funeral. We asked whether we might attend and received nothing but some vague arm waving and mumbling for an answer. It was clear they did not want our company, so we asked them the way to Lirhanda and bade them adieu.

The dusty market place at Lirhanda was almost deserted when we arrived; the few loafers and stragglers present seemed dazed by the heat and glare of the early afternoon sun. They answered our queries as to the location of the *Roho* headquarters with shrugs or blank stares. Then a young boy darted up who volunteered to lead us to the church headquarters. He guided us about a half mile down the road from the market place to a sign which read A.C.O.H.S. and had an arrow pointing towards a path too narrow and steep for our car. We left the car and followed our guide up the path about two hundred yards until we came to a broad close-cropped field which surrounded a large, whitewashed, heavily thatched mud and wattle building. I believe it was the largest mud and wattle structure I ever saw in North Nyanza. Out from under its eaves drifted the somewhat muted strains of familiar Luyia hymns being sung to the accompaniment of hand clapping. We later learned that the sect regularly uses drums on parades but never permits drumming at services held in the mother church. About fifty yards beyond the church, along the edge of the field, our young guide pointed to a series of mud and wattle thatched huts surrounded by neat yards which he said belonged to the former Chief of Isuxa, who is the brother of the High Priest of *Dini Ya Roho*. The High Priest, he informed us, lived in the compound containing several neat but slightly smaller huts just beyond the ex-Chief's.

Then our young guide, evidently feeling his task was accomplished, turned without a word and jogged down the path towards the road and out of sight. The four of us squatted down in the grass near the church building, listening, watching, and wondering what we should do next. All the doors of the church

were closed, and the windows shut to both air and light by the
hinged solid wooden door-type shutters, which are widely
used in North Nyanza in lieu of glass windows or louvred
shutters. The hymns sounded far away as their strains emerged
from under the eaves of the thickly thatched building, but their
spirited tempo and the occasional hiccough and gasp of women
in the congregation were clearly discernible. The church building at first glance looked to be perfectly square, but closer
examination revealed little square-shaped alcoves in each
corner, which were covered over by the main thatch to form
four little roofed corner porches.

Several minutes passed and, as the tempo of the singing
increased, the da-da-da-da-da-da-da-da-da and other broken
syllables of people 'speaking in tongues' began to filter out from
under the thatch. Then a huge, bearded man appeared at the
entrance of the privet hedge surrounding the High Priest's
compound. Stout and over six feet tall, his stature and girth
were accentuated by his high white turban and ankle length
flowing white cassock. Over the cassock he wore a sleeveless,
scarlet-coloured garment which was rather like a waistcoat
worn backwards so that it buttoned up the back. A strip of white
cloth sewn on the front of the vest formed the outline of a huge
droplet. The droplet, since it was nothing more than the part of
the vest outlined by the white strip, appeared a startling scarlet;
and right in the middle of the droplet was embossed a small
white cross. The front of his turban was embossed with a
sizeable red cross. The bearded elder's appearance, as he
approached us, was rendered awesome not only by his size and
the startling uniform but also by the penetrating and ominous
appearance of his eyes. Happily, as he drew close, his awesome
visage melted into the look of a kindly and paternal man who
had perhaps just arisen (or been aroused) from a nap.

He greeted us and asked if we spoke Swahili. We introduced
ourselves and our two Tiriki friends, using the Tiriki dialect
which is virtually identical to that spoken in Isuxa, and
explained that we were students from America living with the
Tiriki for two years in order to study their customs and history.
We expressed our regret at not having been able to accept the
invitation to visit the Roho church in Tiriki because of our
forthcoming trip to Uganda, and then added that we didn't

want to return to America ignorant about a church group as important in Tiriki and North Nyanza as the A.C.O.H.S. The bearded elder then introduced himself as Kefa Ayubu, the High Priest of the A.C.O.H.S. and offered to do whatever he could to help us. I said we would be very glad to visit the service going on in the church, if he thought it wouldn't be too much of an interruption. Kefa Ayubu went over to a side door, opened it a crack, and after peering in entered and closed the door behind him. After several moments he reappeared at a different door and beckoned us to come in. As we entered the darkness of the church interior, the sound of singing, clapping, hiccoughing and babbling almost overwhelmed us. Someone immediately closed the door behind us, and we were led by Kefa along the side wall of the church, out into one chancellery or wing, and then up behind a large, whitewashed cross made of pounded earth, which apparently served as a sort of altar piece to a raised platform. There we were ushered to four folding chairs which faced the congregation and were directly to the left of more chairs occupied by the four bearded, robed and turbaned presiding priests or elders, who acknowledged our arrival with brief nods but without interrupting their hand clapping in time with the singing and dancing of the congregation. Kefa Ayubu drew up a chair to the extreme right of the elders. On our way in it had been hard to do more than see where we were stepping because the dark interior of the church was such a marked contrast to the brilliant midday sun. Once seated on the elevated platform, however, a weird sight unfolded before us as our eyes grew accustomed to the dimness. The centre portion of the church was rather like an arena, clear of benches or chairs. On the hard-packed earth floor several dozen long-robed kerchiefed women were writhing, jumping and dancing, more or less in rhythm with the singing and clapping which was being supplied by a group of less inspired or less energetic women who stood in the back and left hand wings and by the men who stood in the right wing. The gyrations of the women consisted mostly of short, fairly rapid hops done with both feet at once while nodding and throwing the arms up over the head in a jerky fashion.

At any given time about a dozen of the dancers (the number varied a bit from moment to moment) were apparently in or near a state of dissociation, hiccoughing, uttering nonsense syllables, and staggering unsteadily as they jumped about; and usually out of this number three or four were weaving so heavily that the nudges of the dancers all around them were no longer always sufficient to keep them on their feet. Once fallen to the ground such a woman sometimes was successfully pulled to her feet by other dancers and continued to dance herself; but, in other cases, she was unable to rise again even with help and simply lay twitching and trembling while the other dancers sidestepped and swirled around her. The whole scene was distinctly Dantesque; the small bit of light which filtered into the church from under the eaves silhouetted the nodding, perspiring faces and flailing arms of the dancers against the whitewashed interior walls of the church.

The church was built in the shape of a cross with arms of equal length. The big, whitewashed earth cross divided the elders' wing at the front of the church, with its raised platform, from the congregation. On the raised platform, behind the seats for the elders (and guests) was an altar table, cloth draped, but otherwise bare except for two tastefully arranged vases of evergreens. A number of red and white banners used in processions were stacked in both corners of the wing. The three other wings of the church belonged to the congregation; the left and rear wings, bare of any benches, chairs or furnishings, were for the women and children, and the right wing, which had an ample supply of movable chairs and benches, was used by the men.

The singing, dancing and trance seizures continued for perhaps ten minutes after we had been ushered to seats beside the elders. A woman member of the congregation occasionally led the switch to a new hymn, which was always taken up without pause or change of the basic tempo. Then Kefa Ayubu lifted his right hand, and the singing stopped immediately. All the dancers stopped too, except for perhaps a dozen women who, evidently in a state of dissociation, continued their leaping, flailing, rolling on the floor, and incoherent babblings. Most of these women stopped of their own accord in three or four minutes, but members of the congregation took it upon themselves to restrain and rub the arms of several women who were twitching and rolling most violently and showed no signs of coming around on their own. Finally, rather like popcorn that

had finished popping, all the women quieted down and arranged themselves in rows on the floor of the left and rear wings
and in the centre of the church, silent, orderly, and attentive,
their legs together and stretched out straight in front of them.
During the interim the men in the right wing sat down on their
folding chairs and benches. Only when all was quiet did the
elders on the platform take their seats, and we followed their
example. Kefa then led the seated congregation in a very
restrained song of prayer, sung without hand clapping or any
instrumental accompaniment (there were no musical instru-
ments in the church). The contrast between this and the fren-
zied singing and dancing which had just preceded was very
striking indeed.

After the prayer Kefa turned to us and in a stage whisper
asked if we had anything to say to the congregation. My wife
and I each spoke in turn, introducing ourselves, and then I
explained our presence in much the same terms we have used
earlier when speaking to Kefa outside the church. Kefa next
nodded to the two Tiriki who had accompanied us. The elder
of the two got up, introduced himself and his friend, and
explained in somewhat shaken tones that they were neighbours
in Jebdulu, Tiriki, of the two Americans, and members of the
Friends Church in Jebdulu. The congregation remained as it
had while my wife and I were talking, passive but apparently
friendly, and he felt encouraged to continue. In phrases much
more eloquent than our limited knowledge of Lutiriki permitted,
he reiterated and elaborated on what we had just said, em-
phasizing our decision to come directly to the mother church
to learn about the A.C.O.H.S. when we were unable to accept
the invitation of the Tiriki A.C.O.H.S. elder and when the
Maragoli A.C.O.H.S. members we had met on the road were
reluctant to receive us. Our Tiriki friend then closed with some
well turned phrases about there being many mansions in God's
house and about members of all sects and all peoples being
brothers.

When we were finished, Kefa offered a prayer in which he
blessed the four of us and thanked God for our visit. Then he
presented a sermon which was primarily for our benefit—very
likely the sort he usually gives for strangers. At any rate it was
concise and beautifully presented. He began by giving a brief

history of the A.C.O.H.S. He said that he had originally been a member of the Friends Church. In 1928 he and some of the others in the Friends congregation had begun to feel God's spirit (*Roho*); and Mr. Chilson, who was one of the principal Friends missionaries at that time, approved of and encouraged this 'quickening of the Spirit within'. But then in 1929 Mr. Ford became head of Kaimosi Mission, and Mr. Chilson was transferred to the Congo (actually Ruanda Urundi). Mr. Ford didn't approve of the Holy Spirit, Kefa said, and finally in 1932 he told those who were dancing and being possessed that they would either have to stop or leave the church. Kefa didn't go on to relate how A.C.O.H.S. had actually become organized and had reached its present form, but simply concluded his brief history by recalling that he had gone to school at Kaimosi with the father of the younger Tiriki who was with us at the church.

Then Kefa's tone changed from narrative to expostulatory. He read several Biblical texts, the first being the one our elder Tiriki friend had alluded to—John 14: 1–6 ('In my Father's house are many mansions . . .'). The second text was Acts 1: 10 ('And while they looked steadfastly towards heaven as he went up, behold, two men stood by them in white apparel . . .'). The third text was John 15 ('I am the true vine, and my Father is the husbandman . . . '). Then he briefly explained the relevance of these Biblical quotations to Christian living in general and to the practices of his church in particular. 'Different Christians worship each in their own way,' he said. 'The Friends think that their more quiet mode of worship is the best, and God has provided them with a house, while we, who lay more stress on the workings of the Holy Spirit have built our own house and our own Church. Inspired by the vision the disciples had when Jesus was lifted to Heaven, we have adopted the wearing of white robes . . . ', &c. During this part of the sermon Kefa interjected an occasional 'Hallelujah', to which the congregation would immediately respond with a rousing 'Hallelujah'. Otherwise the congregation remained passive but attentive during the sermon.

At the sermon's conclusion Kefa again led one of the soft prayerful hymns. Then one of the leaders who had been presiding before our arrival got up and led a short prayer. When he finished, he gave the nod to a woman in the congregation who immediately got up and led a hymn with hand clapping. Then another prayer was offered by one of the leaders sitting with us on the platform. He was followed by another woman song leader. This time the tempo and the amount of hand clapping began to pick up after a few verses; and after the uninterrupted singing of two or three hymns, many of the women began to dance and soon the possession started again.

We followed the example of the elders and stood clapping, observing the congregation; the drama and excitement was as intense as before; but I began to get the feeling that I was seeing a repeat performance of the same show. Whereas before I had found it thrilling, now I was just finding it tiring. I leaned over to the elder sitting nearest to me and whispered that we ought to leave soon before the late afternoon rains arrived and made the roads difficult. He smiled, nodded and spoke to the High Priest, who called a halt to the singing. As soon as the swooning and rolling had died out, he announced that we were leaving, led a brief prayer, ushered us down around the congregation to the back and out the door we had entered. As we stood outside the church bidding our farewells and adjusting to the dazzling sunlight, the hymn-dancing began again, seemingly far away as the sound emerged from under the eaves. Kefa invited us to return to visit with him at length after our Kampala trip, but he admonished us to let him know in advance and pick a day other than Sunday. Before we passed out of earshot on the path towards the road, we heard the hiccoughing and 'speaking in tongues' begin again. As we were driving back to Tiriki, we noted with surprise that there were no signs as yet of the late afternoon rains. We felt that we have been in the church most of the afternoon; but actually the total visit, from the time we first arrived at the church, had taken no more than an hour. A feeling of elation buoyed us almost all the way home, but by supper time the sense of excitement had subsided and my wife and I felt quite exhausted.

The visit to the Roho headquarters church service was an exciting and fatiguing experience for us all. Perhaps the lingering suspicion that we had intruded upon a basically hostile, maybe actively anti-European, group accounted in part for our feelings—our two Tiriki friends being anxious because of their association with us. Kefa Ayubu, of course, made it clear at the time of our departure that our arrival in the middle of a church service without previous warning was not particularly to his liking; but other than this very legitimate feeling, any hostility towards us, if it existed, remained unexpressed or imperceptible; and neither the elders nor the congregation showed any signs of being embarrassed by our presence. I think the principal factor which made this service so exciting and fatiguing for us was the seeming unpredictability and lack of formal control over the trance seizures, and the large portion of the congregation involved in the possession states. This lent the feeling that at any moment the rest of the congregation, and then the elders, and finally perhaps ourselves might be swept up by an uncontrollable frenzy. The four of us had on a number of occasions previous to this visit seen women swoon and fall into trances at church services of several denominations in Tiriki; but they had always been the odd case in a situation where the primary object was simply worship through group singing rather than through the encouragement of possession. Also, the effect at the Roho service described above was heightened by our confinement in a dark crowded, arena-like room where the only avenue of quick escape seemed to be up through the thatched roof.

In the months that followed, my wife and I witnessed in Tiriki several more instances of possession during Christian church services which involved a fair portion of the female congregation. The proportion of dissociated persons was never as high in these subsequent instances, nor was the onset of the possession so rapid; but again no apparent steps were taken to ritualize or control the nature of the possession or the actions of the possessed, other than the role of the elders (who apparently themselves never became possessed) in terminating the singing and dancing and the actions of other non-possessed members of the congregation in 'bringing around' those who remained in dissociated states. As long as the church leaders themselves were not possessed, there seemed to be no difficulty in terminating the possession among members of the congregation at large. On several occasions we saw male members of the congregation speak in tongues and join in with the dancing; but their efforts were dignified and restrained as compared with the women, and never did we see a man fall down in a swoon. It was widely reputed that some of the church leaders of Roho and several leaders in Pentecostal sects occasionally became possessed during regular church services, but we never witnessed this ourselves and are unable to say precisely how on such occasions the group possession is regulated and terminated.

African ethnography attests to the widespread occurrence of dissociated states and spirit possession in one form or another all over the continent, both within a pre-Christian or pagan context, and also, in recent years, incorporated into Christian worship. My wife and I had the opportunity to witness a case of pagan spirit possession in Acholi, Uganda, just a few days after our visit to the Roho service.[1] It was a much more highly structured and more ritually elaborated affair than possession in Abaluyia church services. Furthermore, only two people were actively involved and actually possessed, the ritual specialist, and her novice-client. The entire set of ritualized events leading up to, highlighting and dispelling the trance were carefully outlined ahead of time to the client and onlookers before the session began. In contrast to this, possession states in separatist and mission Christian services in North Nyanza are commonly for exoteric rather than esoteric ends; and they are participated in primarily by the laity rather than by ritual specialists and initiate-clients.

My Tiriki informants declare there was nothing in traditional Tiriki culture comparable to the group spirit possession so common today among the Pentecostal congregations and several other independent sects. Indeed the only instances of trance states or possession that they remember as having any currency before the advent of Pentecostal missionaries were the spirit possession techniques employed by a clan of ritual specialists living among the Terik and the trances of a few neurasthenic individuals in Tiriki, some of whom might eventually win recognition from the Tiriki elders as prophets or seers (*bangoli, mu- ba- -ngoli*). Tiriki all agreed that trances among women were most unusual, never socially condoned, and that a Tiriki woman was never granted the status of seer or prophetess. The Tiriki recognized, however, that occasionally trance-prone women in Isuxa and other Abaluyia tribes gained reputations as prophetesses. All in all there is a rather meagre

[1] Kindness of Paula Hirsch Foster, Gulu, Acholi.

tradition among the Abaluyia concerning the utilization of trance states; in Tiriki, trance states were actively discouraged among the women folk and only occasionally utilized by the men as a tool for prophetic insight. Trances were not traditionally employed by a group or social collectivity in Abaluyia tribes as a modality of religious expression.

Group trance states and spirit possession had by 1955 become a widespread, indeed almost a characteristic, aspect of Christian worship in North Nyanza. Possession was a topical matter widely under discussion and dispute during our stay in Tiriki, not only among church leaders but also among parishioners and pagans. The Tiriki have no specific word to refer to the phenomenon, generally simply using the descriptive phrase *xugwa hasi*, 'to fall down', or 'to become downcast'. Swooning, speaking in tongues and falling to the ground during worship services are felt to be the result of possession by a spirit or spirits or by the imminence of such possession. The Christians inevitably use the word *Roho* when referring to the spirit or spirits involved. *Roho* is a Swahili word which the Abaluyia added to the Luyia lexicon by the early missionaries. It is regularly employed in the Luragoli translation of the Bible as the word for 'spirit' or 'ghost', and is inevitably used, for example, in the Luyia rendering of the phrase 'The Father, the Son, and the Holy Ghost' (*Dada, Mwana, na Roho Mutakatifu*). Possession by *Roho* is regarded by Abaluyia Christians as a somewhat fearful, awe-inspiring thing (*shindu xuriya*), never to be treated lightly. The pagans concur that the 'falling down' of the Christians is a serious business, and they also attribute it to possession by a spirit—probably an evil spirit (*shinanyenzo*) of one sort or another—and tend to ridicule '*Roho*' as being a mendacious Christian label for any one of a number of evil spirits or ghosts. Indeed, they generally view possession among the Christians as simply more evidence of the lax, dangerous state of affairs, both social and supernatural, arising from Christianity.

Christians in Tiriki differ widely in their feelings about the place and significance of possession in Christian worship. All, certainly all Tiriki who profess Christianity, feel there are two kinds of *Roho*, the *Roho* of God (*Roho gwa Nyasaye*), or the 'true *Roho*' (*Roho Mutakatifu*), and the *Roho* of Satan (*Roho gwa satani*). Theological interpretations of '*xugwa hasi*' run the gamut from the view that it is clearly Satan-inspired to the belief that the highest kind of spiritual union with the Holy Spirit often, if not always, involves the worshipper's falling into a trance. Leaders and members of *Dini Ya Roho* ascribed to the latter point of view, whereas adherents of churches such as the Friends, whose leaders in varying degrees disavowed and attempted to discourage all cases of spirit possession among their members, usually interpreted *xugwa hasi* as evidence of sin in one's heart and the presence of the spirit of Satan (*Roho gwa satani*). The Tiriki Friends generally believe that, indeed (in contrast to seventeenth century English Quakers) the true presence of the Spirit of God (*Roho gwa Nyasaye*) is always a calm and serenity producing experience.

A third view widely held by those in sects which condone but do not actively encourage possession among their parishioners (for example, many members of Dini Israel and some Salvation Army members held this view) is that 'falling down' (*xugwa hasi*) is not the result of possession by *Roho* per se, but rather the result of the Holy Spirit and the Spirit of Satan each struggling simultaneously within the person to try to win his heart.

Leaders of the sects employing or condoning possession by the Holy Spirit have worked out simple theologies which put limits upon and give a legitimate place to spirit possession in their church services and worship practices. Kefa Ayubu, together with several other elders from *Dini Ya Roho*, gave me the following account of their beliefs concerning the Holy Spirit.

The Holy Spirit (*Roho Mutakatifu*) often comes to a Christian believer while he (or she) is singing and worshipping, but it may also come while the believer is praying alone or even while walking along a path or roadway; on other occasions the Holy Spirit comes in a dream. The inrushing and the presence of the Holy Spirit does not necessarily make the possessed person dance (*xu-syeba*), fall down (*xugwa hasi*), or speak in tongues (*xu-lomoloma*). Indeed in most instances the person possessed knows of the presence of the Holy Spirit because of the feeling in his heart, but he gives no outward sign. It is only the women, and by no means all the women, who regularly become so excited when possessed by the Holy Spirit that they fall down and in other ways lose control of their actions. Most men are strong enough to be able to brace themselves (*xu-dinya*) so that the coming of the Holy Spirit doesn't make them swoon, except perhaps when they first experience it or on those rare occasions when they experience an extraordinarily powerful inrushing of the Holy Spirit.

Satan is an ever-present reality who at any moment may arouse a person's greed or passions and tempt him to commit sin (*bwoni, bw- -oni*). The Spirit of Satan (*Roho gwa satani*) may enter a person's heart in just the same manner as the Holy Spirit; thus, they believe you must ever be on guard. A person can recognize whether it is the spirit of God or of Satan by the nature of the feelings and thoughts that the possession brings. Kefa and his elders asserted that dreams, verbal instructions, auditory messages, and even thoughts and feelings that are not associated with a trance state, but which simply rise during the day, can be sorted out as being either of God or of Satan according to whether they are in harmony with the teachings of the preachers and the Bible, or whether they are avaricious, darkly evil, and in general against the teachings of Christ.

It is the obligation and duty of every Christian to reject and drive out the spirit of Satan and the evil works his spirit inspires and also to help all others who might be so afflicted. The major technique employed in casting off Satan's spirit, and the temptations, mistakes, and crimes it inspires is confession. All evil, whether merely felt and contemplated or actually committed, should be confessed as soon as possible. Through confession, the elders assert, Satan's spirit—which inspired the sinful feeling, thought or act—may lose its hold over the person and then, through contrite and sincere supplication of the Lord, the Holy Spirit may be brought to fill the person's heart. Public confession is an integral part of the regular service for worship in *Dini Ya Roho*, everyone reciting his lesser sins (*bwoni*) aloud at the same time. (Our visit to the Roho service at Lirhanda occurred after public confession had already been held.) In addition, at some services, particularly those held during the week, members of the congregation are encouraged to stand up and publicly confess more serious 'sins' one at a time. After group confession, the presiding elder leads a prayer asking God's forgiveness for all those who have confessed their sins. On those occasions when individuals confess separately, each confessor is urged by the presiding elder to hold back nothing and to finish his confession by contritely asking God for forgiveness. After each confession the attending elders all step forward, lay their hands upon the kneeling confessor's head and ask, in the name of the Lord, that Satan's spirit be cast out for good and that the sinner be forgiven. Occasionally a sinner lacks the courage to confess his sin(s) publicly; then he is expected to seek out the elders and in private to confess before them and receive their absolution and benediction.

Members of *Dini Ya Roho*, in addition to public or private confession of sins (*xu-luganila bwoni*), are also expected to confess to and ask forgiveness of any person or persons towards whom they harbour evil feelings; the person confessed to, for his part, is expected to forgive and to ask God to bless the confessor. Everyone is also expected to confess before the elders the nature and content of any unusual dream, vision, or message received either while asleep or while possessed. In most instances the recipient can himself correctly judge whether the communication is inspired by Satan or God, confess the former type, and draw strength from the latter. In cases where a person is uncertain, however, or when a person feels he has received special divinely inspired insight, he is urged to relate the matter to the elders, either in a public meeting or privately. Kefa and his elders say it is their responsibility to interpret and utilize such messages for the good of the recipient and the congregation as a whole and either to praise the recipient and rejoice with him, or, if the message seems Satan-inspired, to council him and pray for his forgiveness and well being.

Hymns, both words and tunes, are frequently first inspired by the dreams and visions of members of the congregation; and after review and perhaps modification by the elders, they may be accepted by the congregation at large and become widely sung.

The elders also receive visions and insights from dreams which they too must evaluate for Satan's influence. Those which they judge divinely inspired are often interpreted as offering divine insight into problems vexing the elders. Kefa and his elders refused to give specific examples when pressed about this, simply offering hypothetical cases of the insight which a dream or vision might afford an elder, for example, about the condition of the heart of a visiting stranger and whether he was

a man of good will. They insisted, however, that judgements
and prophetic insights which the church elders receive while
possessed by the Holy Spirit contribute much to their wisdom
and are an important factor in the ability to lead their congregations well.

Kefa and his elders claim that the *Roho* congregation depends
on the elders' judgement in matters such as the interpretation of
dreams deciding whether a particular vision is God or Satan
inspired and the like. The elders, for their part, turn directly to
the Bible. It is from the wisdom and inspiration the Bible offers
that they know how to evaluate and judge both their own and
their parishioners' dreams and visions. Kefa and his elders at
Lirhanda claim they have no say in the selection of local parish
leaders; nor do they run any sort of theological seminary or
training centre for Roho church leaders. Certainly if the parish
leaders' insight as to what is good and what is evil is derived
primarily from the Bible, a level of literacy in the vernacular
sufficiently high to permit the reading of the Luragoli Bible
would be a helpful requisite for parish leadership. Unfortunately, however, I failed to make a systematic tally of the literacy
rate of *Roho* parish leaders.

My investigation of the *Dini Ya Roho* was far from exhaustive,
but inquiries at Lirhanda and cursory contacts with the sect in
Tiriki and Maragoli lead me to believe that the authority of
Kefa and his elders over the many parishes of the *Dini Ya Roho*
throughout the District is principally confined to the organization of occasional combined parish parades and joint worship
services and to serving as the formal intermediary between all
the local parishes and government officials, namely the District
Administration and the Kenya Police. In 1943 the District
Administration first demanded that the *Dini Ya Roho* choose a
high priest who would have authority over and responsibility
for the actions of all the local parishes. Previous to this the sect
had merely been a collection of local parishes claiming origin or
initial inspiration from the group of preachers and parishioners
who broke away from the Friends Mission in 1932. In order to
comply with the District Commissioner's request, the church
adopted the English name of 'African Church of the Holy Spirit'
commonly abbreviated to A.C.O.H.S., and set up a formal
organizational hierarchy of quarterly, monthly, and local

meetings or parishes, which is closely modelled after the organizational system of the Friends Church in East Africa. Not all of the parishes known popularly as *Roho* became part of this A.C.O.H.S. Another separatist church, also called 'Roho' with similar banners and costumes, has its headquarters among the Luo in Central Nyanza District. Also, within the A.C.O.H.S. church, there is apparently a great deal of variation from parish to parish both as regards ritual and dogma and attitudes towards Europeans. All the A.C.O.H.S. parishes officially recognize Kefa Ayubu as their High Priest and employ him as the major representative when dealing with the District Administration and the Kenya Police. His real authority, however, and his role in church affairs other than as official spokesman when dealing with the British authorities, is questionable, and there is considerable evidence that many local parishes have an enormous, almost schismatic, degree of autonomy.

There occurred during our stay in North Nyanza a number of new attempts at separatism which were thwarted by active administrative intervention permitted under the Mau Mau emergency regulations. Generally these would-be separatists were persuaded to take up membership in another mission group or to form a new local branch of one of the independent sects. As a result of this current governmental intervention and virtual prohibition of new sect formation, there were only about a half dozen well-established and officially recognized independent sects in the southern portion of North Nyanza during our stay in the region, but the intra-sect squabbles and quasi-schisms continue with little sign of change.

With only one exception, all of these officially recognized southern Abaluyia independent church organizations prohibit beer drinking and polygyny for their members. Here they adhere to the traditional Protestant mission line. In the formal organization of both their local parishes and their centralized church organization, they also follow rather closely the model of one or another mission group. The one exception is an offshoot of a currently proscribed Kikuyu independent church known as *Karinga*. In 1953, upon the suggestion of a *Karinga* emissary from Kikuyu, the North Nyanza branch changed its name to 'Orthodox' and claimed affiliation with Greek Orthodox Christianity, which had a few African adherents in

Kampala, Uganda. Then after the fact, so to speak, leaders of the North Nyanza Orthodox Church made a number of attempts to get in touch with the Uganda African Orthodox group. Finally, in 1955, eight of the leaders of the North Nyanza Orthodox Church went to Kampala to visit them; and early in 1956, the 'Assistant Patriarchal Vicar of East Africa' briefly toured North Nyanza, visiting with these new adherents to his church. Unfortunately, I never had the opportunity to meet this gentleman or to become acquainted with his purportedly Greek Orthodox group in Kampala. The North Nyanza group, however, on the suggestion of the Uganda Orthodox Patriarchate, shored up their claim to Orthodoxy by adopting a number of innocuous ritual innovations such as crossing themselves and saying 'Father, Son and Holy Ghost' (*Dada, Mwana, na Roho Mutakatifu*) whenever entering the church. In contrast to the other separatist churches in North Nyanza, beer drinking and polygyny are encouraged in this sect. Clearly not only is the connexion between the North Nyanza and the Uganda Orthodox Churches merely nominal, but also the bond between the Tiriki and the other branches of the North Nyanza Orthodox Churches (some of which appear to be rather anti-European in orientation) is more formal than real. The Tiriki branch is composed primarily of rather conservative, generally pro-Administration, middle-aged Tiriki elders and their families. They seek the spiritual advantages and the new respectability of Christian church membership without the penalties of monogamy, giving up the beer drinks, or of resorting to subterfuge in these two areas of behaviour which are traditionally so important in Tiriki men's lives. In conclusion it should be noted that the Orthodox Church is the only denomination in Tiriki (and probably in all of North Nyanza) in which women do not far outnumber the men.

I shall now narrow my focus and try to offer some insight into the character of separatism in Tiriki in particular by examining in detail the Church of Israel, Tiriki Branch. The Church of Israel originated in the neighbouring tribal location of Nyangori in the early 1940's under the inspiration and direction of a Maragoli immigrant to Nyangori named Daudi Paulo Zakayo Kivuli. Kivuli started his career as a Christian preacher in the Pentecostal Church in the early 1930's. Then, in 1939, he became involved in a leadership dispute with several other African Pentecostal preachers and the European head of the Pentecostal Mission in Nyangori. This was finally resolved in early 1942 when Kivuli resigned from the Pentecostal Mission with a number of his supporters and formed his own new African Israel Church.

Kivuli's new church grew rather slowly for the first five years or so; but starting around 1949, its membership began to pick up. Kivuli is able to converse and preach not only in Luragoli, which is understood by all the southern Abaluyia tribes, but also in fluent Terik and Luo. As a consequence, his following grew to include peoples from these tribal groups as well as from Abaluyia tribes. Today (1956) the African Israel Church has over five thousand registered members, plus nearly five thousand more 'attenders'. The church has congregations in most of the North Nyanza Locations and also in portions of Central and South Nyanza Districts. The vast majority of Kivuli's followers are Maragoli who live in North and South Maragoli Locations, in Nyangori Location, and in Kisii, South Nyanza. Kivuli's first adherents in Tiriki were Maragoli immigrants to Tiriki who lived close to the Maragoli and Nyangori borders and attended Israel Church meetings in those locations. At present, however, the Tiriki branch of the Israel Church has grown to be the largest separatist group in Tiriki Location and has a following primarily made up of birthright Tiriki.

The initial impetus to the recruitment of birthright Tiriki into the Israel Church arose from Chief Amiani's desire to keep *Dini Ya Roho* from spreading to Tiriki. Chief Odanga of North Maragoli was a supporter of *Dini Ya Roho*, and he tried to encourage the growth of the sect during its early years, not only in his own location, but also in neighbouring areas, including Tiriki. Chief Amiani, it will be recalled, was a Salvation Army member in his later years, and he was much involved at this time in the proselytical efforts of the Salvation Army throughout the district and the province, as well as in Tiriki. Thus he did not take kindly to Odanga's efforts to recruit in Tiriki for *Dini Ya Roho*. It will be recalled that from 1939 to 1946 Nyangori was an integral part of Tiriki Location. During this period Amiani employed Kivuli to translate for him when he held meetings with the Terik living in Nyangori. The two men were on very good terms; and when Kivuli formed the Israel Church, Amiani encouraged those living under his jurisdiction who belonged to *Dini Ya Roho* either to forsake it for the Salvation Army or to switch their allegiance to the Israel Church, which like *Roho* was unaffiliated with any mission group and believed strongly in the importance of the Holy Spirit.

In 1943, several Tiriki members of *Dini Ya Roho*, on the suggestion of Amiani, went to visit Kivuli at his church headquarters in Jebrok, Nyangori. They stayed as guests of the Israel Church for a week and subsequently joined the sect. After their return to Tiriki they were unable to persuade the other Tiriki *Roho* members to follow them into the Israel Church, and consequently they remained a very small group for the next several years without any parish of their own, obliged to attend Israel Church meetings held outside of Tiriki, and to depend on the occasional visits of Israel pastors. Amiani's hope of diverting Tiriki *Roho* members into the Israel Church never really materialized, but his efforts did engender the conversion of several birthright Tiriki to the religious sect of his friend Kivuli.

Three people are generally remembered in Tiriki today as having been instrumental in establishing the Tiriki branch of the Israel Church. One is a woman named Leya Leba, who was among the original small group who broke off from *Roho* to join Dini Israel in 1943. She has been very busy as a preacher and organizer of women's prayer and work groups in the Israel Church ever since she joined. She is mainly remembered, however, for having brought her son-in-law, Joseph Ganila, into the Israel fold. The second 'founder' is Thomas Asoga, who joined the original Tiriki Israel group shortly after its inception in 1943 and acted as its informal leader until 1947. Asoga is more remembered today for his unusual spirituality than for his role as a church organizer and parish leader. He was prone to have visions and dreams which served as the inspiration for his religious prophecy; he also sometimes fell into trance states, during which he spoke in tongues. Asoga died early in 1955, but by 1956, less than a year after his death, his memory was universally honoured by members of the Tiriki Israel Church and by many Christians of other sects as well, as one who truly had the power of prophecy, the power to communicate directly with God, and to look right into the hearts of men and see both the good and evil which lay within.

The third person credited with 'founding' the Tiriki branch of the Israel Church is Joseph Ganila, the son-in-law of Leya Leba. Ganila, in 1947, shortly after his conversion to the Israel Church, organized the first Israel parish in Tiriki; he has remained right up until the present (1956) the head of the Tiriki branch of the Israel Church. Thomas Asoga is revered today as having been the one true prophet (*mungoli*) of the Israel Church in Tiriki and its main source of spiritual inspiration. His talents, however, did not extend to the organizational sphere, and he never actually set up an Israel parish in Tiriki, remaining content to have himself and his Tiriki followers hold membership in the Israel parish at Jebrok, Nyangori. Joseph Ganila is no mystic and has never made any pretensions of possessing the power of prophecy, but he clearly has a talent for organization. Under his continuing guidance and direction the Israel Church, Tiriki Branch, grew from the original parish he instituted at Mahanga, Tiriki, in 1947, to the largest, most rapidly growing independent church in Tiriki with twelve active Tiriki parishes in 1956.

Ganila's life history conforms to a pattern quite typical of successful contemporary Tiriki leaders, and it will be outlined in Chapter IX (pp. 274–8) which discusses the tribe's current leadership. I shall confine myself here to mentioning a few of the incidents which preceded his conversion and assumption of Tiriki Israel Church leadership. Ganila, as a young man prior to Second World War taught in Friends Primary Schools. He was educated at Kaimosi Mission and was a member of the Friends Church. In 1943 Ganila enlisted in the King's African Rifles and saw duty both in Ethiopia and in Burma. While in the Army, he developed a strong curiosity about things religious and frequently attended the religious services of the Catholics and of several Protestant denominations. After his discharge from the K.A.R. in 1946, he started systematically exploring the different Christian sects represented in Tiriki in hopes of finding one that would suit his fancy more than the Friends. He visited Pentecostal, Salvation Army, and *Roho* services and found himself particularly drawn to the Pentecostals; but he never felt strongly enough attracted to any of them to decide to switch his affiliation from the Friends. Then in 1947, Ganila had a religious experience. He recounts that the Holy Spirit possessed him, and he knew he had finally found God. Both Ganila's wife and his wife's mother, Leya Leba, were overjoyed and urged him to go and confess his sins to Thomas Asoga. Joseph heeded their advice; and Asoga, after listening to his confessions and welcoming him to the Israel fold, advised him to go directly to Zakayo Kivuli at Jebrok. Joseph went to Kivuli, joined the Israel Church, and shortly thereafter, together with Leya Leba and Thomas Asoga, founded the Israel parish at Mahanga. Thomas became the head preacher (*mwilwazi mw- bi- -ilwazi*), Joseph the clerk (*mulindi mu- ba- -lindi*), and Leya the head of the women's activities (*mulindi wa salasini ya baxali*) of the new parish.

Towards the end of 1947 Joseph arranged to go and live at Jebrok in order to serve a sort of apprenticeship under Zakayo Kivuli. He stayed at the Jebrok headquarters of the Israel Church (which is known as 'Nineveh' among the Israel congregation) for two years, along with five other apprentice leaders who came from Central Nyanza. They studied under Zakayo and acted as his personal assistants. Since Zakayo did not supply his apprentices with food or clothing, Joseph found it necessary to hold a job as clerk at Kaimosi Mission power mill during this period. Jebrok is about eleven miles from Kaimosi, and Joseph commuted almost daily either by foot or bicycle; thus, the apprenticeship could not have been too demanding during weekdays. In 1949, when his apprenticeship was completed, Joseph returned to his homestead at Mahanga in Tiriki and assumed the headship of the Mahanga Israel parish. He also gave up his clerkship at the Kaimosi saw mill and resumed his pre-war occupation of primary school teacher. From 1949 until our departure from Tiriki in 1956, Ganila taught on successive years at several different unaided primary schools under the administration of the Friends and the Roman Catholics. Thomas Asoga, after Ganila's assumption of the Mahanga parish headship in 1949, was freed from administrative type tasks, which apparently he never relished, and expanded his activities as preacher and prophet within the

Israel Church at large, devoting an increasing amount of time to visiting different parishes.

. . . . .

The account that follows is a brief résumé of the organization and activities of the Tiriki Israel Church. It is based on what my wife and I observed while attending a number of Israel Sunday services, prayer and 'remembrance' services, on countless informal chats with Tiriki (both Israel members and non-members) about the sect, and upon a number of rather extensive interviews with Tiriki Israel leaders.

The Israel Church organizational hierarchy is modelled after that of the Friends Church in Kenya. At the lowest level, several local village pastoral groups, each of which holds regular Friday sunrise and Sunday noon services under the direction of its parish preacher (*mwilwazi*), are organized for business purposes into a 'Monthly Meeting' (*Libugana lya Salisini*). The 'Monthly Meeting' is held at the end of each month and is attended principally by the male elders of the local pastoral meetings, although all members of the local meetings are free to attend if they wish, and is presided over by the 'Leader of the Monthly Meeting' (*Mulindi wa Salisini*). The women have their own monthly meeting which handles matters of particular interest and importance to them. At the next higher organizational level, several monthly meetings are joined together to form a Quarterly Meeting (*Libugana lya Gwalide*—Gwalide being an adaptation of the English word 'quarterly') which meets regularly every three months both for worship and to settle common business. Then at the apex of the organizational hierarchy is the founding church, 'Nineveh', at Jebrok, to which all Israeli members and adherents are urged to pilgrimage each Christmas. The Friends have their comparable 'Yearly Meeting', to which all local meetings are urged to send representatives, and their 'General Secretary' of 'Yearly Meeting', who acts as the principal spokesman of the entire East African Friends congregation. At this uppermost level the Israel organization diverges somewhat from the Friends model, for Kivuli is the founder and perennial High Priest of the Israel Church, whereas the General Secretary of the yearly meeting is chosen by the yearly meeting at large and has no prior claim to his office.

Originally the Nineveh Church and the quarterly and monthly meetings formed the entire hierarchical framework of the Israel Church organization. As the church grew, however, and spread far beyond the boundaries of Nyangori and Maragoli, Kivuli decided to establish 'mission branches'. Today there are three mission branches, one in Central Nyanza, which oversees the quarterly and monthly meetings of that region; one in Bunyoro Location, North Nyanza, which presides over the quarterly and monthly meetings of the westernmost portion of North Nyanza, and one with its headquarters at Mahanga in Tiriki. The three mission branches are each under the authority of a minor priest (*musaalisi mudididi*) who is directly answerable to Kivuli. Kivuli himself presides in lieu of a minor priest directly over the quarterly meetings of Maragoli and Nyangori.

Joseph Ganila is (1956) the 'minor priest' who presides over the Tiriki Mission branch of the Israel Church. The Tiriki Mission consists of two quarterly meetings. The larger one, known as Tiriki Quarterly Meeting, has its headquarters at Mahanga and has jurisdiction over three monthly meetings, one in Tiriki, one in Isuxa, and one in Idaxo. The other quarterly meeting, with its headquarters in Eastern Tiriki near Kaimosi Farms, not only contains East Tiriki Monthly Meeting, but also Kapsabet Farms, Eldoret, and Nakuru Monthly Meetings, all of which lie outside of North Nyanza in or near urban centres or European farm areas.

The Mission 'minor priests' are responsible for regulating and integrating all religious activity within their respective mission areas. Each mission priest is in charge of the three-day period of instruction and prayer held every three months for the leaders of all the monthly meetings in his mission area; his authority, formally at least, at all times overrides that of the quarterly meeting leaders in matters of dogma and administrative policy. The quarterly meeting organization brings the local parish meetings together at quarterly intervals for worship, and its leader is responsible for arbitrating disputes and answering queries that have not been satisfactorily settled at the local and monthly meeting level and for informing the local pastors of all decisions and innovations made at the mission level and at Nineveh.

There is only one monthly meeting in Tiriki proper, Mahanga

Monthly Meeting. Since Mahanga also serves as the centre both of the Tiriki Quarterly Meeting and of the Tiriki Mission Branch, Israel activities at Mahanga pretty well reflect the tone of the entire Tiriki Israel membership. I have in consequence chosen to examine the Mahanga parish and monthly meetings in some detail and have based most of my generalizations about Tiriki Israel church services, dogma, and belief on material gathered from their leaders and from observations of and participation in church activities at Mahanga and at affiliated village Israel parishes.

Johana Inyanje is the head of both the Tiriki Quarterly and the Mahanga Monthly Meetings. Johana is a man in his late thirties or early forties, lean, and of imposing stature. He has a primary school education and is a carpenter by trade. Intelligent, high-strung, and with an arresting but rather benign and permissive manner, Johana occasionally has visions and is beginning to earn a reputation as a prophet. He engages in frequent preaching missions to outlying congregations, often in conjunction with carpentering jobs in off-location areas and towns. Inyanje is Joseph Ganila's principal assistant in Mission Branch affairs and often serves as his personal emissary at church meetings, both within Tiriki and at outlying areas. Conversely, when Inyanje is away from Mahanga on carpentering jobs or preaching missions, Ganila assumes direct responsibility for the activities of Tiriki Quarterly and Mahanga Monthly Meetings.

There are seven local or village meetings in the Mahanga Monthly Meeting. Each village meeting (*libugana lya lidala*) is under the care of a local pastor (*mulindi wi lidala*). The local pastors are formally appointed by their monthly meeting leaders, and the quarterly meeting leaders by their respective mission branch priests, or by the High Priest Kivuli himself. In practice, although no formalized system of voting is utilized, the appointments in each case must fairly well concur with the feelings of the subordinates and parishioners involved, for there is the ever present possibility of individual church members switching their affiliation to another denomination and, in addition, the possibility that a discontented leader might break off or transfer his allegiance and carry a large portion of his parishioners with him.

All the principal leadership positions in the Israel Church are
occupied by the men. This, of course, is in harmony with
traditional Abaluyia practice, in both secular and religious
affairs, of debarring women from top leadership roles and of
confining them to secondary authority positions except in situations exclusively involving women and children. Ilwanda, one of
the seven parishes belonging to Mahanga Monthly Meeting, is
unusual in having a woman for a pastor. In Joseph Ganila's
own words, 'She's a woman, but she's a good leader!' Ganila is
the first to admit, however, that the members of Ilwanda parish
would certainly not tolerate a woman for a pastor, whatever
her leadership and preaching skills, if they had any male
members eligible for the job. As things stand, however, there
are no men in Ilwanda Meeting except for several elderly
polygynist converts; and no polygynist is allowed to become a
leader in Israel. Although women are excluded from all pastoral
and general church leadership, women do regularly have their
own auxiliary groups within the church organization and their
own leadership positions within these groups. Every Monthly
Meeting has an auxiliary women's Monthly Meeting with its
formally appointed women leaders. The Mahanga Monthly
Meeting has four such leaders. Leya Leba, the mother-in-law
of Joseph Ganila, is the principal leader, and she is assisted by
three leaders of equal rank, one of whom acts as the secretary of
the Women's Monthly Meeting. Leya Leba's informal status as
the leading woman member of the Tiriki Israel Church is confirmed and further re-enforced by her holding this highest of all
women's positions at Mahanga, the principal Tiriki Monthly
Meeting. The Women's Meetings hold worship services
exclusively for women every month, which all the women of the
affiliated local parishes are urged to attend.

The Women's Monthly Meeting provides the only regular,
formally appointed leadership positions for women in the Israel
Church. There are, however, several other women's groups
organized at the parish level which supply opportunities for
informal or semi-formalized leadership among the women.
Probably the most important and active of these groups are
the women's work groups (*zishiliga*). The work group is
organized ostensibly by the parish pastor to assure the regular
fulfillment of certain maintenance activities which by their

nature are traditionally relegated to the women folk. Periodic smearing of the church floors and walls with a mixture of cow dung and water is, for example, one of these tasks. Also the women's work group is expected to help with the farm work of a sick parish member if circumstances in her homestead are such that she seems to need this sort of help. The women's parish work groups serve principally, however, as the ongoing organizational basis for informal work bees in which participants successively work each other's fields and end the day by drinking tea, singing hymns and praying together at the homestead of the person who has been helped that day. Then each local meeting has its group of elderly women members who take a leading hand at funerals and who are regularly called on to shave the head of the new born infant of a parish member a few days after its birth (in accordance with traditional Luyia custom) and pray for its well being. These women elders have no appointed leader, but they are all recognized by the congregation at large as being people of importance because of their age and their willingness to participate fully in these sorts of activities. Finally, each meeting has several women who are widely recognized as having musical talent and who are regularly called upon by the pastor to act as song leaders at worship services.

The Israel Church holds views about sin and the importance of confession which are similar in many details to the beliefs and practices of *Dini Ya Roho* outlined earlier in this chapter. Regular Sunday Israel services in Tiriki include spoken group confessional and supplication to God for forgiveness of sins, and in addition the regular early morning Friday services held in local Israel parishes devote a major portion of the total worship period to public confession of sin, both on a group and an individual basis.

Joseph Ganila and other Israel leaders in Tiriki assert that a 'sin is a sin' (*bwoni ni bwoni, buzwa*) and that before God there are no distinctions between different kinds or degrees of sin. Church members of good standing they assert, after they have been in the Israel Church for several years, learn to recognize sin whatever its guise when they see or experience it, and without any qualifications or fuss to rid themselves of its hold simply through public confession. Israel leaders say, however, that such a state of enlightenment is not arrived at rapidly or easily. Thus, for pedagogical reasons, Israel preachers frequently categorize sins according to the parts of the body in which they reputedly originate, and urge their parishioners to examine themselves with the aid of one or another anatomically based typology of sins, such as the following:

(1) Sins of the head, i.e., mistakes in judgement, such as erroneously telling someone it is only a five minutes' walk to someone's homestead when actually it is more like a half hour walk.

(2) Sins of the heart, e.g., feeling anger or malice in your heart towards a neighbour or friend.

(3) Sins of the loins, e.g., lusting after someone else's spouse.

Sins of the loins are seldom confessed in mixed company, women being especially reticent in such cases. Indeed, Israel members, both male and female, claim one of the most important aspects of the Women's Monthly Meeting is that its monthly worship service, because it is not attended by men, allows the women to confess publicly those sins which they would feel ashamed to confess before the menfolk—notably sins of passion, including lustful phantasies, dreams and desires. Also, a principal task of the leaders of the Women's Monthly Meeting is to hear confessions which women are even embarrassed to confess before the female congregation and to be available for these sorts of confessions during the intervals between the regular Women's Monthly Meeting for worship. Segregated and private opportunities for confessional are not necessary, it is claimed, for Israel members of long standing who have achieved great spiritual strength. Such people, assert Ganila and other Israel leaders, have strength enough to confess publicly and without restraint any sort of sin to which they might fall victim.

Tiriki Israel leaders have developed additional and more elaborate divisions and categorizations of sin, which map both a sin's point of origin and subsequent flow through the body. For example, they assert that the head not only contains the mind, which may make false judgements, but in addition contains four of the five sense organs. Each of these senses, the elders feel, is a potential source of sin; indeed it is usually one or another of the five senses which initiates sin. Thus most sins start with the head. You may see something you fancy and want to steal it. Initially, this is a sin of the head—specifically of the eyes, the elders claim; but if the heart agrees with the head and longs for the object, it becomes a sin of the heart. Next you may get up and walk to the spot where the object is; and thus, what started out as a sin of the head and became a sin of the heart or chest is now a sin of the legs. There are comparable sins of the ears, for example, to overhear something, and then to start to spread rumours on the basis of this. Such a sin which originates with the ears also becomes a sin of the mouth, because one spreads the rumours with the mouth. But it still remains only secondarily a sin of the mouth; the elders feel 'A true sin of the mouth is one where the individual deliberately goes around saying something which isn't true.'

Sins generally flow from the head to the chest and thence either to the arms and legs or to the loins. Sins of touch, however, may start in the loins, the hands, or any part of the body and thence flow to the heart either to be cast out or passed on again to another sector of the body. The heart controls the flow of sin in the body, either preventing or aiding its passage from one part to another. If your heart is filled with God's Holy Spirit, then sin, wherever it enters your body, cannot harm you or control you; you simply confess it, and its harmful effects are gone. Satan's spirit, however, may try to capture your heart directly, and under its evil influence you may instigate or aid and abet all manner of sin.

Confession of sin helps a person avoid committing evil acts. Ultimately, however, all sin is related to the condition of a person's heart, and the principal purpose of confession is to free the heart from sin's control. Israel rhetoric indulges heavily in what might be termed metaphorical reductionism. Certain key concepts—for example, 'adultery'—are widely used in a number of metaphorical contexts. Adultery, according to Israel theology, is in its most literal sense sleeping with someone else's wife, and as such it is a sin of the loins. In addition, however, and more significantly, it is a sin of the heart, because it is the heart which does the lusting and allows the loins to do such a thing. And by extension, according to Israel thinking, lusting after another person's spouse is also adultery because your heart is desirous of and might permit actual adultery. Finally, any covetousness or desiring of what is not yours is also adultery because it involves the same condition of the heart. Thus the truly enlightened and diligent member of the Israel Church may confess the sin of adultery even if he merely covets a neighbour's rooster or his pocket knife. This means, of course, that the outsider or neophyte attending an Israel service may be surprised or shocked to hear the church leaders and the most respected members of the congregation confess to having committed the most heinous sins; indeed he may note that the apparent frequency and seriousness of sins confessed seems to be greater for the church elders and leaders than for the neophytes.

The preceding paragraphs in no way afford a complete or systematic inventory of Israel beliefs concerning sin; each preacher, and indeed each individual, has his own particular catalogue of sins and method of spurring his memory to reveal sins he has committed but forgotten. Another popular way of classifying sins is to relate them to the days of creation as described in Genesis. Sins of the first day when God created the heavens, for example, are wanting the sun to come out when it is behind a cloud or wanting the moon to go away—perhaps so that one can steal something under the cover of darkness. A sin of the second day, when God created the earth, is, for example, not wanting to walk on the earth because it is hot and dusty or because it is cold and muddy. On the third day God created the animals, and to kill an animal or insect needlessly is a third day sin. Israel doctrine urges all its members to confess all sorts of 'sins' at public confessional but not in detail; one is expected to confess merely that he has committed a first, second or third day sin, rather than actually describe the nature of the transgression. Regardless of the eagerness and diligence a believer evinces in trying to remember and confess his sins, it is believed that some sins will inevitably be forgotten; but such forgotten sins may reveal themselves in dreams. Thus, the content of one's dreams should be carefully reviewed for sin, and sinful dreams confessed.

Why all the concern about the confession of sin? Israeli leaders preach that confession frees the individual, particularly the individual's heart, from the sin or sins that happen to be present and thus enables the person to receive God's Holy Spirit (*Roho Mutakatifu*) more fully. It is believed that sin left unconfessed will not only very likely sooner or later involve the sinner in difficulties with his fellow man, but also, through delivering him into the hands of Satan, may relegate him to eternal hell fire after death. Sin confessed and rejected, however, and the Holy Spirit earnestly sought in its stead, lead the person to a way of life which will probably be revered and praised by his fellow man and assure him after death of a place in heaven.

The Israelis place almost as much importance on the receiving of the Holy Spirit as do the *Dini Ya Roho*, but their beliefs leave much less room for, and in general attach little positive significance to, actual dissociated or possession states (*xugwa hasi*) arising from the presence of the Holy Spirit. Occasionally Johana Inyanje 'speaks in tongues' when under the influence of the Holy Spirit, and Thomas Asoga is reputed to have done so fairly frequently. Their mutterings are 'interpreted' by Joseph Ganila and other church leaders and sometimes proclaimed by them to be evidence of God's inspiring presence. Also, occasionally, not only recognized prophets such as Inyanje but others in the congregation as well, have dreams the contents of which they reveal to the elders and which may be proclaimed as a message from God or as worthy material for a new hymn. Several women in the Israeli Church have gained reputations because of the hymn melodies and lyrics which they have made up, avowedly from Divine insight granted through their dreams.

Inyanje, Asoga and other Tiriki Israeli leaders did not and do not, in most instances, fall down (*xugwa hasi*), tremble, and apparently lose control when filled with the Holy Ghost, as so many of the women and some of the elders of *Dini Ya Roho* are wont to. Indeed, the Israel leaders interpret such behaviour as evidence of unconfessed sin. They say that a person writhes and falls around when possessed by the Holy Spirit because of the struggle going on within him between the Holy Spirit of God and the spirit of Satan. Each spirit wants control of his heart; and the individual, refusing through ignorance or fear to confess and thereby rid himself of sin inspired by the spirit of Satan, is tossed about and perhaps thrown down by the efforts of the Holy Spirit to capture his heart. The Israeli elders and congregation rejoice when they see a neophyte tremble and fall down, for here is evidence of the Holy Spirit struggling for a victory;

but such behaviour on the part of a person long in the church is viewed as evidence of unconfessed sin which he should by now know better than to overlook or hold back. In all cases the person who loses control of himself is encouraged and exhorted by his peers and elders to calm down, and to seek out and confess the sin that is troubling him and thereby assure the victory of the Holy Spirit in his heart. Members of Israel say that the widespread falling down among the *Roho* members is merely evidence of the large amount of unconfessed sin among their congregation.

The Israel dogma about the nature and importance of the Holy Spirit is quite simple and straightforward. The Bible, the leaders of Tiriki Israel explain, speaks about the Father, the Son, and the Holy Spirit. Today, however, Israel dogma asserts, only the Holy Spirit is important. The Father has finished his work, which was to perform the acts of creation, make the heavens, the earth, &c. The work of the son, Jesus, is also completed. He came down to earth, died for our sins, made possible salvation for all those who believe in Him. God no longer sends prophets as in the Old Testament; if God were to send Jesus again, for example, men would only kill him again. Consequently God doesn't want men to see Jesus again in living form and instead of sending prophets or another Jesus, God nowadays communicates to men directly through the Holy Spirit to man's heart. Recent and contemporary prophets like Thomas Asoga and Johana Inyanje are people whose hearts are particularly open to the prophecies of the Holy Spirit (*Roho Mutakatifu*). They are not, however, prophets in the Old Testament sense; they are not leaders of men. Rather they are simply those who, time and time again, are acknowledged by the church leaders and the congregation at large to have received messages in their hearts of significance to the well being of the church community. Leaders in the Israel Church are quick to point out that any one may be able to prophesy occasionally; even women and children. But only rarely does someone come along who can prophesy frequently and consistently throughout the years, and who is consequently worthy of being regarded as a prophet (*mungoli*).

Israel leaders accede that today, as in former times, pagans may acquire the power of prophecy. They claim that both pagans and true believers in the Israel Church may be inspired by the working of the Spirit (*Roho*) in their heart, but that there is a crucial difference between the pagan and the Christian prophets. The difference is that pagan prophets are inspired by the spirit of Satan (*Roho gwa Sadani*) while the true Christian prophets are inspired by the Holy Spirit of God (*Roho Muta-katifu wa Nyasaye*). Israel leaders do not universally agree that the pagan prophets of pre-European times were Satan inspired —there is a difference of opinion over this—but they all agree that ever since the coming of the Christian message to North Nyanza those worshippers and prophets who retain their pagan orientation are definitely inspired by the spirit of Satan.

Members of the Church of Israel in Tiriki hold views concerning the ancestor cult and the nature and reality of sorcerers and witches which are essentially identical with the beliefs of Tiriki Christians of other denominations. It will be recalled from Chapter VI (pp. 162–6) that virtually all Tiriki Christians accept and believe in the continuing reality and influence of these forces and agents in that they now feel they are all manifestations of the evil powers of Satan. It will be recalled that the ancestor cult *per se* no longer concerns Christians much, and that its ritual aspects have been largely abandoned even by the pagans. Christians widely recognize and admit there are those among their number who are confessed witches (*baloji*) and others who know and on occasion practice various kinds of sorcery. I know of no case where a Christian has confessed to having practised sorcery (*bubila*, &c.) after his conversion to Christianity, but there are Christians who, when accused of witchcraft have acceded that under the compulsion of the witchcraft force within them (*buloji, bu- -loji*) their shadows might have gone forth while they were sleeping and committed one or another act of evil. In those cases where a Christian is accused or suspected of witchcraft, and even more particularly on those occasions where the accused is willing to admit that he might have been involved in witchcraft—though of course against his waking will, the accused is urged to confess his involvement and to pray to God for forgiveness and for strength to cast out the witchcraft propensity once and for all. The elders and congregation then join in prayers for his deliverance from the forces of evil.

Christians of all denominations in Tiriki generally believe that prayer affords a powerful shield against all kinds of misfortune or evil, particularly against sorcery. Israel members feel, however, that protection against sorcery and other Satanic evils is certain only while one is actually engaged in earnest prayer and worship. To forgo prayer for even one day is to permit a large enough chink to develop in one's spiritual armour so that one may be reached by the harmful medicine of a jealous person, or perhaps have one's heart directly invaded by Satan's spirit. Many Christians feel that their Christian beliefs arouse the wrath of pagan sorcerers and witches and that they consequently become the spiritual target of evil medicine. Thus they feel a need to be prayerful, not only to stay free of Satan's spirit, but also to escape the dangers of malevolent sorcery. Tiriki Christians, both in the Israel Church and in other denominations, apparently lack any very well formulated theory or concept as to how prayer protects a person against sorcery and other evil. Generally they seem merely to regard it as a sort of universal protective medicine (*lunyasi lulahi*). Some Christians profess, however, that prayer itself does not protect one against sorcery and other evil; rather it brings one in communication with God, and it is God's strength that brings protection.

Hymn singing is another way highly favoured among Tiriki Christians, both of worshipping God and of warding off evil forces. In addition, some sects, notably the Salvation Army, Pentecostals and Israel, do a lot of drumming as an accompaniment for their marching, hymn singing and dancing. Members of these sects feel that drumming is a particularly effective deterrent to the powers of Satan and his human agents. These three sects, particularly the Israels, favour the use of large speaking tubes or megaphones by congregation members, both in their regular worship services and parades and when performing solitary prayer and hymn singing. These megaphones are made locally out of old kerosene cans; and when spoken or sung through, they produce a rather nasal sounding resonance strongly reminiscent of the Bob Burns 'bazooka'. The popular name for these speaking tubes is 'Bible' (*ibayibu, i-, zi- -bayibu*), and is probably derived from their being so frequently used by zealots for reciting Bible verses.

A district administrative ordinance prohibits all drumming, both pagan and Christian, from sundown to sunup except at funerals and on other rare occasions when special administration permission may be obtained. There is no ordinance against the use of the *ibayibu*, however, and on many a morning silence is broken well before dawn by one or another religious enthusiast who has risen early to indulge in a round of hymn singing, preaching, and praying to God, and, incidentally, to the entire sleepy populace within earshot—perhaps a half mile radius. Sometimes such a worshipper may be moved to 'speak in tongues' through his trumpet even before the crack of dawn, but usually such ardour doesn't arise until the sun has risen sufficiently to dispel the chill of the night. At the crack of dawn drumming begins at the homesteads of various zealous Christians and sometimes at local churches scattered across the countryside, and thence until about an hour after sunup the sounds of worship rend the morning air. Friday mornings are particularly noisy because the Israels regularly hold early morning parish services that day, but on almost any day of the week at least a few pious individuals within easy earshot are up before dawn shattering the stillness with praises of God.

A church member who owns a drum or speaking trumpet treasures it as a highly valued possession. Pagans, and Christians of relatively quietistic persuasion, have on occasion been moved to snatch and destroy drums and trumpets because of the racket they produce, and this has simply added to the fierce possessiveness with which their owners guard and care for them. One Israel matron told me with some pride,

'The pagans and even some of the Christians don't like my drumming; some of them would even like to destroy my drum. They know it dispels their evil powers, and it makes them angry; so, I just keep drumming all the more.'

The Israel Church in Tiriki, unlike *Dini Ya Roho*, has no testimony against the use of traditional medicines for helping to alleviate illness or against seeking medical aid at mission hospitals or government medical dispensaries. They do feel, however, that the ultimate cause of illness is probably due to transgressing God's law, to sorcery, or to some other sort of Satan-inspired evil. It is consequently common practice for

Israel congregation members to visit the home of an ill member, singing songs, beating the drums, and praying to God to bring strength and protection to the ailing person. Also, of course, the stricken person is admonished to confess whatever sins are on his heart.

Hymn singing, often through speaking trumpets and to the accompaniment of drums and hand clapping, is a very important aspect of Israel services for worship. In addition, the congregation often dances—a sort of shuffling hop—to the singing and drumming. Singing, drumming and dancing activities occupy perhaps as much as half of the total time spent in group worship by the Israel churches. The hymn book printed by the Friends Mission in Luragoli dialect is a regular part of an Israel leader's equipment, and in addition is owned by a fair portion of the congregation. The hymns in this book are sung widely by Friends, Pentecostal, Salvation Army and Israel congregations. Some of the tunes and lyrics are inspired by American Missionary evangelical hymns; others which have lyrics and melodies made up by African converts tend to follow fairly closely the Mission hymn model, both as regards tempo and lyric message. The most popular and most widely sung hymns among the Israel Church members are not found in the Friends Luragoli Hymnal but are much more spirited hymns which are usually created, become popular, and are replaced by new hymns within a matter of a year or less. These popular 'hit' hymns flow back and forth across denominational boundaries, churches of several denominations in one area, for example, favouring a hymn which was dreamed up (literally in many instances) by an Israel member, and another month preferring a Pentecostal hymn.

The Israels, Pentecostals, and Salvation Army congregations are constantly making up new hymns with lively tunes that can easily be danced to, while the Friends, who prohibit all dancing, generally reject the more spirited hymns in favour of slow tempos, dignified and sometimes rather dirge-like.

A number of people in Christian circles, mostly women, have gained considerable fame as hymn composers. They usually claim that inspiration for their hymns, both lyrics and tunes, comes to them in dreams. The following is the lyric of a hymn which was very popular in the spring of 1956. The woman who composed it, a member of the Friends Church, claimed that both tune and lyrics were revealed to her in a dream. The tune is melodious and fairly gay, about as gay as the Friends seem willing to tolerate, and it was widely sung in early 1956 among all the sects in eastern Tiriki including the Israel Church.

Mu Lidala Lilahi

Mu lidala lilahi	In the good village
Mu lidala lilahi	In the good village
Zingelosi bibixa zingubu zindabu	Angels wear bright clothes
Mu lidala lilahi	In the good village
Mu lidala lilabu,	In the bright village,
&c.	&c.
Mu lidala lyu buyanzi	In the joyous village
&c.	&c.
Mu lidala ha Yesu	In Jesus' village
&c.	&c.
Mu lidala mwigulu	In the village of heaven
&c.	&c.

The words of another hymn, also very popular in 1956, are given below. This has a much more lively melody and lends itself well to dancing. People say it originated with the *Dini Ya Roho;* it was probably the most popular hymn among the Tiriki Israels in the spring of 1956, but it was not sung by the Friends except when they were attending inter-denominational memorial services.

Yohana Wa Gura Wanyola Ixabi

Yohana wa gura wanyola ixabi	John has won and found grace
Yohana wa gura wanyola ixabi	John has won and found grace
(Refrain)	
Roho ni Roho	Spirit is Spirit
Roho lwanda!	Spirit rock!
Roho ni Roho	Spirit is Spirit
Yaxanga shuluheni	Flash like the lightning!
Isaac wa gura wanyola ixabi	Isaac has won and found grace
&c.	

(The names of whomever the singer or the congregation chooses may be inserted in each verse, sometimes Biblical names, sometimes living people of outstanding character or virtue. After each verse, the refrain is repeated.)

Often instead of the above verses, the following verses are sung with the same refrain:

Israel balelo benyanga ixabi	The Israelis today need grace.
Israel balelo benyanga ixabi	The Israelis today need grace.
(*Refrain*)	
Bajeshi balelo benyanga ixabi	The Salvation Army members today
&c.	need grace.
Bafulenzi balelo benyanga ixabi	The Friends . . . &c.
Babenda balelo benyanga ixabi	The Pentecostals today . . . &c.

.   .   .   .   .

Early in this chapter I briefly described the visit my wife and I made to a *Dini Ya Roho* Sunday Service and outlined some of the beliefs which this, the oldest of North Nyanza independent churches, holds concerning possession by the Holy Spirit, the workings of the spirit of Satan, and the importance of confession. Then I traced the growth of the Israel Church in Tiriki, outlined its organizational framework, and listed some of its dominant beliefs and ritual practices. Next I shall outline some of the common characteristics of the three separatist churches in Tiriki, and note whether or not these characteristics are similar to or at odds with mission church practices. I shall conclude this chapter by analysing some of the factors which have contributed both to the success of the Israel Church, Tiriki Branch, and to the relative lack of success of *Dini Ya Roho* and Karinga, and which have tended generally to inhibit Christian separatism in Tiriki.

Separatist and Mission Churches in Tiriki: Similarities and Differences

Adolescent male circumcision is almost universal among the Abaluyia tribes, but only the Tiriki have taken over the Nandi-type initiation practices essentially without modification, and only the Tiriki have through the years fought mission-inspired efforts to change or eliminate the traditional initiation. The Friends and other Protestant mission groups have opposed or worked to modify circumcision and initiation customs among all the Abaluyia tribes, but only among the Tiriki has their interference in this area unwittingly become a real stumbling block or deterrent to the acceptance of Christianity.

Generally in North Nyanza, Abaluyia have shed much of the
traditional ritual surrounding circumcision, just as they have
abandoned many aspects of the ancestor cult, and have merely
continued to insist upon the actual performance of male circumcision sometime after the onset of puberty; the missions,
for their part, have generally acquiesced to the Abaluyia
insistence on circumcision and have contented themselves with
merely urging their youthful members to be circumcised either
at a hospital or medical dispensary or at rites held by Christian
converts especially for Christians. All independent churches in
North Nyanza are at present, I believe, essentially neutralist in
their policy concerning circumcision, not regarding it as a
concern of the church. The Tiriki branches of the Israel and
Orthodox churches are partial exceptions to this because they
do go so far as to admonish their youth never to go to the
hospital or medical dispensary for circumcision, but instead
either to join in the Tiriki Christian ceremony conducted by
Sagwa (see pp. 138–40) or to be circumcised and initiated in
the traditional Tiriki non-Christian ceremony.

The Tiriki Israel leaders explicitly take the position that
circumcision ceremonies do not really fall within the province
of the church. They recommend that their youth follow a procedure as regards circumcision which will not conflict with
Tiriki custom, but they feel that the actual decision should be
up to the youth and his family rather than the church. It should
be noted, however, that Joseph Ganila is actively working for a
return to one circumcision and initiation ceremony for all
Tiriki youth to replace the present practice of separate rites for
Tiriki Christians and Tiriki pagans. He favours the establishment of a single ceremony short enough to be performed in its
entirety during the summer school vacation so as not to disadvantage Tiriki students. He feels that something could be
worked out which might incorporate Christian ritual while at
the same time preserving the essential features of the traditional
Terik-Tiriki initiation. Ganila feels that Chief Hezron, who like
himself was initiated in the traditional Tiriki manner and
favours such a combination, should be able to work out a
satisfactory new ceremony.

The Orthodox Church elders in Tiriki are said to favour the
traditional pagan form of Tiriki circumcision and initiation

ceremony. Unfortunately, I failed to obtain a comprehensive picture of the official view of the Orthodox Church in North Nyanza concerning circumcision; consequently, I cannot say in what manner or degree the Tiriki Orthodox leaders conform with or differ from the official position and the position of Orthodox congregations in other Abaluyia tribes.

The sex ratio of the Tiriki Israel and *Roho* parishes is generally about the same as in the Mission parishes; among the adults, women outnumber the men more than two to one, while in actual attendance at church services they generally outnumber the men about five to one. Clearly the women have generally had more to gain and less to lose through church membership than the men in Tiriki; thus it is not surprising to find this anomalous sex ratio. It will be recalled that Tiriki women were traditionally relegated to a secondary role in the ancestor cult. They had to content themselves with the subsidiary sacrificial and propitiatory rites held at the women's shrine situated by the senior wife's cooking stones for most of their religious needs, and with occasional sacrifices and rites held by the senior men of the homestead, perhaps partially on their behalf, at the homestead ancestral shrine. The Christian church not only has relieved its women members of any religious dependence upon the menfolk of the homestead but also apparently has made them feel that they are participating fully in the really important religious rites and worship of the times. It will be recalled that in addition, women were freed of all beer brewing obligations by joining the Protestant missions. The Israel Church offers the women of Tiriki the same general religious and social advantages as Protestant mission church membership, with perhaps a few additional new and appealing elements of ritual; but it provides no major rituals or religious practices not already widely followed by one or another of the mission churches. Even dream interpretation and spirit possession are widely practised in some of the mission-affiliated parishes, particularly those of the Pentecostals, albeit not always with the full support or knowledge of the European missionaries. Thus the current success of the Israel Church in drawing women members from the mission churches and other separated churches seems to be based primarily on the more compatible nature of the Tiriki Israel leadership. I shall speak more of this later in the chapter.

Now that the Israel Church has established a substantial and rapidly growing membership in Tiriki, undoubtedly some women are switching to Israel because it seems to be the coming church, and others are following co-wives, neighbourhood friends and work partners into the Israel Church so that their old patterns of sociability and cooperation will be disrupted as little as possible.

The sex ratio of the Orthodox Church membership in Tiriki affords a striking contrast to all the other denominations in the tribe, both mission affiliated and separatist; women in this sect barely outnumber the men. Another striking aspect of Tiriki Orthodox membership is its large proportion of elderly people, especially older men. Many of the men in the Tiriki Orthodox congregation are approaching, or have already reached, the judicial elder age grade. Generally Tiriki men who were Christians in their younger days have forsaken or been deprived of Church membership by the time they become active as judicial elders—in the majority of cases because they have started attending the elders' beer parties or because they have become polygynists. The Catholics in Tiriki also have a high proportion of elderly members, but in contrast to the Orthodox Church, the aged adherents are mostly women. It is noteworthy, however, that several Tiriki judicial and ritual elders, highly respected by their pagan peers, are avowed Catholics.

Catholic and Orthodox policies have one common element which is at variance with all other Christian groups in Tiriki, namely, they have no testimony against alcoholic beverages. They make no effort to prohibit the production of African beer, nor do they try in any way to discourage or curb the consumption of African or European type beer or any sort of alcoholic beverage so long as their use does not appear to be excessive or conducive to disorderly social behaviour. Given the advantages to be gained by younger women from belonging to a church which prohibits its members either to brew or consume beer, it is probable that the membership of younger women in the Catholic and Orthodox denominations is discouraged by the absence of such a prohibition. Conversely, Tiriki women past child-bearing age have always been allowed to have their own beer pot at local drinks and occasionally, when the senior elders feel inclined to permit them to do so, even to join the circle drinking from the main pot. The old women traditionally helped organize and supervise the brewing activities of the younger women, but they were not (and are not) expected to supply the labour for brewing. Thus the elderly women who like beer are able to avoid or rebuff taunts of other women that they are 'ignorant pagans' and receive whatever other personal satisfactions may accrue through joining the Catholic or Orthodox Church, while at the same time not forfeiting their beer-drinking prerogatives.

Prohibitions against the use of alcohol serve to curtail the church membership of middle aged and elderly Tiriki men. Those older Tiriki men who are unwilling to lose or weaken their elder's status by withdrawing from social and ritual beer drinking may join the Catholic or Orthodox Church with impunity.

The Orthodox Church not only allows beer drinking but also is the only Christian sect in Tiriki which condones polygyny and in no way penalizes its polygynist members. Polygyny, of course, is not crucial to the attainment of full status as a Tiriki elder, but it is usually a distinct advantage for an elder to have a younger wife to help with the farm work and homestead chores. Also elders of substance and vigour are expected to inherit a deceased clan brother's wife, or at least they are viewed with more favour by their peers if they are willing to do so. Many Tiriki elders are polygynists. Thus it seems probable that the Orthodox Church's success in drawing elder male members is in part due to its permitting polygyny. The Orthodox Church indeed has a higher proportion of elderly male members than all other Christian sects, including the Catholics; but its total membership (as of 1956) remains comparatively small. The relatively large proportion of elders in the Catholic Church and the even higher proportion in the Orthodox Church suggest that restrictions against drinking and polygyny deter elders from joining other Christian groups. Granted this probability, it becomes striking that the vast majority of Tiriki elders prefer to remain pagan, even in those portions of the tribe where the Catholic and Orthodox denominations have flourishing parishes. Thus it would seem that none of the Christian sects have much appeal for most of the Tiriki elders; they mostly seem to find what remains of the traditional religious practices sufficient for their needs, or at least preferable to what the Catholic or Orthodox churches offer them.[1]

Unfortunately it was impossible for me to ascertain with accuracy the total membership of any of the churches of Tiriki. Records or accurate information on church membership by tribal group do not exist for the Friends or the Pentecostals. The other church groups have records from which one can obtain a fair picture of total membership of people living within the tribal boundaries of Tiriki, but criteria by which members are distinguished from attenders, novices or catechists vary with each denomination. Thus the ranked estimates of church group size which I give below must be labelled 'impressionistic', based as they are on varying sorts of information, both written and oral, and on personal observation. The estimates include children from early school age (6–7) on up and regular attenders as well as official members. In other words the estimates are intended to reflect the number of 'self-proclaimed' affiliates or members of the different denominations, as of 1956.

The Salvation Army and the Friends lead the list, probably with several thousand affiliates and members each. The Israels and the Pentecostals are second, both with about a thousand Tiriki followers. The Catholics are third, with five hundred catechists and members. The Orthodox is fourth, with two or three hundred adherents; and the *Dini Ya Roho* is smallest with probably not more than a hundred Tiriki affiliates. The small number of Catholic converts can be attributed in part to the rather short time that a Catholic priest has been resident in Tiriki—only around ten years. The Friends, of course, have been resident and active in Tiriki since 1902, and the Salvation Army and Pentecostals have been proselytizing in the area for

---

[1] Developments since 1959 make it appear that fear of joining an organization suspected by the British Administration of having subversive connexions may have been the major deterrent to the elders joining the Tiriki Orthodox Church. In my brief return visit to Tiriki in June, 1961, I found that many erstwhile pagan elders have joined the Tiriki Orthodox since 1959, and several have become Orthodox parish priests. They are still polygynists, and still drink beer; but they now wear big cross pendants under their shirts, and faithfully attend the Orthodox service for worship every Sunday morning before going to beer. Apparently once the Mau Mau Emergency was declared over in 1959, many Tiriki elders, who had been increasingly attracted to the Tiriki Orthodox Church, no longer felt afraid of being members of an organization with former Kikuyu connexions, and quickly joined the Church.

more than twenty-five years. Clearly, however, the length of activity in Tiriki is not the major factor in a denomination's success. The Israel Church, which established its first parish in Tiriki only eight years ago, now far exceeds the Catholics in its number of Tiriki adherents; and conversely, the *Dini Ya Roho*, which has been active in Tiriki for almost twenty-five years, has the smallest Tiriki following of any established church group in the tribe. The Israel Church, Tiriki Branch, while still far behind the Friends and the Salvation Army in total number of Tiriki adherents, is at present drawing many converts from all the other denominations in Tiriki and appears to be far exceeding all of them in its current rate of membership (and affiliate) increase.

The Success of the Tiriki, Israel Church

I shall now endeavour to sort out the principal factors under-lying the popularity and rapid growth of the Israel Church in Tiriki. Quite clearly prohibiting alcohol tends to favour the growth of church membership, attracting several younger women for each elder they repel. Also, rules against polygyny probably tend to attract more people than they discourage. The Israel Church follows the lead of the Protestant missions in Tiriki in its rules against polygyny and also in its official stand against alcohol. (In Israel as well as the Mission churches, a woman can be married to a polygynist without affecting her church standing; but a pagan polygynist who is converted to the Israel church is forbidden to take any more wives upon pain of excommunication, and he is not allowed to assume a position of leadership in the church unless he divorces all but one wife.) Rules against polygyny are probably viewed with favour by the majority of younger women in Tiriki since they are claimed, particularly by mission preachers, to help elevate the dignity and status of women's position in society and to be a mark of 'civilization'. Also they probably have a certain appeal for the younger men because they tend to foster not only a decrease of the status within the family of the old men relative to the younger men, but also they help disbar most elders of high repute within the community from membership within the church, thereby leaving most leadership positions within the church vacant for the younger men. Similarly, prohibitions against drinking work to preserve church leadership for the younger men since community beer drinks, in any case, have not yet become of much ritual and social importance to them. The prohibition against alcoholic beverages is seldom broken by Israel members, either through attendance at the local community beer drinks or through drinking at informal beer and liquor parties of the younger men, but clearly the prohibition is commonly ignored by both Israel leaders and younger male members during the initiation ceremonies. Israel leaders concentrate on proscribing participation in everyday beer drinks and on decrying the evils of intoxication.

The Tiriki Israel Church has made few innovations in matters of ritual and dogma. Instead, its leaders have proven themselves highly adept at utilizing practices of other denominations of proven popularity. Also they carefully organize and conduct their worship services with a polish and flair superior, in my judgement, to that of *Dini Ya Roho* and the Salvation Army, and vastly superior to that of most mission church services. The special costumes, insignia, flags, marching and drumming are adaptations of Salvation Army practices, while the public confession of sins and the laying on of hands has, at one time or another, been practised by several mission groups, including the Friends. Pentecostal services supply a precedent for the seeking of visions and the extolling of trance-like states; dancing occurs widely in Pentecostal services and is not discouraged by the Pentecostal missionaries so long as it remains restrained enough to be viewed by them as a joyous inrushing of the Holy Spirit. The *Dini Ya Roho*, of course, considerably expanded the Pentecostal preoccupation with ecstatic religious worship and preceded the Israel Church in transferring much of the traditional Abaluyia concern with dreams and dream interpretation to a Christian context.

The rich ritual eclecticism of the Israel Church undoubtedly contributes to its present day success. Most important, however, to its rapid growth and substantial contemporary following is the peerless skill with which Joseph Ganila and his followers have developed a church organization in Tiriki which remains essentially respectable and legitimate in the eyes of both British Administrative officers and Tiriki mission Christians, while at the same time winning the general approval of the

Tiriki pagan elders. This is quite a *tour de force*, because the criteria of respectability and legitimacy are considerably different—although they overlap—in the case of each of these three groups.

The British Administration demands, above all else, that the churches be disciplined and maintain control over their members, and that the church leaders do not use their positions either to disguise or to sanction political activity. The European missionaries and most of their African converts are vehement in their denunciations of any separatist group which does not demand strict monogamy of its members; and, of course, the Protestant missions strongly denounce any deviation from alcoholic abstinence. In the doctrinal sphere there is a good deal of conflict between different mission groups, but they all oppose any deviation from a strict Trinitarian viewpoint, and all the Protestant sects are ill disposed towards any deviation from a rather fundamentalist and literal interpretation of the Bible.

The Tiriki elders vary enormously in the interest they take in details of the religious ritual and dogma of both mission and separatist churches; some are well informed sceptics or agnostics; the majority, however, feel rather indifferent about Christian theology and view differences between the different church groups as of doubtful significance. Most pagans simply judge church groups, both mission-affiliated and separatist, primarily by the sorts of Africans they recruit and utilize as church leaders. The criteria they use for evaluating the worthiness of church leaders are essentially the same that they apply to leaders in the tribal administrative bureaucracy. These criteria, very briefly, are as follows:

First, a worthy leader must be a member in good standing of the Tiriki age group organization; i.e., initiated in the traditional Tiriki manner, and a supporter of the true initiation customs and age group practices. Second, he must have skill as a leader of men; he must have social presence, be well spoken, and know how to keep a crowd in order. Third, he must be able to deal with the British Administration; he should have the respect and general support of the Administration so that he can be an effective spokesman for his constituents (his parishioners) in situations where their wishes or interests conflict with the fiats or policies of the Administration. Finally, he must champion the cause of education for Tiriki youth. Most of the contemporary Tiriki pagan elders are either illiterate or have received only the most rudimentary primary school education. They frequently and vociferously blame the missions and the mission schools for weakening the traditional respect of the youth for the elders' position and authority, but they almost universally recognize that positions of political and economic power and privilege increasingly fall to those with the most education, and constantly criticize the missions for not supplying more and better educational facilities for Tiriki youth.

The four criteria of leadership listed above are met only by a small minority of leaders and pastors in both mission and separatist churches. Most of the African leaders of mission churches in Tiriki are either people from other tribes who have no loyalty to Tiriki initiation and age groups, or they are Tiriki tribal apostates who have publicly revealed or disavowed the initiation secrets and in consequence been cursed by the elders. In contrast, the top leadership in Tiriki of both the Orthodox and the Israel separatist churches are in the hands of men of good standing in the age group organization, but they are the only two sects in Tiriki where this condition is widely met. The head of the Tiriki Orthodox church, like Joseph Ganila the Tiriki Israel head, is a skilful and commanding leader; but the Orthodox Church, unlike the Tiriki Israel Church, is so suspect because of its erstwhile Kikuyu connexions that the British Administration tends to discredit the worthiness or loyalty of its leaders, thus strongly limiting their effectiveness as intermediaries between their parishioners and members of the Administration. In addition the principal Tiriki leaders of the Orthodox Church, in contrast to the top level Israel leaders, are either little interested in or unable to campaign effectively for an increase in the quality and number of schools. With little or no schooling themselves, they are further handicapped from the outset in any campaigning they do for more schools by the widely remembered role that their parent church, *Dini Karinga*, took in developing the now proscribed independent schools in Kikuyu. Thus of all the church groups in Tiriki, only the Israel Church, Tiriki Branch, has top leadership which the elders truly respect and trust.

The British Administration in Kenya has viewed all church

groups, both mission affiliated and separatist, with considerable uneasiness since the outbreak of Mau Mau; and the North Nyanza Administration makes an effort to keep close tabs on all church activity in the District. The Israel Church, however, probably has the best reputation in District Administrative circles of all the separatist churches. Most of the credit for this must go to Daudi Kivuli, the founder and High Priest of the Israel Church. Under his firm and talented leadership, *Dini Israel* had grown, even before Ganila's conversion in 1948 and its subsequent spread to Tiriki, into a disciplined and, relative to other separatist sects, conservative church with a fairly large following in Nyangori and Maragoli. Kivuli has proved singularly successful among separatist leaders in preventing disgruntled elements within Israel parishes from breaking off and forming separatist splinter groups. Today (1956) the Administration feels that the *Dini Israel* is one separatist church which can be fairly well depended on not to foster or countenance political subversion among its members or to produce quixotic cult groups which might quickly mushroom and spawn anti-European or other troublesome movements. Certainly in Tiriki most people today are very much concerned about whether or not they belong to or are considering joining an organization which is looked on with suspicion by the Administration. Younger men don't want to jeopardize their chances of finding desirable jobs and attaining administrative posts by becoming involved in a religious group which is, or might well be later, proscribed or labelled as subversive. The women do not concern themselves much with such economic and political considerations, but they generally do want to belong to a church in which testimony presented on their behalf before the African district court or the local elders will be viewed with favour.

In the sphere of education, all the separatist churches are handicapped by their inability to run schools of their own. Even in cases where separatist churches might find funds and personnel to run their own schools, the District Administration under its current policy does not allow them to open schools. European missions run nearly all schools in the district, and in Tiriki the mission monopoly on education is complete. Chief Hezron has hopes eventually of establishing a non-denominational District Education Board school there, and in theory at least, all schools regardless of their denominational affiliation accept and retain students solely on the basis of their academic merit, provided they do not prove to be major disciplinary problems. I found no conclusive evidence that the mission schools at present practice favouritism towards their own members, but many people in Tiriki feel they favour the children of their affiliates. In any event, the separatist churches suffer considerable loss of prestige in many African's eyes because they are obliged to depend on mission schools for the education of their younger members. Kivuli, Ganila, and most of the lesser leaders in the Israel Church do everything they can to encourage and facilitate the schooling of the children in their congregations. Both Kivuli and Ganila accept with apparent good grace the refusal of the Administration to allow them to start schools of their own at the present time and rationalize the reasonableness of this position with their parishioners by pointing out the financial burden it would put upon the congregation, even with a District Education Board subvention. They also stress the difficulties of finding properly qualified teachers, and the pitfalls of settling for anything less than the best possible teachers. Ganila has let it be known that he feels the District education authorities will probably permit *Dini Israel* to open some schools before long, but that the really important thing is to support Chief Hezron's efforts to get a District Education Board school in Tiriki, and to fight for the proliferation of non-denominational schools throughout the tribe and the district. In other words, Ganila champions the cause of education and at the same time tries to make a virtue of Israel's having no schools by on the one hand campaigning for more and better schools of all sorts and intimating that *Dini Israel* could very soon start its own schools if it wants to, and on the other hand by declaring it is a positive and progressive virtue not to be involved in parochial education because non-affiliated District Education Board schools are a much more satisfactory sort of solution in the long run.

One controversial area remains to be discussed in this evaluation of the Israel Church's current success in Tiriki, namely the position of the dream or vision prophet (*mungoli*) and the utilization of his revelations. It is fairly characteristic of reformers and ambitious leaders, both in mission-affiliated congregations and

separatist sects in North Nyanza, to claim that divine sanction
for their actions has been bestowed upon them in a dream or
vision sent by God. Both the missionaries and the District
Administration have come to view with suspicion any Christian
leader (and to suspect even more any secular leader) who claims
divine insight and sanction for his actions directly bestowed
through his dreams or visions. They generally feel that the early
Pentecostal missionaries in North Nyanza unwittingly spawned
a monster by preaching and encouraging the great value of
direct mystical revelation and insight. Of course, nothing comparable to the pandemic traditional Abaluyia concern with
dreams and dream interpretation existed in the American and
Canadian backgrounds of these Pentecostal missionaries. At
first they were surprised and delighted, and then appalled and
worried, along with the administrators and missionaries of
other denominations, by the almost explosive speed and force
with which their notions were accepted, modified and utilized
by Abaluyia Christians.

Most of the responsible elements in Tiriki, including the
pagan Tiriki elders, are as profoundly disturbed as the missionaries and District Administration by the tendency of disgruntled
or ambitious religious leaders to see support for themselves
through dreams and visions. Clearly part of their concern is
derived from their knowledge of the Administration's current
attitude towards such things and their desire to avoid the close
government surveillance which befell the more conspicuous
supporters and followers of the dream-inspired prophet of the
anti-European *Dini ya Misambwa* after its suppression in 1948.
In addition, however, the Tiriki traditionally regarded dreams
and visions as always subject to the interpretation of the ritual
elders and never in themselves as bestowing authority, either
religious or political, upon the dreamer or prophet. The Tiriki
claim that they alone among the Abaluyia tribes subordinated
and controlled dream prophecy and interpretation in such a
circumscribed manner.

Traditionally a man occasionally came along in Tiriki who
earned a reputation for himself as a prophet (*mungoli*) because
his dreams or visions, as evaluated and interpreted by the elders,
so often seemed to predict correctly future events, or shed insight
on one or another imminent social problem. In this manner a

man's fame as a prophet occasionally spread, but always his prophecies carried ritual or political authority only so long as they were endorsed by the tribal elders. The Tiriki say that there were never any instances among the Tiriki themselves of prophets assuming the roles of ritual or political leaders by virtue of their powers of prophecy, but they claim that prophets did occasionally usurp special positions of great authority among the Nandi and Terik.

Joseph Ganila, alone among all the church leaders in Tiriki, has consistently utilized prophecy in a manner which conforms with the pagan elders' tradition derived expectations, namely to re-enforce but never directly to establish his priestly authority. It was noted earlier in this chapter that Johana Inyanje, Ganila's first assistant, is a man of great personal charm and eloquence who is prone to have dreams and visions. Inyanje's dreams, always subject to the interpretation and veto of Ganila himself, are most likely a drawing card to Tiriki Israel membership and probably have further stimulated the interest in and growth of dream confession and interpretation within the Tiriki Israel Church. Ganila himself does not dream; his God-given genius, he asserts, is his reason. It is his role, he claims, to determine, with God's aid, whether a particular dream is a revelation from God or from Satan, and if from God, to interpret its message. Ganila helps maintain the devoted following of the feminine portion of his congregation through his eloquent prophet assistant. But it is through his successful subordination of mystical revelation to his own priestly authority that Ganila has won much of the confidence and approval of his clerical subordinates and the respect of the Tiriki pagan elders.

Ganila's control over and utilization of powers of prophecy have given vision and dream prophecy a strictly subordinate but nevertheless legitimate and meaningful place within the framework of the Tiriki Israel Church. He has apparently not only assuaged the British Administration's concern about such activities but also evoked the tacit, if not active, support of the pagan tribal elders because he manages them in a way which is consonant with traditional practice.

VIII

The Tiriki Authority Structure

MOST of the ultimate power sanctions in Tiriki have shifted during the last fifty years from the religious realm, presided over by the ritual elders, to the political realm, over which the British have final authority. True, the status and role of women has in large part been preserved and enhanced through the Christian churches, but church leadership, which is of course in the hands of the men, has in no way succeeded in establishing itself on a par with the British-sponsored tribal government in Tiriki.

The Tiriki elders are clearly willing at present to support the British authorities and the tribal administration which they have evolved because the British have maintained a semblance of their traditional prestige in the face of erosive forces such as the appearance of hostile missionaries, and indifferent or hostile mission-educated African converts. The tribal elders, in turn, continue to serve as an important judicial adjunct to, and legitimizing force for the contemporary tribal bureaucracy. The tremendous growth of new networks of social interaction and new types of activities and inter-dependencies, especially in the economic sphere, both within the tribe and with people living beyond, has produced a situation that demands administrative and legislative institutions not found in the indigenous political structure.

Neither tribal government nor even sub-tribal legislative bodies as such, can be said to have existed in Tiriki in pre-European times. Sub-tribal councils of warriors and elder warriors were occasionally held with judicial and ritual elders for purposes of augury and divination prior to cattle raids. These councils, while instrumental to the starting of a raid or series of raids, did not in themselves alter the normal pattern of conventional social obligations or responsibilities, and thus they could hardly be classed as legislative groups. Special larger meetings involving warriors and elders from two or more sub-tribes were occasionally held in times of crisis caused, for example, by a series of devastating enemy raids, by prolonged drought, by an epidemic, or by some other natural disaster which disrupted the normal cycle of activities. At such times special patterns of inter-community and inter-sub-tribal co-operation might be temporarily established, courses of military or economic action evolved, and/or evocative or lustral rituals developed to destroy the witches and solicit the aid of the ancestral spirits. Any initiated Tiriki could speak at such a crisis meeting, and in matters of warfare the advice of distinguished warriors and elder warriors was heavily counted upon. Final responsibility for the people's well-being, however, rested in the hands of the judicial and ritual elders; and their active support or at least passive acceptance was needed before propositions of younger members of the tribe were generally accepted and carried out. Such general meetings of warriors and elders of several sub-tribes held at times of crisis were the nearest thing the Tiriki had to tribal government.

The British, by appointing Tiriki war leaders to serve as tribal Chiefs and sub-tribal headmen during the initial years of their administration, indeed chose men who would have been expected to initiate action in situations connected with raiding and defence, but they thereby removed the ultimate tribal judicial and legislative authority from the elders and conferred it upon a single man of a junior age grade. Thus the Tiriki Chiefs were not only subject to censure and dismissal by the British (as are all Abaluyia Chiefs) but they were also more dependent on the British than many (perhaps all) other Abaluyia Chiefs for any authority within the tribe, other than that which the tribal elders might choose to extend to them as their military representative. The tribal Chiefs prior to Amiani are not remembered today as either having ignored the elders' wishes or having failed or refused to show the tact and deference traditionally expected when dealing with their elders. Amiani, however, not only used his British-conferred powers to increase his personal wealth and the number of his dependent followers, often at the expense of other Tiriki, but also followed some policies quite inimical to the wishes of most of the Tiriki elders. As has been seen, the British authorities failed to support his stand on initiation because of the riots it engendered, and finally removed him from the Chieftaincy when unrest became so widespread that the District Commissioner and others became convinced that Amiani was no longer able to keep the peace within the tribe.

From the time when the British first established a tribal Chieftaincy in Tiriki until 1947, the Chief and the tribal elders have served as the *de facto* legislative body of the tribe, with the traditional power of the elders generally proving subordinate to the British-conferred authority of the Chief. In 1947 this situation was somewhat changed through the formal establishment in Tiriki of a tribal advisory body known as the Tiriki Location Advisory Council. The Tiriki and other tribal advisory councils are the extension to the tribal level of the sort of advisory council that was first established in North Nyanza at the district level in 1924. The district council, known as the Local Native Council until 1951, and since then as the African District Council, is comprised of the Chief and generally two other representatives from each tribe in the district.

The African District Council (A.D.C.) has assumed over the years a position of fairly great influence and prestige in the eyes of the Tiriki. All the major economic and social affairs of the district are debated by this group, and certain district administrative tasks, such as the care of many of the roads, and the regulation of the principal tribal markets, are permanently under its jurisdiction. To be sure, the motions and decisions of the A.D.C. are always subject to the modification and veto of the District Commissioner, who is the permanent president of the council. Because its legislative functions are strictly subordinate to the authority of the District Commissioner, its activities in effect are limited to debate, recommendation, and the regulation of certain established responsibilities such as tribal markets. Representatives to the A.D.C. are appointed by the tribal Chiefs in consultation with their headmen and tribal elders; the District Commissioner reserves the right to veto unsuitable appointments.

Ever since its founding in 1924, appointees to the A.D.C. from Tiriki have tended not only to be chosen from the younger and relatively more educated segment of the tribe, but also until Hezron became Chief in 1946 they were allied to the Chief by kinship, or some other fairly clearcut personal bond.

Advisory councils were extended to the tribal level in 1948 and 1949, largely through the British-encouraged efforts of the

African District Council. In A.D.C. debates held during 1948 it was decided that the establishment of tribal location advisory councils should be encouraged in all Abaluyia tribes. It was also decided that all tribal matters should be discussed by the Location Advisory Councils of their respective tribes before being brought to the A.D.C. In 1949 rules for the Location Advisory Councils were formalized in a constitution drawn up and ratified by the African District Council. The constitution laid down the rules both for the selection of Location Advisory Council (L.A.C.) members and for the general duties and responsibilities of the Location Advisory Councils.[1] The L.A.C.s

[1] The constitution for the Location Advisory Councils specifies that members of each Location Advisory Council should be selected as follows:

Two members are to be elected from each of the *olugongo* areas (sub-tribal areas), two members are to be appointed by the Chief, and two members are to be appointed by the District Commissioner, all for three year terms.

The constitution goes on to say that Location Advisory Council members cannot have a record of any criminal convictions, and they may be removed for inefficiency with the approval of the District Commissioner. The A.D.C. members are also to be L.A.C. members, and the Chief is to act as the chairman of his tribe's L.A.C. The constitution specifies that the Chief is to follow the majority decision of the L.A.C., and that either the Chief or the L.A.C. members have the right to appeal a decision to the A.D.C. (Jack Mowrer, *The North Nyanza African District Council* (E.A.I.S.R. Library, Makerere College, Kampala, Uganda: unpublished manuscript, 1954), pp. 25–26).

The North Nyanza Location Advisory Councils derive revenue from a rate collected at the same time as the annual poll tax. The money from the rate is used to pay the salary of a L.A.C. secretary, for educational assistance to those families too poor to pay tuition fees for their children, for tribal athletic programmes, for subsistence fees to L.A.C. members (transportation and food allowances are, for example, paid to each Tiriki L.A.C. member every time he attends a L.A.C. meeting), for community development, stationery costs, and miscellaneous expenses.

The nature of community development varies from tribe to tribe. In Tiriki, for example, an historical committee was established in 1954 as part of the tribal community development programme. The committee was established ostensibly to record Tiriki history for posterity while some of the old men are still alive who remember the tribal traditions as they were before the coming of the Europeans. Most of the L.A.C. community development money set aside for this committee was spent paying travelling and food allowances to the elders selected to partake in the meetings, and paying a modest salary to an appointed secretary of the committee whose job it was to arrange the meetings and record the historical information agreed upon by the elders. Tiriki elders seldom feel inclined to dwell for long upon historical matters without the euphoria engendered by African beer and the occasional additional reward of some freshly slaughtered mutton or beef, so the expenses incurred by historical committee activities were substantial, amounting in 1955 to a total of sh. 1,272/- (seven shillings to one dollar).

One might well argue that an historical committee could not be considered part of community development, but Chief Hezron was quite eloquent in his

are indeed primarily *advisory* bodies, advising both their respective Chiefs and the A.D.C. The advice of a tribe's L.A.C.,
for example, is usually followed by the A.D.C. in matters such
as the selection of sites for new schools, churches and markets
within the tribe. Also the L.A.C.'s recommendations as to who
should get licences to open new shops in A.D.C. markets within
the tribe are usually approved.

The Tiriki L.A.C. appears at first glance to be little more than
a sounding board for Chief Hezron's policies and decisions.
Indeed, even unpopular innovations introduced by Chief
Hezron on orders from his British superiors, such as the implementation of laborious soil conservation measures or an
increase in the annual poll tax, are generally accepted and
supported by the L.A.C. members with a minimum of dissent.
Only nine of the twenty-one members of the Tiriki Location
Advisory Council (twenty-two when the Chief himself is
included) are more or less directly beholden to the Chief for
their Council appointments[2]; the majority who do not hold their
office by virtue of the Chief are nevertheless generally as supporting of the Chief as the others. Most of the Tiriki L.A.C.

---

assertions that the future well-being of a tribe could be greatly aided by a proper
understanding and appreciation of its own history. Almost certainly the establishment and most of the activities of the Tiriki historical committee in 1954–56 did
much to increase the elders' feeling that they were again receiving some of the
respect and the honour from the tribe which they feel is their due.

The Tiriki historical committee was established in Tiriki primarily through the
efforts of Chief Hezron and the L.A.C. They were much encouraged, to be sure,
by a sympathetic British District Officer, John Rowlins. The historical committee
was started before any plans had been made to undertake an anthropological
study in Tiriki. Indeed one small factor furthering the decision to choose Tiriki
as a site for anthropological research was the interest of the tribe in their own
history as manifest by their establishment of the historical committee. My wife and
I were welcomed by the historical committee, and particularly during the first
months in Tiriki we worked in close conjunction with it. Quite aside from the
considerable information we gained from attendance at the historical committee
meetings, the committee's existence and the welcome they gave us probably
considerably facilitated our initial acceptance by the tribe.

[2] Four of the total of sixteen regular Tiriki Location Advisory Councillors
(seventeen if one includes the Chief) are chosen by Chief Hezron (two are his
L.A.C. appointees, and two are his District Commissioner approved choices for the
A.D.C.), and in addition, the five Tiriki sub-locational headmen attend and participate as voting members in the Tiriki Location Advisory Council meetings;
this means there are nine Tiriki L.A.C. members directly or indirectly dependent
on the Chief for their L.A.C. appointments, out of a total of twenty on Tiriki
L.A.C. members (twenty-two if the Chief is included).

members are from the younger (elder warrior age grade), better-educated segment of the tribe, but this age group (with the exception of the Maragoli immigrants) regard Hezron as a champion of their interests just as much as the pagan elders do. The several members of the L.A.C. with Maragoli or anti-initiation sympathies have long since learned of the general disapproval engendered by letting either of these sympathies take an apparent part in their opinion formation. The contemporary (1955) Tiriki L.A.C. members either hold Hezron and most of his policies in the same high regard as do a majority of the tribe or they are aware enough of public sentiment to keep their disagreements to themselves. Whenever an issue comes up that is truly unpopular, Hezron is usually as acutely aware of this unpopularity as his councillors and works with them to forestall or modify the issue. When nothing can be done to forestall the unpopular move, Hezron generally declares it to be an inevitable change stemming either from higher British authorities or from economic or other factors lying outside the tribe's power to control or influence. Hezron's stature in the eyes of the L.A.C. and the tribe is great enough so that usually little further dissent arises on such occasions.

A hierarchy of salaried bureaucratic tribal officials (see Chapter IV, pp. 109–15, for a description of this hierarchy) carry out most of the administrative duties of the contemporary Tiriki tribal government. They are responsible for the collection of the annual poll tax, for the implementation of any official edict or innovation such as a new soil conservation ordinance, and are the principal peace officers within their respective administrative areas. They are also the official judicial spokesmen of their areas; but here they defer to the opinion of the judicial elders, except on those occasions when they feel they can depend directly or indirectly on the power of the British Administration to back up their unpopular decisions. In the legislative field the salaried tribal officials have little real power, in spite of their membership in the Tiriki Location Advisory Council. Legislative activity in the tribe is still primarily initiated by the Chief, working together with his Location Advisory Councillors and in close collaboration with the British District Officer. The Chief is also always careful to solicit directly or through his councillors the opinion, and eventually the assent, of the judicial elders for legislative-type decisions. The elders, although they sometimes force a compromise upon the Chief, as they did over the issue of shortening the length of the initiation period (see Chapter V, p. 147), in the end either actively support or passively comply with the rulings of Chief Hezron. Most important, few of the elders question Hezron's right to make legislative decisions for the tribe so long as they are consulted when the decisions are being made.

The contemporary Tiriki governmental bureaucracy is able to implement and carry out certain organizational changes of a legislative type that the indigenous non-centralized political structure probably could not have handled successfully. No Tiriki, either young or old seriously wishes to return to the pre-European system of tribal controls, and most Tiriki seem quite content with the workings of the contemporary tribal political machinery. It will be recalled that the present-day tribal government was not designed specifically with the Tiriki in mind; rather, it is a system the British have evolved for the district as a whole to bring orderly centralized government to the segmentary type tribes of North Nyanza, while at the same time (in accordance with the British ideals of 'indirect rule') preserving and utilizing as much of the indigenous authority systems as feasible.

All evidence indicates that the British administrators believed that Tiriki, along with the other Abaluyia tribes, were primarily organized on a clan basis. They assumed since tribal Chieftaincies were conspicuously absent (with the exception of the Wanga tribe), that each Abaluyia tribe was controlled politically by several major genealogically-linked clans of roughly equal influence and authority. In every tribe the British administrators attempted to find a leader of one of the major clans (the seniormost or most influential clan, if there was such) to act as tribal Chief. Then, through the decades, several successive systems of administrative hierarchies have been instituted for the Abaluyia to aid the tribal Chiefs in maintaining effective tribal government. The current (1956) hierarchy is, of course, the *olugongo* system, consisting in practice of salaried Chief, headmen, sub-headmen, and unsalaried *maguru*, with the Location Advisory Councillors (who receive no salary for acting in this capacity) serving as legislative advisors to the Chief (see

Chapter IV, pp. 103–6, 109–10, for an account of the nature of the different tribal administrative systems that were successively instituted in Tiriki and the other Abaluyia tribes). These administrative systems have worked with varying success in different tribes over the years, and there is no reason to believe that the contemporary system does not work as well in most tribes as any of those tried previously. In Tiriki, however, the contemporary system seems to be working very much better than in other Abaluyia tribes which have been subjected to roughly similar sorts of European contact and economic change. It seems appropriate, therefore, to point out some of the unique aspects of the indigenous Tiriki social structure that may have made it easier for the Tiriki to adjust themselves to and utilize the contemporary British-imposed tribal political system.

The substitution of the *olugongo* system for the preceding *mlango* system (see Chapter IV, pp. 101–10) encouraged the establishment of tribal subdivisions on the basis of territory, divorced from clan affiliation, and consequently also indirectly helped discourage nepotism in the recruitment of tribal officials. A series of rather diffuse criteria, centring principally around social presence, a commanding personality, integrity, responsibility, and European-type schooling, became the principal official requirements for leadership candidacy. The *olugongo* system of tribal administration and leadership recruitment is of course quite in keeping with the traditional Tiriki pattern of subordinating clan and kinship loyalties to more inclusive, initiation-based loyalties and of applying primarily criteria of suitable age, personality and demonstrated competence when choosing a leader.

Two factors apparently underlay the British decision to shift from the *mlango* to the *olugongo* system of tribal administration. First, in most tribes, officials selected according to clan tended to dispense administrative largess and judicial decisions on the basis of their clan and lineage affiliation, leaving the members of the smaller clans and lineages also residing in each administrative region greatly disadvantaged. Second, under the *mlango* system the British-appointed tribal Chief, generally selected from the largest or the apparently most influential clan of the tribe, was given no new explicit power sanction through which he could obtain the immediate loyalty of people other than his own clansmen. Of course, he had the mercenary police force the British allowed him to keep, and he also had the ultimate backing of British military forces, but so long as the traditional concepts of clanship were being officially upheld as the legitimate basis for political power within the tribe the Chiefs were generally obliged to look to their own clansmen or to mercenaries for most of their immediate aid and support. The formal structure of the *mlango* system seemed to reinforce the traditional predominant Abaluyia pattern of a non-centralized 'stateless' tribal organization where the major clan groups were in 'segmentary opposition'.[1] It supplied no new organizational symbols or concepts through which tribal regions could readily adapt themselves to centralized tribal political systems. Left unchecked, the multiple clan-based foci of loyalties that prevailed in each tribe under the *mlango* system tended to cancel each other out (just as they did in pre-European times) leaving the tribal Chief a rather ineffectual political figure. The Tiriki were fortunate in already having a nascent basis for pan-tribal corporate action, and criteria for the appointment of and loyalty towards leaders which subordinated clan affiliation to other considerations.

The frequency of nepotism is perhaps as great in Tiriki as in most other Abaluyia tribes, but in Tiriki nepotistic considerations carry much less weight in political and judicial decisions. Given a choice between two equally qualified men, a Tiriki will always lend his support to the man who is his clansman or close kinsman, but a Tiriki who develops fixed political loyalties on this basis is subject to the ridicule not only of tribesmen of other clans but of many of his own clansmen as well. Probably the Tiriki tendency to give only secondary consideration to clan and kin loyalties was a significant factor in Amiani's ability to build up a strong tribal following prior to his repudiation of the initiation customs, and most likely it is instrumental in Hezron's success and popular support even in those parts of Tiriki where his own clan (*Bamuli*) is hardly represented at all.

Another factor which may have facilitated the Tiriki's acceptance of the contemporary tribal bureaucracy is the Tiriki age grading system. This not only delegates social roles and

[1] See M. Fortes and E. E. Evans-Pritchard, eds., *African Political Systems* (London: Oxford University Press, 1940), pp. 13–15.

responsibilities on the basis of age and thereby establishes a simple division of authority on a basis other than clan or lineage affiliation,[1] but more important, it gives a fairly clearcut precedent for middle-aged men (men roughly of the 35 to 50 year age bracket) filling the organizational and administrative positions that have been created by the tribal bureaucracies. Certainly today it is primarily men of this age bracket (those who in traditional times would for the most part have been the elder warriors) who hold most of the administrative posts within the British-sanctioned tribal government. Men of this age grade would in traditional times have been organizers of community defence and advisers and councillors to the warrior age grade. Today, as traditionally, it is men of this age grade who chair the meetings (*zimbego*) held a number of months after an important man's death to decide about the distribution of his property and care of his family.[2] Consequently the British preference for younger men for bureaucratic tribal posts is felt to be proper and fitting. It is generally seen, not as an usurpation of the major power positions from the elders by the younger men, but instead as an appropriate assumption of an ever-increasing number of executive duties by those men just junior to the elders, men who, after all, always have performed such functions.

A final factor probably of significance to the smooth running of contemporary tribal affairs in Tiriki is the degree to which organizational activities are still handled in a manner harmonious with the traditional social structure.[3] Traditionally the middle-aged men generally took a more active role than the elders in the initiation of new social action as well as in carrying

[1] One can argue that role authority divisions based on age can be found in all societies; nevertheless Tiriki age grading gives a more formal, more openly proclaimed, and more elaborated set of role divisions based on age than those found in other Abaluyia tribes.

[2] The judicial and ritual elders act as the final judges at such meetings, but a younger man is chosen to act as the spokesman and mouthpiece for the elders. Except that he be a member of the deceased's clan, the choice of spokesman is not made on the basis of genealogical propinquity to the deceased, but rather an effort is made to find a well spoken younger man of good character, sagacity and tact.

[3] Here I am using 'organizational' and 'structure' in a manner consonant, I believe, with Professor Firth's use of the terms 'social organization' and 'social structure'. See Raymond Firth, *J.R.A.I.*, Jan–June, 1954, pp. 9–17, and Robert Redfield, *The Little Community* (Chicago: University of Chicago Press, 1955), pp. 34, 42–43.

it out; but for such social action to become firmly established and widely accepted, the active approval, or at least the passive assent, of the elders had to be attained. To be sure, the sort of organizational decision or social innovation being proposed partly determined what age group would be most actively involved in its consideration and inception. Even in the religious realm, however, which was traditionally the province of the eldest members of the community, younger men sometimes played important roles as innovators. The following is an illustration:

It will be recalled from Chapter VII (p. 222) that traditionally there were a small number of men in Tiriki, some young, and some older, who were recognized by the ritual elders as having powers of prophecy. It was believed that this power was granted them by the ancestral spirits. These prophets (*bangoli*) received messages from the ancestral spirits through dreams (*maloro, li- ma- -loro*) or visions (*maloli, li- ma- -loli*). The power of prophecy was not believed to be inherited, and thus was not confined to particular clans or lineages. A prophet became known as such through revealing to the ritual elders one or more of his dreams and visions that he felt gave portent of some future event. If such a prophecy were actually fulfilled, ritual elders began to take an active interest in the person's dreams and visions, and thenceforth any dream or vision he might have that seemed to shed light on the outcome of a future event or a proposed project such as a cattle raid, was given careful consideration by the ritual elders. Thus slowly a person might gain a reputation as a prophet. The elders always retained the right to interpret or reject the dreams and visions of a prophet, and there is no memory of a major community project or innovation having been undertaken in traditional times solely on the basis of a prophet's dream or message. Even when a prophet reached elderhood it was necessary, before he could successfully recruit others to take action on the basis of his vision or dream, for him to have the continuing endorsement of other ritual elders for the insight or innovation that his prophetic powers revealed. Thus a prophet, whether young or old, could offer assurances or even suggestions for new modes of social action on the basis of his special visions, but the elders, particularly the ritual elders, always decided whether and how such insights might be used.

Today there are no longer any pagan *bangoli* to be found in

Tiriki, but there are a few men recognized as such within Christian religious groups. Within churches in Tiriki, contrary to instances in other Abaluyia tribes, the Christian dream prophet (*mungoli*) has been relatively unsuccessful in achieving and maintaining church leadership primarily through his prophetic powers. Several proclaimed Christian prophets, however, such as Johana Inyanje cited in Chapter VII (p. 197), have become honoured assistants to church leaders. These church leaders use their prophet assistants, much as the ritual elders did, to support and confirm their own policies, even while deriving most of their authority as church leaders from other sources.

In traditional times younger men could be innovators in tribal affairs, not only in their own province of tribal defence, but also in the religious sphere, through becoming accepted as prophets. In all spheres, however, the general acceptance of a younger man's insights and suggestions was contingent upon the approval or at least the passive concurrence of the elders, while in the religious sphere the active sponsorship of the elders was demanded. In short, while people from all age groups might propose innovations to tribal custom and policy, the judicial and ritual elders held the final power of veto for all such innovations, and in the judicial and religious spheres their active endorsement was required.

Summary and Conclusions

Much or this chapter has been devoted to outlining the development and significance of the contemporary tribal bureaucracy. I shall conclude by reviewing several factors that probably have facilitated the incorporation of this alien structural complex into the Tiriki social system.

Fifty years ago most of the ultimate power sanctions of the tribe were in the hands of the elders; today a high proportion of the basic power sanctions have been transferred to the British administrators, with the tribal bureaucrats, and particularly the tribal Chief, acting as their agents. Superficially, at least, the younger men seem to have gained a great deal of power and the elders seem to have lost most of their power. Thus one would expect the prestige of the elders and the respect shown them by the tribe in general to have diminished a great deal, and

in consequence their utility as a judicial body and as arbiters of
local disputes to have shown a marked decline. This decline,
however, has not been nearly so great in Tiriki as in the other
southern Abaluyia tribes that have undergone comparable
European contact. Perhaps this is partly due to the Tiriki pagan
elders' experience in 1927 of having gained British Governmental sanction to continue the pagan initiation rites in spite of the
efforts of Chief Amiani to abolish the traditional ceremonies.
The 1927 experience clearly demonstrated to the Tiriki that,
although the elders were formally subordinate to their Chief in
political affairs, the Chief was subordinate to the British
Government, and that the British Government could be moved
to prevent a Chief taking action that violated the basic traditions of his tribe. The Tiriki elders look to the British Administration today, not with veneration or patriotic fervour, but with
a hardheaded appreciation of where the ultimate power sanctions now lie that do most to preserve the tribal *status quo*. They
clearly perceive that the ultimate tribal authority which once
lay in their hands now belongs to the British. They are inclined
to speak of the British Administration with respect and generally do what they can to bolster its prestige within the tribe.

Chief Hezron, for his part, strongly supports and regularly
utilizes the elders in their judicial capacity. He also tries,
whenever possible, to carry out political, economic, and social
reforms with the elders' active assent and aid. Thus Chief
Hezron, with British Administration backing, makes use of the
Tiriki elders' traditional roles as legitimizers of the innovations
and organizational decisions initiated and carried out by the
younger men. The elders, for their part, sensing that much of
their present status depends upon the backing they receive from
the British Administration and its tribal officers, tend to give
their full support to most of Chief Hezron's policy decisions.
For the present, at least, a felicitous mutually helpful balance
of power exists between the middle-aged men and the elders.
From the former are recruited the bureaucratic-type administrators who handle most of the executive and legislative tasks;
the tribal elders, in return, as it were, for being allowed to
retain most of their judicial duties and prerogatives, support
and lend their mantle of traditional legitimacy to most of the
administrators' decisions and innovations.

IX

The Contemporary Tiriki Leader

THE preceding three chapters have shown how the contemporary church groups and tribal government supplement and also conform to major elements of traditional Tiriki social structure. This chapter will outline briefly the nature of the principal contemporary community and tribal leadership roles in Tiriki (1954–1956), and will examine some of the implicit criteria which are usually fulfilled by people holding these positions. Two brief biographical sketches of church leaders and two sketches of administrative leaders of tribal renown will be presented. These will be followed by an outline of the 'modal' or typical career pattern of both church and administrative leaders, which will illustrate the important functions that church affiliation and leadership, and age group membership usually play in the attainment of tribal leadership.

Types of Contemporary Tiriki Community and Tribal Leadership

Leadership in every major field of social endeavour in Tiriki is restricted by the same sex and age qualifications that regulate the assumption of the principal social statuses and roles. A female, for example, has no possibility of gaining formal recognition as a community tribal leader; indeed, even informally a woman seldom achieves much continuing influence over menfolk outside of her homestead. To be sure, a few female herbalists enjoy a certain prestige in the eyes of the men within their own and immediately neighbouring communities; also within the framework of the Christian church organizations several elderly women are held in high esteem and informally exert considerable influence upon male as well as female members of their respective churches. With these few exceptions acknowledgement of any women as being personages of importance is strictly limited to the community or sub-community, and to exclusively women's affairs.

Age is also a factor that more stringently delimits leadership recruitment than it does in most societies where age grading is less formalized. The referential and vocative term *musaxulu*

237

which can be roughly translated as 'elder', is generally applied
to all men of the judicial age grade or older. Its feminine
equivalent, *mushele* (*mu- ba- -shele*) is normally used for all women
past childbearing age. Age in itself brings a certain social pre-
eminence. No matter how poor or disliked or how ineffective as
a judicial or ritual elder he may be, a man of the judicial or
ritual age grade will be addressed as 'elder', and will be shown
at least formally the deference and consideration due all elders
(the only regular exceptions to this are the feeble minded
(*basilo mu- ba- -silo*) and the insane (*balalu mu- ba- -lalu*) who
survive to an elderly age). Except for those elders living in
Tiriki who have not been initiated according to the Tiriki
custom or who have been cursed by the elders, active participation in all judicial affairs of the community and a place at the
elders' beer drinks are privileges open to all elders—and only to
elders.

Most elders, if their health permits, regularly attend the
judicial meetings (*biina shi- bi- -ina*) of their community and sub-
community, and also take their place around the elders' beer pot
when a beer drink (*malwa*) is held. At conversation over beer the
elders form and reaffirm opinions about current or pending
judicial cases and other community and tribal affairs. There are
generally about two dozen elders so occupied in each Tiriki
community. These elders are simply known as 'the community
elders' (*basaxulu wu luhya*), or as 'the important elders' (*basaxulu
bagali*—literally, the 'big elders'). Today several elders are often
to be found in a community who are neither welcomed at the
beer drinks nor regularly participate in the community judicial
proceedings either, because they are Christian leaders who scorn
such activities and/or because they have been cursed by the
elders. Such an elderly *persona non grata* is nevertheless generally
addressed and referred to as 'elder' (*musaxulu*), and is shown the
deference by all younger people generally granted people of his
age, though he is seldom considered or called a 'community
elder' (*musaxulu wu luhya*).

Any discussion of contemporary Tiriki leadership must begin
with a description of community leadership, for the community
(*luhya*) remains the social unit of most significance in preserving
the peace, administering justice, and in carrying out the edicts
and decisions initiated or transmitted by the members of the

British-spawned tribal bureaucracy. In most Tiriki communities one elder serves as the informal nexus of authority. This man, recognized by nearly all community members as being the person with most influence and prestige in community affairs, has no formal title, and as often as not lacks any major formal power position in the community or tribe. Such an informal community leader is apt to be either an older member of the judicial age grade or a younger member of the ritual age grade. Younger judicial elders are generally chosen to serve as sub-community *maguru*, and there are usually several ritual elders in the community senior in years to the informal community leader who are acknowledged to be the community's outstanding ritual leaders (*basaalisi bagali*). Further, such an informal community leader is usually not an initiation chief (*mwimili wi idumi*).

What, then, is the basis of the informal community leader's authority? In common with all important Tiriki leaders he must have social presence, be a persuasive public speaker, and also possess tact; further, he must have demonstrated over the years an extensive knowledge of traditional custom and judicial procedure. In short, he must be a person who is respected for his knowledge as well as for his eloquence. An informal community leader usually belongs to one of the larger clans in the community. Clan connexions are of aid in a number of ways to the attainment of high community status. For example, it adds to a man's reputation to have a large number of offspring; and the proximity of clansfolk facilitates the borrowing of cattle with which to pay bridewealth—an essential element in the acquisition of wives and legitimization of offspring. Seldom is the informal community leader the wealthiest man in the community either in terms of cash or cattle (*muruji, mu- ba- -ruji*), or in terms of homestead size and grain stores (*muhinda, mu- ba- -hinda*). Perhaps in pre-European times relatively great wealth was a more important factor in the attainment of leadership positions; today, however, with ample cash income available for those men who are willing to work away from the tribe for extended periods, those who remain at home a good deal of their lives, participate extensively in community affairs, and win the confidence of the community are seldom as wealthy as some of the men who have focused the greatest portion of their energies on economically remunerative work that keeps them away from home for extended periods. Certainly today a man does not derive his power and influence in the community primarily from his ability and willingness to dispense economic largess.

The contemporary informal community leader has almost inevitably held a number of administrative-type positions in his younger years; usually while still in the elder warrior age grade he held a post in the British-sponsored tribal government, sometimes as headman (*mlango*), sometimes merely as an attendant or policeman (*askari*). Usually he also has a record of work outside the tribe which reflects a greater than ordinary willingness or capacity to undertake and carry out managerial jobs, such as being a foreman on a European farm, or other jobs requiring organization of and responsibility towards other people. Seldom has he had extended dealings with mission groups in Tiriki—if for no other reason than because, as has been pointed out in previous chapters, such contact generally involved certain violations of the initiation oaths or responsibility that alienated a man from his pagan peers. Nevertheless, such a leader, even though illiterate, usually has a reasonable working knowledge of Swahili which was useful during his employ as a government servant and/or a farm foreman, &c., and he has more than average knowledge of European life and customs for a Tiriki of his age group. Finally, and this is probably a *sine qua non* for such leadership, the informal community leader has more than average knowledge of sorcery.

It will be recalled that Tiriki elders too old to want to father children are, because of this fact, able to use certain kinds of sorcery to bring about the demise of their enemies without fearing the automatic counter-sanction of sterility. Indeed, they are expected to use such sorcery to hasten the undoing of Tiriki outcasts or uninitiated undesirables. Tiriki youths learn of this sorcery in initiation, and Tiriki men who have attained the judicial elder age grade may be taught how to make and use the medicine involved by the ritual elders. There are also other magical practices not specifically associated with the Tiriki customs, and it is believed that witches (*baloji*) use various kinds of harmful medicines and rituals to bring misfortune, disease, and death both to neighbours and to kinfolk.

A witch's basic motive for his (or her) harmful actions is believed to be simple bad 'heart' or character either inherited 'through the blood' or acquired by magical treatment and instruction from a practising witch. It is inconceivable to a Tiriki that a person generally suspected of being a witch could become an informal community leader; even to have had a paternal grandfather or father who was widely rumoured to be a witch is quite enough to disqualify a man from ever becoming an elder of great authority in the community. If a man is free from suspicion of being a witch, however, skill in one or another of several forms of divination add to his prestige and leadership potential, while skill in using a particular magical potion known as *bubila* is of very great aid in gaining the deepest respect of the community. Indeed, in many Tiriki communities the informal community leader is a practitioner of *bubila*.

It seems pertinent to give a brief discussion of *bubila* here because of its frequent association with informal community leadership. The Tiriki generally believe that the essential active ingredient of *bubila* is a medicine made of various specific roots, herbs and animal organs. The practitioner of *bubila* (known as a *mubila*, *mu- ba- -bila*) knows how to concoct this medicine and then how to use it to bring sickness and death to his enemies. The *bubila* medicine transmits its harmful qualities via the practitioner's breath. The *mubila* first puts a plug of the medicine in his mouth, and then faces his unsuspecting victim and speaks to him in 'gentle tones' (*maxoba madolo*), often muttering a thinly veiled threat such as 'tough days are coming' (*maduxu madinyu gizanga*). Within a few days the victim begins to feel badly and manifests one or more of the symptoms widely purported to result from *bubila*. These symptoms range from indigestion (*xusalila munda*) to various aches, chills and fevers also generally associated with malaria (*murengo*). But the victim's difficulties do not stop here; instead of lessening or disappearing in a normal fashion, symptoms increase; appetite disappears, further indigestion may ensue, and quickly the sufferer grows thin and loses strength. Finally, swelling may appear in the abdomen or in the limbs, and in the last throes, as death approaches, it is reported the skin may turn blotchy with whitish patches and readily peel off, 'like the skin of a roasted banana'. (The final symptoms of swellings and blotchy rotten skin are the same, it will be remembered, as those said to await the man who betrays the initiation secrets.)

Only a *mubila* has the medicine with which to cure the malady caused by *bubila*. The fee for the cure is considerable, generally being today about equivalent to the value of one sheep or goat which has to be paid before treatment starts, with at least that much additional payment after the cure is completed. Generally a victim turns to the nearest of kin whom he knows to be a *mubila*, because such a near kinsman can generally be prevailed upon to charge a less heavy fee and extend credit for the final payment more graciously.

The Tiriki report that the art of *bubila* was first developed in the neighbouring tribes of Idaxo and Isuxa; thence its knowledge and utilization spread to Tiriki and other Abaluyia tribes. Only men may become *babila*. Its knowledge is transmitted in much the same manner as other specialized crafts and skills—generally from a father to one or more of his sons, and often to a sister's son. It is also possible for a younger man to induce a *mubila* to accept him as an apprentice even though they are in no way related. In all cases, regardless of whether the teacher and apprentice are related, the knowledge is imparted to the apprentice in exchange for services rendered; in most cases where the apprentice is not the practitioner's own son the exchange also involves the apprentice making payment of livestock or, today, cash. It is reported that the apprentice cannot practice his art until his mentor has died.

A *mubila* has power to kill or cure, but in no way does his magical knowledge impart to him an inherently evil or malicious disposition such as is characteristic of the witch (*muloji*). It is believed entirely possible that a witch might gain knowledge of *bubila* and use it for his own anti-social purposes. This seems only to enhance the feeling that men of good standing in the community who are in no way suspected of being witches but who are *babila* are a desirable, even a vital, community asset.[1]

---

[1] For fairly extensive discussions of *bubila* and *babila* see Günter Wagner, *The Bantu of North Kavirondo*, Vol. I (London: Oxford University Press, 1949), pp. 132–143, and, 'The Abaluyia of Kavirondo', *African Worlds*, ed. by Daryll Forde (London: Oxford University Press, 1954), p. 47.

The twenty-five years that have passed since Wagner's investigations have probably tended to make the Abaluyia, both Christian and pagan, ever more wary about discussing or even freely admitting to the continuing activities of *babila*

The informal community leader's functions are primarily judicial and political in nature. Nevertheless, it is clear that a necessary adjunct to his pre-eminence in these spheres within the community is a knowledge of and skill in magic (especially *bubila*) equal to or nearly equal to that of any other men in the community. To summarize, the informal community leader in Tiriki today usually has the following attributes: (1) he is a man with a fair number of clansmen and kinsmen living in the community; (2) he combines a certain aggressiveness but eloquence of speech with ability as an arbitrator and an extensive knowledge of local affairs and tribal custom; (3) his life career has given him more than average experience for men of his age bracket in directing the activities of Africans and in dealing with European employers and administrators; (4) his experience with Europeans, however, has never led him to renounce or divulge the secret Tiriki initiation customs; (5) he has a reputation as a practitioner of sorcery. Usually his magical reputation is based on his supposed knowledge of *bubila*, the magical complex which above all others seems to concern the contemporary Tiriki, both pagan and Christian. Through his skill with *bubila* not only does an informal community leader effectively discourage people from treating his opinions lightly, but also it enables him to assure the community that the use of *bubila* by irresponsible or anti-social members of the group may be effectively counteracted by him.

---

with educated outsiders. It was after more than a year of almost continuous residence in Tiriki, the acquisition of rather intimate knowledge of one Tiriki community and fairly detailed knowledge of several others, and a fair degree of facility in the Tiriki language, that the contemporary Tiriki concern over *bubila* became apparent to my wife and me. Our knowledge of the subject was greatly augmented when after nearly a year in Tiriki one of our Tiriki employees was striken seriously ill purportedly by *bubila*.

There are aspects of *bubila* mentioned by Wagner that my investigations failed either to confirm or refute. This is clearly due, in part, both to tribal variations in the *bubila* complex and also to changes in the nature and practice of *bubila* during the last twenty-five years. My wife and I both feel that our knowledge of the contemporary significance and practice of *bubila* and other magical activities in Tiriki, including the contemporary role of the witch (*muloji*), is far from complete. For example, a number of factors suggest that in Tiriki the malevolent activities of a witch are seldom if ever directed against his or her immediate agnates, while activities of a *mubila* who is not a *muloji* may be sometimes so directed. Unfortunately such relationships, with their interesting structural implications, were neither adequately confirmed nor refuted by the data gathered.

It may be that in traditional times a man's skill in magic was not such a necessary adjunct to his attainment of highest respect as a judicial elder. Without question the very aged men—the ritual elders—were the religious leaders of the community and were also formally, at least, the principal practitioners of magic for socially approved ends. Today, however, as a group, the ritual elders have largely vanished from the public eye, and perhaps, as a result there has developed a greater dependency on the judicial elders for aid in matters of witchcraft. The Tiriki elders say there were traditionally three principal types of community leaders, with usually one outstanding leader of each type. These were, the ritual elder (*musaalisi mugali wu luhya*), the judicial elder (*musaxulu mugali wu luhya*), and the war leader (*mwimili wi lihe wu luhya*). The contemporary phenomenon of a single informal community leader, renowned both as a political-judicial figure and as a magical practitioner, has very likely become common only in the last generation. Today, the informal community leader is the man who more than all others draws together and represents community opinion on matters brought before the community by the tribal government's official community leader, the sub-headman. The sub-headman is usually a man of elder warrior age grade, and his leadership position can be roughly correlated with the traditional community war leader, even though the duties he performs are quite different. Traditionally, however, each community often had two or three war leaders with war horns, while today the office of community sub-headman can be bestowed upon only one man in the community at a given time.

The community sub-headman is nominated for his position by the sub-tribal headman in consultation with the elders of the community. The headman's choice generally reflects the preferences of the community elders, especially as they are articulated by their informal leader. The tribal Chief makes the actual appointment after the qualifications of the nominee have been reviewed and approved by the European District Officer in charge of southeastern North Nyanza tribes. Both the British and the Tiriki expect the sub-headman not only to represent the British Administration and tribal government in his community, but also to defer to the community elders' judgement in matters pertaining to local affairs and customary law, and to refer to his headman all cases where serious conflict exists between British administrative demands and local custom or sentiment.

A sub-headman receives a certain formal deference from the members of his community, and from all members of the tribe who know or deal with him. This deference is primarily an out-growth of his position as an agent of the Chief. People recognize the immediate value of complying with their sub-headman's requests and of staying in his good favour, as it is helpful, indeed almost essential, to have his support when carrying disputes to the court of the headman or Chief; for it is he who often serves as a key witness both in the tribal and district African court systems. The sub-headman also has the right to arrest anyone in the community for misconduct, and demand that they appear before the court of the headman or the Chief. In the case of major crimes such as manslaughter or murder it is his duty immediately to report such an event to the nearest Kenya Police station and to do whatever he can to aid in the apprehending of the person or persons involved. The sub-head-man in effect serves as the local constable. The sub-headman, for his part, knows that the informal support of the community, and thus his ability to perform his official duties efficiently, depends on continued sponsorship by the judicial elders and especially their informal head. Furthermore he, probably even more than other people in the community, fears and wants the continual backing of the informal community head's magical prowess.

Within the community circle no one would suggest that the sub-headman is more important or more influential than the community elders, or that he has as much power (*zingulu*) and should receive as much respect as the informal community leader. Within the broader context of tribal affairs, however, the sub-headman is granted recognition, resulting from his position in the tribal bureaucracy, which neither the community elders nor the informal community leader can expect to receive. Throughout the tribe an elder may be known and praised for his past incumbency of one or another tribal governmental position and for other formally established leadership positions, past or present, including initiation leadership, but seldom if ever is a man known throughout the tribe as a result of being an informal community leader. In short, a distinction may be drawn between tribal leadership and community leadership. Recognition as a tribal leader is virtually confined to younger men predominantly of the elder warrior age grade who hold one or another office or position in the contemporary British organized tribal government. The leading contemporary community elders, and particularly the informal community leaders, are apt to be men who formerly occupied one or another tribal administrative position; and it seems fairly safe to predict that the coming generation's informal community leaders will be generally drawn from the younger men who during the present decade will occupy one or another tribal administrative post.

The following is a list of the principal contemporary leadership offices that Tiriki generally view as of indisputable significance and as bringing their incumbents tribe-wide recognition. They are listed in order of the prestige generally accorded them, the first position being held in highest general esteem:

(1) Tribal Chief.

(2) African District Court elder (only one Tiriki was a member of the African District Court in 1954–56).

(3) Initiation chiefs. (This is the only traditional authority position that regularly carries tribe-wide deference and recognition. Perhaps during initiation periods the deference granted them exceeds that shown the District Court elder, and equals, more or less, that given the Chief, but when initiation is not being held this would not be so. It should be pointed out that the deference granted the initiation elders is not openly manifest at formal tribal administrative functions. An initiation chief would never, for example, be granted a seat of honour, nor seldom introduced to a British official at a tribal function arranged on behalf of the British Administration; he would, however, be given a choice seat among the places reserved for the tribal elders—if he chose to attend such a function. This lack of recognition within the contemporary tribal administrative structure neither reflects nor markedly detracts from the respect and honour more generally accorded these men by the tribe.)

(4) African District Council members.

(5) Headman of the five Tiriki sub-locations.

(6) Location Advisory Council members.

(7) Secretary to the Chief, and tribal tax collector. Although

the formal deference granted these two salaried functionaries is great, the esteem in which they are held informally varies enormously with the incumbent. The tax collector's position, as one would suspect, is a particularly difficult one. Holders of these offices are younger men who have achieved a higher educational level than average for either headmen or sub-headmen.

(8) Sub-headmen of the twenty-seven contemporary Tiriki 'community' administrative divisions.

(9) African District Council market inspector for Tiriki and Nyangori Locations; Chief's askaries (policemen and orderlies), &c. (In this last category the deference granted the incumbent is probably as much a function of the personality of the office holder as it is of the office itself.)

There is one more major category of tribal leadership to be found in contemporary Tiriki—namely, the church leaders of tribal renown. These leaders consist of pastors who are officially recognized as being the heads of the Tiriki branch or portion of their respective denominations, plus several Christian pastors without official positions of eminence who are nevertheless widely regarded as men of great importance and influence in the Christian community because of eloquence as preachers or other admired clerical attributes. A distinction must be made, just as in the political realm, between local or 'village' (*lidala*) church leaders, and church leaders of tribal renown and influence. There are scores of local congregations in Tiriki today each with its own pastor; indeed, two or three local churches are to be found in most communities. Not only does each of these local congregations have a pastor, but each also has one or more alternate pastors as well, plus church elders. Many, probably most, local churches in Tiriki are regularly attended by only a half dozen men or less and perhaps one or two dozen women. Nearly every regular male attender at any given time holds one (or more) official position of leadership within his church group. In effect, all regular adult male church attenders can and do from time to time claim to be church leaders. The head pastor, however, has a position clearly superior to the other members of the local church, and in terms of regularly granted community deference he alone can be thought of as a local church leader of community standing. From this base of at least seven Protestant denominations and nearly a hundred local parishes, each with its official pastor, there have emerged only about a dozen contemporary Tiriki pastors who have tribe-wide reputations as church leaders and who are known to most adult Tiriki Christians.

Education and Contemporary Tribal Leadership

Fair facility in reading and writing both the vernacular (more precisely, *Luragoli*, the Luyia dialect that the Friends missionaries chose for their translation of the Bible and for primary school instruction) and Kiswahili,[1] is a virtual *sine qua non* for candidacy to contemporary tribal leadership. Today most Tiriki, including the pagan elders, concur with both the British Administration and the missionaries in feeling that literate people should hold the major administrative jobs both in tribal government and church organizations. Indeed nearly all Tiriki both young and old agree that at least a primary school training is a valuable asset for all. Twenty years ago, however, when the present generation of administrators were of school age, the importance of literacy was not widely perceived in Tiriki. The majority of Tiriki men now in their thirties or forties have never regularly attended school; consequently most men of this age bracket are either completely illiterate or have only a feeble knowledge of reading and writing gained from literate friends or from sporadic attendance of the adult literacy

[1] Although English is becoming increasingly important in business and governmental affairs and has recently been introduced into the regular primary school curriculum, Kiswahili still remains, at the tribal level, the principal commercial and administrative *lingua franca* of North Nyanza. See W. H. Whiteley, 'The Changing Position of Swahili in East Africa', *Africa*, Vol. XXVI, No. 4, pp. 343–53, for a general discussion of the declining importance of Swahili. If the current trend in North Nyanza continues, very likely by 1970, and perhaps sooner, English will have largely replaced Swahili as the *lingua franca*. At present, however, the number of Tiriki competent in English are very few, and Swahili still remains the language used in the North Nyanza African District Council Meetings, and the language in which both the Location Advisory Council minutes and the African District Court records are written. In short, while competence in spoken and written English is very rare (probably in 1956 limited to several dozen Tiriki) and by no means a requirement for the tribal bureaucrat, ability to speak and read Swahili is virtually mandatory for the attainment of most tribal positions of authority.

The tribal circumcision chiefs are not being considered in this discussion since their offices are in no way part of the contemporary British fostered tribal bureaucracy. In point of fact, however, several of these elders have conversation ability in Swahili, but probably none of them are literate.

classes sometimes held by missionaries of African Christians for prospective or new church members.

Today's Tiriki tribal leaders are mostly recruited from the relatively small proportion of men who regularly attended mission schools for several years during their childhood and/or adolescence. Primary school education in Tiriki has always been exclusively in the hands of the missions, and it has been a regular mission policy to include Christian education in the primary school curriculum. Thus primary school education and Christianity have become inexorably linked in people's minds. Indeed the same Swahili-derived word, *musomi* (*mu- ba- -somi*), —literally, 'one who reads'—is commonly used in Tiriki (as in the rest of North Nyanza and much of East Africa) to denote both 'student' and Christian.

A generation ago most Tiriki fathers were not only unconvinced as to the utility of literacy but also were loath to have their children go to mission schools because of the many non-Tiriki Africans and undesirables (*badamanu*) attending the schools and because of the hostile attitude the missionaries (especially the Friends) took towards many traditional customs, particularly the initiation ceremonies. A large portion of the students attending classes at Kaimosi and other schools within Tiriki at that time were either Maragoli who lived within walking distance or youths boarding at Kaimosi who came from more distant tribes. Nevertheless, a few pagan Tiriki fathers did allow one or more of their sons to attend mission primary school, and some others, glad for the income it brought their family, were willing for their sons to work on the Kaimosi Mission coffee plantation and at other mission jobs. In most cases the missionaries made an hour or more of daily primary school instruction mandatory for all their child employees. Thus a generation ago a number of Tiriki youth of pagan parentage learned to read and write, either because of the unusual foresight of their parents, or because of the economic motive that lured their families into letting them seek employment at the mission.

Most Tiriki youths who attended mission schools during this period followed their illiterate age peers into the traditional initiation ceremonies sometime during their early or middle teens. This, of course, was in direct violation of the mission

injunction against Tiriki initiation, and was generally viewed
by the missionaries and African Christians as 'backsliding'—a
deplorable return to pagan ways. After returning from initiation,
some of the former mission pupils felt disinclined to return to
school where they would be obliged to mingle on a basis of
equality with the uncircumcised children and with the youths
who had not been initiated according to Tiriki custom; many,
however, re-applied for school entrance only to find that both
the European missionaries and most of the African teachers
were against their being allowed to re-enroll as students. Some
missionaries claim that Tiriki youth who had been good
students and helpful obliging members of their class generally
would return from initiation surly in manner, difficult to
manage in the classroom, and no longer able to apply themselves to their studies effectively. Even as early as the late 1920's
the general demand for education had grown enough among the
Maragoli and other tribes so that the Tiriki mission schools
were overcrowded, mostly with these non-Tiriki students; consequently, it became almost a matter of policy not to readmit
Tiriki who had participated in the traditional initiation rites.
A few Tiriki youth were circumcised at the mission hospital.
They, of course, were able to complete their schooling without
interruption simply by arranging to have the operation performed during a school vacation.

A number of Tiriki were readmitted to school after traditional initiation, but usually not until they had first been employed away from the tribe for a number of months or even
years. Several of these readmitted students received teacher's
training and then taught in mission primary schools for varying
lengths of time. Also several Tiriki teachers were recruited from
the handful of Tiriki youth circumcised either at the hospital
or in the Maragoli manner and who consequently did not have
their education interrupted. In order to hold a job as a teacher
in a mission school, a man is expected to be formally affiliated
with a Christian church; reasonably regular church attendance,
monogamy, and church membership for all his children are
virtually mandatory aspects of this affiliation, while abstention
from all alcoholic beverages remains a basic rule of Protestant
church membership which teachers in Protestant mission schools
are expected to honour—even if they themselves are Catholics.

Many teachers in Tiriki serve as their church's clerk or treasurer, and sometimes they aspire to the clerkship of their denomination's regional or tribal organization. Others become local pastors, in which case the reputation they derive from being a pastor generally soon overshadows their reputation and prestige acquired through teaching.

The Tiriki generally view a teacher as a man of fairly great importance (*mugali xadi*) principally by virtue of the greater *entrée* his education gives him to the European world and because of the comparatively large salary he receives as a teacher which allows him to dress better, to have a larger, better equipped and furnished home, and to entertain in a more lavish and more European manner than most of his neighbours. But these attributes do not make a leader (*mwimili*) in the judgement of most Tiriki. In contrast, a village pastor is generally regarded as a real leader (*mwimili ligali*). In recent years a large proportion of the local pastors have been recruited from the ranks of the schoolteachers. The modicum of status derived from schoolteaching, skill in reading and writing, and familiarity both with missionaries and church organization mediated by their teaching experience, are all forceful factors leading to the frequent choice of schoolteachers and ex-schoolteachers as local pastors. Of course, not all men with school teaching experience make acceptable pastors. Generally only those who in the eyes of their parishioners show the traditionally expected leadership attributes of eloquence in speech (as manifest in preaching), a commanding social presence, and promise as organizers and arbiters are chosen as local pastors. Other men with teaching experience but not so gifted in all of these ways may become church elders, preachers, or church clerks, but seldom become or remain village pastors. In conclusion, it should be noted that probably more than half of the local pastors to be found in Tiriki have never been schoolteachers, but for the most part they are literate and have had mission school training. Schooling is almost a *sine qua non* for becoming a church pastor, while schoolteaching further facilitates the gaining of such a position.

Church Leadership as a Route to Tribal Political Leadership

Once a young man has become a local pastor his leadership ability inevitably receives regular scrutiny from all segments of

the community. The pagan elders, as well as all other members
of the community, attend Christian weddings, funerals, and
many other church affairs that their Christian neighbours and
kinfolk arrange. Also it is an increasingly common practice for
church pastors to represent in court those womenfolk whose
husbands are away and whose kinsmen cannot conveniently
represent them. In short, once a man achieves the position of
local pastor he gains the public eye; he not only becomes subject
to the continual observation of his Christian parishioners but is
also under the repeated scrutiny of the community political
leaders and judicial elders.

The local pastor, if he shows ability as a leader, generally
soon moves on either to more responsible positions in the church
hierarchy (sometimes facilitating his own promotion by switching denominational affiliation), or he gets appointed to a
position in the tribal administration.

An analysis of the life histories of a sample of contemporary
tribal governmental leaders and tribally recognized and proclaimed church leaders reveals that most of these men have held
posts either as mission teachers or as local pastors, or both,
preceding their rise to tribal renown. Several tribal leaders have
held positions of tribal eminence both in the church and tribal
governmental organizations. In nearly every case where this is
true, however, such leaders have been forced, during Hezron's
Chieftaincy, to forfeit their eminence in either the tribal administrative or the religious realm. This separation of Christian
church leadership and tribal leadership, so long favoured by the
pagan tribal elders, has been greatly aided and abetted by Chief
Hezron. In the present decade an increasing number of Tiriki
tribal officials, following Chief Hezron's personal example, have
started publicly drinking beer and in addition have in many
cases acquired more than one wife. As a result they have lost
their church membership or at least have been disqualified
from church membership.

Today a marked cleavage exists between top level Tiriki
leadership in the tribal political and the church realms. Most
of the important contemporary tribal leaders are *bona fide*
initiated Tiriki who have not been cursed by the initiation
elders. The men who have consistently maintained and worked
to augment their church-based tribal eminence are in almost

every case those leaders who are not welcome at community beer drinks either because they are not initiated in the Tiriki manner or because they are outcasts. Furthermore, these men rejected by the tribal elders have, with few exceptions, lost or relinquished their tribal positions during the last six years. Clearly to have been initiated in the traditional Tiriki manner and never to have violated the initiation oaths are important requisites to the attainment and maintenance of tribal administrative eminence in Tiriki today. This is in marked contrast to the situation as late as a decade ago when political power, under the leadership of Chief Amiani, was slipping more and more into the hands of relatively highly-educated Christian men who had either never been initiated in the Tiriki manner or who had betrayed the secrecy of the initiation rites. It will be recalled that, in consequence, judicial and informal support of the tribal administration by the community elders had virtually dwindled to nil.

Below are four brief biographical sketches of contemporary Tiriki leaders of tribal renown. I have selected these four men because they have career histories quite typical of those found in the rather detailed biographies my wife and I obtained in 1955–56 from a sample of Tiriki administrative and church leaders. The sample included all Tiriki holding officially recognized tribal administrative positions above the level of sub-headmen (see pp. 246–7). It also included four sub-headmen, six men in minor or unofficial administrative positions, and twelve leading church pastors. Two of the sketches are of men whose leadership careers in recent years have been diverted exclusively into Church activity. Neither of these men is (nor has been for years) a member in good standing of the Tiriki age group organization. The other two sketches are of men of good standing in the age group organization who have followed the more typical pattern of moving progressively into tribal governmental positions of increasing importance, with a concurrent loss or sloughing off of their church leadership positions. Three of the biographies have been fictionalized in order to protect the anonymity of those being described, but care has been taken to make the sketches embrace without exaggeration those features which probably have most relevance to the nature and success of the respective careers.

Case No. I. Johana Adimuga

Adimuga, the second son of a monogamous pagan father, was born during the harvest season that preceded the great famine of 1906. His paternal grandfather was a famous warrior and keeper of a war horn (*ibumi*); his father also took part in a few skirmishes with the Nandi before these were stopped by the British. It is widely rumoured today that the warrior grandfather in his later years was seen running around at night naked, and that he displayed other undesirable behaviour characteristics of a witch (*muloji*). Some suggest that this was the reason why Adimuga's father left his parental homestead when Adimuga was still a baby and moved with his wife and children to live in the formerly empty land east of Kaimosi Mission. He was one of several Tiriki men who moved to that area with their families soon after the establishment of the Mission and the punitive expedition of 1906 made it secure from Nandi raids.

Prior to the First World War nearby Kaimosi Mission held little interest for most of the Tiriki living in the newly settled eastern region, and the missionaries were rather unsuccessful in attracting Tiriki children from that area for religious instruction or schooling. During the First World War the Mission started the practice of hiring local boys to work on their newly planted coffee fields. Many pagan parents had become willing to have their sons employed by the missionaries and bring home cash to add to the family coffers because of the need to pay poll tax and because of their growing interest in acquiring manufactured articles. The missionaries set aside part of the time the boys spent in their employ for religious and academic instruction. Every morning the boys started their work day at the mission with an hour of worship from about 7:00 to 8:00 a.m., followed by an hour of school work. Then they laboured in the fields from around 9:00 to 2:00. Adimuga and several of his neighbourhood friends started working for the Friends missionaries on this basis in 1915, and Adimuga continued with them until he left to be initiated in the traditional Tiriki manner in 1920.

These five years sufficed to give Adimuga some skill at reading and writing in both the vernacular and Swahili, and also awakened his interest in Christianity. The missionaries gave him the Christian name of Johana. In leaving Mission employment to be circumcised Johana was simply conforming with his

Tiriki peers, including those affiliated with the mission; for it wasn't until later in the decade that the missionaries succeeded in persuading any of the Tiriki youth to forego the traditional initiation.

Nearly two years passed after his emergence from initiation before Johana again sought European employment. This time he found work on one of the newly opened European settler farms near Eldoret, about 60 miles northeast of Tiriki. Between 1922 and 1925, Johana held three different jobs of successively higher status. First, he was a 'shamba boy' (gardener), then an assistant at a power mill, and finally a houseboy. Early in 1926 Johana returned to Kaimosi Mission to work as a cook for one of the missionaries. Nineteen twenty-seven proved to be a turning point in Johana's life. He took two steps that year that had the effect of committing him strongly to Christianity and to Friends Mission membership. One of these was his public confession of the initiation secrets at the 1927 Tiriki initiation time, and the other was his marriage to a Christian girl, a Friends Mission convert.

Friends missionaries, it will be recalled, succeeded in 1927 in persuading a group of young Tiriki men who were mission affiliated or converts to stand up in a Friends Meeting composed of both men and women from a number of Abaluyia tribes, and 'confess the circumcision secrets', i.e., reveal the nature of the secret Tiriki initiation rites. Johana was one of the dozen or so Tiriki Christians who joined Chief Amiani in this public violation of the initiation oath of secrecy. Johana's own remarks in 1955 as to why he took this step are not too helpful in assaying his underlying motives. He simply states that some of the ceremonies were not good, since they were pagan and called on the ancestral spirits instead of God, and that the missionaries were admonishing the Tiriki men to prove that their commitment to God was their first commitment by 'confessing' the secrets; so he joined with the others in making the public revelation. He also adds, however, that he now feels the missionaries were wrong in attacking Tiriki initiation, and he strongly supports the secret Tiriki Christian ceremony instituted by Sagwa. In talking with Johana about his past, and in comments gleaned from others about him, I learned several things which seem quite pertinent to his having taken this step. First Johana and the

Friends missionary for whom he started to cook in 1925 quickly
developed a strong mutual bond of respect and affection; thus
the advice of his employer and of other missionaries probably
began to carry considerable weight with Johana. Second, Chief
Amiani was Johana's maternal uncle (*xoza*), and he apparently
put considerable pressure on Johana to follow his lead in confessing the circumcision secrets. Third, Johana wanted to marry
a young girl of non-Tiriki parentage who lived in Tiriki. She
was from a community just beyond the mission boundary which
was in large measure made up of African Friends' converts,
many of whom were immigrants to Tiriki from other Abaluyia
tribes. She was a devout Friends convert, and on her insistence
they laid plans to have a Friends Church wedding. This, of
course, further increased Johana's contact and involvement
with the Friends missionaries and their converts.

It remains impossible to evaluate with certainty the importance of the above factors in Johana's decision to reveal the
initiation secrets. Indeed some other factor we have not considered may have been the crucial one. For example, it was and
remains difficult for a man to cope with the rumour that one of
his immediate agnatic forebearers was a witch, because of the
general supposition that the same propensity will most likely
be inherited by some, but not all of the male descendants. In
mission circles, witchcraft was felt to be satanic-inspired
ignorance or evil which could be conquered by belief and faith
in God; thus within the mission group the taint of witchcraft was
consistently repudiated or nullified by prayer and piety and did
not work as a potential threat to one's position. The consequences for revealing the initiation secrets, however, were clear
cut. Johana and all the other Tiriki who were involved in the
revelation were promptly cursed at a special meeting of the
circumcision elders held in a circumcision grove, and later
publicly cursed by the elders standing as a group by the edge
of the mission property. In addition, for a number of years
thereafter they were harassed in many little ways and frequently
threatened with physical violence by the enraged pagans.
Johana was more fortunate than several other confessees in not
having his house burned, or being beaten. He avoided some of
the tumult that immediately followed the confession by quickly
leaving the mission's employ and again finding work on a farm

near Eldoret. But early in 1928 he took leave from his job at Eldoret long enough to be married at Kaimosi Mission in one of the first church weddings ever held for a Tiriki.

Shortly after Johana's wedding the Kaimosi Mission head asked him to return to the mission to work so that he might be trained to be a schoolteacher. The Friends missionaries had been having singularly little luck in recruiting Tiriki men who would remain steadfast workers for them, and apparently in Johana they felt they had found a happy exception. Johana returned to Kaimosi late in 1928 and started to work as a cook for one of the mission teaching staff. He received regular academic instruction from the missionaries, and in 1932 he passed his Standard B examination (roughly equivalent to Standard 3 in the current Kenya school system). During these years Johana remained anathema in the eyes of the Tiriki pagans, but the respect in which he was held by the missionaries and the African Christian community steadily grew. The following year, with the full backing of the Friends Mission and the small group of Tiriki Christians, Chief Amiani appointed Johana to be one of Tiriki's representatives on the North Nyanza Local Native Council (forerunner of the African District Council). In addition, Chief Amiani asked him to serve as his personal assistant and emissary, and Johana gave up his job as cook at the mission so he could devote his full attention to these tasks. Shortly thereafter Amiani had the quarrel with the Friends Missionaries which led to his leaving the Friends and throwing himself wholeheartedly into Salvation Army work in the tribe and district. Johana, although he continued to act as Amiani's personal emissary, remained a steadfast member of the Friends Church.

In 1935 the Friends missionaries arranged for Johana to go to teachers' training school outside of the district. The two years there brought a halt to his activities with Chief Amiani, but he retained the post of Local Native Council representative, even though not regularly able to attend its meetings. He returned to Tiriki in 1938 with a primary school certificate, and started a career of schoolteaching in the Friends primary school system. After one year he was appointed to be a supervisor of the Friends Primary unaided schools, a position that he held until he was replaced by a person of considerably higher educational qualifications almost a decade later. In 1944 Johana reached both the zenith and the end of his career as a public servant and personage of political importance in Tiriki. That year Amiani appointed one of his Salvation Army leaders to succeed Johana on the Local Native Council, but in lieu of this office he offered Johana the much more important position of court elder at the multi-tribal Native Tribunal which met at Mbali in Maragoli. The missionaries strongly urged Johana to turn down the court elder job on the grounds that he was better equipped both by training and temperament to serve his church and tribe as school supervisor. They argued that indeed he was the only Tiriki so equipped, while there were a number of other Christians who might fill the Native Tribunal position most satisfactorily. Johana heeded the missionaries advice and turned down the Tribunal appointment. I am not clear about why Johana decided to follow the missionaries' advice. Johana himself merely says that he saw the wisdom of their remarks. It seems likely that he sensed the difficulties inherent in accepting a job where he would have been obliged to be arbiter in disputes involving Tiriki, many of whom held him to be a traitor; and in order to take this job he would have had to give up his position as school supervisor in which he dealt almost exclusively with missionaries, and mission African affiliates who supported and admired him.

Since 1944 Johana has devoted himself unstintingly to teaching and to church affairs. After he was replaced as primary school supervisor in the late 1940's he returned again to primary school teaching. In the early 1950's it looked as though he might have to retire from primary school teaching because his own educational qualifications were no longer sufficient to allow him to teach in District Education Board aided primary schools. But he was permitted to continue to teach in one of several unaided Friends Primary schools that the Friends still operate, and recently, in consideration of his long practical experience, he was allowed to teach Standard I in an aided Friends school.

In the early 1940's Johana and several other Tiriki Friends affiliates living in his community started their own local Friends parish so that they no longer would be obliged to go several miles to Kaimosi Mission for worship. After several years it was officially recognized and established as a new Parish of the

East African Friends Meeting, and Johana was appointed its pastor. Since then it has considerably increased its membership and has become one of the leading Friends parishes in Tiriki.

Today most of Johana's age group peers are actively participating in the judicial affairs of the community; most join regularly in the local beer drinks, and many have either taken a young previously unmarried girl or accepted the young widow of a clansman as a second wife. The vast majority of his age group who were Christians have either in effect abandoned, or have been officially excommunicated from, their church affiliations. Johana remains a teetotaler, and monogamous; he takes no part in the judicial activities of the community except occasionally when he is a plaintiff, or serves as a witness. The community at large tends to let him go his own way, while they go theirs. The community elders when possible, however, use their influence to keep him from assuming an authoritative or conspicuous position in local affairs; for example, his best efforts to be granted a plot at the local market on which to build a shop were blocked by local leaders who successfully obtained the ear of the headman and the Chief, who have final say in such matters. Johana identifies primarily with the other Tiriki men of his age group who are steadfast Christians, most of these having been among the group that revealed the initiation rites and were cursed by the pagan elders in 1926. Among these men, and in the eyes of the North Nyanza Christian community at large, he has achieved and retained a position of respect and eminence. He regularly plays an important role in the Province-wide activities of the Friends Yearly Meeting. The Friends Yearly Meeting of East Africa embraces all the Friends meetings in East Africa, but nearly all Friends meetings are in fact located in the North and Elgon Nyanza Districts of Nyanza Province. Throughout Tiriki, regardless of the contempt in which some Tiriki men still hold him, Johana is recognized as one of the principal Christian leaders in the tribe.

Case No. II: Petro Waxala

Petro was born shortly after the start of the First World War. He is a younger son of a Maragoli who married a girl from one of the larger Tiriki clans and then moved to Tiriki, on to some land made available to him by his wife's family; this was shortly before Petro was born. It is not too common in North Nyanza for a man to move into his in-laws' land, but even as long ago as the First World War a severe land shortage had developed in Maragoli which induced (and continues to induce) many young Maragoli to emigrate whenever and to wherever the opportunity arises. Petro, who spent his entire boyhood in Tiriki, tends to ignore his Maragoli connexions; it is noteworthy that when I first asked him his clan he gave me his mother's clan instead of his father's.

Petro's family were all pagans, and his first contact of consequence with Christian missionaries occurred when he went to Kaimosi Hospital in 1928 at the age of about thirteen to seek treatment when he accidentally cut himself with a large bush knife (*panga*) when helping to clear a field. He was confined to a hospital ward for several weeks, and afterwards for a number of months he was obliged to return to the hospital at frequent intervals to have his bandage changed. During his long period of convalescence Petro accepted the missionaries' invitation to enroll in the Kaimosi primary school. He proved an apt pupil and after finishing his primary schooling in only two years, he went on with his intermediate schooling.

In the autumn of 1931 the Tiriki pagan elders began preparations for circumcision. Petro was the proper age for circumcision, and he found himself unwittingly made a pawn in the struggle between the Friends missionaries and the Tiriki pagans. It will be recalled (see Chapter V, p. 129) that in 1927 the North Nyanza District Commissioner had been obliged to intervene to prevent rioting triggered by efforts of Friends Mission converts to interfere with and discourage the traditional initiation rites. In order to assure no further violence the District Commissioner had decreed that henceforth the Christians were in no way to interfere with the circumcision and initiation ceremonies of the pagans and vice-versa. Friends missionaries in 1931 claimed the handful of Tiriki youth under their tutelage who were ready for initiation as converts to their church, and they were very anxious to prevent them from joining the traditional Tiriki ceremony. The pagan elders, on the other hand, did everything they could to make them enter the regular ceremony. The missionaries placed two alternatives before their Tiriki students of circumcision age. One was to take part in the Christianized non-secret ceremonies carried out by Christian converts in Maragoli, Idaxo, and other tribes. The other alternative, which they favoured even more strongly was for the boys simply to go and be circumcised at Kaimosi Hospital. This, it will be recalled, was of course a number of years before Sagwa had started a secret Tiriki-type Christian ceremony.

Petro had become a prize pupil at Kaimosi; he considered himself to be a Friends convert, and wanted very much to continue his education without interruption. Joining a Maragoli or Idaxo Christian initiation ceremony would not only have made Petro an outcast in the eyes of the other Tiriki, but would in addition have seriously jeopardized the position of his father, who was already regarded with some suspicion because he was a stranger from another tribe. Thus the only tenable choices for Petro were either to be circumcised at the hospital or to defy the missionaries and join the Tiriki ceremony. Petro and two or three other Tiriki youth studying at Kaimosi Mission chose the former alternative. The majority of their student peers from Tiriki, however, left the mission, or were 'forcibly abducted', and were circumcised in the traditional ceremonies, with a resultant break in their schooling which either served to terminate their education, or temporarily disadvantaged them in attaining further mission schooling.

Those circumcised at the hospital were regarded with new esteem by the missionaries. On the other hand, they found themselves estranged from their own communities and widely viewed by their Tiriki peers as cowards who had chosen hospital circumcision in order to escape the rigours of traditional circumcision rites. Thus Petro's life became even more heavily linked to the mission and the missionaries. He continued his intermediate and secondary schooling without interruption, and in 1935 was sent by the mission to Nairobi for teacher's training. He completed this course in 1937, and returned to Tiriki to become headmaster of a Friends primary school. He was just twenty-two; not only was he probably the youngest but he was also one of the most highly trained African teachers in the Friends school system at that time. It is noteworthy that more than fifteen years were to pass before any Tiriki initiated in the traditional manner (and most of these were initiated in Sagwa's

Christian ceremony) succeeded in attaining a formal education comparable to Petro's.

Between 1937 and 1954 Petro served as headmaster of several Friends schools, and then as a school supervisor. In addition he held several different positions of considerable responsibility at Kaimosi Mission, and in the Friends African Yearly Meeting.

In 1947 Chief Hezron appointed Petro to serve as one of the Tiriki representatives to the African District Council. As an A.D.C. member Petro automatically got a seat on the Location Advisory Council, where Chief Hezron chose him to be the Location Council recording secretary. At first blush it seems surprising that Hezron would have chosen a mission-circumcised Tiriki to be such an important spokesman for the Tiriki tribe. But two factors must be kept in mind when considering his appointment to these posts. First, Petro never himself condemned the Tiriki initiation ceremonies or betrayed any tribal secrets. Also, he was personable, respectful in his manner towards the elders, resolute and forthright. All agreed that he could not be considered a true Tiriki because of his failure to be initiated; however, most people who knew him had come to feel that he hadn't ducked out of initiation because of cowardice but that he simply had been the victim of bad counsel from the missionaries. The second and more crucial factor is that Chief Hezron was most anxious to combat from the inception of his Chieftaincy the notion widely held in North Nyanza that the Tiriki were poorly educated and backward as compared to the other tribes in the southern part of the district. Petro was appointed to the A.D.C. post and L.A.C. secretaryship probably primarily because there was no other Tiriki born man available who had anything like as much education as Petro, or his command of English. By the early 1950's the situation had changed; several young initiated Tiriki had completed schooling that put them educationally more or less on a par with Petro. In 1953 Chief Hezron appointed one of these younger men to replace Petro on the African District Council. Petro responded by immediately resigning from his position of Location Advisory Councillor and Secretary.

The loss of his A.D.C. position, although not entirely unexpected, came as a blow to Petro. For about a year prior to this he had had a deepening interest in Christianity and church affairs, and this loss of political status focused his energies even more strongly on religious matters. For several years Petro had been gradually losing his position of special favour with the missionaries. It has been the pattern in North Nyanza over the last two generations for African school teachers to reach the peak of status and prestige as teachers shortly after beginning their teaching careers; thereafter their standing in the profession generally falls quite rapidly because of the successively higher educational attainments of young men (and now also young women) just starting out as teachers. Petro found himself, even before he was forty, being rapidly outranked by young teachers. His Tiriki age peers were of course just beginning to take an active interest in local judicial affairs in anticipation of the time when they would be the community elders; activity which was closed to him because of his hospital circumcision. Thus Petro could find no alternate paths for maintaining his status in traditional community activity. Kaimosi Mission has typically done little to alleviate or compensate for status loss of their older teachers, except to encourage them to become more active in evangelical work and thereby gain influence and prestige within their own parishes. Petro, indeed, has found solace and a new outlet for his talents in religion and pastoral activity, but not in a way, as we shall see, that the Friends missionaries would have predicted or that the African Friends have found congenial.

Petro traces his strengthened interest in matters religious to a dream he had one night towards the end of 1952. He dreamed he was driving along a road with one of the principal missionaries from Kaimosi. The missionary was driving. Suddenly Petro grabbed the steering wheel and tried to drive the car himself; the car ran off the road into a ditch and was smashed. The missionary was unhurt, and walked away leaving Petro, who was injured and pinned in the wreckage, to fend for himself. At this point Petro awoke, and stricken with terror and remorse, he woke his wife, called her to come and pray with him, and spent the rest of the night in prayer, beseeching God's mercy, and promising to give up his sinful ways and lead a truly Christian life. Petro, prior to this incident, was already an assistant pastor in a Friends parish, and held important posts in the East African Friends Yearly Meeting; but after this he became much more pious. He became very active in leading special prayer groups, and much more zealous and very regular in his periods of private prayer, meditation, and Bible reading.

About a year after this dream, and only a short while after losing his position on the A.D.C., Petro reports that he had a vision while walking down a path not far from his home. He likens it to St. Paul's experience on the road to Damascus. He experienced a blinding light and fell in a swoon. He said he knew from that instant onward that he had found the Holy Spirit and that thenceforth he must devote his life to Christ and preaching the Word of God. (To my knowledge Petro is not an epileptic and has never had an epileptic seizure. The Tiriki are very afraid of any sort of epileptic seizures, believing them contagious; and they are quick to spread the word if they see someone have a fit; thus I think it is safe to assume that Petro has never had a seizure that looked like epilepsy which lasted long enough for anyone to see.)

In the months that followed Petro greatly increased the time he devoted to prayer and evangelical preaching. He preached repentance of sins and salvation with a vehemence and emotional ardour that gripped the hearts of some of his parishioners, while it disturbed and began to antagonize others. Also he became more and more interested in possession by the Holy Spirit and the seeking of prophetic signs and portents. Indeed he himself with increasing frequency was possessed by the Holy Spirit, i.e. fell into trance states, sometimes while praying privately, and sometimes in public worship services. Sometimes when possessed he simply swooned and on other occasions he babbled incoherently. Possession by the Holy Spirit, and 'speaking in tongues' are quite common, it will be recalled, among Pentecostal members and in most of the separatist sects. But both the Friends missionaries and the Friends African membership had consistently regarded such behaviour with distaste and suspicion ever since the early 1930's, when the split had occurred which led to the formation of the separatist 'African Church of the Holy Spirit'. Thus most of the Friends leadership began to regard Petro with considerable concern—a concern which rapidly turned to alarm when some of the Friends who heard his preaching also began to fall into possession states. The counselling of the Friends missionaries and the African church elders proved completely ineffectual in curbing Petro: instead the spiritualist emphasis of his preaching and worship increased. Also he began the practice of interpreting the spiritual message of the dissociated speech, dreams and visions which he and his followers more and more frequently experienced.

By the late spring of 1954, Petro had collected around him a devoted group of disciples who saw it as their Christian duty both to convert the heathen and to try to revitalize the Friends and all other Christians. They preached a form of worship leading to salvation that leaned heavily on confession of sins and experiencing the immediate presence of the Holy Spirit. The Friends elders and missionaries demanded even more vehemently that Petro and his followers modify and temporize their views; but their exhortations merely triggered Petro's group to denounce in prayers and sermons those Friends who were trying to muzzle the preaching of salvation. At the Friends Yearly Meeting held in August 1954, the Friends elders decided Petro's preaching and general religious behaviour had grown so antithetical to Friends beliefs and practices that he should be placed on probation if he did not agree to put an immediate end to his present type of preaching. He refused to agree to this, and consequently was informed that he was on probation and could no longer preach in the Friends Church. After his regular membership in the Friends Church had been withdrawn, the missionaries quickly decided that Petro should no longer work for the Friends school system. Petro now refers to this as the time when the Friends 'cursed' him.

In the weeks that followed, Petro continued to meet for regular prayer and worship, in spite of the protests of Friends leaders, with a growing group of devotees drawn mostly from the ranks of the Friends. When forbidden to meet in Friends church buildings, they simply met outdoors or in their own homes. Petro now, of course, had no job or other regular responsibilities, so he devoted himself more completely than ever to his religious activities. Soon he proclaimed his group to be a new and independent religious body. The Friends were very alarmed by this, both because they didn't want to lose the membership of his growing number of followers, and also because all mission groups had been specifically counselled by the British Administration to quash all attempts at schismatic

20

leadership that might arise within their ranks. The Administration had forbidden the formation of any new religious sect during the Mau Mau emergency, which was then at its height, fearing that Mau Mau cells or other seditious groups might use them to cover their activities or further their aims. The Friends notified the Administration, and the local European District Officer made it very clear to Petro that he could not form a new religious sect, and that if he continued to hold religious meetings not sanctioned by an established church group he would be arrested and perhaps detained indefinitely. Petro, by this time, had no use for Friends leadership, and also showed no inclination whatsoever to join one of the already existing independent churches and thereby be subordinate to a new set of leaders, probably all of whom were considerably less educated than he. Fortunately the District Officer perceived the impossibility of his continuing within the Friends Church and suggested that the Friends invite the Pentecostal Mission to consider Petro and his following for membership in their church, since Petro's theological leanings and practices seemed to be closer to the Pentecostals than any other Mission group. This was a rather bitter pill for the Friends to swallow, because for years they had been trying to discourage the Pentecostal missionaries from proselytizing and winning converts in what they considered to be Friends regions, but the Friends followed the District Officer's suggestion. The Pentecostals agreed to consider Petro's group for membership, and thanks in large measure to the tact and diplomacy of the District Officer, Petro finally agreed that he and his following should join the Pentecostal Church.

The Pentecostal Church has generally supported and encouraged Petro. He was made the pastor of a new Pentecostal church—established, after some dickering with the Friends, close to the Friends church where he had formerly preached, and conveniently close to the homes of Petro and most of his congregation. Today (1956) Petro not only fulfils the duties of parish pastor, but he also spends a lot of time as a travelling missionary for the Pentecostals, helping to conduct revivals in Nairobi and other urban centres throughout Kenya. Since joining the Pentecostal church Petro has become less preoccupied with spirit possession, interpretation of dreams and the like, but he still maintains a keen interest in such matters. He avidly reads any tract he can find on mysticism, and also has a strong interest in faith healing. Today Petro has the respect of the Pentecostal missionaries and African clergy, and he continues to hold the devoted loyalty of his own parishioners. All indications are that he is finding his life as pastor and evangelist both challenging and rewarding.

Case No. III: Mattayo Lusiza

Lusiza was born in 1911 into one of the older and larger Tiriki clans. His father and paternal grandfather, although not men of particular distinction, were respected community elders. The family homestead was less than a mile from Kaimosi Mission border, and Lusiza as a young boy frequently used to graze his father's livestock on the fringes of mission land. In 1919, when he was only eight, he was invited by the missionaries to come and work on the coffee plantation. His parents, generally hostile towards the mission and the missionaries, consented to his working there for pay. Thus he joined a number of other boys from Tiriki and nearby tribes in the established daily routine of early morning prayers and an hour of schooling followed by four or five hours of work in the fields.

Lusiza proved an apt pupil in the daily classes at the mission, and during his four years of employment there he learned to read and write in the vernacular with some fluency; but the sober round of prayer, study, and work on the coffee plantation did not stir his imagination as much as the prospect of working in a European town. In 1923, Mattayo, as he was called by the missionaries, accompanied one of the young men of his village to Eldoret, and there found a job as a houseboy in a European home.

The autumn of 1927 was circumcision time; Mattayo left his job in Eldoret, went home, and joined the traditional ceremony. He returned to Eldoret in 1928 and during the next five years held several positions in European households. Then in 1933 Mattayo was invited by the headman (*muliyango*) of his region in Tiriki to return home and become his clerk. Mattayo who had continued his education on his own while in Eldoret, had by this time acquired considerable fluency not only in speaking but also in reading and writing Swahili. The headman was one of Mattayo's clan elders, someone towards whom he had always felt a great deal of respect and affection. Although there was no regular salary or wage connected with the job, Mattayo accepted the headman's offer, returned to Tiriki, and served as his clerk and personal assistant for the next two years.

Early in 1935 Mattayo had the opportunity to take a market inspector training course at Kakamega. The headman he had been working for encouraged him to go. Leaving his Tiriki bride of just a few months at home, Mattayo left for Kakamega, and spent the following year there training and apprenticing as a market inspector. After he completed his training, Mattayo stayed on as an assistant inspector at the large Kakamega market. Kakamega is only thirty miles from his home community in Tiriki, so he was often home weekends. The job was appealing, not only because Kakamega was at that time a rather lively gold mining town, as well as the District Administrative centre, but also because it had one of the larger markets under the control of the District Administration. Furthermore, Mattayo enjoyed the distinction of being an employee of the District Administration. The limitations of the job, however, soon began to make themselves felt. Advancement in rank and pay in market inspection were limited and slow in coming; also he was soon transferred from Kakamega, and during the next few years, found himself frequently stationed in much less interesting spots than Kakamega, and further from his home. A man in Tiriki receives quite a bit of respect and praise from his peers and elders for being an assistant market inspector, but he is still unable to take any noteworthy role in local and tribal affairs if he is able to get home only infrequently and on short occasions. Mattayo was a rather talented organizer and leader of men; he was also ambitious. Thus it is not surprising that at this point in his life he followed the example of so many enterprising Tiriki of his generation and turned to the Christian Church for further opportunities for training and leadership.

Mattayo had nominally been a Friend ever since his childhood employment and instruction at Kaimosi. There is no evidence, however, that he had regarded his church membership very seriously, and after his initiation and consequent loss of favour with the Friends Missionaries and elders he had taken very little active part in Friends affairs. It will be recalled that in the early 1930's the Salvation Army had become established in Tiriki and North Nyanza under the talented leadership of Chief Amiani. Amiani recruited many of the early leaders in the Salvation Army from tribal administrators and assistants who had previously either been pagans or members of the Friends Church. Mattayo first became interested in the Salvation Army while serving as headman's clerk. His headman, however, was one of those who remained a pagan in spite of Amiani's efforts to convert his subordinates. Mattayo also desisted from joining the Salvation Army until 1936—which was the period when he was being transferred so frequently from one North Nyanza market to another. In the autumn of 1937, Mattayo took several months' leave from his market inspector job in order to attend the Salvation Army training school in Nairobi. After his return to North Nyanza, he took a very active role in the Salvation Army leadership, and during the next eight years he became increasingly known and respected throughout the district as a zealous church member and a skilful organizer and leader of the outdoor parades and services for which the Salvation Army is renowned.

Mattayo kept up his peripatetic existence as market inspector until 1945, when he was appointed to be produce inspector at Kaimosi Farms, a collection of European homesteads bordering Tiriki to the east. His job there was to check the grains and vegetables marketed by African farmers living on and cultivating (with the European owners' consent) plots on these farms. For the first time in over a decade, Mattayo was employed near enough his own community so that he could be home every weekend. He soon became a very popular leader in Tiriki Salvation Army circles, and in 1946, he was appointed 'Sergeant Major' in charge of all Salvation Army activity in eastern Tiriki.

Mattayo continued to serve as Kaimosi Farms produce inspector until 1953. He kept up his activities as a Salvation Army leader, and in addition became renowned in eastern Tiriki as a dispeller of *bubila*, a strongly feared form of sorcery. Mattayo had learned the art of *bubila* in the early thirties when he was serving as the headman's clerk, and was much in favour with the local elders. One of the elders, who knew the art, instructed him. It will be recalled (pp. 240–1), that the Tiriki believe *bubila* is occasionally employed by men, both good and evil, who have scores to settle. Knowledge of how to employ *bubila* to kill someone also entails knowledge of how to cure a victim. Witches (*baloji*), it is said, sometimes attain knowledge of *bubila*, and then employ it for their own nefarious purposes. Thus it is normal to find in every community at least one elder of importance and influence who is a *mubila* and can be counted on to help protect good people from being victimized and killed by this dreaded form of sorcery. Tiriki Christians felt particularly vulnerable to *bubila* because in many cases they had so estranged themselves from the pagan elders that whenever they sought out an elder who was a *mubila* for a cure either they received his outright refusal or else they were afraid that he might not really be working for a quick or complete cure, even if he said he was. In the late 1940's a number of severe illnesses occurred among Christians in eastern Tiriki which everyone, both Christian and pagan, became convinced were due to *bubila*. Mattayo quickly made his knowledge of *bubila* available to the Christians, and he is generally credited by Christians of all denominations with having saved the lives of a number of victims, and with having brought the outbreak to a halt by demonstrating to the witch or witches responsible that their efforts were in vain. It is noteworthy that Mattayo's efforts as a *mubila* on behalf of the Christians apparently did not estrange him from the pagan elders.

Late in 1953 Mattayo petitioned for and obtained the job of market master in the North Nyanza marketing sub-district that included Tiriki and Nyangori. At last he was able to live at home all the time and commute daily by bicycle to the markets throughout his area.

For the first time since he had served as the headman's assistant he was in a position to enter into everyday community affairs. He was still too young to take a regular role in the judicial activities of the community elders, but he began frequently to represent at the local courts women members of the Salvation Army who were involved in litigation. The elders of his clan and of his community quickly came to regard him as a man to be trusted; he found himself more and more frequently called upon to serve as a witness in property exchanges or family border disputes and settlements, and to help organize and chair post-funeral inheritance settlements of prominent members of his clan.

In the summer of 1953, Mattayo was nominated by the men of his sub-tribe to represent them on the Tiriki Location Advisory Council. His nomination was accepted by the Chief, and he became a regular member of the tribal administration.

Mattayo's career as a church leader survived his becoming a Location Council member by only a few months. In the spring of 1954, he inherited a second wife. She was a woman in her early thirties who had several children by her deceased husband, who was Mattayo's clan brother. All Christian churches in Tiriki, both mission affiliated and separatist, with the *de facto* exception of the 'Orthodox Church', which had no following in eastern Tiriki at that time, forbid their members to become polygynists, even through wife inheritance. The churches' official view of wife inheritance was that the clan of the deceased man can make some arrangement for his widow and children, such as having her marry a widower, a young unmarried man, or remain celibate while her deceased husband's brothers took care of her and the children. In practice, however, it is rare indeed to find a man who will take even a young widow as his only wife, and quite unrealistic to expect either the deceased's clan brothers or the widow herself to tolerate her not remarrying if she is still young. Thus Mattayo had the wholehearted support of the clan and community elders for his action, and indeed the understanding sympathy of some of his Christian confreres. Salvation Army rules, however, specifically forbid all men who are polygynists from holding leadership positions, and places on probation anyone already a member who becomes a polygynist. Mattayo resigned from his Sergeant Major position before the Salvation Army took formal action to remove him; today, in recounting the incident, he merely says that he got weary of his work as a leader in the Salvation Army, and left it. His automatic placement on probation did not estrange him from his Salvation Army and other Christian friends, and he still considers himself to be a Christian with a denominational preference for the Salvation Army. After being put on probation, Mattayo started quite openly to attend local beer parties with his pagan peers and also to drink European beer when being entertained by or entertaining Chief Hezron.

An election by secret ballot was held for the first time in Tiriki in early June 1956. The Kenya Administration had decided to prepare the African population for the inevitable advent in the near future of widespread, perhaps universal, suffrage in the Colony, by starting with secret ballot elections for members to the most local of the officially recognized administrative bodies. In North Nyanza these are the Location Advisory Councils. All tax-paying males, plus indigent elders who had obtained an official tax waiver, were eligible to vote. The elections in each sub-tribe were supervised by British District Officers. They had the responsibility of explaining to the local voters the system of different shaped coloured chips used to distinguish each candidate so that illiterate voters would know how to indicate their choice when they entered the privacy of the small hut containing the ballot box. Mattayo was elected to the Tiriki Location Advisory Council by an overwhelming majority, and for a second term represented his area in that quasi-legislative tribal body. The election could hardly be regarded as secret, as we conceive of it, because the District Officer was continually present in the hut which served as a ballot booth, both to keep laying out the chips, and to make sure that the voter in each case only voted for one candidate. It was clear from informal discussions and comments we overheard before and after the election that the Tiriki generally viewed the new method of election as rather diverting and amusing, but that they had absolutely no faith in its secrecy. However, Mattayo was clearly, secrecy or no secrecy, the choice of the local elders, and it was amusing to see their efforts after the election to try and trace down who the handful of people were who had cast their votes for the other two local candidates.

About two months after his election to the Location Advisory Council, Mattayo was appointed by Chief Hezron to be sub-headman of his local area, replacing an older man who was generally liked locally, but whom the Chief and District Officer had come to feel was getting somewhat more interested in the local round of community beer drinking and judicial activities than in being the Chief's local representative. This appointment occurred several weeks after we left Tiriki to return to the United States, so our knowledge of it is entirely second hand. Mattayo was obliged to resign his job as market master in order to take on the sub-headman's job. The latter in one sense can be considered as a lower position than the former, since its salary would ordinarily be no greater, and it is a Location or tribal appointment at the lowest official level, instead of a District appointment that requires special training. Mattayo apparently had no hesitancy, however, about accepting the job as sub-headman. Of course it meant that he no longer was obliged to bicycle rather long distances, frequently twenty or thirty miles over hilly, often muddy roads each day—something about which he complained to me on several occasions—and also that by becoming sub-headman, he was able to increase greatly his influence in his own community and sub-tribe.

Mattayo's career illustrates clearly the zig-zagging between participation in mission and church affairs, and pagan activities, which is typical of most men who are leaders in the Tiriki tribal administration today. As a young boy, prior to initiation, he received regular employment and primary schooling at Kaimosi Mission. Then he turned his back on the Mission in order to be initiated in the traditional Tiriki manner. He subsequently rejoined the church, this time the Salvation Army, while still a young man, and received a bit more formal schooling at the Salvation Army School in Nairobi. This was at a time when his age group (*Mayina*) still occupied the traditional warrior age grade. Several years later, after he had married and his age group had reached the age where traditionally they would have been regarded as elder warriors, he became really active in the Salvation Army, however, and found within that organization an outlet for his proclivities as a leader and organizer. Then, as Mattayo was approaching the height of his administrative career, and his age group was nearing traditional judicial elder status, he took a second wife and lost his church membership.

It is very unlikely that Mattayo will ever again be much involved with, or a leader in, church activities unless it be a separatist church such as the Orthodox which condones both beer drinking and polygyny. On the other hand, it wouldn't be at all surprising to find that ten or fifteen years from now Mattayo, although probably no longer holding any official tribal administrative posts, had come to be the most influential elder in his community, an elder not only with diplomacy and skill as an arbitrator, but also one with a knowledge of *bubila*, who is recognized as the true power behind the scenes in community affairs.

Case No. IV: Joseph Ganila

I make no attempt in this account to disguise the identity of the person whose career is being discussed. He is Joseph Ganila, who, it will be recalled from Chapter VII, became the leader of the Tiriki Israel Church.

Ganila belongs to the Bumbo clan, Tiriki's second largest. His father, who died in 1931, was a renowned warrior, as was his father before him. Ganila, the youngest of three sons, was born shortly after the end of the First World War. He spent his childhood at his parental homestead in the community of Mahanga, about a half mile or so beyond the Kaimosi Mission's northern boundary. Ganila, who grew up in a pagan family, had little contact with Kaimosi Mission until 1928 when he joined some of his peers in seeking employment on the mission coffee plantation.

Religious instruction and schooling in the 'three R's' for two hours each morning before work in the fields was still the routine imposed by the mission on its youthful employees, and Ganila proved to be one of their more apt pupils. In 1931 Joseph forsook his mission job and studies in order to be circumcised and initiated in the traditional Tiriki manner. The following year he sought re-employment on the mission plantation, and unlike some of his peers, he succeeded in persuading them to take him back again. Ganila's academic progress was, of course, slow because the actual instruction periods were for only an hour a day, but by 1935 he had completed Standard 3 and the missionaries, feeling he showed academic promise, encouraged him to go on with his schooling. Joseph started to study full time at Kaimosi Intermediate School in 1936, and by 1939 he had successfully completed Standard 6 and some teacher's training. He went on for another year at Kaimosi to finish his 'T-4' (primary school) teacher's training, and in 1940 he started teaching at the newly-opened Friends primary school at Muhudu in northern Tiriki.

Joseph recalls that the Muhudu Primary School, where he started his teaching, and which he opened (i.e. was the first teacher), was the first school to be established in northern Tiriki. Before then the number of school attenders from the northern portion of the tribe had been very small indeed, and these few had been obliged to attend the primary school at Kaimosi Mission, which was not only inconveniently far for many children, but also was staffed and attended principally by Maragoli and other non-Tiriki, thereby putting Tiriki students at a disadvantage. Joseph says he was the first Tiriki-born and initiated man from the Bumbo sub-tribal region of northern Tiriki to complete his primary school teacher's training. Thus he regards himself as an educational pioneer in his home region on two counts. Joseph also recalls with some sadness that the material rewards of pioneering in education at Muhudu were nil. After one year he left Muhudu to seek employment at Nairobi, because the students' parents had failed to pay him a single cent for a whole year of teaching.

Joseph worked for a number of months in Nairobi as a clerk in an engineering firm. Then in August 1942, he joined the King's African Rifles. Assigned to the Eleventh Division, he was trained and worked as a lorry and motorcycle mechanic, and spent a number of months overseas with his unit, principally in Burma.

Joseph was discharged from the Army in May, 1946, and returned to Tiriki. He very soon married a local Tiriki girl, spent a number of months getting his house and homestead in order, and then got a job as clerk at Kaimosi Mission power mill. While in the Army Joseph had developed a strong interest in religious matters. He had attended the worship services of many Christian denominations and also learned something of Moslem and Buddhist practices. When he returned to Tiriki he found that the Friends mode of worship did not particularly answer his present religious needs, and he started systematically investigating the other denominations with followings in North Nyanza. The Pentecostals appealed to him more than any other group with a substantial following in Tiriki, but he did not feel sufficiently drawn to them to forsake his Friends membership and join them. Joseph's wife, through her mother, Leya Leba, had become interested in, and then converted to, the *Dini Ya Israel*, which had its headquarters and principal following in the neighbouring tribal location of Nyangori. It will be

recalled from Chapter VII (p. 193) that Ganila himself was
converted to the Israel Church in 1947, following a sudden and
powerful religious experience that convinced him that he had
been possessed by the Holy Spirit. Shortly after his conversion,
Ganila and two other Israel converts in Tiriki founded the first
Israel parish church in Tiriki at Mahanga. I shall briefly
summarize in the following paragraph the material I presented
in Chapter VII (pp. 192–4, 196–9, 223) on Joseph's leadership
activities in the Israel Church.

Late in 1947 Joseph started serving a two-year religious
apprenticeship under Zakayo Kivuli, the founder and High
Priest of the Israel Church. During his apprenticeship Joseph
lived at Jebrok, Nyangori, the Israel Church headquarters, and
commuted daily by bicycle the dozen or so miles from Jebrok
to his clerical job at the Kaimosi Mission power mill. In 1949,
his apprenticeship completed, Ganila returned to his home at
Mahanga and assumed the headship of the Mahanga Israel
parish. He also started teaching primary school again and left
his power mill job. After the Second World War the awakened
popular interest in education throughout Tiriki triggered the
opening of many new primary schools, including several in the
relatively conservative northern region of the tribe. Between
1949 and 1956 Ganila taught in several of these newly-opened
schools. There is no need to retrace here Ganila's activities as
head of the Israel Church in Tiriki. It is sufficient to note that
under his skilful guidance and leadership the Israel membership in Tiriki grew in six years from a handful of followers at
Mahanga to embrace seven large and active parishes. Ganila
succeeded as has no other modern Tiriki religious leader in
combining a talent for organization and administration with
a keen awareness of traditional Tiriki attitudes towards leadership and the place of dream prophecy.

Ganila's success as the leader of the Tiriki Israel Church,
together with his school teaching activities, quickly won him
the respect of his peers and the elders of his community, and in
the early 1950's he was chosen to represent Bumbo sub-location
in the Tiriki Location Advisory Council. As Ganila's popularity
both as a church and secular leader grew in Tiriki, his rapport
with Kivuli, the High Priest of Dini Israel, deteriorated. In
1955, and again early in 1956, Joseph had some rather severe

altercations with Kivuli. The immediate causes of the disputes appear rather trivial; in one case, for example, a rather bitter debate was triggered by a remark Ganila made about Kivuli's putting too much writing on the banners he and his Nyangori followers carried in parades. There is evidence, however, that the underlying friction stemmed from Ganila's gradually having assumed virtually complete independence from Kivuli in his handling of Tiriki Israel church affairs, not only in matters of ritual and practice, but also in the financial sphere. It is noteworthy that Ganila never took any overt steps to establish Tiriki Israel's complete independence from Kivuli. Almost certainly if Ganila had declared Tiriki Israel's independence, the District Commissioner would have intervened and thwarted him, because of the policy which prevailed in Kenya during the Mau Mau emergency of prohibiting the formation of any new separatist sects; and Ganila was quite aware of this.

In May 1956, Ganila was elected to represent his sub-location for another term on the Tiriki Location Advisory Council in the first secret ballet election ever held in Tiriki. By this time he had firmly established himself as a popular and respected leader in both religious and secular affairs in his home area, and Chief Hezron had come to view him as one of the tribe's most promising young leaders. Then his activities as a religious leader came to a quick demise. In the summer of 1956, shortly after my wife and I had departed from Tiriki and returned to the United States, Kivuli called a special business and worship meeting at Jebrok to discuss the state of the Israel Church organization, particularly the Tiriki branch. The upshot of the meeting was that Ganila was voted out of the leadership of the Tiriki branch of the Israel Church, purportedly by an assembled multitude of Israel members including representatives from the Tiriki branch. Ganila responded by resigning from Israel Church membership.[1] Unfortunately I have not been able to obtain Ganila's version of what happened at this meeting. Kivuli appointed in Ganila's stead, not Inyanje, who had been Ganila's principal assistant, but another Tiriki Israel preacher, apparently well regarded in Tiriki, and generally

[1] Personal correspondence with Mr. F. G. Welbourn, Makerere College, Kampala, Uganda.

conforming and subordinate in his relations with Kivuli. The
Israel Church continues to this day (1961) to have a strong
following in Tiriki, but its rapid growth in Tiriki stopped after
Ganila was replaced.

Early in 1957 Ganila found new scope for his leadership
ability, but in the political rather than the religious field. Several
older illiterate or meagrely-schooled Tiriki headmen were
retired, creating vacancies in the tribal administrative bureaucracy. Ganila was offered and accepted one of these vacancies,
the position of headman of Bumbo sub-location. He is still
serving as headman today (1961).[1]

Ganila's career pattern deviates in one respect from that of
most of his peers in the tribal administration. After losing his
church membership at the time of life when he was becoming
most heavily involved in tribal administration, he again joined
the church. It is reported that in 1959 Ganila rejoined the Israel
Church, but that he has remained strictly a lay member. All
reports, however, indicate that he remains very popular with
his peers, and in the good graces of the community and sub-
tribal elders.

The Contemporary Administrative Career Pattern

The characteristic career pattern that emerges from an
analysis of the biographies of contemporary tribal administrative
leaders is a 'W'-shaped zig-zagging back and forth between predominantly pagan and predominantly Christian socio-religious
affiliations. The contemporary tribal leaders, generally born
into pagan families, for the most part attended mission schools
during part of their boyhood and early adolescence. There they
were instructed in 'the three R's' and Christianity and also

---

[1] In 1959 the five Tiriki sub-tribes were divided, and their boundaries redrawn
to form a total of ten sub-tribal divisions. The tribal administration was reorganized
so that each of the new sub-tribes was put in charge of a sub-chief. The office of
sub-headman was abolished, and the old office of headman was replaced by that of
sub-chief. Each of the sub-chiefs is in charge of an area about half the size of the
former sub-tribal division which was presided over by the headman. He no
longer, however, has the assistance of any subordinate administrative appointees.
Joseph Ganila is the sub-chief of the new Bumbo sub-tribe.

Tiriki at present has eleven sub-chiefs; one sub-chief is in charge of each of the
ten sub-tribes, and the eleventh sub-chief serves as a replacement whenever any
of the sub-chiefs is on leave, and on other occasions serves as the chief's administrative assistant.

attended and frequently joined the Christian church. Then they retired, sometimes eagerly, sometimes perforce, from school life to traditional circumcision and the subsequent six months of initiation and seclusion. This action, viewed by the mission authorities as an extremely unfortunate return to paganism, marked the end of most initiates' school careers. Nearly all of the contemporary tribal leaders, however, were recruited from those Tiriki youth who managed, usually after a delay of several years, to return to mission schools to complete elementary teachers' training and then to obtain jobs as teachers in mission schools. Then, either during or following their careers as teachers, they generally moved from church positions of lesser importance to local pastorships and there gained recognition as up-and-coming community leaders. The next step was usually to a position in the tribal administrative bureaucracy. Often at this point in their careers two or more positions (e.g., school teacher, religious leader, and/or tribal functionary) were held at the same time; it was common, however, for a man to give up his job as a schoolteacher soon after he could find sufficient income from other sources to prevent a decline in his living standard resulting from the loss of his teacher's salary. Finally, after firmly establishing themselves in one or another tribal administrative position, men who have gained renown as tribal leaders have usually gradually moved into the sorts of activities which are traditionally expected of important men as they approach elderhood. Most such men have started to attend the community beer drinks, and many have taken a second and then perhaps a third wife. Thus the leaders, by participating in activities that for the second time estrange them from the Christian churches, have helped themselves gain further approval of their leadership status from the community elders and from Chief Hezron.

To summarize, contemporary Tiriki tribal leaders received virtually indispensable instrumental aid to attaining positions of tribal authority through the education they obtained from the missions and from the training in leadership gained as pastors in one or another local church organization. One of the essential props, however, to security and success as a contemporary tribal political leader is continued membership in good standing in the Tiriki age group organization—initially achieved, of course, by undergoing traditional Tiriki initiation. Church positions of tribe-wide renown, while in several cases used by contemporary tribal leaders as stepping-stones to their present tribal administrative eminence, are generally tenaciously held to and faithfully filled only by those Tiriki men of leadership ability whose chances for attainment of or continuing success in tribal administration are hampered by not having undergone the Tiriki initiation or by their betrayal of the initiation secrets.

Chief Hezron has used his British-vested authority to uphold the sacredness of the Tiriki initiation rites. Chief Amiani, in contrast, wielded similar British-backed power so as to weaken, or at least temporarily cast aside, the traditional concepts of authority implemented and formalized through the initiation rites and the age grading system. Chief Hezron, indeed, has chosen to encourage a new pre-occupation with the initiation ceremonies and age group organization. Thus we have the contemporary employment of these traditional elements of Tiriki social structure as mechanisms for maintaining and enhancing tribal solidarity, for roughly assigning different types of authority positions to different age grades, and for implicitly bestowing a mantle of indigenous legitimacy upon Hezron's contemporary tribal leadership.

X

Changing Tiriki Social Structure: Summary and Conclusions

WERE Tiriki to be revisited today by administrators or missionaries who had dealings with the tribe fifty years ago, they would undoubtedly be struck by the enormous changes that have come to both the people and the country. Heavily-forested areas through which elephants occasionally roamed are now densely populated and cultivated. Instead of narrow, tortuous trails they would find a network of well-kept dirt roads, regularly traversed by buses and trucks transporting people, livestock, farm produce, charcoal, and manufactured products between the tribal area and the railheads at Kisumu and Eldoret. European-type clothing has everywhere replaced the traditional skins of the men and the women's pubic tassels. No longer are groups of young men found practising with spear and shield and bow and arrow between occasional cattle raids; today members of the traditional warrior age grade regularly lounge at the community market places when 'home on leave' from work off-tribe. The market places harbour many drastic innovations; the symmetrically laid out tin-roofed brick-walled general stores, butcher shops, tailor shops, maize-grinding mills, and tea houses, all offering goods or services for money, present a startling contrast to the occasional barter and exchange carried on at central meeting grounds in pre-European times.

The absence of thorn fences around homesteads, the relative scarcity of large homesteads with many huts centred around a dusty central courtyard, and the difficulty of distinguishing where one homestead ends and the next begins would all offer clues as to changes from the indigenous family and neighbourhood organizations. The schools, crowded with children on weekdays and with church meetings on Sundays, are an even more striking innovation. In other areas the changes have apparently been less drastic. The games played by young children as they tend their infant charges have undoubtedly changed somewhat in character, but their play groups, and also the clusters of women hoeing in the fields, would probably strike a familiar note to the former administrator. The fact that the women's work groups are now organized according to church affiliation, and that probably only the children's play groups continue to approximate the traditional type neighbourhood social patternings, would not be immediately apparent. The sight of the elders gathered to hear a case, or drinking beer in a banana grove, would seem familiar enough, but the uniformed tribal administrators chairing local and sub-tribal meetings, and bicycling back and forth between their constituencies and the tribal centre, would again be a radical departure from the traditional scene. The tribal centre itself, with its typewriter-equipped offices, comfortable rest houses for touring officials (and anthropologists), its maternity ward and medical dispensary, reflects not only revolutionary changes in knowledge and technology, but also the functioning of a centralized tribal administration where formerly no such thing even existed.

Initially Tiriki might look, to a European visitor, like a society that is trying to turn its back on the past and is rushing to become an integral part of the modern industrial world. More careful examination reveals that the Tiriki are quite conservative in some ways. Indeed, a fair number of interesting juxtapositions of old and new that to the outsider might seem almost paradoxical have occurred in this process of change. Also the observer soon realizes that here is a society where, in spite of all the changes, restlessness and factionalism are minimal, a strong sense of social continuity and order is manifest, and a fairly high level of general morale prevails. This is especially striking when the Tiriki social climate is compared with that in neighbouring Maragoli or nearby Bunyoro.

The ongoing activities of both the women and the tribal elders afford striking examples of the apparently contradictory aspects of Tiriki social change. The women look a bit anachronistic as they continue to work the fields exclusively with short-handled hoes; yet these same women are the segment of the tribe that has perhaps most eagerly and most universally accepted the innovation of a new religion. Of course the paradox disappears when it is discovered that the women had little vested interest in the traditional religion and that the religious innovations of Christianity have supplied the women with a social and ritual context within which they can preserve many of their traditional patterns and beliefs in spite of the extended absences of their menfolk. Tiriki women are conservative after all. The elders also look anachronistic as they gather, day after day, to listen to and judge local disputes; furthermore, their love for good company and discussion around the beer pots remains essentially unchanged. These same elders, however, are the most steadfast apologists for the contemporary centralized tribal Chieftaincy—an institution which has no traditional Tiriki counterpart. The apparent radicalism of the elders in this sphere clearly becomes an aspect of their social conservatism when the larger social context is examined and understood. It will be recalled that since the demise of the major ritual role of the seniormost ritual elders it is primarily because of the continuing support of the new tribal administration, with its Colonial Administration backing, that the elders' position as respected judicial leaders and preservers of the sacred initiation customs remains secure. The women and the elders, while conservative, are not reactionary. Both these groups have maintained a good deal of continuity with their pre-European traditions by more or less unwittingly seeking out and accepting the support of certain far-reaching social innovations.

The younger Tiriki men, of both today and a generation ago, may be likened to 'progressives'. They have forsaken cattle raiding (against their will, to be sure), adopted the practice of working for extended periods away from their homelands. They have turned to the European for skills in reading and writing, in many technological areas, in combating disease, for scientific knowledge, cosmological insight, and religious dogma. Today, however, we have the second generation of post-contact progressive young men. The first generation of young progressives are now the conservative tribal elders; the very generation that two decades ago was so taken with exploring, trying to exploit, and accepting the European world now strives to maintain the integrity of the traditional age-graded statuses, and uses the European's authority to help accomplish this. This state of affairs—where the younger men are eager for change and the elders are the more conservative, but where both groups interact in a mutually helpful manner—clearly has a precedent in the types of relationships traditionally maintained by the age group system. It will be recalled that men of the junior age grades were traditionally expected to initiate and carry out social innovations, but always subject to the senior age groups' counsel and veto. There was, in effect, an ongoing division between initiators (the 'progressives') and the legitimizers (the 'conservatives') of social change.

Factionalism is a recurrent theme in the accounts of many relatively homogeneous and stable societies suddenly caught up in the vortex of European-induced social change. With the demise or in the absence of strong progressive-conservative factionalism, a rather disorganized multiplicity of relatively ineffectual splinter factions is common. The latter situation seems to characterize, for example, contemporary social conditions in North and South Maragoli. A pagan-Christian factional division pervaded the Tiriki social scene in the 1920's and 1930's, with the pagans retaining the more conservative orientation. Recently, however, particularly within the last decade, this division has become of little consequence, and 'progressive' versus 'conservative' orientations have again become aligned predominantly according to age grades.

It is my opinion that the ongoing patternings of the age group organization underlay, and certainly supported, this recent resolution and control of factionalism in Tiriki. The age grades, each grade with its formally ascribed status, role, and social orientation, in effect supply the Tiriki with a set of built-in, mutually interdependent social factions that cover the field from 'progressive' to 'conservative'. Also it is noteworthy that the age group organization functions in such a manner that a modicum of social adaptability and flexibility is perforce demanded of its members; for all men who live out their full three score and ten years must succeed and adjust to several formally delineated changes of status, role and social orientation. To summarize, the Tiriki have a social system that aligns its male members into several social groupings, each of which must fulfil and maintain an ascribed set of social expectations; and these expectations run the gamut from 'progressive' to 'conservative'. Through the decades, each age group must acquiesce and adjust to several major formally structured social changes which entail progressive shifts towards conservatism.

The Tiriki age group system worked to maintain an ongoing

social 'steady-state' in pre-European times, wherein the values
and social patterns of the tribe as a whole varied but little from
one generation to the next. The elders, particularly the ritual
elders, held most of the ultimate power sanctions whereby the
continuity of the traditional social order was maintained and
the occasional necessary organizational innovation legitimized.
Today members of these two seniormost age grades are ill-
equipped to have final say about current organizational decisions. In many instances they haven't the physical energy to
keep abreast of organizational demands; also they are crippled
by their relative lack of formal education and by limited experience during their formative years with many emergent contemporary problems. The age group system, with its traditional
age-graded status allocations, would probably have proved a
troublesome heritage rather than an asset had not events
conspired to transfer the major power sanctions from the elders
to the hands of the younger administrative age group members.

The disfranchised or unfranchised elements in the tribe—
namely the tribal strangers, outcasts, witch suspects, and, last
but not least, the women—formed the principal membership of
the Christian faction that successfully neutralized the enormous
power of the elders; and they did it, of course, by destroying the
ritual elders' virtual monopoly of supernatural power sanctions.
The efforts of the Christian faction were more or less triggered
and coordinated by Chief Amiani, who was led both by temperament and expediency to utilize these less integrated
elements in the tribe to bring about a religious revolution, and
thus deprive the senior elders of their effective supernaturally-
backed authority in all areas except initiation; and of course it
was the British Administration that prevented the elders' defeat
in the area of initiation.

It is interesting that the traditional clan structure remains
essentially intact after the replacement of the ancestor cult by
Christianity, which provides no explicit re-enforcement for clan
groupings. Nothing, however, in Christian practice or dogma
precludes the maintenance of most of the traditional lineage
sentiments and practices concerning exogamy, social obligations, and inheritance; furthermore, the pervasive ideological
motif of remembrance was not seriously curtailed by the coming
of Christianity.

The ideological aspects of the initiation rites (*idumi*) seem if anything to have been re-enforced since the demise of the ancestor cult. Even as their role as intermediaries between the living and the ancestors was rapidly dwindling to nil, the ritual elders, with British protection, began working with added vigour to preserve and enhance the quasi-religious initiation rites and the complex of social statuses and interrelationships which they promulgate and maintain. The tribal administration, under the leadership of Chief Hezron, has, with Colonial Administrative encouragement, aided and abetted the elders' efforts, both as guardians and practitioners of the traditional initiation rites, and also as judges and administrative advisors. Thus the members of the judicial and ritual age grades have become staunch supporters of the contemporary tribal administration. The senior age groups have in effect become a House of Lords, with important ritual functions, significant, even though limited, advisory and veto powers, and important judicial duties.

Individual personalities have certainly played their part in producing the contemporary social system. The brash, forceful Amiani did much to institute the office of a strong tribal Chief, which remains an integral aspect of the contemporary social structure. He also encouraged, perhaps even precipitated, the activities of the out-group Christians that led the conservative elders to become apologists for the British Administration, and, under Hezron, strongly to support the administrative efforts of the younger age group members. It is a felicitious event that circumcision chief Sagwa should have become a Christian and thereby have opened the way for the Christian faction to rejoin the ranks of the majority. And it is also good fortune that Chief Hezron has proved to have such astute political sensitivity and has been so adroit at bringing the Christian and pagan factions together.

The emergence of fortunate leadership has facilitated the current happy resolution of Tiriki administrative problems. Also, of course, the nature of the British Administration, the missionary groups, and other outside contacts and influences have greatly effected the course of events. For example, the British penchant for fostering reforms within the framework of existing indigenous political institutions whenever possible and the mutual British and Tiriki commitment to distinctive, separate executive and judicial governmental leaders, have together fostered the evolution of the current tribal administration. This does not alter the fact, however, that the ongoing social structure of a society continually limits, and in large measure defines, the types of leadership that emerge as well as the nature of the reforms that can be carried out.

The importance of the Tiriki age group organization, in spite of its temporary resurgence, is clearly on the wane. The role allocations it ascribes are becoming fused with the offices maintained by the administrative bureaucracy; and where not so fused they are becoming blurred by new forms of status achieved through education and wealth. Furthermore, European-type education and progressive experience within the administrative bureaucracy are coming to be more important for the attainment of administrative offices than experience and achievement measured by the standards of the traditional age group organization. Nevertheless, the age group organization and its indigenous outgrowth, the multi-clan community and sub-tribal organizations, clearly have greatly aided the Tiriki in evolving and accepting their contemporary bureaucratic administrative structure, which manages to cope fairly successfully with the countless problems and many innovations arising from and demanded by the tribe's growing interdependence with other parts of Kenya and the modern world. The Tiriki are fortunate to have had an indigenous social system that has proved adaptable to change and capable of providing considerable aid in maintaining social integration and integrity during the revolutionary changes of the last fifty years.

Bibliography

APPLEBY, A. A. *A First Luyia Grammar*: Enlarged Edition with Exercises. Butere, Kenya: Church Missionary Society, 1951.

DUNDAS, K. 'The Wanga and Other Tribes of the Elgon District,' *Journal of the Royal Anthropological Institute*. London, 1913.

EISENSTADT, S. N. *From Generation to Generation*. Glencoe, Illinois: The Free Press, 1956.

FALLERS, LLOYD A. *Bantu Bureaucracy*. Cambridge: W. Heffer & Sons, Ltd. (no date).

——(ed.). *The King's Men: Leadership and Status in Buganda on the Eve of Independence*. London: Oxford University Press, 1964.

FEARN, HUGH. *An African Economy; a Study of the Economic Development of the Nyanza Province of Kenya, 1903–1953*. London: Oxford University Press, 1961.

FIRTH, RAYMOND. 'Social Organization and Social Change,' *Journal of the Royal Anthropological Institute of Great Britain and Ireland*, Vol. 84, pp. 1–20.

—— 'Some Principles of Social Organization,' *Journal of the Royal Anthropological Institute of Great Britain and Ireland*, Vol. 85, pp. 1–18.

FORTES, M., and EVANS-PRITCHARD, E. E. *African Political Systems*. London: Oxford University Press, 1940.

Friends African Mission Annual Reports, Kaimosi, Kenya.

HILL, M. F. *Permanent Way: the Story of the Kenya and Uganda Railway*. Nairobi, Kenya: East African Railways and Harbors (no date).

HOBLEY, C. W. 'Anthropological Studies in Kavirondo and Nandi,' *Journal of the Royal Anthropological Institute of Great Britain and Ireland*. London, 1903, pp. 325–59.

HOLLIS, A. C. *The Nandi, their Language and Folk-lore*. London: Oxford University Press, 1909.

HOYT, ALTA HOWARD. *Bantu Folklore Tales of Long Ago*. Wichita, Kansas: Day's Print Shop, 1951.

HUMPHREY, NORMAN. *The Liguru and the Land*. Nairobi: The Government Printer, 1947.

HUNTINGFORD, G. W. B. *The Nandi of Kenya*. London: Routledge & Kegan Paul, Ltd., 1953.

JACOBS, ALAN H. 'Age-Class Systems and Political Organization in East Africa,' *Anthropology Tomorrow*. Chicago: student publication of the Department of Anthropology, University of Chicago, Vol. IV, No. 3, pp. 29–37.

LEVINE, ROBERT, and SANGREE, WALTER H. 'The Diffusion of Age-Group Organization in East Africa: A Controlled Comparison,' in *Africa*, Vol. XXII, No. 2, April, 1962, pp. 97–110.

Low, D. Anthony, and Pratt, R. Cranford. *Buganda and British Overrule, 1900–1955*. London: Oxford University Press, 1960.

Luragoli–English Vocabulary. Kaimosi, Kenya: Friends Africa Mission Press, 1940.

'Minutes of the North Nyanza African District Council.' Kakamega, Kenya, 1955.

Mowrer, Jack. 'The North Nyanza African District Council.' Unpublished manuscript, 1954. East African Institute of Social Research Library, Makerere College, Kampala, Uganda.

'Nyanza Province Annual Report.' Kisumu, Kenya: Office of the Provincial Commissioner. Reports for 1913 through 1939.

Peristiany, J. G. *The Social Institutions of the Kipsigis*. London: George Routledge & Sons, Ltd., 1939.

Ravenstein, E. G. 'Vocabularies from Kavirondo, British East Africa,' collected by Mr. C. W. Hobley, *Journal of the Royal Anthropological Institute of Great Britain and Ireland*. London, 1899, pp. 338–42.

Redfield, Robert. *The Little Community*. Chicago: The University of Chicago Press, 1955.

Rowe, John Allen. *Kaimosi: An Essay in Mission History*, unpublished Master's thesis, Department of History, University of Wisconsin, 1958.

Sangree, Walter H. 'The Bantu Tiriki of Western Kenya,' in *Tribes of Sub-Saharan Africa*. Edited by James Gibbs. New York: Holt, Rinehart and Winston, Inc., 1965.

—— 'The Social Functions of Beer Drinking in Bantu Tiriki,' in *Society, Culture, and Drinking Patterns*. Edited by David J. Pittman and Charles R. Snyder. New York: John Wiley & Sons, Inc., 1962.

—— *Structural Continuity and Change in a Bantu Tribe: The Nature and Development of Contemporary Tiriki Social Organization*. Unpublished Ph.D. thesis, Department of Anthropology, University of Chicago, 1959.

Schapera, I. 'Christianity and the Tswana,' in *Cultures and Societies in Africa*. Edited by S. and P. Ottenberg. New York: Random House, 1960.

Steere, Douglas & Dorothy. *Friends Work in Africa*. London: Friends Home Service Committee, 1955.

Sundkler, Bengt C. M. *Bantu Prophets in South Africa*. London: Lutterworth Press, 1948.

Taylor, John U. *The Growth of the Church in Buganda; an Attempt at Understanding*. London: S. C. M. Press, 1958.

Thompson, Joseph. *Through Masai Land* (new and revised edition). London: Sampson Low, Marston & Co. (no date).

WAGNER, GÜNTER. 'The Abaluyia of Kavirondo (Kenya),' in *African Worlds*. Edited by Daryll Forde. London: Oxford University Press, 1954.
—— *The Bantu of North Kavirondo*, Vol. I. London: Oxford University Press, 1949.
—— *The Bantu of North Kavirondo*, Vol. II. London: Oxford University Press, 1956.
—— 'The Changing Family among the Bantu Kavirondo.' Supplement to *Africa*, Vol. XII, No. 1, 1939.
—— 'Maragoli Land Tenure.' Unpublished manuscript, 1946 (in the possession of Walter H. Sangree).
—— 'The Political Organization of the Bantu of North Kavirondo,' in *African Political Systems*. Edited by M. Fortes and E. E. Evans-Pritchard. London: Oxford University Press, 1940.
WELBOURN, F. B. *East African Rebels, a Study of some Independent Churches*. London: S. C. M. Press, 1961.
WHITELEY, W. H. 'The Changing Position of Swahili in East Africa,' *Africa*, Vol. XXVI, No. 4, pp. 343–53.
WILTSEY, ROBERT. *Age Class or Sets, and Age Grades*. Unpublished manuscript, University of Rochester, 1959.

Glossary of Tiriki Words

-gura - ma-	butter, grease, oil	61
-guru li- ma-	unsalaried local headman	114
guxu, guxu, baguxu	grandmother, grandchild. Also sometimes used as a term of respect or affection between persons of differing generations	33
-higa - ma-	cooking hearth	38
-hinda mu- ba-	person wealthy in terms of homestead size and grain stores	239
-hindila bu- -	adulthood	82
-hoda mu- mi-	tinful (approximately 20 oz.) of native beer	73 n.
-hya lu-, zimbihya	meeting place, market, community	52
-iha mw- bi-	bride; male initiate just emerging from seclusion	62
-ihwa mw- bi-	sister's child	9
-iluxa mw- mi-	lustral ceremony, ritual	10
-ilwazi mw- bi-	head preacher, pastor	194
-ima mw- mi-	custom	39
-ina shi- bi-	judicial meeting; court	238
-ixo bw- -	incest	9
-izuxulu mw- bi-	greatgrandchild; greatgrandparent	10
-janganyigo mu- ba-	mixed, alien (Swahili-loan) group, clan (Swahili-loan)	7
jilo mu- mi-	tabu: forbidden behaviour	53
-jizi mu- mi-	homestead	9
-lago -il - ma-	rule, regulation, law	139
-lalu bu-	madness	32
-lalu mu- ba-	insane person	238
-lambo mu- mi-	corpse	42
-lango m- mi- ⎫ *-liyango mu- mi-*⎭	headman; door	105
-libwa shi- bi-	archway built at homestead entrance to welcome bride or returning initiate	63
-lina, mu- ba-	friend	28
-lindi mu- ba-	leader; clerk of Friends Meeting	194
-loji bu-	witchcraft substance	205
-loji mu- ba-	witch	39
-loli li- ma-	vision	234
-lomoloma xu-	to speak, speak in tongues, prattle, chat	185
-loro li- ma-	dream	234

-luganila xu-	to confess	187
-luri mu- ba-	scout	72
-lumindi, bu- -	murder	5
-lwa - ma-	beer	6
-mbodoxa i- zi-	jealousy	41
-mbumi i- zi-	war horn	86
mulugulu	'off tribe'	xxxvi
-mwabo a- ba-	brother; parallel cousin; sometimes also cross cousin	9
-mwamu mu- ba-	'black man', Negro	88 n.
-nani gu- ma-	mythical man-eating giant	39
-nanyenzo shi- bi-	evil spirit	40
naxobizala, naxobizala (singular and plural)	in-law of adjacent generation (a term used with avoidance behaviour)	28
-ngoli mu- ba-	dream prophet, seer	183
-ngolole i- zi- *-ngolose i- zi-*	initiation mask	56
-ngulu - zi-	strength, power	163
-nini shi- bi-	shadow; spirit	42
-nyega xu- *(-suha xu-)*	to curse	130
-nyungu i- zi-	large earthenware pot	64
-oni bw- -	sin	186
-rembe mu- mi-	Erythria Abyssinica	90
-rende mu-, ba-	neighbour	18 n., 28
-rima bu-	anger	41
-ruji mu- ba-	person wealthy in cattle and/or cash	239
-rumbi shi- bi-	initiation seclusion hut	52
-saalisi mu- ba-	ritual elder who prays to the ancestral spirits	36
-sabo li- ma-	sleeping hut for adolescents	61
-sambwa lu- zi-	ancestral shrine	34
-sambwa mu- mi-	ancestral spirits	30
-saxulu bu- -	elderhood	82
-saxulu mu- ba-	(male) elder	36
-saza mu- ba-	adult male (circumcised)	66
-sejerele lu- zi-	rubbing stick used for divining	18
-sejese shi- bi-	stick protruding from the centre of the hut roof	17
-sela bu- -	thin eleusine gruel	60
-senende i- zi-	a creeper vine used in making initiation headdresses	53

senje, senje, basenje	paternal aunt, i.e., father's, sister (and father's sister's husband)	13
-sexa lu- zin-	beer tubes	37
-shebela xu-	to sponsor an initiate	52
-shebi mu- ba-	circumciser	50
-shele, mu- ba-	elderly woman	238
-shiliga i- zi-	work bee	160
-sibwa lu- zi-	carved baton carried by initiates leaving seclusion	63
-silo mu- ba-	fool, feeble minded person	238
-sisi i- zi-	cooking section of the hut	66
-siyala mu- ba-	cross-cousin	9
-sobi li- ma-	bull roarer	53
-somi mu- ba-	literate person, student; Christian	249
-somo lu- zi-	territorial unit	xxxviii
-soni shi- bi-	shame; shameful thing; kin whom you may marry	11
-subuhedeman i- zi-	sub-headman	110
-suha xu- ⎫ *-nyega xu-* ⎭	to curse	130
-sumadi i- zi-	traditional leather cloak for male elders	56
-sungu mu- ba-	'white man', European	88 n.
-swa lu- -	state of ritual impurity; state of ritual danger	10
-syeba xu-	to dance	185
-syuxa xu-	to haunt	43
-syuxu shi- bi-	vengeful ghost	41
-walagi i- zi-	'home brew' illegally distilled liquor	xxxvii
xoza, xoza, baxoza	maternal uncle	15
-xula li- ma-	age group	xxxviii
-xulu bu- -	circumcision song(s)	74
-xulu mu- ba-	initiates	52
-xwana bu- -	ritual contamination arising from the birth of twins	37
-xwasi mu- ba-	(brother–sister) in-law	13
-xwi bu- -	bridewealth	14
-yayi mu- ba-	boy	51
-zu in- zin-	house; sub-clan	8
-zuxiza li- ma-	remembrance gathering (usually at the ancestral shrine)	36

Appendix I

Male Speaking

* Letters indicate terms used for both reference and address
** Numbers indicate terms used only referentially

Tiriki Term (S) (Pl.)	Rough English Equivalent
*A *Guga, Baguga*	Grandfather, grandson; great-grandfather, great-grandson
B *Guxu, Baguxu*	Grandmother, granddaughter; great-grandmother, great-granddaughter
C *Dada, Badada*	Father
**1 *Ise*	Father
D *Mama, Bamama*	Mother (and mother's brother's wife)
2 *Nyina*	Mother
E *Xoza, Baxoza*	Mother's brother
F *Senje, Basenje*	Father's sister (and father's sister's husband)
G *Amwabo, Bamwabo* / *Amweru, Bamweru*	Sibling, same sex
H *Mbozwa, Bambozwa*	Sibling, opposite sex
3 *Musiyala, Basiyala*	Cross cousin
I *Mwana, Baana*	Child (male, female)
J *Mwihwa, Biihwa*	Sister's child
4 *Shizuxulu, Bizuxulu*	Great-grandparent, great-grandchild
5 *Shisoni, Bisoni*	Great-grandparent (used to refer to great-grandparents only if all known members of the great-grandparental generation are deceased)
6 *Muguga, Baguga*	Ancestor, ancestress (usually restricted to agnatic ancestor)
R *Basanje* / *Bamwayi*	Parent(s) of child's spouse

I—Male Speaking

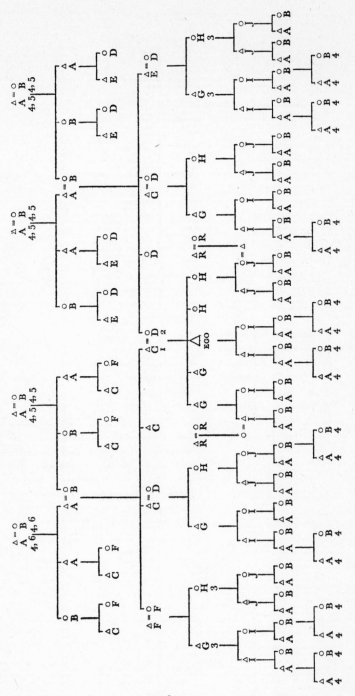

Appendix II

Female Speaking

* Letters indicate terms used for both reference and address
** Numbers indicate terms used only referentially

Tiriki Term (S.) (Pl.)	Rough English Equivalent
*A *Guga, Baguga*	Grandfather, grandson; great-grandfather, great-grandson
B *Guxu, Baguxu*	Grandmother, grandchild; great-grandmother, great-granddaughter
C *Dada, Badada*	Father
**1 *Ise*	Father
D *Mama, Bamama*	Mother (and mother's brother's wife)
2 *Nyina*	Mother
E *Xoza, Baxoza*	Mother's brother
F *Senje, Basenje*	Father's sister (and father's sister's husband); brother's child
G *Amwabo, Bamwabo* *Amweru, Bamweru*	Sibling, same sex
H *Mbozwa, Bambozwa*	Sibling, opposite sex
3 *Musiyala, Basiyala*	Cross cousin
I *Mwana, Baana*	Child (either sex)
4 *Shizuxulu, Bizuxulu*	Great-grandparent, great-grandchild
5 *Shisoni, Bisoni*	Great-grandparent (used to refer to great-grandparents only if all known members of the great-grandparental generation are deceased)
6 *Muguga, Baguga*	Ancestor, ancestress (usually restricted to the agnatic line)
R *Basanje* *Bamwayi*	Parent(s) of child's spouse

22

II—Female Speaking

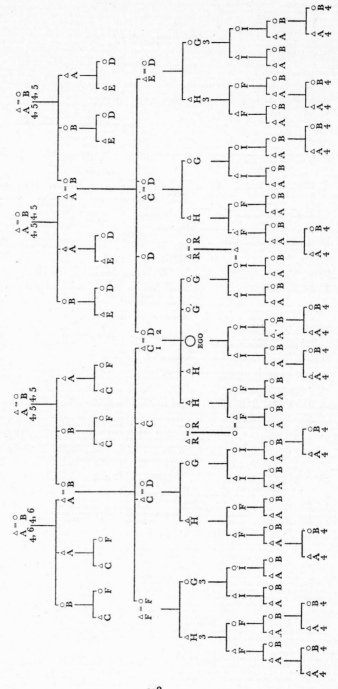

Appendix III

Affinal Kin: Male

* Letters indicate terms used for both reference and address
** Numbers indicate terms used only referentially
? Question mark indicates that investigator is somewhat uncertain
  about the term used in this relationship

Tiriki Term		Rough English Equivalent
(S.)	(Pl.)	
*A	Guga, Baguga	Grandfather, grandson; male in-law of adjacent generation
B	Guxu, Baguxu	Grandmother, granddaughter; female in-law of adjacent generation
F	Senje, Basenje	Wife's brother's child; wife's father's sister (?)
G	Amwabo, Bamwabo ⎫ Amweru, Bamweru ⎬	Sibling, same sex
H	Mbozwa, Bambozwa	Sibling, opposite sex
I	Mwana, Baana	Child (either sex)
J	Mwihwa, Biihwa	Sister's child
K	Muxali, Baxali	Wife, woman
L	Muxayo, Baxayo	Senior wife, great wife
M	Muxwasi, Baxwasi	Brother- or sister-in-law
N	Mulamwa, Balamwa	Wife's brother's wife
O	Basagwa, Basagwa	Wife's sister's husband
**7	Naxobizala	In-law of adjacent generation (avoidance relationship)

III—Affinal Kin: Male

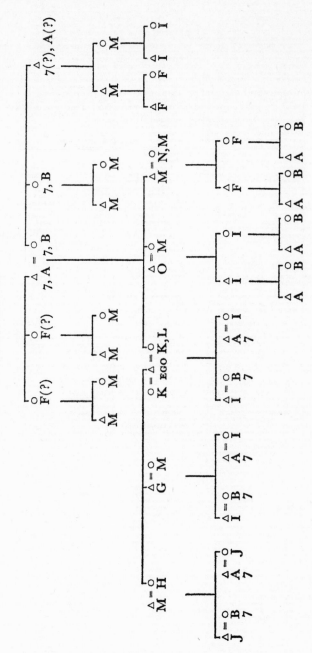

Appendix IV

Affinal Kin: Female

* Letters indicate terms used for both reference and address

** Numbers indicate terms used only referentially

? Question mark indicates that investigator is somewhat uncertain about the term used in this relationship

Tiriki Term (S.) (Pl.)	Rough English Equivalent
*A *Guga, Baguga*	Male in-law of adjacent generation (grandfather, grandson)
B *Guxu, Baguxu*	Female in-law of adjacent generation (grandmother, granddaughter)
F *Senje, Basenje*	Brother's child; brother's child's spouse; husband's father's sister (?)

Tiriki Term (S.) (Pl.)	Rough English Equivalent
G *Amwabo, Bamwabo*	Sibling, same sex
Amweru, Bamweru	Sibling, opposite sex
H *Mbozwa, Bambozwa*	
I *Mwana, Baana*	Child (either sex)
M *Muxwasi, Baxwasi*	Brother- or sister-in-law
**7 *Naxobizala*	In-law of adjacent generation (avoidance relationship)
P *Musaza, Basaza*	Husband, man
Q *Ambalixayo, Bambalixayo*	Co-wife; husband's brother's wife

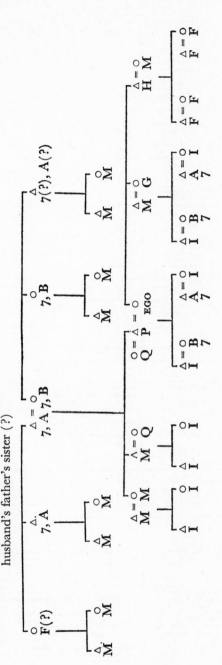

301

Index

Abagusii, 124 n.

Abaluyia, xxxv; clan land ownership concepts, 29, 83; District of North Nyanza, 98, 98 n.; *mlango* headmen, 105–6; Tiriki, a frontier community, 27–8

Abashiseza clan, 99

Acholi, 183

Adimuga, Johana, *pseud.*, 254–59

Administration, British, xxxii–iii, 102–4, 109, 132, 142–3, 229, 236; District, xxxii–iii, 98, 98 n., 99; Hobley, first Administrator, 99–101

Administration, tribal, Tiriki, xxxiii, 105, 224, 229–30, 282; age grading and, 232–3; Chief's authority, 225; consonance with traditional social structure, 232–5, 233 n. 3; establishment of sub-tribes in 1959, 278 n.; judicial elders and, 224, 230; leader career pattern, 278–80; summary, 117–19; tribal elders and, 168–9, 236; under Amiani, 103 ff.

Adultery, Israel Church, 201–2; tests of fidelity, 159

Affinal, kin, 299, 300, 301, 302; ties, 142

African District Council (A.D.C.), 84, 226–7, 257, 262; forest, xxxviii; market inspector, 247

African District Court elder, 246

Afterlife, pagan *vs.* Christian concepts, 164

Age grades, 48; elder warrior, 68, 69; five, 68; initiate, 68, 69; judicial elder, 68, 69; leadership and, 283; list of names of, 69, 70, 70 n.; overlap of duties of, 71; ritual elders, 68, 69, 72; tribal administration and, 232–3, 233 n. 1; warrior, 67, 69, 70

Age group (*lixula*), xxxviii, xxxix, 48; beer drinks, 74; brotherhood (*idumi*), 44, 95; changeover, 75–8, 81–2; corporate nature of, 74–5; funerals, 74; summary, 81–2; Terik same as Tiriki, 79

Age group organization, age grades, age groups, Tiriki, xxxiii, xxxix, 44; brother (*mugugwa*), 66; comparison of Tiriki, Kipsigis and Nandi, 75–81; cursing and expulsion of *idumi*

Age group organization, *contd.*—
revealers, 67; formal incorporation into, 66; on wane, 287; social change and, 283–5; structure and function of, 67–75

Aged, attitudes towards, 30–33; supernatural power and the, 30

Agriculture, fields owned by men, 159; women's major role, 153, 155. *See also* Work bees

Aligula, Johnston T. B., xi

Amiani, Chief, 102–3, 107, 119, 167, 191–2, 225–6, 236, 253, 257, 269, 280, 285–6; appointed Chief, 102; appointed headman, 127; beer brewing ruling and, 135–6, 158; break with Friends, 133–4; circumcision and initiation and, 128–33; conversion to Christianity, 1927, 127–8; end of reign, 140, 225–6; estrangement from Christians, 1939, 138; Maragoli immigration policy, 137–8; pagan elders' wrath, 131–3; political powers, 132; resignation, 107; retirement, 1946, 127 143; Salvation Army and, 133–4; selling of land to Maragoli immigrants, 108–9

Ancestor cult, 30, 33–7, 78; Christianity and, 163, 205; demise of, 166–9, 285–6

Ancestors, beseeched by ritual elders, 45; custom traced to, 39; founding, 3

Ancestral shrine (*lusambwa*), 34, 36; decreasing in number, 35, 166; nature of, 36–7, 46; supplications at, 36–7; women's, 38

Ancestral spirits (*misambwa*), 30, 33–43, 164, 166–9; age groups and, 74–5; intolerance of witches, 40, 44; Maragoli beliefs, 35; supplications of, 34–5, 225

Anger (*burima*), of sorcerer, 41

Anglicans, 171

Army (*ibololi*), 92–3; leaders as British-appointed headmen, 99–100

Arson, burning of Christian homes by pagans, 129

Askari, tribal police and messenger, xxxvii, 103, 240, 247

302

Index

Asoga, Thomas, 192–4, 203
Authority, age grades and, 232–4, 236; age group organization and, 236, 285; attitudes towards, 170; British Administration as ultimate source of, 236; elders as former source of, 236; sanctions, secularization of, 169; shift from ritual to younger age grades, 285
Authority structure, Chapter VIII; diagram, 111–12; intimate, informal nature of, 118–19; of Bantu-speaking peoples, xxx–i; of independent churches, xxx–i; summary of contemporary tribal, 117–19
Avoidance behavior (naxobizala), 67
Ayubu, Kefa, Roho High Priest, 177, 180, 182, 185–8

Banana groves, for beer drinks, xxxvii; for memorial church services, xxxviii
Bechuanaland, 171
Beer, brewing and conversion to Christianity, 135–6, 158, 162; brewing by men, 136; Catholics and, 162, 213–14; drinking by contemporary tribal administrators, 252; drinking tubes (zinsexa), xxxvii, 37, 73 n.; drinks, xxxvii, 166, 283; drinks and age group solidarity, 73–4; drinks and initiation, 56–61; drunk by the cup, 73–4 n.; for ancestral supplication, 36–7; Hezron's position concerning, 271; leadership and, 238, 252, 279; Orthodox Church and, 190, 213–14; pagan attitude towards abstainers, 150; prohibition by Protestant Christian groups, 149, 218, 271; prohibition of and church membership growth, 216–17
Bible, in Luragoli, 122, 124, 188; ibayibu megaphones, 206–7; Israel Church, 204; reading, 163; reciting of verses, 206
Blackwater Fever, 102
Boundaries, tribal, Tiriki-Nandi, 101
Bride, 63; initiation bride, 62–4
Bridewealth, 14, 15, 21–3, 154; elopement and, 22; father's responsibility towards son, 21–2; sibling bond and, 15; son's responsibility towards father, 22
Broken pot ceremony, 11

Brotherhood, initiation, 44, 95
Brother-in-law (muxwasi), 13, 28
Bull roarer (lisobi), 53
Bunyoro, 114, 134, 282
Bureaucracy, tribal, see under Administration, tribal, Tiriki.
Bus, Kisumu-Eldoret, xxxvii
Bwali, community first fruits, 87; pre-planting, sub-tribe, 38; times of crisis, 88

Cash crops, 156 n.
Catholics (Mill Hill Mission), 161 n., 162, 193; beer drinking and, 213–14; membership in Tiriki, 215
Cattle, bridewealth and, 154; herding during initiation, 60; lending of, 154; raiding, 86, 101, 154–5; reference to in initiation, 64; size of herds, 155; social influence and, 154, 239. See also Livestock
Census, communities censused, xii
Central Kavirondo District, 98 n., 107 n. 1
Central Nyanza District, 107
Change, age group system and, 283–4; economic vs. political and religious, 153–162; Tiriki between 1902 and 1956, Chapter X
Changeover, of age groups, 76–7
Chicken, sacrificed at ancestral supplication, 36
Chief, the, 225–6, 230–1, 236, 246; contemporary court authority structure and, 117–19; diagram, 111; duties and privileges, 100; early Tiriki Chiefs, 99, 100, 101, 102; Paramount Chief (Mumia), 103; power of tribal, 132; recruited from war leaders, 225; sons sent to Kaimosi schools, 126. See also Amiani; Hezron Mushenye
Chief, initiation, 50, 148–9, 246
Childbirth, offerings at women's ancestral shrine, 38
Children, play, work, xxxvi
Chilson, Arthur, 100, 180
Christian, adherents, number of Tiriki, 172, 215–16; ancestral spirits and, 163–4; beer drinking and, 213–15; ghosts and, 163–4; growth of anti-Maragoli sentiment, 138; membership and polygyny and drinking,

Christian, *contd.*—
216–17; poison and, 163; religious groups; xxxviii, remembrance services, 165–6; sorcery and, 163; takeover of community religious functions, 88; Tiriki initiation, 139–40; witches and, 163–4
Christianity, ancestor cult and, 163; beer drinking and, 149; blamed for spoiling the land, 88; current importance of, 169; -pagan factionalism, 120, 127; -pagan hostility over initiation in Tiriki and Nyangori, 107–8, 127; spread under Chief Amiani, 127–36; women and, 158
Church, xxxviii; growth of membership, 122 *et passim*, 215–16; leaders, four biographies, 251–67; leadership, local *vs.* tribal, 247–8; leadership and beer drinking, 271; leadership and polygyny, 271
Church Missionary Society (Anglican), 161 n.
Churches, breakaway, *see* Independent; denominations and women's work groups, 160–1; independent, xxix, xxxi, xxxii, Chapter VII; Mission, xxix; Protestant sects, xxxi; separatist, *see* Independent; women and, 157–62
Circumcision, Abaluyia in general, 211; at mission hospital, 250, 261; Christian views towards, 129; circumcised person, not in Tiriki *idumi* (*jebusabageni*), 58; circumciser (*mushebi*), 50; grove (*gabunyonyi* or *shibanda*), 49, 50, 94, 128; mission circumcision, 139; operation, 54–5, 139; resultant contamination, 55; Tiriki-Terik, 4. *See also* Initiation
Civil servants, *see under* Headman, *mlango*
Clan, 44, 46; Abashiseza clan of Wanga, 99; alien, 7; Baluxoba, 99; basis for tribal government, 231–2; basis of *mlango* headman system, 104, 105, 230–2; Christianity and, 285; differences from Abaluyia norm, 5; distribution among many communities, 96; histories and origin myths, 3–4, 20; exogamy, 10, 12–13; formation, 7; inheritance and, 24; lands, 27; list of major clans, 7; *liguru* and, 116;

Clan, *contd.*—
lubamba, xxxviii–ix; Maragoli land ownership, 27, 29, 32, 46–7, 97; *olugongo* headmen, 106, 230–2; ownership of land, 5–6; segmentation, 7, 9; size, 6–7; social functions, 4–5; structure survives collapse of ancestor cult, 285; sub-clan, *vs.*, 24; Terik, 6
Clerk, Christian Church (*mulindi*), 194
Clitoridectomy, 62, 96 n.
Clothing, of initiates, 56; of Tiriki men, xxxvii
Coffee planting, 155, 156 n.
Community (*luhya*), 87–91; *bwali* first fruits, 87–8; chart, sub-location, 112; courts, 117; defense, 87; elder, 45; initiation seclusion huts, 91; *isubuhedeman* divisions today, 110; judicial duties, 88; keeper of horn, 86; leaders, three traditional types, 244; leadership, 239–45; meeting places, origin of, 84; multi-clan nature of, 96; overcrowding of, 91; ritual unit, 87; size, 91, 91 n.; sub-community (*liguru* area), 117; sub-headman, 244–6; witches and, 40
Confession, by Amiani, 131–2; Dini Ya Roho churches and, 186–7, 199–204; initiation, 53–4; Israel Church and, 199–204; of initiation secrets by Christians, 128, 255; of initiation secrets and Christian steadfastness, 131; of sins in Christian Church, 194
Converts Christian, beer brewing and, 135–6; Catholics, 161–2; conversion of Amiani, 127; death and, 122–3; early Friends, 122, 125–7; rate of conversion, Tiriki, 127
Cooperative work groups, 160
Corporate group. *See* Age group; Clan; Sub-clan
Corpse, burning of, 165, 165 n.
Cosmological beliefs, Tiriki, 39; change in, 164
Counsellor, initiation, 52, 60
Countryside and landscape, Tiriki, xxxvi
Courts (community, *luhya*), 88–9, 117, 118; church pastors and, 159; divisional, 106; *liguru's* sub-community, 116–18; limitations on jurisdiction, 88; Native Court of Appeals, Kakamega, 103–4; supervision of native

Courts, *contd.*—
tribunals and court fees in 1913, 102; withdrawal of formal Administrative sanction from Chief's courts, 106
Courtship, during initiation, 61, 63
Cross-cousin, 9
Curse, against Christian betrayers of initiation secrets, 129–31, 256; against witches, 40; elderhood and, 238; elders' against witches, 67, 126; father's sister's, 15; for revealing initiation secrets, 62; grandparents and, 31–2; mother's brother's (*xoza*), 19; nature of, 130
Custom (*mwima*), origin of, 39

Dance (*xusyeba*), for deceased elder, 165; in Christian services, 139, 166, 178, 185, 208, 217; initiation, 53, 57, 60, 64
Death, causes, 42–4; of first Christian convert, 122–3; and reincarnation (initiation), 60
Denominations, Christian, 161 n.; women's work groups and, 160
Dialect, Tiriki, *vs.* Maragoli, Idaxo, Isuxo, xvii
District, *see* North Nyanza
District Commissioner, 102, 107 n. 1, 108, 129, 133–4, 168, 225–6, 228, 260
District Education Board, 145, 146 n., 220–1, 258
District Officer, 266, 272
Divining, Christians and, 167; disease and, 163; initiation date and, 51; learning of, 18 n.; prior to raiding, 72–3, 224
Dream, 43, 192, 203, 212, 217, 222–3, 265; Christian conversion and, 263; inspiration for Christian hymns, 187; prophets, 221, 234–5; Satan- and God-inspired, 187–8
Drumming, initiation friction drum, 64; prohibition against, 207; used by church groups, 173, 175, 206–7
Duka, local shops, stores, xxxvii
Dungu, Joshua, 126

East Indian, traders and shopkeepers, 153 n.
East Tiriki, 105, 129; dissolution as an administrative unit, 110; Shimoli, Assistant Chief, 105

Eating, behaviour of initiates and uniniated, 66
Economics, changes, women, 157; weak Tiriki orientation towards, 153; women's hoe agriculture and, 153
Education and schools, championing of, 216; Chief Hezron and, 144; Christianity and, 144, 249; church pastorship and, 251; District Education Board, 145, 146 n., 220–1; growth of literacy, 248; initiation and, 147, 261–2; leadership and, 144, 219, 248–51, 279; Maragoli and, 145; Mission and, 145–8, 146 n., 249; pagans and, 249; separatist churches and, 251; tuition fees, 157
Elder warriors, 68–9; community leadership and, 240, 244; defensive warfare raids, 86; executive type duties, 117; property settlement meetings and, 233
Elders, xiii; ancestor cult, 30–5; beer drinking, xxxvii, 238, 282–3; initiation and, 51 *et passim*, 168; ritual elders, 35; sub-clan and, 41; supernatural powers, 41–2; witches and, 40; work, xxxvi. *See also* Elders, community
Elders, community, 45, 96, 238; British Administration and, 236, 283, 286; contemporary administration and, 236–7, 286; estrangement of, 22–3; inheritance and, 24; land, 228; *liguru* and, 116–17; secrecy and, 240–2; young men and, 116
Eldoret, 255, 267
Election, of Hezron, Chief, 144; secret ballot, 272
Elgon Nyanza District, 83; tribes of, 98 n.
Elopement, 10, 22
Employment, at Kaimosi Mission, 254, 267; community leadership and, 240; encouraged by rinderpest, 1910, 123, 155; motives for, 156–7; outside of district, 102, 123, 155–6, 156 n., 255, 267–8, 281
English, literacy in, 248 n.
Entrance, archway (*shilibwa*), 63
Epilepsy, 264
Erythrina Abyssinica, 90
Evans-Pritchard, E. E., 83
Executive, separate from judicial, 287

Terik, *contd.*—
Nandi offshoot, xxxix, 6; Nyangori Location and, 107, 109; population distribution, 51, 51 n. 1; role in age group changeover, 77–8; sub-tribe, 92–3; raiding (cattle), 101, 154; territorial organization, 87; -Tiriki differing views on armies, 93–4; -Tiriki *idumi*, 48–9
Territorial organization (*lusomo*), xxxviii; divisions, 85; summary, 96–7; traditional, 83 *et passim*
Thompson, Joseph, 83
Tigoi, Friends school, 141
Totemic Terik clans, 6
Traders, 153 n.
Tribal bureaucracy, developed by British, xxxix
Tribal police. *See Askari*
Tribe, boundaries, Tiriki, 27–8; brotherhood based on common initiation, 95–6; Kaimosi Mission as boundary, 100; leadership, 246–7; Location Advisory Council, 226–9; territorial sub-division, 85; traditional corporate action, 224–5; traditional unity, 95–6
Tswana, 171
Twinship, resultant contamination, (*buxwana*), 37

Uganda, 171

Vernacular, spelling of, xvii–xix; use of by investigators, xi
Victoria, Lake (where witches' ghosts are sent), 40, 44, 87, 100, 130, 164
Vihiga, Friends Mission at, 122
Village (*lidala* or *lusomo*), Christian, 115 n.; and political leadership, 114–15
Visions, 192, 197; in case of religious conversion; interpretation of in separatist Christian churches, 187–8, 222

Wage labour, on European farms and East African urban centres, xxxvi
Wagner, Günter, xxxiii, 11, 13, 98 n., 126 n.
Wanga, Abashiseza clan, 7, 99; Chiefs and Chieftaincy, 99, 230; communities, 83–4; *liguru* and, 114 n. 3; moated villages, 86; *olugongo* and, 106; tribe, xxxv

Warfare and raiding, 101, 154–5; Abaluyia in World War I, 123; abolition by British, 67; defence, 86–7; raiding, 72, 92–3; training during initiation, 67
Warrior, age grade, 67, 70–1, 81–2, 155; leaders, 94, 99, 225; purification of, 37, 73; Terik, 103
Waxala, Petro, *pseud.*, 259–67
Wealth, in cattle and cash (*muruji*), 154, 239; in homestead size and grainstores (*muhinda*), 239; status and, 154, 157, 239–40
Wele, Northern Abaluyia 'high God', 39
Wendt, missionary killed by Nandi warriors in 1905, 101
Whiteman, European (*musungu*), 88, 88 n. 2
Widow, care of, 24–6; inheritance, 25, 214; inheritance, church view of, 271
Wiltsey, Robert, 81 n. 1
Witch (*muloji*), 39–40, 243 n.; antiwitchcraft ordinance, 167; Christianity and, 163, 167, 205; community leadership and, 241–2; conversion to Christianity and, 125–6; haunting ghost of, 44; inherited taint, 256; jealous nature, 41; position in traditional society, 126–7, 126 n.; sorcery and, 130–1 n., 240, 270; traditional leadership and, 126
Women, agriculture and work bees, xxxvi, 159–61; beating of Christian wives, 135; changing status and duties of, 157–8, 224; Christian Church and, 282–3; clitoridectomy of, 62, 96 n.; economic status in husband's family, 158; Israel Monthly Meeting, 198–200; limited leadership opportunities of, 237; mother-in-law and, 161; section of hut (*isisi*) forbidden to initiated men, 66; social change and, 282; subordinate to men, 153
Work bees, women's (*zishiliga*), 160, 281–2; in churches, 198–9, 282
World War I, 123, 155–6, 254; Tiriki in, 156

Yawoha. See Roho
Yearly Meeting, 195